ALL THINGS MUST PASS AWAY

ALL THINGS MUST PASS AWAY

Harrison, Clapton, and Other Assorted Love Songs

BY KENNETH WOMACK
AND JASON KRUPPA

For Phala Helm (1931–2020)
All things must pass away

I had no ambition when I was a kid other than to play guitar
and get in a rock 'n' roll band. I don't really like to be the guy
in the white suit at the front. Like in the Beatles, I was the one
who kept quiet at the back and let the other egos be at the front.

—George Harrison

It's very difficult to explain the effect the first blues record
I heard had on me, except to say that I recognized it immediately.
It was as if I were being reintroduced to something that I already knew,
maybe from another, earlier life. For me, there is something primitively
soothing about this music, and it went straight to my nervous system,
making me feel ten-feet tall.

—Eric Clapton

Thus, many a melody passed to and fro between the two nightingales,
drunk with their passion. Those who heard them listened in delight,
and so similar were the two voices that they sounded like
a single chant. Born of pain and longing, their song had the power
to break the unhappiness of the world.

—Nizami Ganjavi, *Layla and Majnun*

All things pass
A sunrise does not last all morning
All things pass
A cloudburst does not last all day

—Timothy Leary, *Psychedelic Prayers After the Tao Te Ching*

CONTENTS

PROLOGUE
Hammersmith Odeon, December 1964

FOR ERIC CLAPTON, MEETING THE BEATLES—and especially George Harrison—was a turning point. It was December 1964, and the Yardbirds, with nineteen-year-old Clapton playing lead guitar, were one of the supporting acts for "Another Beatles Christmas Show," which comprised twenty-one dates at London's Hammersmith Odeon. As it happened, the Yardbirds were sixth on the bill behind the Fab Four, of course, along with Freddie and the Dreamers, DJ Jimmy Savile, Sounds Incorporated, and Elkie Brooks. The brainchild of Beatles manager Brian Epstein, the Christmas shows proved to be a seasonal hit in 1963, and the 1964 installment would equal, if not eclipse the previous year's take. For the Beatles, the Christmas shows would be a tiresome affair, especially after having experienced a whirlwind of global fame across that incredible year. Not only would they perform two sets per day for eighteen of the Hammersmith Odeon dates, but they would also be decked out in full costume for a series of comedy sketches, including one that required them to dress up, Eskimo-style, as Arctic explorers in search of the Abominable Snowman.

Meeting the world's most famous band was a big deal for Clapton. Years later, he would remember vividly the moment in which the group strode into his orbit. "Hanging out backstage at the Odeon was where I had my first meeting with the Beatles," he later recalled. "Paul played the ambassador, coming out to meet us and saying hello. I remember him playing us the tune of 'Yesterday,' which was half-written, and asking everyone what they thought. He didn't have the words yet. He was calling it 'Scrambled Eggs,' and singing

'Scrambled eggs . . . Everybody calls me scrambled eggs.'" For Eric and the other Yardbirds, meeting the Beatles in the flesh seemed surreal. "The Beatles were then in another world to us," he remembered. "They were stars and climbing fast."

In their own way, the Yardbirds were also on the move. Eric joined the band after sixteen-year-old lead guitarist Anthony Topham was forced to quit the group by his parents, who preferred that their son concentrate on his schoolwork as opposed to performing nightly in a music club. At first, the band seemed like the perfect fit for Clapton, who listened to the Yardbirds' regular set at London's legendary Crawdaddy Club. "They were playing good R&B, songs like 'You Can't Judge a Book' by Bo Diddley, and 'Smokestack Lightning' by Howlin' Wolf," Eric remembered, "and for me, just the fact that they knew these songs was enough for me to enjoy them." Fancying himself as a blues purist, Eric couldn't resist the opportunity to be Topham's replacement, and besides, Eric later wrote, "for the first time in my life, I now had a full-time job as a musician."

During his first three months with the Yardbirds, Eric reveled in the opportunity to perform the blues night after night. As he recalled, "What I immediately liked about being in the Yardbirds was that our entire reason for existence was to honor the tradition of the blues. We didn't write any songs at first, but the covers we chose to do defined our identity." The Yardbirds enjoyed a regular gig at the Crawdaddy courtesy of their manager Giorgio Gomelsky, the up-and-coming promoter who operated the club in the back room of the Station Hotel. Still smarting after losing out to Andrew Loog-Oldham in his effort to rep the Rolling Stones, Gomelsky was determined to transform the Yardbirds into a world-beating success.

For Gomelsky, Eric seemed like the perfect vehicle to accomplish this end. As a member of the Yardbirds, Clapton was making his name as a virtuoso soloist at the Crawdaddy. Gomelsky even played a part in deriving the guitarist's famous nickname. As Eric recalled, "While most other bands were playing three-minute songs, we were taking three-minute numbers and stretching them out to five or six minutes, during which time the audience would go crazy, shaking their heads around manically and dancing in various outlandish ways. On my guitar I used light-gauge guitar strings, with a very thin first string, which made it easier to bend the notes, and it was not uncommon during the most frenetic bits of playing for me to break at least one string. During the pause while I was changing my string, the frenzied audience would often break into a slow handclap, inspiring Giorgio to dream up the nickname of 'Slowhand.'"

Clapton's nickname would endure, although his tenure with the Yardbirds would prove to be decidedly short-lived. By the time that the band shared the bill with the Beatles at the Hammersmith Odeon, Eric could barely conceal his disgust as the group charted a new direction under Gomelsky's management and, in particular, as bassist Paul Samwell-Smith assumed a leadership role. For Eric, the writing was on the wall: with Samwell-Smith as his mouthpiece, Gomelsky intended to fuel his ambitions for the Yardbirds by recasting them as hitmakers, as opposed to blues-breakers. Those six-minute blues effusions would soon be replaced by three-minute tunes with commercial appeal. The December 1964 release of the band's first long-player rendered this last point indubitably clear for Clapton. Entitled *Five Live Yardbirds*, the album offered a study in contrasts. On the one hand, it depicted Eric and the band in full blues power back in their club days, yet on the other, it stood as a stark reminder for Eric of the band's imminent transition away from their blues-laden sound.

For Eric, the final straw arrived in the form of "For Your Love," the single that would radically alter the Yardbirds' identity. Composed by Graham Gouldman, who would later find stardom of his own with 10cc, "For Your Love" had been originally intended as a vehicle for the Beatles. Indeed, Gouldman's manager had gone so far as to enlist a colleague to get a copy of the demo into Epstein's and the Beatles' hands at one of the Hammersmith Odeon Christmas shows. In his heart, Gouldman knew that it was all for naught—John Lennon and Paul McCartney were not in the habit of shopping for compositions, given the renown they enjoyed as songwriters. The song eventually found its way into the hands of Gomelsky and Samwell-Smith, who produced a February 1, 1965, Yardbirds session at IBC Studios. Clapton had championed Otis Redding's "Your One and Only Man" as the Yardbirds' next single, losing out to Samwell-Smith, who preferred the Gouldman tune. After they completed "For Your Love," Samwell-Smith wouldn't entertain any notions about recording the Redding tune. As Clapton later recalled, "Sam did his first and everyone just said, 'Oh, that's it. No need to try yours.' So I thought, 'Fucking hell!' and I got really upset and bore a grudge, and I think that when they said it I actually made up my mind that I wasn't going to play with them anymore. It was like kids, you know." Besides, he was already fed up with the group's new power dynamics. In addition to installing Samwell-Smith as music director, Gomelsky had also announced—via an official memorandum, no less—that if any of the Yardbirds had any suggestions or concerns, they were to be submitted to the manager or Samwell-Smith for consideration.

If Clapton held any notions of remaining in the band, they clearly ended when the group recorded "For Your Love." Samwell-Smith's arrangement called for very little in the way of guitar pyrotechnics; in fact, much of the song consisted of lead singer Keith Relf, drummer Jim McCarty, and a raft of session musicians, including Brian Auger on harpsichord. Clapton and rhythm guitarist Chris Dreja appeared exclusively on the song's up-tempo middle eight. Years later, Auger would recall thinking, "Who, in their right mind, is going to buy a pop single with harpsichord on it?" As events would demonstrate, Auger had dramatically misread the British pop music marketplace. In short order, "For Your Love" would nestle in for a lengthy stay near the top of the charts. But Clapton had already had his fill of the Yardbirds. On March 5, the day of the single's release, he visited Gomelsky's office in Soho for what seemed like an inevitable showdown. To Clapton's great surprise, the meeting was a relatively brief affair—and without fireworks in the slightest. As Clapton later recalled, Giorgio calmly "told me that it was quite clear that I was no longer happy in the band, and that if I wanted to leave, then he wouldn't stand in my way. He didn't exactly fire me. He just invited me to resign. Totally disillusioned, I was at that point ready to quit the music business altogether." Even still, Clapton recommended that Gomelsky and the group consider another up-and-coming session man named Jimmy Page. Concerned about the cloud hovering over Clapton's departure, Page suggested that the Yardbirds try his friend Jeff Beck instead. Without missing a beat, Beck joined the band for their very next show in Croydon on March 5.

Years later, Eric would come to realize that his decision to leave the Yardbirds was influenced by factors he didn't have the experience or maturity to understand in his early twenties. On the one hand, he was copping an attitude entrenched in a purist philosophy, while on the other, he was chagrinned by the way his guitar work sounded in the studio. "I was developing a very purist attitude toward music and thought that it really ought to be just live," he later observed. "My theory was that making records, first and foremost, was always going to be a commercial enterprise and therefore was not pure. It was a ridiculously pompous attitude, considering that all the music I was learning from was on records." But it wasn't just purity that concerned him, Clapton admitted. "In truth, I was just embarrassed because, in the studio, my own personal inadequacy was there for all to see. But it wasn't just me, and as exciting as it was to be actually making a record, when we listened back and compared it to the stuff we were supposedly modeling ourselves on, it sounded pretty lame."

Eric would also chalk up his behavior during this period to his need to feel hip and informed. "The truth is," he later admitted, "I was taking myself far too seriously and becoming very critical and judgmental of anybody in music who wasn't playing just pure blues. This attitude was probably part of my intellectual phase. I was reading translations of Baudelaire and discovering the American underground writers like Jack Kerouac and Allen Ginsberg while simultaneously watching as much French and Japanese cinema as I could. I began to develop a real contempt for pop music in general, and to feel genuinely uncomfortable about being in the Yardbirds. No longer were we going in the direction I wanted, mainly because, seeing the runaway success of the Beatles, Giorgio and some of the guys had become obsessed with getting on TV and having a number one record."

As the 1960s progressed, Clapton would discover, time and time again, that he still had a lot of growing up to do—and worse yet, that his pattern of scuttling bandmates over the lofty, high-minded principles of youth was only just beginning. Indeed, it would be a pattern that Clapton would repeat over and over again across the years. Besides, there was no doubt that the Beatles loomed large in Eric's world, too. Meeting them at the Hammersmith Odeon back in December had been—and always would be—one of the great highlights of his life. And, as it turned out, the significance of Clapton meeting the Beatles was very much a two-way street. As it happened, the Fab Four knew all about the Yardbirds, who had recently shared a package tour with Billy J. Kramer and the Dakotas. Epstein made sure that the Beatles learned about the ecstatic response that the Yardbirds had received from the audience.

As Clapton and the Liverpudlians lounged around backstage at the Hammersmith Odeon, the young, self-important guitarist quickly discovered that he was rankled by John Lennon's irreverent, put-down humor. Ringo Starr and Paul McCartney were plenty nice—even if the Beatles' bassist tried a bit too hard in the welcome-wagon department. But for Eric, meeting George Harrison, the Fabs' twenty-one-year-old lead guitarist, was the highlight of his experience that day.

"I just met him then," Harrison later said of the Odeon encounter, "but really didn't get to know him. I met him again when the [Lovin'] Spoonful were at the Marquee [in April 1966], and John and I went down and were just sort of hanging about backstage with them. . . . I can remember just seeing Eric, 'I know him. I'm sure I know this guy, and he seems like, you know, really lonely.' I remember we went out and got in a car and went off to [John] Sebastian's hotel, and I remembered thinking, 'We should've invited that guy, 'cuz I'm sure we know him from somewhere and he just seemed, like, lonely.'"

Eventually, they bonded over their shared obsession with the electric guitar. "He seemed to like what I did," Eric later wrote, "and we talked shop a lot. He showed me his collection of Gretsch guitars, and I showed him my light-gauge strings, which I always bought from a shop called Clifford Essex on Earlham Street. I gave him some, and this was the start of what was to eventually become a long friendship." Harrison would later remember that seeing Clapton was "like looking at myself." To his mind, they not only shared a deep reverence for the craftsmanship associated with pursuing the electric guitar, but also with the way that the two young men engaged the world. Clapton wasn't "a leader sort of person," Harrison came to realize. "It's the same with me. I need someone to encourage me to do things."

As those tender moments in rock history unfolded, Clapton and Harrison would develop a loving personal and professional friendship that would endure for decades, the kind of association that could overcome virtually any obstacle. They would also emerge as each other's staunchest, most steadfast supporters. They would root for each other from the sidelines—and many times, standing across from each other, guitars in hand, on the world's greatest rock 'n' roll stages. Clapton would observe, in awe, as Harrison developed into one of the finest songwriters and guitarists of his generation. And for his part, Harrison would cheer his friend on as Clapton pursued one of his most heartfelt ambitions, one that he had fashioned out of the ashes of his Yardbirds experience. In the uncompromising sweet bloom of youth, Clapton vowed that someday he would record an honest-to-goodness blues album. And Harrison—in ways that neither of them could ever possibly have imagined—would help him see his dream made real.

1 | THE QUIET BEATLE

IN CONTRAST WITH ERIC, George's first musical love affair wasn't with the blues. In fact, his earliest memories weren't even musical in origin, but rather, of a religious nature. During his preteen years, he had come to recognize an inherent irony in his fellow Liverpudlians' approach to spiritual matters. Years later, George would recall his fascination with the strange intermingling of commerce and religion—and, ultimately, vice—that he observed in the neighborhood around his family's Upton Green home. Growing up in the city's Speke district, George remembered that "priests used to come round to all the houses in the neighborhood collecting money. We weren't particularly bad, but there were some really awful families in some houses. They'd switch all the lights off, turn the radio down, and pretend they were out. My dad was making probably £7/10 shillings a week, so a donation of five shillings, which he would give, was quite a lot of money. I never saw people out of work at that time. I was probably too small to notice. When you're young, you're just dealing with day-to-day things, as opposed to following world politics or anything else outside your life."

What really troubled young George was that his father's hard-earned money went toward the construction of yet another cathedral. "Before that," George reflected, "there was a temporary church in a big wooden hut. It had the stations of the cross around it, and that's my earliest remembrance of wondering, 'What is all this about?' Okay, I could see Christ dragging his cross down the street with everybody spitting on him, and I got the gist of that; but it didn't seem to make any sense. I felt then that there was some hypocrisy

1

going on, even though I was only about 11-years-old." Even at that tender age, George recognized that "it seemed to be the same on every housing estate in English cities: on one corner they'd have a church and on the other corner a pub. Everybody's out there getting pissed and then just goes in the church, says three 'Hail Marys' and one 'Our Father' and sticks a fiver in the plate. It felt so alien to me. Not the stained-glass window or the pictures of Christ; I liked that a lot, and the smell of the incense and the candles. I just didn't like the bullshit. After Communion, I was supposed to have Confirmation, but I thought, 'I'm not going to bother with that, I'll just confirm it later myself.'"

Throughout the rest of his life, George did just that. Indeed, his spiritual quest would become a key factor in the Beatles' creative inspiration and musical direction. As with so many of his later moments of intellectual recognition, George didn't look back after his epiphany regarding the hypocritical relationship that existed between churchgoing and drinking. "From then on," he recalled, "I avoided the church, but every Thursday a kid would come round to herald the arrival of the priest. They'd go round all the streets, knock on the door and shout, 'The priest's coming!' And we'd all go, 'Oh, shit,' and run like hell up the stairs and hide. My mother would have to open the door, and he'd say, 'Ah, hello, Mrs. Harrison, it's nice to see you again, so it is. Eh, be Jesus.' She'd stuff two half-crowns in his sweaty little hand and off he'd go to build another church or pub."

George grew up in arguably the most traditional and convivial of the future Beatles' households. George's father, Harold Harrison, had formerly worked as a steward on the White Star Line before landing employment as a Liverpool bus driver. Harold met Louise French, a grocery shopkeeper, in 1929, and they married the following year. In short order, the Harrisons had two children, Louise and Harry. In 1941, the Harrisons' third child, Peter, joined their growing brood, and on February 25, 1943, George was born. Given Harold and Louise's meager occupations, the Harrisons lived in a succession of council houses. In a rare moment of good fortune, the Harrisons were chosen to relocate from the modest neighborhood surrounding Arnold Grove into a new council house on Upton Green in Speke.

Among his family, George was known by his nickname Geo (pronounced as "Joe"). In his schoolboy days, George had been an exceptional pupil at Dovedale Primary, yet he had transformed, by his adolescence, into a largely disinterested student at the Liverpool Institute. As he later recalled, it "was very pleasant being little and it was always sunny in the summer," yet by the time he was promoted to grammar school, it was "raining and cloudy, with old streets and backward teachers." George's no-nonsense way of looking at the world didn't help matters. In short order, he concluded that "I didn't like school. I think it was awful; the worst time of your life."

By his teen years, George's blunt way of understanding the world was in full bloom. And he came by it naturally. George's self-confidence and ability to speak and behave honestly found their origins in his family life. "I had a happy childhood," he remembered, "with lots of relatives around." Years later, Hunter Davies interviewed George's parents while compiling an authorized biography of the Beatles. George's mother, Louise, was "jolly, very friendly and outgoing," Davies wrote, while "Mr. Harrison is thin and thoughtful, precise and slowly deliberate." George's sister-in-law remembered the Harrisons as being "tolerant, sensible, loving people. They were so warm and brought you into everything." But it was George's schoolmate Paul McCartney who came to understand the true fount of his friend's fun, albeit forthright demeanor. "Louise was lovely, but quite a hard lady, too, in some ways, but soft as toffee on the inside," Paul recalled. "She'd always tell you how she felt, Louise."

And it would be Louise who ensured that the Harrison home was filled with music, courtesy of the BBC radio airwaves. George's earliest memories were marked by a continuous musical soundtrack, one that was highly varied and directed by his mother's whimsy and wide-ranging tastes: "In those days," he fondly recalled, "the radios were like crystal sets. Well, not quite. The radios had batteries: funny batteries with acid in them. You had to take the battery down to a shop on the corner and leave it with them for about three days to charge up. We'd listen to anything that was played on the radio: Irish tenors like Josef Locke, dance-band music, Bing Crosby, people like that. My mother would always be turning the dial on the radio until she'd found a station broadcasting in Arabic or something, and we'd leave it there until it became so crackly that you couldn't hear it any more. Then she'd tune in to something else."

As with so many other British teenagers, George's earliest musical passions had been inspired by skiffle. A jazz-oriented musical style derived from the blues, ragtime, and folk music during the 1920s in the American South, the skiffle boom took the UK by storm in the 1950s. Led by Lonnie "The King of Skiffle" Donegan, skiffle dominated the British charts, including, most notably,

Donegan's cover version of Lead Belly's reading of "Rock Island Line," a folk tune about traveling along the Chicago, Rock Island, and Pacific railroads. Born as Huddie William Ledbetter, Lead Belly popularized a number of folk songs, including "Goodnight, Irene," "Midnight Special," "Cotton Fields," and "Boll Weevil." In the autumn of 1956, George attended a Donegan concert in the company of his older brother Harry. Together, they were captivated by the performance. After purchasing his own copy of "Rock Island Line," George begged his mother to purchase a three-quarter-sized, Dutch-made Egmond guitar. His early efforts at playing the guitar were met with abject failure. Several months later, though, he was buoyed by the imported American sounds of Elvis Presley, and he turned his attentions back to the guitar with a renewed vigor. Along with his friend Arthur Kelly, George began taking weekly lessons from a local guitarist who worked out of a nearby pub known as the Cat. "He taught us a few basic root chords straightaway," Kelly recalled. "The first number we learned was 'Your Cheatin' Heart,' by Hank Williams. We hated the song but were thrilled, at least, to be changing from C to F to G7." Not long afterward, George and Arthur launched a skiffle band of their own. Known as the Rebels, the group also included George's brother Pete on tea-chest bass. For the most part, their performances were limited to playing a handful of songs in George's bedroom. At one point, though, they played a gig at the local British Legion, where they served as the opening act for a magician.

By this point, George's interest in skiffle—with its blues-tempered origins—had led him to expand his musical tastes toward rockabilly and country and western sounds, having discovered such legendary American guitarists as Chet Atkins and Carl Perkins. During this same period, he caught Eddie Cochran's live act in Liverpool, and he saw his destiny laid out before him. During Cochran's performance, George remembered a "funny break in-between songs. He was standing at the microphone and as he started to talk he put his two hands through his hair, pushing it back. And a girl, one lone voice, screamed out, 'Oh, Eddie!' and he coolly murmured into the mike, 'Hi, honey.' I thought, 'Yes! That's it—rock 'n' roll!'" Buoyed with new levels of musical excitement, George sharpened his skills by devoting hour upon hour of painstaking practice to mastering the sounds that he heard on Radio Luxembourg and the American records that he and his friends found—and, for the most part, shoplifted—at Lewis's department store along the banks of the Mersey.

Meanwhile, George's friendship with Paul had begun to develop during their schoolboy days together at the Liverpool Institute. Paul had even taken to hanging out at the Harrisons' sociable home on weekends. In July 1957, fifteen-year-old Paul had joined sixteen-year-old John's skiffle band, the Quarry Men, and it was only a matter of time before he began working to add George to the group's ranks. After taking in the Quarry Men's December 1957 performance at Wilson Hall, George met up with the band at a West Oakhill Park skiffle club. As the Quarry Men looked on, George played a slick, note-perfect rendition of "Guitar Boogie," a fairly complicated composition that caught the group's attention—just as George had planned. He followed up "Guitar Boogie" with a scrupulous cover version of "Raunchy." Intuitively realizing that he was in the presence of a budding virtuoso, the now seventeen-year-old John overlooked George's tender age of fourteen and invited him into the group. "We asked George to join us because he knew more chords," John later remarked, "a lot more than we knew. We got a lot from him."

Harrison would remember things somewhat differently. "The Quarry Men had other members," George recalled, "who didn't seem to be doing anything, so I said, 'Let's get rid of them, then I'll join.'" George's new role in the band brought an end to guitarist Eric Griffiths, who was nonchalantly dismissed after John and Paul simply neglected to invite him to a rehearsal, leaving drummer Colin Hanton to share the news with the erstwhile Quarry Men guitarist. Shortly thereafter, bassist Len Garry came down with tubercular meningitis, and his condition understandably led to his estrangement from the band. Only Hanton remained from Lennon's original Quarry Men lineup, but the difference in overall quality was unmistakable. With John, Paul, and George as the band's trio of budding guitarists, their sound had noticeably improved. They were hardly yet professionals, to be sure, but their creative energy was clearly blossoming like never before.

At this juncture, George's membership in the Quarry Men should have been the tonic that the band needed to enter a new phase of musical fusion. Yet over the next eighteen months, the group performed just seven gigs, the majority of which were private parties. Indeed, two of the Quarry Men's shows were made possible by the Harrison family, including a December 20, 1958, wedding reception for George's brother Harry, and, ten days later, a New Year's Day performance at Wilson Hall, for which George's father served as chairman. For the Quarry Men, 1958 would be a year of triumph and tragedy, a period in which John and Paul discovered themselves as songwriters, only to suffer the mind-numbing pain of inexplicable loss when John's mother, Julia Lennon, died in a roadway accident in July 1958. Meanwhile, John had begun to overlook his difference in age with George, who—in spite of being nicknamed as the Quiet One at the height of Beatlemania—talked incessantly about a wide range of subjects. "When George was a kid," Lennon recalled, "he used to follow me and my first girlfriend Cynthia. We would come out of the art school together and he'd be hovering around. . . . Cyn and I would be going to a coffee shop or a movie and George would follow us down the street two hundred yards behind. Cyn would say, 'Who is that guy? What does he want?' And I'd say, 'He just wants to hang out. Should we take him with us?' She'd say, 'Oh, okay, let's take him to the bloody movies.' So we'd allow him to come to the movies with us."

Although their gigs may have been few and far between, the Quarry Men shared a dream of making an honest-to-goodness record of their own. In June 1958, the Quarry Men—John, Paul, George, and Colin, along with pianist Duff Lowe—recorded a demo at P. F. Phillips Professional Tape and Disk Record Service, which, in truth, was nothing more than a back room in the home of Percy Phillips, who had built a primitive recording studio with a Vortexion reel-to-reel tape recorder, an MSS portable disc-cutting machine, and a trio of microphones. Under Phillips's watchful eye, the group cut a 78-RPM single for the bargain-basement price of seventeen shillings. The bandmates' lack of funds ensured they would be going "straight to vinyl," which meant that they would be recording directly onto a shellac disc. It also meant the band had to turn out flawless takes in order to get their money's worth. For their first number, the Quarry Men laid down a cover version of Buddy Holly's "That'll Be the Day" with John on lead vocals. The recording was highlighted by a rollicking guitar solo from George, who enjoyed an audible shout of encouragement from one of the other Quarry Men to "honky tonk!"

For the single's B-side, Paul recommended that they perform an original composition, "In Spite of All the Danger," which he had composed with George. It was a big moment for the youngest Quarry Man, but it was hardly a harbinger of things to come when it came to proving his songwriting talent among the likes of Lennon and McCartney. Composed in the style of Elvis Presley's "Trying to Get to You," "In Spite of All the Danger" was a surprisingly catchy ballad about the anxiety of newfound love, complete with a "doo-wop" backing vocal arrayed against Duff's tinkling piano. Despite its crude production, the band's first recording was a major triumph in the Quarry Men's eyes, especially given the amateurish conditions of Phillips's studio and the haste with which they worked that day.

While the "That'll Be the Day" b/w "In Spite of All the Danger" single had afforded the Quarry Men with a genuine thrill, by early 1959, the future of the group was very much in question. After a gig at the Pavilion Theatre in Lodge Lane, the band enjoyed several pints as a form of post-show celebration. The result was nothing short of disastrous, as the Quarry Men's second set proved to be an unmitigated drunken mess. On the way home on the bus that night, Paul erupted, blaming Colin for holding the band back musically. John's boyhood friend Pete Shotton intervened, getting off of the bus a stop early with Colin, who was effectively dismissed from the Quarry Men's ranks. Having reached a crossroads, the group began to drift apart. Having turned sixteen, George took up work as an apprentice electrician, while John and Paul continued pursuing an academic track. Eventually, George began auditioning for another band, including the popular Liverpool group Rory Storm and the Hurricanes. Known for the flamboyant antics of their handsome leader Storm (born Alan Caldwell), the explosive sounds of lead guitarist Johnny "Guitar" Byrne, and the slick drum work of Ringo Starr (born Richard Starkey), the Hurricanes came to the conclusion, as others had before them, that George was simply too young to take seriously. Not content with biding his time, George began performing with other groups, including, most notably, the Les Stewart Quartet.

The Quarry Men's saving grace—and likely the Beatles', for that matter—came about because of George's association, brief as it was, with the Les Stewart Quartet. In August 1959, George and his new bandmates were invited to be the inaugural act at Liverpudlian Mona Best's Casbah Coffee Club. Yet on August 12, the day of the opening, Stewart and bass player Ken Brown fell into a ferocious argument after Brown had missed a rehearsal in order to help decorate the club. Stewart subsequently refused to perform that evening, and a desperate Brown asked George if he knew anyone who could take the band's place. In short order, George located John and Paul, and the Quarry Men—with Brown on bass—opened the Casbah, where they enjoyed a regular Saturday-night engagement for the foreseeable future. Their gigs at the club were especially noteworthy because John and George had recently acquired electric guitars of their own—a pair of Höfner Club 40s—with amplification courtesy of Brown's Watkins Westminster amp. As it turned out, the band's run at the Casbah would be decidedly short-lived. In October, Brown was forced to miss a performance because of a bad cold. When the Quarry Men received their meager pay at the end of the night, an agitated Paul felt that Brown did not deserve his regular fifteen-shilling cut. Mona Best ignored his arguments and paid the bass player anyway. With that, John, Paul, and George were through with Brown, which effectively brought their regular engagement at the Casbah to an end. During this period, George replaced his Höfner Club 40 with a three-pickup Futurama electric guitar. "It was difficult to play," he later recalled, and the strings were about a "half-inch off the fingerboard . . . but nevertheless it did look kind of futuristic."

At this juncture, George's ambitions were decidedly simple: all he really wanted to do was play as often as possible and hone his abilities as a guitarist. If it hadn't been for Allan Williams, his future life as a musician might not have unfolded in the company of the other Beatles. John and his art-college roommate, Stu Sutcliffe, had taken to hanging out in Williams's Jacaranda Club. During this period, John famously talked Stu into using his prize money from an award-winning painting in order to purchase a bass guitar. The bandmates, which now included Sutcliffe and thirty-two-year-old drummer Tommy Moore, rebranded themselves as the Beatals in a sly reference to beat music and the late Buddy Holly's Crickets. Acting as the group's manager, Williams talked them into scrapping their handle in favor of the Silver Beetles and sent them on the road as the backing band for singer Johnny Gentle (born George Askew). For the nine-date tour of Scotland, the musicians adopted stage names, save for John and Tommy. Stu dubbed himself Stuart de Staël, as an homage to Nicolas de Staël, the Russian abstract artist. Paul took the name Paul Ramon, while George called himself Carl Harrison in honor of his guitar hero, Carl Perkins.

While the wide-eyed Liverpudlians relished their days on a bona fide rock 'n' roll tour, George held no illusions about the experience: "That was our first professional gig: on a tour of dance halls miles up in the North of Scotland, around Inverness. We felt, 'Yippee, we've got a gig!' Then we realized that we were playing to nobody in little halls, until the pubs cleared out when about five Scottish Teds would come in and look at us. That was all. Nothing happened. We didn't really know anything. It was sad, because we were like orphans. Our shoes were full of holes and our trousers were a mess, while Johnny Gentle had a posh suit. I remember trying to play to 'Won't you wear my ring around your neck?'—he was doing Elvis's 'Teddy Bear'—and we were crummy. The band was horrible, an embarrassment. We didn't have amplifiers or anything."

As it happened, the tour ended in calamity when Tommy quit the band after a harrowing car accident at the tail end of their Scottish jaunt. The now-drummerless group's salvation finally came, from of all places, some seven hundred miles to the east in the port city of Hamburg, West Germany. Williams had sent another Liverpool group, the rhythm and blues combo Derry and the Seniors, to Hamburg for an extended—and very successful— engagement at Bruno Koschmider's Kaiserkeller Club on the city's notorious Reeperbahn, a street in Hamburg's St. Pauli area, as well as the epicenter of the city's red-light district. Yet the band still lacked a drummer, the final, necessary ingredient for embarking upon their German adventure. The answer to their problems arrived in the form of eighteen-year-old Pete Best, Mona Best's strapping son who played regular gigs with Ken Brown's new band, the Black Jacks, at the Casbah, where John, Paul, and George had begun hanging out of late. With a two-month booking at Koschmider's Indra Club in the offing, Paul wasted little time inviting Pete—along with his brand-new set of Premier drums—to join the group. After a hasty audition on August 12 that he couldn't possibly have failed, Pete was offered membership in the band, provided, that is, that he was willing to go abroad—and soon. In the process, the group dropped "Silver" from their name and settled, once and for all, upon the Beatles as their handle.

For George and the other musicians, Hamburg proved to be a paradise of revelry and vice. But musically, it was the making of them, as they performed long sets, night after night, and in the process, grew artistically by veritable leaps and bounds. In early October, Koschmider closed the Indra, which was too slatternly for its own good, and transferred the Beatles to the Kaiserkeller. With its rotting stage and its rough clientele, it was only marginally better than the Indra. When the Beatles began to flag after their lengthy evening gigs, Koschmider would encourage them to "Mach schau!"—or to "Make show!" in his broken English. With the exception of Pete Best, the bandmates had taken to swilling beer onstage in combination with the multicolored amphetamine Preludin pills, or "Prellies," that they ingested to stay awake. They responded to Koschmider's entreaty to "Mach schau!" by evolving a bizarre stage act that included a goose-stepping John, who wore swastikas, and shouted "*Sieg Heil!*" and castigated the audience as a bunch of "fucking Nazis."

As George later recalled, the Kaiserkeller was the Beatles' proving ground as musicians. "In the Kaiserkeller, we had to start earlier and finish later. They'd double us up with the other band, so we were alternating—first with Derry and the Seniors and then Rory Storm and the Hurricanes. In the contract, we had to play for six hours and the other band had to play six hours, so it made into a twelve-hour set. We'd do an hour, they'd do an hour and it seemed to rotate like that, day in and day out, for tuppence a month. But when you're a kid you don't care, really." The best part, according to George, was that "we had to learn millions of songs. We had to play so long we just played everything." In short, "Hamburg was really like our apprenticeship, learning how to play in front of people."

The Beatles' first sojourn in Hamburg proved to be short-lived after Koschmider's local rival, Peter Eckhorn, had begun luring stage acts away from the Kaiserkeller. In November 1960, the Beatles followed suit by defecting to Eckhorn's Top Ten Club. As they prepared to play the Top Ten, though, the police—perhaps at Koschmider's vengeful urging—inspected Harrison's passport and deported the seventeen-year-old for being ineligible to obtain a work permit. After he was "booted out of town," George gathered up everything he owned to make the journey back home. "I had an amplifier that I'd bought in Hamburg and a crappy suitcase and things in boxes, paper bags with my clothes in, and a guitar. I had too many things to carry and was standing in the corridor of the train with my belongings around me, and lots of soldiers on the train, drinking. I finally got to Liverpool and took a taxi home—I just about made it. I got home penniless. It took everything I had to get me back." After a few evenings in Eckhorn's employ, Paul and Pete decided to sneak back to the Bambi Kino in order to retrieve the belongings that they had left behind in their haste to escape the Kaiserkeller. As a farewell prank, Paul and Pete set fire to a condom and accidentally ignited the rotting tapestry in their quarters behind the cinema. Although the fire quickly extinguished itself in the dampness of the walls, Paul and Pete were arrested and deported from the country in short order. Within a fortnight, John began his own journey by train back to Liverpool.

As it happened, John, Paul, George, and Pete didn't regroup until late December, when they played a series of dates at the Casbah. A December 27, 1960, performance at the Litherland Town Hall proved to be a significant turning point in the Beatles' career. Having been billed by DJ Brian Wooler as "Direct from Hamburg!" the Beatles offered up a searing performance—accented by John's acquisition of a 1958 Rickenbacker Capri 325 electric guitar, with its trademark scaled-down neck, back in Hamburg in November. The audience included Mona Best, her son Rory Best, accounting student and future Beatles roadie Neil Aspinall, and promoter Brian Kelly. With Chas Newby standing in on bass for Stu, who remained back in Hamburg with his fiancée, photographer Astrid Kirchherr, the concert began with Paul exploding into a powerful rendition of "Long Tall Sally." "Everyone—the whole lot—surged forward toward the stage," Kelly remembered. "The dance floor behind was completely empty. 'Aye, aye,' I said to myself. 'I could have got twice the numbers in here.'" Quite suddenly, the Beatles had taken Liverpool by storm with their energizing and highly professional post-Hamburg stage act. "It was that evening that we really came out of our shell and let go," John recalled. "This was when we began to think for the first time that we were good." As for George, the experience had been a whirlwind. "We probably looked German," he remembered, "very different from all the other groups, with our leather jackets. We looked funny and we played differently. We went down a bomb."

From that moment on, there was a new, palpable forward momentum in the Beatles' story. By the time that they began a fourteen-week engagement at the Top Ten Club in Hamburg in April 1961, George had turned eighteen and was eligible to obtain a work permit. At the same time, the group decided effectively to end their relationship with Williams by denying him his commission. Williams was understandably infuriated by what he perceived to be a decidedly underhanded move, but the Beatles—still smarting over the incident with Brown back at the Casbah in October 1959—weren't about to pay *anyone* who hadn't worked materially toward the group's success. Ensconced once again at the Top Ten Club, the band played numerous shows with fellow Briton Tony Sheridan (born Andrew Esmond Sheridan McGinnity), a skilled guitarist and vocalist who was known as "The Teacher" among his fellow expatriates. Later that year, he would play an unexpected role in the band's destiny. As George later recalled, "Tony Sheridan had an up-side and a down-side. The up-side was that he was a pretty good singer and guitar player, and it was good to play along with him because we were still learning—the more bands we saw and heard the better. He was older than us as well and was more hardened to the business, whereas we were just getting into it, more bouncy and naïve. On that basis, it was good to have Sheridan there; but at the same time, he was such a downer. He'd fled from England—some kind of trouble—and was always getting into fights. I remember he managed to cut the tendon in his finger on a broken bottle in a fight—fortunately, not on his guitar-playing hand. When he used his guitar pick after that, his injured finger stuck right out."

As it turned out, Stu's tenure in the Beatles was to be short-lived. In the band's early days in Hamburg, he had been the talk of the Reeperbahn for his unusual haircut. Astrid had succeeded in persuading Stu to alter his hairstyle to a "French cut" by reshaping his locks to lie atop his forehead rather than towering above it, Teddy Boy style. Although they teased him relentlessly, John, Paul, and George eventually adopted Stu's look as their own, and the famous Beatle haircut was born. Stu eventually quit the band, having grown tired of Paul's criticism regarding his skills as a bass player.

George and the Beatles' next opportunity to venture into a recording studio came at the bidding of German bandleader Bert Kämpfert, who caught their act with Sheridan at the Top Ten Club. He subsequently offered Sheridan a contract with Polydor Records and enlisted the Beatles as his backup band. For Sheridan's recordings, the Beatles temporarily rebranded themselves as the Beat Brothers. In German slang, *Pidels*, which sounds a lot like *Beatles*, is the plural form of penis; it was a connotation that Kämpfert was entirely unwilling to risk. The three-day session took place in late June 1961, and despite working as Sheridan's supporting act, John, Paul, George, and Pete were thrilled to be making a record—*any* record. For the A-side of Sheridan's single, they recorded a rollicking version of the traditional standard "My Bonnie (Lies over the Ocean)," with George on lead guitar and harmonies by John, Paul, and George. For the B-side, they recorded yet another standard, "When the Saints Go Marching In." To their great delight, they were also allowed to record "Cry for a Shadow," an instrumental that George and John, with his whammy bar in full force, had composed as a parody of the work of Cliff Richard and the Shadows, who were enjoying enormous success in Great Britain at the time. On the final day of the sessions, Sheridan offered renditions of Jimmy Reed's "Take Out Some Insurance on Me Baby" and Hank Snow's "Nobody's Child." For the Beatles, though, the highlight was their own recording of "Ain't She Sweet," which featured a kinetic lead vocal performance from John.

After Stu's resignation from the Beatles, Paul was forced to handle bass duties after George and John refused to even consider the notion. "I doubt I would have picked up the bass if Stuart hadn't left," McCartney later remarked. "I certainly didn't start playing it by choice: I got lumbered with it." In short order, Paul purchased a custom-made, left-handed Höfner 500/1 bass—the violin-shaped instrument with which he is most often associated. By this juncture, George had upgraded through a succession of guitars. In 1957, he replaced his Egmond with a Höfner President, an acoustic that cost him thirty-two guineas. It also proved to be a source of endless distraction from George's schoolwork. In class, he would invariably be "looking out the window, thinking about how I could be practicing a guitar, while they were trying to teach me Pythagoras."

In November 1959, George enjoyed a significant upgrade when he purchased a Futurama, the guitar with which he began the Beatles' Hamburg residencies. With its resemblance to the much-coveted Fender Stratocaster, the imported Futurama was a steal at fifty-five guineas. As Harrison recalled, "Paul came with me when I bought the Futurama. It was on the wall with all the other guitars and Paul plugged it into the amp but couldn't get any sound out of it, so he turned the amp right up. The guitar had three rocker switches and I just hit one and there was an almighty 'boom' through the amplifier and all the other guitars fell off the wall. My mother signed the hire-purchase agreement for me. That is, one pound down and the rest when they catch you." Not long after Paul bought his Höfner violin bass, George made yet another upgrade, replacing the Futurama as his primary electric guitar with a Gretsch Duo Jet. He associated the instrument with the likes of his guitar heroes, legendary figures like Eddie Cochran and Chet Atkins. George purchased the Duo Jet secondhand for ninety pounds from a merchant seaman. As Harrison later recalled, "I saved up for years and years to get a guitar [like this]. I got £70 and felt I was gonna get murdered if anybody knew I had it in me pocket."

By the time they returned to Liverpool during the summer of 1961, the Beatles had established themselves as a bona fide Northern phenomenon. A key part of their cracking stage act featured John, Paul, and George each taking his share of lead vocals on the group's vast repertoire of cover songs. This democratic division of vocal duties was no mere novelty, but a critical part of the band's identity during this period. At this point, George got as much time in the spotlight as John and Paul, an important equilibrium that would persist until the end of 1962, when the power structure within the band began to shift. As they consolidated their fame in their hometown, the group established the sub-basement-level Cavern Club as their *de facto* headquarters. Over the course of the next few years, the Beatles settled in for more than 280 performances at the Cavern, the springboard from which they finally made their name—at least in the region. That August, Polydor released the 45-RPM single "My Bonnie" b/w "The Saints," credited, as promised by Kämpfert, to Tony Sheridan and the Beat Brothers. The song eventually earned the fifth spot on the West German charts and sold more than a hundred thousand copies. The record became a central aspect of the Beatles' growing legend on October 28, 1961, when a patron named Raymond Jones entered NEMS (North End Music Stores)—the largest record outlet in Liverpool and throughout the North—and requested a copy of the Beatles' "My Bonnie" from the store's owner, twenty-seven-year-old Brian Epstein. At the time, he operated two NEMS outlets in Liverpool, including stores on Great Charlotte Street and Whitechapel, the latter of which was fewer than two hundred yards away from the Cavern Club.

In his autobiography, *A Cellarful of Noise*, Epstein claimed to have been unfamiliar with the Beatles before Jones's visit on that fateful day: "The name 'Beatle' meant nothing to me though I vaguely recalled seeing it on a poster advertising a university dance at New Brighton Tower, and I remembered thinking it was an odd and purposeless spelling." Curious about the identity of the mysterious band, on November 9, he attended a lunchtime performance by the group at the Cavern in the company of his assistant manager at NEMS, Alistair Taylor. They descended into the cellar, where the club's DJ, Bob Wooler, announced that Mr. Brian Epstein of NEMS was in attendance. Mesmerized by their performance, Epstein met with the Beatles backstage, where he was greeted by George: "Hello there. What brings Mr. Epstein here?" As with so many others who encountered the group, Epstein enjoyed their charm and good humor. But more importantly, he was impressed with the reaction that they garnered from the kids in the audience. "They gave a captivating and honest show and they had very considerable magnetism," he wrote in his autobiography. "I loved their ad-libs and I was fascinated by this, to me, new music with its pounding bass beat and its vast engulfing sound."

By the time he left the Cavern, Epstein had already decided that he wanted to manage the Beatles. During a December 10 meeting, the group accepted Epstein as their manager, later inking a formal, five-year contract with him on January 24, 1962, at Pete Best's house. As a show of good faith, Epstein pointedly declined to sign the contract in order to allow his clients to withdraw from the agreement at any time. As the months unfolded, he instructed the band to improve their demeanor on stage—no more swearing, no more eating between songs. For his part, he saw to it that their standing fee at the Cavern Club was doubled, and he vowed, more importantly, to earn them a record deal with a major label. In short order, Epstein began expanding his contacts throughout the music world. As part of this effort, Epstein played "My Bonnie" for Ron White, the marketing manager for the monolithic EMI (Electric and Musical Industries), as well as to Tony Barrow, the *Liverpool Echo*'s music reporter who also served as a publicity representative for Decca Records. Epstein was known for the brash confidence that he brought to such meetings, often touting the Beatles' destiny as being "bigger than Elvis." Impressed with the Beatles' sound, Barrow contacted Dick Rowe, Decca's chief A&R (Artists and Repertoire) man, and Rowe dispatched one of his producers, Mike Smith, to Liverpool. On December 13, Smith visited the Cavern and was suitably impressed with the band's energy and charisma. That same evening, Smith told Epstein that "we've got to have them down for a bash in the studio at once. Let's see what they can do."

2 | ABBEY ROAD

ON MONDAY, JANUARY 1, 1962, the Beatles arrived at Decca's Broadhurst Gardens recording studios. Signaling his serious interest in the group, Mike Smith allowed them to perform fifteen songs—auditions typically consisted of just two or three songs—for the label's consideration. Most tunes were staples from their stage act, including "Till There Was You," "The Sheik of Araby," "Three Cool Cats," and "Bésame Mucho," as well as three early Lennon-McCartney originals: "Like Dreamers Do," "Hello Little Girl," and "Love of the Loved." As Lennon later recalled, "I remember when we made our first recording. We didn't sound natural. Paul sang 'Till There Was You' and he sounded like a woman. I sang 'Money,' and I sounded like a madman. By the time we made our demos of 'Hello Little Girl' and 'Love of the Loved,' we were okay, I think." Of the three vocalists, Harrison notably sounded the most assured on the four tracks where he sang lead.

As Harrison and his bandmates awaited Decca's verdict, EMI's Ron White sent his formal rejection to the group in mid-January, claiming that the label already had plenty of vocal groups under contract at the time. On February 1, Dick Rowe offered Decca's response, curtly reporting that "groups with guitars are on the way out." Besides, Rowe added, the Beatles "sound too much like the Shadows." As it happened, the Decca saga was not quite over. Fearing that the label would lose its valuable retail record contracts with NEMS, Rowe traveled to Liverpool on February 3 in order to hear the band for himself. As Smith's superior and Decca's A&R head, Rowe felt that he owed Epstein this courtesy. But when he arrived at the

Cavern, Rowe was waylaid by the regular throng of kids packing themselves into the Cavern's sweaty archways to see the Beatles. Rowe returned to London, where, several days later, he met with Epstein yet again in order to assuage the manager, who felt as though he had been slighted by the music conglomerate. "You have a good record business in Liverpool," Rowe told him. "Stick to that." Having now been rejected by EMI and Decca, as well as by two other major British record firms, Pye and Philips, Epstein was crestfallen as he left Decca House.

But his fortunes would shortly change when he visited Bob Boast, the manager of London's flagship HMV record store on Oxford Street. Although Boast had been unimpressed with the Beatles' Decca audition tapes, he recommended that Epstein cut an acetate of the standout tracks for presentation to the city's A&R men. As he cut the acetate in HMV's studio, engineer Jim Foy liked what he heard and duly introduced Epstein to Sid Colman, the general manager of Ardmore and Beechwood, EMI's in-house music publisher. Feeling that it was in the company's best interest to avoid losing the Beatles to their competitors, Colman directed Epstein to thirty-six-year-old George Martin at Parlophone, the bottom of the proverbial barrel among EMI's record labels, which included august HMV and the hit-making Columbia.

With absolutely nothing to lose, Epstein made an appointment to meet Martin on February 13, the day after making the acetate at the HMV. The manager delivered his usual bombastic pitches about the Beatles—that they would be "bigger than Elvis," that they were poised to conquer the world—before offering Martin a sampling of the Decca sessions. For the most part, Martin was unmoved. He was especially flummoxed by the idea that a Liverpool group would somehow unseat an international star the likes of the King. It was simply preposterous. And Martin certainly wasn't willing to stake his reputation on the band without having properly auditioned them. "It's *interesting*," he told Epstein, "but I can't offer you any kind of deal on this basis. I must see them and meet them. Bring them down to London, and I'll work with them in the studio." As it happened, Epstein was loath to return to Liverpool without a record contract in hand—the Beatles' spirits were reaching a new low after the Decca rejection.

Meanwhile, the band was scheduled to return to Hamburg April through May of 1962 for an engagement at the Star-Club, a sterling new venue on the Reeperbahn, where a massive dance floor could accommodate nearly a thousand patrons. During their visit, they learned the awful news that Stu Sutcliffe had died of a brain hemorrhage. The Beatles were understandably devastated. For his part, Harrison held a soft spot in his heart for Sutcliffe, but playing to form, he maintained the forward-looking demeanor that would come to define his nature: "We didn't go to the funeral. That was it: as the man said, 'He not busy being born is busy dying.' But we all felt really sad and I remember feeling worst for Astrid. She was still coming to the shows and sitting there. I think it made her feel a bit better, at least, to hang out with us."

Back in England, Epstein had become absolutely desperate to prove himself to his clients. In a veritable bolt from the blue, he was invited to London by Martin for a meeting on May 9. To Epstein's genuine surprise, Martin agreed to provide the Beatles with a recording contract without having met them, much less auditioned them. In truth, the contract saddled EMI with very little in the way of risk—the Beatles' agreement with Parlophone was known, for very good reasons, as a "penny-per-record contract." While Epstein likely never knew the reasons behind Martin's about-face regarding a contract—the EMI brass was pressuring him to sign the band and appease the influential Northern record store owner—Epstein was ecstatic. After arranging for the Beatles' audition at EMI Studios on June 6, he telegrammed the Beatles in West Germany: "CONGRATULATIONS, BOYS. EMI REQUEST RECORDING SESSION. PLEASE REHEARSE NEW MATERIAL." The Beatles responded with their own telegrams in short order, with Lennon and McCartney having a laugh, while the ever-pragmatic Harrison kept his eye on the prize.

> Lennon: WHEN ARE WE GOING TO BE MILLIONAIRES?
> McCartney: PLEASE WIRE TEN THOUSAND-POUND ADVANCE ROYALTIES.
> Harrison: PLEASE ORDER FOUR NEW GUITARS.

On September 6, the Beatles joined Martin at EMI Recording Studios at 3 Abbey Road in northwest London. Working with Ron Richards in Studio 2, they performed a cover version of "Bésame Mucho," followed by three original Lennon-McCartney compositions, "Love Me Do," "P.S. I Love You," and "Ask Me Why." Afterward, Martin joined the band in the control room above the studio floor to provide his assessment.

No fly-on-the-wall observer of the Beatles would ever have labeled Harrison as "quiet," and in fact, his sarcasm and wit could be just as sharp as Lennon's. In a moment that has since become part of the band's legend, Harrison's snark went a long way toward endearing the Beatles to their future recording manager during the September 6 meeting. After Martin gave them a lecture on various rudimentary aspects of the recording process and a healthy critique overall, he asked, more graciously than really necessary, if there was anything they were unhappy about. Neither Lennon nor McCartney stepped into the opening the producer had given them, but after the band shuffled their feet for a moment, Harrison spoke up: "Well, I don't like your tie." Following Martin's thorough dressing-down, Harrison's concentration on a completely trivial detail struck just the right note of absurdity, breaking the ice with the producer and cueing the other Beatles to follow suit. By the time the four young men had left the studio, Martin had been well and truly charmed.

While Martin liked the band's raw potential and their acerbic sense of humor, he wasn't fond of Pete Best's drumming and thought he should be replaced—at least in the recording studio. For Epstein and the Beatles, too, Best had now become expendable. Lennon, McCartney, and Harrison left the matter in their manager's hands, and Epstein informed the drummer in August that he would shortly be replaced by Ringo Starr, who had resigned from Rory Storm and the Hurricanes almost as soon as he had learned of the Beatles' interest. For Ringo, assuming his new role in the Beatles would be a trial by fire among the band's hardcore Liverpudlian fans: "The first gig in the Cavern after I'd joined was pretty violent," he later recalled. "There was a lot of fighting and shouting; half of them hated me, half of them loved me." As Harrison remembered, "Some of the fans—a couple of them—were shouting 'Pete is best!' and 'Ringo never, Pete Best forever!' but it was a small group and we ignored it. However, after about half an hour it was getting a bit tiring so I shouted to the audience. When we stepped out of the band room into the dark tunnel, some guy nodded me one, giving me a black eye."

When the Beatles returned to EMI Studios on September 4, Martin had them record Tin Pan Alley composer Mitch Murray's "How Do You Do It," which the producer was certain had hit potential, as their debut single. Bowing to Martin's request, the Beatles worked up a competent arrangement and delivered a polished performance of the song, but their hearts weren't in it. Lennon and McCartney pushed back and—in an incredibly brash move considering they didn't have any leverage in the situation—told the producer they would rather stand on their own material than perform generic material by an outside writer. When challenged by Martin to offer a comparable song to Murray's composition, the Beatles launched into a rehearsal of "Please Please Me," a slow number that Lennon had styled after Roy Orbison's "Only the Lonely (Know the Way I Feel)." But Martin felt that "Please Please Me" was "much too dreary" in its current incarnation, and he encouraged the boys to rehearse a more vigorous, upbeat version for their next session. By the time they returned to Abbey Road on September 11, the Beatles had transformed the song considerably. Before that, they would record a new version of "Love Me Do" with session man Andy White in tow, while Starr chipped in on tambourine. Released as the Beatles' first official single on October 5, 1962, "Love Me Do" notched a respectable top-twenty showing on the British charts.

There was no single moment when the Lennon-McCartney-Harrison balance that had characterized the Beatles' stage act in Liverpool and the Cavern shifted, but in retrospect, it becomes clear that the band's next recording session was a signpost on the way to Lennon and McCartney assuming more prominent roles. On November 26, they returned to EMI Studios and recorded an up-tempo version of "Please Please Me." For Martin, that session demonstrated that the Beatles could take constructive criticism, and, most importantly, that Lennon and McCartney could write a hit. When they finished recording, Martin declared dramatically over the intercom from the control room, "Gentlemen, you've just made your first number one record." There would be no more talk of "How Do You Do It" in the wake of "Please Please Me." Martin would challenge them next to give him something *better* than "Please Please Me," and when they delivered, he continued to challenge them.

By Paul's estimate, one notebook of pre-fame Lennon-McCartney songs contained around one hundred compositions. Even if none of those songs were half as good as "Love Me Do," they represented countless hours of the two young men honing their craft together, building a rapport, critiquing each other, pushing each other to improve ideas, and forging what would become an indomitable songwriting team. Harrison's coauthorship with

McCartney of "In Spite of All the Danger" in 1958 and with Lennon of "Cry for a Shadow" in 1961 could hardly compare. Once the Lennon-McCartney partnership reached cruising altitude, Harrison could only watch them soar, and as their songwriting royalties started rolling in and their reputations flourished, he began to wonder how he too could get himself off the ground as a songwriter. But he had a great deal of catching up to do.

By early 1963, Martin's prediction of "Please Please Me" as a chart topper had come true, followed by "From Me to You" and "She Loves You," both of which also hit number one. Martin became more and more confident of the group's abilities, and all four Beatles responded to his encouragement. The commercial-minded producer's attentiveness to the Lennon-McCartney songwriting had helped open the floodgates on their compositions. Later in the year, around the time Lennon and McCartney were penning the song that would finally break them in America, Harrison, with scarcely any encouragement from anyone, was picking away at his first solo tune. Recorded in September, "Don't Bother Me" would, at its core, prove a remarkably prescient sketch of the complicated relationship its composer would have with fame for the rest of his life. But while it was full of its author's sullen charm, it would not replace the transcendent "I Want to Hold Your Hand," recorded in October, as the band's next single.

The American market had rebuffed the Beatles' advances the whole of 1963, but on February 1, 1964, "I Want to Hold Your Hand" reached the top of the *Billboard* charts, followed by the band's epochal appearance on *The Ed Sullivan Show* on February 9, before a television audience of more than seventy million viewers. Beatlemania, which had been born back in the UK in October 1963 after the band's appearance on the ITV variety show *Sunday Night at the London Palladium*, was about to become a truly global phenomenon.

For Harrison, the group's bravura visit to New York City would be memorable in more ways than one. "While we were staying at the Plaza in New York for *The Ed Sullivan Show*," he later recalled, "the Rickenbacker people came and gave me one of their twelve-string guitars. After that trip, I used it a lot. It was a great sound, and in those days the only other type of twelve-string available had a great big fat neck (it would have a high action, be a bugger to get in tune and impossible to mash the strings down). The Rickenbacker had a slim neck and low action. The twelve machine heads were fitted very tidily, and in a way which made it simple to recognize which string you were tuning. The pegs for the six regular strings were positioned sideways while the pegs for the octave-extra six were placed backwards as on old Spanish guitars. John already had a little six-string Rickenbacker, the famous blond one with the short-scaled neck that he later had painted black; so after I was given the twelve-string at the Plaza, John and I both had Rickenbackers and they became synonymous with the Beatles." As the Beatles' fame grew, their slightest gesture could set off profound reverberations, and Harrison's use of the Rickenbacker 12-string on their next project became a case in point. By now, Martin and Epstein acted as the Beatles' brain trust, directing their careers both inside and outside the studio to consolidate the power of Beatlemania. "Brian Epstein and I worked out a plan," Martin later recalled, "in which we tried—not always successfully—to release a new Beatles single every three months and two albums a year. I was always saying to the Beatles, 'I want another hit, come on, give me another hit,' and they always responded."

By the early months of 1964, Epstein and Martin's plan had come to include the annual production of a feature film—a jukebox movie along the lines of *The Girl Can't Help It* (1956) or *Jailhouse Rock* (1957). In addition to producing the Beatles' songs for *A Hard Day's Night*, Martin was tasked with composing the orchestral interludes for the United Artists film, which was set to be directed by Richard Lester, an American transplant who had cut his teeth bringing independent programs to British television, most notably, *The Running, Jumping, and Standing Still Film* with Spike Milligan and Peter Sellers. In November 1963, Lester had shot a television commercial for Smith's potato chips starring a nineteen-year-old model named Pattie Boyd, a rising star in the world of fashion who had been featured in *Elle* and the UK edition of *Vogue*. Lester subsequently cast Pattie as a schoolgirl in *A Hard Day's Night*, where she caught Harrison's eye.

Given the Beatles' breakneck schedule, Lester filmed *A Hard Day's Night* at London's Paddington Station, Twickenham Film Studios, and various other locations across March and April. For Pattie Boyd, the opportunity to be in the film was nothing short of a grand adventure. For their scenes, Lester depicted the Boyd sisters as precocious schoolgirls who unexpectedly find themselves in the Beatles' orbit on a railway carriage. In one scene set on the train, where Pattie Boyd looks on as the band plays "I Should Have Known Better," Harrison plays his new Rickenbacker twelve-string, including a memorable chiming solo. Seeing the film upon its release in August, guitarist Roger McGuinn was instantly struck with the sound of the twelve-string and sought out his own version of the instrument, which would give his band, the Byrds, a distinctly identifiable sound, and consequently clear a path for the burgeoning folk-rock scene the following year.

As for the filming itself, Pattie Boyd later recalled, "The train took us to Cornwall and back, not that I remember much of the scenery. I spent most of the day watching the action, chatting to everyone during the breaks, and waiting to do my bit. The Beatles were so funny together, so quick-witted, and their laughter was infectious. I couldn't understand half of what they said because of the thick Liverpudlian accent—a revelation to me, I'd never heard anything like it. It was impossible to be in their company and not be helpless with laughter." Almost immediately, Boyd began sizing up the individual Beatles: "On first impressions, John seemed more cynical and brash than the others, Ringo the most endearing, Paul was cute, and George, with velvet brown eyes and dark chestnut hair, was the best-looking man I'd ever seen," she later wrote. "At the break for lunch I found myself sitting next to him, whether by accident or design I have never been sure. We were both shy and spoke hardly a word to each other, but being close to him was electrifying."

For his part, Harrison felt Boyd's attraction acutely and couldn't take his eyes off her. Wasting little time, he asked her out, only to be curtly rejected. Boyd later remembered that "as the train neared London and the filming was winding down, I felt sad that such a magical day was ending. It had been pure joy, and I wanted to capture it forever. As if George had known what I was thinking, he said, 'Will you marry me?' I laughed, as I had at all the Beatles' jokes. I scarcely allowed myself to wonder why he had said it or whether he might feel as I did. Then he said, 'Well, if you won't marry me, will you have dinner with me tonight?' I felt awkward and said I couldn't, I had a boyfriend, but I was sure my boyfriend would love to meet him—maybe we could all go out. George didn't think so, so we said our farewells at the station and disappeared into the night." As it happened, Boyd had been living with—and "semi-engaged"—to her boyfriend, photographer Eric Swayne. Within a matter of days, she broke up with him, determined to win a second chance with the Quiet Beatle.

If Harrison had been stung by Boyd's rejection, he didn't reveal it during their next encounter on March 12. "There was a press photo call at Twickenham Studios and each of us schoolgirls had to stand behind a Beatle and pretend to do their hair," Boyd wrote. "I made a beeline for George. He seemed pleased to see me and asked how my boyfriend was. I told him I'd dumped him. He grinned and asked me to have dinner with him." That evening, Harrison and Boyd had dinner at the Garrick Club in Covent Garden along with Epstein, who acted as the couple's chaperone. Boyd revealed, "I didn't resent [Epstein's] presence on our first date—he was good company and seemed to know everything about wine, food, and London restaurants. And perhaps if George and I, two very young, very shy people, had been on our own in such a grown-up restaurant, it would have been too intense. As it was, we had a lovely evening and sat side by side on a banquette listening to Brian, hardly daring to touch each other's hand."

In sharp contrast with Harrison's happy childhood, Boyd's upbringing had been riddled with confusion, abandonment, and abuse. Born on March 17, 1944, in the village of Taunton in Somerset, Pattie Boyd had her life upended when she was eight years old. Her family had moved to Nairobi after the discharge of her father, Colin Boyd, from the Royal Air Force. At the behest of her mother, Diana Boyd, Pattie was sent away to boarding school. As she later recalled, "I had never felt so miserable. I didn't know what I had done wrong, why I was being punished. I didn't understand why my mother didn't want me at home with her. I felt completely and utterly bereft—unloved, unwanted, unimportant. With hindsight, I think I sensed something bad was going on at home but I was too young to know what it was—and that made my insecurity even worse. Every time I had to go back to school I would cry and my mother would smile and say goodbye. I couldn't work out what message she was delivering and it left me feeling confused." The answer finally came when her mother pulled up to her boarding school with a strange man in the passenger seat. Diana introduced the man to Pattie as "your new father." Diana had met and married Bobbie Gaymer-Jones—while Pattie's father embarked on an affair of his own.

Incredibly, things got even worse for Pattie and her younger siblings Colin Junior, Jenny, and Paula. As the Boyd children were coming to grips with their mother's new marriage, Diana and Bobbie announced that they were returning to England and leaving them behind in Nairobi. "I felt as though my world had ended," Pattie Boyd later wrote, "and I don't understand to this day why she did it. Was it too expensive to take us all on the ship? Or maybe Bobbie didn't want us to travel with them. What 28-year-old in his right mind would want three pesky children aged nine, seven, and six competing for his wife's attention? They had only been married for three months when they left. I was desolate." In December 1953, Pattie and her siblings were finally reunited with their mother in London. But their bliss was quickly tempered by their mother's growing family—in short order, Pattie would gain two half-siblings. Worse yet, Gaymer-Jones turned out to be a menacing stepparent. As Boyd later recalled, "My stepfather was a frightening character, and we were all scared of him, including, I think, my mother, although she would never have said so. I thought he was a bully. He had loved his time in the army and treated us as though we were his own personal foot soldiers, wanting his boots polished, his food on the table, the children silent, and everything just so in the house. He was always telling us to stand or sit up straight, always finding fault." Gaymer-Jones's verbal barrages eventually transitioned into terrible beatings that deeply traumatized the Boyd children.

By age seventeen, Pattie was no longer living in her stepfather's orbit. But as it turned out, the man wasn't long for her world anyway. During a family vacation, he announced that he wanted to divorce Pattie's mother, who was subsequently left to raise their sizable brood. Then, Pattie's world took a dramatic turn during her employment as a shampoo girl at Elizabeth Arden, where she was a beautician trainee. In short order, she was discovered by a writer for *Honey* magazine, who suggested that she build a portfolio and seek out modeling jobs. For Pattie Boyd, life in the capital had taken a magical turn. No longer burdened by her years under her stepfather's ironclad rule, she was finally beginning to enjoy the bloom of her youth. As she later recalled, "London belonged to the young. All the old class structures of our parents' generation were breaking down. All the old social mores were swept away. No one cared where you came from or what school you'd gone to, what accent you spoke with or how much money you had. All that mattered was what you could do, what you could create."

By March 17, 1964—Boyd's twentieth birthday—George Harrison had already met her mother. "I took him home to Strathmore Road to meet my family. We arrived in George's beautiful silver Jaguar E-type and everyone was excited," Boyd recalled. "George sat down and told one funny story after another. He was so easy and friendly with everyone, and it was the same every time we went home. My mother adored him, and so did my brothers and sisters." That Easter, Harrison and Boyd were enjoying a lavish Irish vacation in the company of John and Cynthia Lennon. In May, the couples traveled farther afield—this time, to Tahiti, where they took on assumed names in order to throw off the paparazzi. As Boyd later wrote, "John and Cynthia were Mr. and Mrs. Leslie, George was Mr. Hargreaves, and I was Miss Bond. To complete the disguise, Cynthia and I wore wigs and dark glasses." Harrison and Boyd became engaged on Christmas Day in 1965, marrying on January 21, 1966, and settling together in Harrison's Kinfauns home in Esher. Boyd recalled that their wedding "had to be secret—if the press found out, it would be chaotic. I had always thought I'd have a big white wedding, as all little girls do, then have children and live happily ever after—not be divorced like my mother. As a child I thought I'd do anything to avoid divorce—I even considered waiting until I was forty to marry because by that time I would have had my fun and there would be no chance of a marriage breaking up. But there I was, at 21, marrying George, who was all of 22. But I was so happy and so much in love, I didn't care. Divorce didn't enter my head: we would be together and happy forever." As the decade wore on, the glamorous newlyweds took their place as royalty among the Swinging London set.

While Harrison's highly public "private" life was the veritable portrait of romantic success, his life among the Beatles—and as a musician and a budding intellectual in general—was caught in a state of transition. As a guitar player, he had improved precipitously since his Quarry Men audition back in 1958. His solos were concise and memorable, logical and thoughtfully worked-out extensions of the songs themselves. But he was also determined to make his name as a songwriter. In the shadow of Lennon and McCartney, this would be no easy feat. By 1965, the songwriting duo had taken their place among the annals of history's greatest composers. That December, the Granada television network even went so far as to broadcast a special entitled *The Music of Lennon and McCartney*. As one act after another, including the George Martin Orchestra, saluted the songwriters' embarrassment of musical riches, it was clear that the pair had much to celebrate at this comparatively early date in their songwriting career. They had already been feted in numerous ways and in nearly every medium. They had even famously won over William Mann, the *Times*' classical music critic, back in December 1963. In his article, Mann interpreted Lennon's work on "Not a Second Time" as being akin to the Aeolian cadence that concludes Gustav Mahler's *The Song of the Earth*. Lennon would later joke that an "Aeolian cadence" meant nothing to the songwriter, sounding to him like "exotic birds." But he would be lying if he said he wasn't secretly chuffed by receiving such select attention. And then there was McCartney's "Yesterday," for which BBC critic Deryck Cooke extolled him and Lennon as "serious" composers of a "new music."

This environment—where the stakes of authorship were growing increasingly competitive—was a tough world for Harrison to cut his teeth as a composer. "Songwriting for me," he later reflected, "was a bit frightening because John and Paul had been writing since they were three-years-old. It was hard to come in suddenly and write songs. They'd had a lot of practice. They'd written most of their bad songs before we'd even got into the recording studio. I had to come from nowhere and start writing, and have something with at least enough quality to put on the record alongside all the wondrous hits. It was very hard." According to McCartney, he and Lennon had considered including Harrison as a member of their songwriting team back in the Quarry Men days. "John and I had really talked about it," he said. "I remember walking up past Woolton Church with John one morning and going over the question: 'Without wanting to be too mean to George, should three of us write or would it be better to keep it simple?' We decided we'd just keep to two of us."

Even still, the Beatles' brain trust of Epstein and Martin recognized that the group's popularity emanated from all four members and not merely the vaunted Lennon and McCartney. For this reason, they were careful to include showcase numbers by all four of the Fabs. Their debut LP, *Please Please Me*, featured Harrison singing the Lennon-McCartney-penned "Do You Want to Know a Secret" and Starr covering the Shirelles' "Boys." *With the Beatles* included Harrison covering Chuck Berry's "Roll Over Beethoven" and Ringo taking lead vocals on the Lennon-McCartney original "I Wanna Be Your Man." Later, however, during the recording sessions for the soundtrack of *A Hard Day's Night*, Lennon passed "I'm Happy Just to Dance with You" off to Harrison for the simple reason that he didn't want to take the syrupy vocals for himself. Besides, it was "written for George to give him a piece of the action." To John's mind, it wasn't merely the Lennon-McCartney juggernaut that prevented Harrison from landing songs on Beatles albums, but rather "'cause, simply, his material wasn't up to scratch. That's the reality of it. It wasn't a conspiracy. He just didn't have the material."

Gone were the days of Hamburg and the Cavern when Harrison would enjoy nearly equal numbers of lead vocals. Those had been cover versions, of course, and now that the Beatles were moving toward an almost entirely original repertoire, Lennon and McCartney ruled the roost. Harrison recognized that the time was nigh for him to get involved in the band's competitive stakes of authorship. Of his first song, "Don't Bother Me," Harrison would later say, "I was sick in bed. I don't think it's a particularly good song; it mightn't be a song at all. But at least it showed me that all I needed to do was keep on writing and maybe eventually I would write something good." And keep writing he did, though the next song showed there was still a great deal of room for improvement. "You Know What to Do," demoed in the studio in June 1964 with likely accompaniment from Lennon and McCartney, was musically clunky and lyrically bland, betraying its author's lack of identity as a songwriter. They never returned to it, and Harrison wouldn't submit another song for consideration until the following year.

Although he may have envied their output and success, Harrison credited Lennon and McCartney with being supportive along his early journey to becoming a songwriter. "I knew a little bit about writing from the others," said Harrison, "from the privileged point of sitting in the car when a song was written or coming into being." And while he may not have felt that Harrison's material was particularly strong, "John was always helpful. He said things like, 'When you're writing, try to finish the song immediately, because once you leave it it's going to be harder to complete,' which is true. Sometimes, anyway." On some occasions, Harrison would be especially bold and share his unfinished works with Lennon. "I played him a tune one day," Harrison recalled, "and he said, 'Oh, well, that's not bad.' He didn't do anything at the time, but I noticed in the next song he wrote that he'd nicked the chords from it!" Ultimately, for Harrison, "Writing on my own became the only way I could do it, because I started like that. Consequently, over the years, I never really wrote with anyone else and I became a bit isolated. I suppose I was a bit paranoid because I didn't have any experience of what it was like, writing with other people. It's a tricky thing. What's acceptable to one person may not be acceptable to another. You have to trust each other."

By 1965, Harrison began to find his own voice as a writer and started contributing original material regularly to Beatles albums. Although his two songs on *Help!*—"I Need You" and "You Like Me Too Much," both recorded in February—are lyrically thin, they chart encouraging progress musically. By the fall months of that year, during the *Rubber Soul* sessions, he made a considerable leap forward. "If I Needed Someone" takes a page from the Byrds-y twelve-string jangle that Harrison originally helped inspire, fleshed out with luminous, layered three-part harmonies. "Think for Yourself," though, is even stronger, stepping outside of standard pop's boy-girl romance format into something wholly confrontational and challenging, with unexpected twists both lyrically and melodically. What sparked this new depth?

Intellectually, Harrison was on the precipice of embarking on a new spiritual path. Not surprisingly, his journey began by way of his long-held interest in seeking out new acoustic instruments—in this instance, the sitar, the long-necked, multi-fretted Indian lute. He had first come into the orbit of the sitar on the set of the Beatles' second movie, *Help!*, which featured a scene in which a band of Indian musicians performed an instrumental version of "A Hard Day's Night." After listening to the sitar work of Ravi Shankar, the renowned Bengali-Indian virtuoso, Harrison was hooked:

> I had bought a very cheap sitar in a shop called India Craft in London, and it fitted on to the song ["Norwegian Wood"] and it gave it that little extra thing. Even though the sound of the sitar was bad, they [the Beatles] were still quite happy with it. At the same time as I played the sitar, very badly, on the Beatles' record, I began to hear Ravi Shankar's name. The third time, I thought, "This is an odd coincidence." I went out and bought some of Ravi's records, put them on, listened to them and it hit a certain spot in me that I can't explain, but it seemed familiar to me. The only way that I can describe it was my intellect didn't know what was going on and yet this other part of me identified with it. It just called on me.

For Harrison, meeting Shankar would ignite one of the most important associations of his lifetime. As Graeme Thomson put it, Shankar acted as the Beatle's "spirit guide" in many ways. Harrison's budding interest in Eastern music and religion occasioned a reconsideration of spirituality and religion. Indeed, by 1966, George had found himself in the throes of "confirming things for himself" as he had predicted all those years ago: "Nobody I know in the Christian religions seems to have a deep enough understanding of the science of God to be able to translate it into human terms. Church leaders are purveying a kind of nonsense because they don't really understand it themselves. So they blind you with ignorance, like a government does, as if the power of the Church has become reason enough for you not to question anything it says. It's like, 'You don't know anything about Christ and God because we're the ones who own the franchise.'" Through Shankar, George had steeped himself in the literature of Eastern religion and philosophy. These readings had, in short, changed his way of seeing the world and his notions of spiritual transcendence. "I had read enough from the Vivekenandas and Yoganandas," Harrison later recalled, "to comprehend how to see God: by using the Yogic system of transcending through the relative states of consciousness (waking, sleeping, dreaming) to get to the most subtle level of pure consciousness. It is in that level that the individual experiences pure awareness, pure consciousness, the source of all being. Everything in creation is the effect of that pure state of being, the transcendent or the God. God is the cause. And the effect is all three worlds: the causal, the astral, and the physical. I believe absolutely in the power of prayer, but it's like love: people say 'I love you,' but it's a question of 'how deep is your love?'"

For *Revolver*, he enjoyed a previously unheard-of bounty of *three* songs on a long-player, including "Taxman," "Love You To," and "I Want to Tell You." For Harrison, it was a windfall, to say the least. For the whole of the band's recording career, of course, Harrison had languished as the "junior" member of their creative team, a pecking order that was not only reinforced by Lennon and McCartney, but producer George Martin, too. The elder statesman for the Beatles' brain trust had no problem making distinctions among the bandmates and their *individual* talents, determined as he invariably was to get the most out of their *collective* talents. And the Beatles' producer wasn't above playing favorites. The stakes of authorship were significant in a highly competitive group like the Beatles, and to Martin's mind, Harrison was still lagging behind the world-famous songwriting duo as late as *Sgt. Pepper's Lonely Hearts Club Band*, when the producer rejected Harrison's "Only a Northern Song" and suggested that the youngest Beatle go back to the drawing board and give it another go. The result was the shimmering "Within You, Without You," demonstrating Harrison's ability to rise to the challenge of working in a band where two of the members—Lennon and McCartney—had become household names.

Yet by *Revolver*, even Martin could sense a shift, however slight, in Harrison's songwriting fortunes. The producer later wrote that Harrison had "been awfully poor up to then. Some of the stuff he'd written was very boring. The impression is sometimes given that we put him down. I don't think we ever did that, but possibly we didn't encourage him enough. He'd write, but we wouldn't say, 'What've you got then, George?' We'd say, 'Oh, you've got some more, have you?' I must say that looking back, it was a bit hard on him. It was always slightly condescending. But it was natural, because the others were so talented." Martin was equally quick to admit that he, too, fell well short of being on an equal playing field with the likes of Lennon and McCartney, later remarking that "there is no doubt in my mind that the main talent of that whole era came from Paul and John. George, Ringo, and myself were subsidiary talents. We were not five equal people artistically: two were very strong, and the other three were also-rans."

As Harrison began his spiritual quest, he found a strong advocate and supporter in Pattie Boyd, whose skepticism about organized religion was decidedly similar to his own. "Religion, inevitably, played a large part in my education," she later recalled. During her youth, "we had to go to church on Friday evenings and twice on Sundays. I have no idea why I was sent to Roman Catholic convents: we were Church of England. My mother was quite religious and we went to church every Sunday. Yet at school I had a very different experience with priests, nuns, and lots of incense, which I loved. However, I had difficulty accepting much of what I was taught. How on earth could Jesus have been born from a virgin? How could he have risen from the dead? None of the nuns was prepared to explain anything: we had to take it all at face value. None of it was inspirational because they weren't."

As with her husband, Boyd's lifelong concerns about organized religion and what she perceived to be its hypocritical foundations were central aspects of her intellectual makeup. Indeed, it was Boyd who brought the Harrisons into the orbit of Maharishi Mahesh Yogi in the summer of 1967, after seeing a newspaper advertisement. At fifty years old, the Maharishi had been on a journey of spiritual regeneration for much of his life. In 1945, he began a personal program of solitary meditation in the Himalayas that lasted for more than a decade. When he literally came down from the mountain, the Maharishi devoted himself to spreading traditional Indian teachings to the masses, a project that he started in 1957 with the founding of the Spiritual Regeneration Movement, the crusade that would eventually bring him to London during the Summer of Love. His timing couldn't have been better. Of particular interest to George Harrison and Pattie Boyd—and very soon thereafter, the other Beatles—was the Maharishi's development of an increasingly popular technique known as Transcendental Meditation. The Maharishi urged his followers to engage in a pair of twenty-minute daily sessions in which they focused on their mantra, the simple phrase whose repetition promised to open new vistas of spirituality, inner calm, and human consciousness.

For Harrison, there was simply no turning back after experiencing a lecture from the Maharishi at London's Hyde Park Hilton in August 1967. Striving for spiritual growth via Transcendental Meditation afforded Harrison an avenue for living in the material world. And not surprisingly, the Maharishi's teachings would provide him with a new bedrock and approach for his songwriting. "Maharishi used to say that if you have a bow and an arrow, and you can only pull back the bow a little, the arrow won't go far," George later reflected. "But if you can draw the bow right back, you can get the maximum range from the arrow. With prayer, some people are so powerful at doing it that their prayers really work, whereas others might have the intention but not the ability. A strong bloke can lift a heavy weight dead easy. Another guy won't have the strength. Both have the same intention, but only one has manifested the ability to do it. For prayer to really work, you have to do it in the transcendent, as the more manifest the material world is (or the conscious level is), the less effect it has. So the power of prayer is subject to one's own spiritual development. That's why the transcendent level of consciousness is so important, and also why the mantra is so important in reaching that level. The mantra is like a prescription. If you have the right word on a prescription, you get the right medicine."

With an overarching desire to have access to "the right medicine," Harrison began pursuing a lifelong quest for transcendence, a journey that would find the Beatles in the company of the Maharishi at his ashram in Rishikesh in

1968. In terms of his musical growth, Harrison remained confident as always, and he was determined to redraw the songwriting map—not only within the parameters of the Beatles, but as a solo artist and beyond. Martin may have been content with being an "also-ran," but Harrison simply wasn't having it.

3 | LITTLE BASTARD

CLAPTON'S EARLY YEARS—not to mention his progress toward international fame—couldn't be any more different from Harrison's experiences. Though each musician's youth would exert a profound impact upon his musical and interpersonal life, the similarities end there. While Harrison had grown up in a supportive, loving household that imbued him with the confidence to speak his mind, Clapton could only recall a life of introversion. And in contrast with George's formative years and early musical forays, which often involved scads of like-minded kids, Eric's path was often a lonely journey toward discovering his life's work.

As it happened, Clapton came by his shy, inward-looking demeanor out of sheer necessity. Although he was born as "Eric" on March 30, 1945, in Ripley, a tiny village in Surrey, some forty miles north of the English Channel, he was known among his family as "Rick." He grew up in a state of poverty, to be sure, without the benefit of electricity or running water and with only a few hissing gas lamps for warmth. Clapton recalled that his family lived in one of Ripley's old "almshouses," which "was divided into four rooms; two poky bedrooms upstairs, and a small front room and kitchen downstairs. The toilet was outside, in a corrugated iron shed at the bottom of the garden, and we had no bathtub, just a big zinc basin that hung on the back door. I don't remember ever using it." During his earliest years, he remembered feeling as if everyone were talking about him behind his back, or—worse yet—speaking about him in a kind of familial code, often right in front of him. Eric lived in "a house full of secrets," but eventually, the reality of his personal situation became clear: "One day I heard one of my aunties ask, 'Have you heard from his mum?' and the truth dawned on me," he recalled, "that when Uncle Adrian jokingly called me a little bastard, he was telling the truth."

Soon thereafter, Eric discovered that he was being raised by his grandmother Rose Clapp, whom he had believed to be his mother. As long as he could remember, she had reared him as her own with her husband, Jack Clapp, Eric's maternal grandfather. In truth, Rose and Jack had taken Eric into their home after their daughter, sixteen-year-old Patricia Clapton, had given birth to him. Eric was the product of an affair between Pat, as she was known, and twenty-five-year-old Edward Fryer, a Canadian airman who was stationed near Ripley. A pianist in a dance hall group, Fryer had met Pat during one of his gigs as a scratch piano player. Pat learned that Fryer was married and that he had every intention of returning to his wife in Canada and leaving her to fend for herself. Eric had been born in one of the Clapps' upstairs bedrooms. The truth about Eric's illegitimate lineage was a closely guarded secret—and not only from Eric himself. The family made every effort to avoid airing their dirty laundry in Ripley, which, like so many small towns, found its citizenry knee-deep in each other's business. During the years after Eric's birth, Pat pretended to be his older sister until she left Ripley—and her son—altogether.

Eric's earliest love wasn't music, but rather, candy of nearly every kind. In spite of his reclusive nature, he managed to find his way to the village sweet shop. "Ours was run by two old-fashioned sisters, the Miss Farrs," he later wrote. "We would go in there and the bell would go 'ding-a-ling-a-ling,' and one of them would take so long to come out from the back of the shop that we could fill our pockets up before a movement of the curtain told us she was about to appear. I would buy two Sherbet Dabs or a few Flying Saucers, using the family ration book, and walk out with a pocketful of Horlicks or Ovaltine tablets, which had become my first addiction." But the stress and strain of his unspoken heritage took its toll. "In spite of the fact that Ripley was, all in all, a happy place to grow up in, life was soured by what I had found out about my origins," he wrote. "The result was that I began to withdraw into myself. There seemed to have been some definite choices made within my family regarding how to deal with my circumstances, and I was not made privy to any of them. I observed the code of secrecy that existed in the house—'We don't talk about what went on'—and there was also a strong disciplinarian authority in the household, which made me nervous about asking any questions."

Not surprisingly, Eric's overarching insecurity led to an unmitigated hatred of school. He wanted nothing more than to feel anonymous, which meant that competitive athletics were out, not to mention virtually anything "that would single me out and get me unwanted attention." His only solace—outside of sweets, that is—was music. At first, he came to adore music by listening to his grandmother Rose, who loved to play keyboard instruments. "My earliest memories are of her playing a harmonium, or reed organ, she kept in the front room, and later she acquired a small piano," he recalled. "She would also sing, mostly standards, such as 'Now Is the Hour,' a popular hit by Gracie Fields, 'I Walk Beside You,' and 'Bless This House' by Josef Locke, who was very popular in our house and the first singer to captivate me with the sound of his voice." In his braver moments, Eric would sing aloud by standing alone on the stairs leading up to the family's bedrooms. "I found out that one place had an echo," he recalled, "and I used to sit there singing the songs of the day, mostly popular ballads, and to me it sounded like I was singing on a record."

Still, the vast majority of Eric's musical education arrived courtesy of the radio, "which was permanently switched on in the house. I feel blessed to have been born in that period because, musically, it was very rich in its diversity. The program that everybody listened to without fail was *Two-Way Family Favorites*, a live show that linked the British forces serving in Germany with their families at home," he wrote. "We would hear the whole spectrum of music—opera, classical, rock 'n' roll, jazz, and pop—so typically there might be something like Guy Mitchell singing 'She Wears Red Feathers,' then a big-band piece by Stan Kenton, a dance tune by Victor Sylvester, maybe a pop song by David Whitfield, an aria from a Puccini opera like *La Bohème*, and, if I was lucky, Handel's 'Water Music,' which was one of my favorites. I loved any music that was a powerful expression of emotion." It was during this period that Eric fell in love with the blues. It happened, quite expectedly, during an episode of *Two-Way Family Favorites*. "It was a song by Sonny Terry and Brownie McGhee," Clapton recalled, "with Sonny Terry howling and playing the harmonica. It blew me away."

Not long afterward, Eric encountered the sounds of Big Bill Broonzy, an authentic country bluesman from the American South. Broonzy's "Hey Hey" and "Key to the Highway" were among his early favorites. For Eric, "Music became a healer for me, and I learned to listen with all my being. I found that it could wipe away all the emotions of fear and confusion relating to my family." Indeed, music would be his only tonic in 1954, when his mother suddenly returned to Ripley and shook up the nine-year-old boy's life to its core. Married to a Canadian soldier named Frank MacDonald, Pat introduced the Clapp household to her two young children, six-year-old Brian and one-year-old Cheryl. Clapton remembered traveling to Southampton to meet her ship that brought her from West Germany, where she was living with MacDonald at the time. "Down the gangplank came this very glamorous, charismatic woman, with her auburn hair up high in the fashion of the day," he wrote. "She was very good-looking, though there was a coldness to her looks, a sharpness. She came off the boat laden with expensive gifts that her husband Frank had sent over from Korea, where he had been stationed during the war. We were all given silk jackets with dragons embroidered on them, and lacquered boxes and things like that."

But it would take more than gifts and meeting his half-siblings to salve Eric's longstanding emotional wounds. "One evening, when we were all sitting in the front room of our tiny house," he wrote, "I suddenly blurted out to Pat, 'Can I call you Mummy now?' During an awful moment of embarrassment, the tension in the room was intolerable. The unspoken truth was finally out. Then she said in a very kindly way, 'I think it's best, after all they've done for you, that you go on calling your grandparents Mum and Dad,' and in that moment I felt total rejection." Once again, at his family's urging, he was entreated to continue referring to his mother as his sister, a ruse that would continue into his adulthood. Meanwhile, back at school, Eric's troubles fitting in with his classmates went from bad to worse. At this juncture, he wasn't merely a social misfit, but a naive one at that. His behavior came to a head when he discovered a work of "homemade pornography" while playing on the Ripley village green. "It was a kind of book," he recalled, "made of pieces of paper crudely stapled together with rather amateurish drawings of genitalia and a typed text full of words I had never heard of. My curiosity was aroused because I hadn't had any kind of sex education, and I had certainly never seen a woman's genitalia. In fact, I wasn't even certain if boys were different from girls until I saw this book." Spotting one of the schoolgirls from his class, Eric tried out one of the phrases from the book on her: "Do you fancy a shag?" In short order, he was summoned to the headmaster's office, where "I was bent over and given six of the best. I left in tears, and the whole episode had a dreadful effect on me, as from that point on I tended to associate sex with punishment, shame, and embarrassment, feelings that colored my sexual life for years."

Eric's life changed for the better when, at the age of twelve, he met John Constantine, a new kid at school who hailed from a middle-class family. Like Eric, John was a misfit who eschewed cricket and football in favor of mod-looking clothes and 78-RPM records. As the school's outcasts, Eric and John were subject to constant ridicule, and they even earned a nickname among their peers as "the Loonies." Eric spent much of his free time at the Constantines' home on the outskirts of Ripley. For one thing, John's family had a "radiogram," which combined a radio and gramophone—often attractively encased in a piece of wooden furniture; in the States, the radiogram was known as a "console." Radiograms often sported larger loudspeakers than standard radios or gramophones; hence, they were much-coveted devices in the 1940s and 1950s. The Constantines' radiogram was the first such entertainment system that Eric had ever seen, and he was transfixed by the device. He was equally entranced by John's copy of Elvis Presley's "Hound Dog," which the boys played over and over. As Clapton recalled, "There was something about the music that made it totally irresistible to us, plus it was being made by someone not much older than we were, who was like us, but who appeared to be in control of his own destiny, something we could not even imagine."

Better yet, the Constantines owned their own television set. Suddenly, Eric had access to the latest British television programs, including Val Parnell's *Sunday Night at the London Palladium*, the most popular variety show of the day. "One night they had Buddy Holly on the show," Eric remembered, "and I thought I'd died and gone to heaven. That was when I saw my first Fender guitar. Jerry Lee Lewis was singing 'Great Balls of Fire,' and the bass player had a Fender Precision Bass. It was like seeing an instrument from outer space, and I said to myself: 'That's the future—that's what I want.'" Not long afterward, Eric purchased his very first record album, *The "Chirping" Crickets*, featuring Buddy Holly belting out such classics as "That'll Be the Day," "Not Fade Away," and "Oh, Boy!" Meanwhile, Eric matriculated at age thirteen to Hollyfield Road School, some thirty minutes outside of Ripley in Kingston-upon-Thames. Given its proximity to London, Hollyfield thrust him into an entirely different social set, one with ready access to the city and a more arts-oriented outlook. For the first time in his life, Eric began to feel as though he belonged. "We would study normal things like history, English, and math," Clapton remembered, and then "a couple of days a week we would do nothing but art: figure drawing, still-lifes, working with paint and clay. For the first time in my life, I actually started shining, and I felt like I was hitting my stride in every way."

By this juncture, the skiffle boom was in full force across the British Isles. While John, Paul, George, and Ringo were caught up in the same musical phenomenon some two hundred miles to the north, Eric found himself longing for a guitar to call his own. While they had very little to spare in the way of disposable income, his grandparents took him to Bell's Music Store to place a down payment on a bottom-of-the-barrel starter guitar. "The instrument I had set my eyes on was a Hoyer, made in Germany and costing about two pounds," Clapton recalled. "An odd instrument, it looked like a Spanish guitar, but instead of nylon, it had steel strings. It was a curious combination, and for a novice, it was really quite painful to play. Of course, it was a case of putting the cart before the horse, because I couldn't even tune a guitar let alone play one. I had no one to teach me, so I set about teaching myself, and it was not an easy task."

For his first number, Eric tried out "Scarlet Ribbons," a folk song that had been popularized by Harry Belafonte, although Eric preferred the blues-oriented cover version by Josh White. "I learned it totally by ear, by listening and playing along to the record," Clapton later wrote. "I had a small portable tape recorder, my pride and joy, a little reel-to-reel Grundig that Rose had given me for my birthday, and I would record my attempts to play and then listen to them over and over again until I thought I'd got it right." Unfortunately for Eric, the cheaply constructed guitar offered little in the way of action. The strings were arrayed too high above the fingerboard, rendering the instrument very difficult to play. Not surprisingly, he broke a string soon after bringing the guitar home, which forced him to learn how to play the Hoyer as a five-stringed instrument. Even still, Eric was thrilled to own a guitar of his very own. "Though I still hadn't quite got to grips with the actual playing of the guitar, I wanted to look like I knew what I was doing and tried to cultivate the image of what I thought a troubadour should look like. I got a Biro and I wrote on the top surface of the guitar, in huge letters, the words LORD ERIC because I thought that's what troubadours did."

Years later, Clapton would realize that play-acting as a troubadour was shrewd preparation for life as a rock 'n' roll star. "Guitar playing—it's like a bluff," he said. "Covers up all your wimp things." Still caught up in his own protracted wimpy phase, Eric balanced his five-string guitar playing with his ongoing musical education courtesy of Robert Johnson. At Hollyfield, Eric came into the orbit of Clive Blewchamp, a school chum who was a tried-and-true blues fanatic. For Eric, discovering the music and legend of Robert Johnson was a genuine turning point. "It was almost like I'd been prepared each step to receive him," Clapton recalled. It was "like a religious experience that started out by hearing Chuck Berry, and then at each stage I was going further and further back, and deeper and deeper into the source of the music, until I was ready for Robert Johnson." In addition to the Mississippi native's otherworldly blues-playing, Eric was caught up in Johnson's mystique, especially the myth that Johnson had sold his soul to the devil at a lonely, midnight crossroads in exchange for his incredible skills as a blues guitarist.

Johnson's records left Eric in a state of emotional abandon. Clapton later recalled that, not unlike himself, "it was almost as if he [Johnson] felt things so acutely he found it almost unbearable. Eric immersed himself in Johnson's music. During his all-too-brief lifetime, Johnson pursued his mastery of the Delta blues as a traveling performer. His work was captured in a pair of recording sessions in San Antonio and Dallas in 1936 and 1937, respectively. Incredibly, the resulting twenty-nine extant recordings of his music mark the sum total of his preserved output. Eric had been particularly inspired by stories about Johnson's days in a cheap San Antonio hotel room, where the shy guitarist would play the blues facing into a corner because of an innate bashfulness and lack of confidence—qualities that Eric identified with explicitly. The young guitarist vowed that "following this man's example would be my life's work. I was totally spellbound by the beauty and eloquence of songs like 'Kindhearted Woman,' while the raw pain expressed in 'Hellhound on My Trail' seemed to echo things I had always felt. I tried to copy Johnson, but his style of simultaneously playing a disjointed bass line on the low strings, rhythm on the middle strings, and lead on the treble strings while singing at the same time was impossible to even imagine." Eric knew that his quest for learning the fabled blues man's playing style was only just beginning.

By this point, Eric's starter guitar simply wouldn't do. One Saturday, he found himself wandering around a Kingston flea market, when he happened upon a Washburn guitar. The vintage guitar originated in Chicago—a touchstone for a young blues aficionado like Eric. He would never forget the moment he first laid eyes on the instrument: "I saw a very odd-looking guitar hanging up on one of the stalls," he remembered. "It was acoustic but it had a very narrow-shaped body, almost like a medieval English guitar, and a painting of a naked woman stuck on the back of it. Intuitively, I knew it was good. I picked it up and, though I didn't play it because I didn't want anyone to hear, it felt perfect, like a dream guitar." As it happened, the pinup had been varnished over, much to Eric's chagrin. "It was difficult to scrape this off without damaging the wood, and it pissed me off that someone had done this to such a beautiful instrument. At last I had a proper guitar, meant for folk music. Now maybe I could become the troubadour that I thought I was meant to be."

When he turned sixteen, Eric changed schools yet again, leaving Hollyfield for the Kingston School of Art. He would later recall the "tremendous sense of belonging" that he felt during this period—both at the Kingston school, as well as among the expanding circle of musicians and artists that he had come to know. "In those pre-hippie, beatnik days, it did seem to be all about the music. Drugs were rare, and even the drinking was fairly moderate." In those days, crowds of musicians and beatniks would gather on Eel Pie Island in the Thames, near Twickenham. Always struggling to fit in with his peers, Eric took to playing his Washburn in the company of Dave Brock, who would later found the space-rock group Hawkwind. Eric slowly began to come out of his shell, especially when "we'd all jump on the train and go up to London to the folk clubs and pubs around Soho, places like the Marquess of Granby, the Duke of York, and the Gyre and Gimble coffee bar in Charing Cross." In those days, the folk scene was beginning to reach its zenith, and Eric became enamored with a guitarist known as Buck, who played a twelve-string guitar, and Wiz Jones, who performed Irish ballads and folk tunes, along with the occasional Lead Belly song. Eric would sidle up to the musicians to get a closer look at their hands, so that he could mimic their playing style. Then he would go home to his Washburn, practicing for hours and learning that evening's music.

During this period, Eric also returned with a vengeance to the music of Big Bill Broonzy. As with his studies of Robert Johnson, Eric threw himself headlong into the Chicago blues man's music and performance style. In many ways, Broonzy was a natural inspiration for Eric. The blues legend enjoyed a wide-ranging repertoire that included forays into hokum blues, country blues, urban blues, ragtime, jazz, folk music, and spirituals. By 1938, Broonzy's musical prowess had become so revered that he was selected to sit in for the late Robert Johnson at the "From Spirituals to Swing" concert at vaunted Carnegie

Hall in New York City. Johnson had recently died at age twenty-seven under mysterious circumstances—perhaps the devil had come for him, after all? Across his lifetime, the prolific Broonzy composed more than three hundred songs. As for Eric, the young guitarist devoted himself to learning Broonzy's finger-picking technique, "which was to accompany yourself with your thumb, using the thumb to play eighth notes on the bass strings while you pick out a riff or countermelody with your fingers. This is a staple part of blues playing in one form or another and can be developed into a folk pattern, too, like clawhammer, where you move your thumb rhythmically between the bottom strings alternately while picking out the melody on the top strings with your first, second, and sometimes third fingers." For his practice sessions, Eric would play along with the record until he felt as if he had mastered the song, then he would record his efforts on the Grundig and assess the results. Using this picking technique, Eric mastered an array of material, including the Bessie Smith song "Nobody Knows You When You're Down and Out," the bluegrass staple "Railroad Bill," and Big Bill Broonzy's "Key to the Highway."

On occasion, Eric would attach himself to his contemporaries, while continuing to pursue the music of the great bluesmen at home. One such person was Gina Glaser, an American folk singer that he had met around school. He recalled being "star-struck" by the woman—and especially by her hard-wrought life and her "world-weary aura." She had a young child whom she was raising as a single mother, and she had posed as a nude model for Kingston art classes. In Clapton's memory, "she had a beautiful, clear voice and played an immaculate clawhammer style. I was smitten with her, and I think she found me attractive, but she was twice my age, and I was still pretty green around women." Observing the American folk singer in close quarters seemed to afford Eric new levels of confidence, as did his emergence as a regular at a Kingston pub called the Crown. With his guitar playing on an upward trajectory, he began playing in a corner of the Crown, with a billiard table as the only barrier between him and the "suave crowd of beat people" who frequented the pub. Eric especially admired the other regulars' "affluence": "The guys wore Chelsea boots, leather jackets, matelot shirts, and Levi 501s, which were incredibly hard to find—and a kind of harem of very-good-looking girls moved around with them. Bardot was then the icon for women to follow, so their uniform was tight jumpers, slit skirts, and black stockings with duffel coats and scarves. They were very exotic, very fast, and very well educated, a tight group of friends who seemed to have grown up together." Eric admired them from afar—it became his fervent ambition to be accepted by them, "but since I was an outsider from the word go, and working-class, the only way I could really get their attention was by playing the guitar."

While Eric's playing improved by leaps and bounds during this period, his schoolwork took a nosedive. When he had first enrolled at Kingston, Eric had been determined to hone his skills as a draftsman in order to pursue a trade beyond graduation. At Kingston, he had accepted a place in the graphics department, as opposed to fine arts, where the majority of his fellow students had enrolled. To Eric's mind, he had made a grave mistake—his heart simply wasn't into graphics, and his motivation ebbed considerably. Always a keen observer of his peers, Clapton remembered lunching in the canteen and seeing "all the students come in from fine art, long-haired, covered in paint, and looking completely detached. They were given almost total freedom, developing their talents as painters or sculptors, while I was set to do projects every day, designing a soap box, or coming up with an advertising campaign for a new product. Apart from a short period when I managed to get into the glass department, where I learned engraving and sandblasting, and became quite interested in contemporary stained glass, I was bored to tears." Of course, Eric's core issue wasn't really his suitability for graphics or fine arts, but rather, his obsession with music, which was "ten times more exciting, ten times more engaging, and as much as I loved art, I also felt that the people who were trying to teach me were coming from an academic direction that I just couldn't identify with. It seemed to me that I was being prepared for a career in advertising, not art, where salesmanship would be just as important as creativity. Consequently, my interest, and my output, dwindled down to nothing."

In short, Eric resolved that he would drop out of Kingston at the end of the current term in favor of his music. But to his surprise and dismay, he received his assessment at the conclusion of the term, only to learn that Kingston's administration had decided to disenroll him. "I knew my portfolio was a bit thin," he later wrote, "but I really believed that the work I had done was good enough to get me through. To me it was much more creative and imaginative than most of the other students' work. But they were judging by quantity, and they booted me and one other student out, just two of us out of 50, which was not good." For Eric, there were a number of ramifications: first—in keeping with his earlier desire to leave Kingston—his dismissal proved to be a rite of passage: "I got brought up short by the sudden realization that all doors weren't going to open up for me for the rest of my life, that the truth was that some of them were going to close. Emotionally and mentally, the shit hit the fan." Second, and perhaps worse yet, his dismissal forced him to gird his courage and be honest with his grandparents, to whom he had been lying for several years—namely, by telling them that he was attending school when in fact he had been wandering the streets, guitar in hand, and lounging about in pubs, watching the world go by.

Eric's grandfather Jack Clapp was predictably matter-of-fact, albeit stern. "You've had your chance, Rick," he told his grandson, "and now you've chucked it away." He pointed out that if Eric wanted to continue living in the family home, he would need to contribute financially to the household. A master plasterer, bricklayer, and carpenter, Eric's grandfather offered him a position as his "mate," at an impressive wage of fifteen pounds per week. The opportunity opened Eric's eyes, not only to the demanding nature of his grandfather's profession, but also to the man's distinctive and unflinching skill level. "My grandfather really was brilliant with his hands, and watching him plaster an entire wall in minutes was exhilarating," Clapton recalled. "It turned out to be a valuable experience, even though it seemed he was being extra-tough on me, which I'm sure was because he wanted no suspicion of nepotism. I learned that he worked, and lived, from a very strong set of principles, which he tried to pass on to me." Eric took particular notice of the other work on the building sites that he frequented with his grandfather, identifying two schools of thought when it came to pursuing a profession. A vast number of the other workers were "skivers," who only worked when the foreman was present. The others were laborers like his grandfather, who put in a full workday, doing a solid job from start to finish. Simply put, he "had no time for skivers, and so, to a certain extent, like me in later years, he was slightly unpopular and a bit of an outcast. His legacy to me was that I should always try to do my best, and always finish what I started." For Eric, these were lessons that—in good times and bad—would never be far afield from his outlook on professional life.

Of course, working with his grandfather afforded Eric with the free time away from school to fall into a more adult routine and continue honing his skills as a guitarist. With his Washburn on its last legs, he desperately needed the wages from his newfound profession in order to purchase a replacement. Prior to working for his grandfather, Eric had agreed to accompany his grandmother to West Germany, where his estranged mother was living with her husband Mac, who was stationed there on an air-force base, and her three children. To Eric's chagrin, he learned that he would need to cut his hair before joining his family in the dining hall. "Almost as soon as I arrived, Mac told me that I would have to get my hair cut before I could go into the mess," Clapton recalled. "I was horrified by this request, since my hair was not even particularly long by the standards of the day, but it seemed that the offensive part was that you couldn't see the top of my ears." In short order, "they gave me a crew cut and I felt alone and humiliated. I moped around a lot for the remainder of my stay." Things got even worse when his half brother, Brian MacDonald, sat down on top of the ailing Washburn, breaking the guitar's neck in half. "I was gutted," Eric recalled. "He was the sweetest kid, totally in awe of me, and it was an accident, but there and then I vowed internally that Pat and her entire family could go to hell."

Sadly, at this juncture, Eric began to withdraw yet again, losing his grip on the self-confidence that he had worked hard, and for so long, to acquire. Resolving to no longer trust anyone, he returned to Ripley badly in need of a new guitar. Back at Bell's Music Store, he caught a glimpse of a semi-acoustic guitar, a double-cutaway Kay. Eric recognized the instrument from Alexis Korner's recent performances at the Marquee Club on Oxford Street. Among blues devotees, Korner was enjoying a kind of hero status for having established the first R&B band in the UK. For Eric, the opportunity to play a guitar like Korner's was too good to pass up. The double-cutaway design afforded the player with easy access to the upper echelons of the fretboard. Eric came to realize that the Kay was a poor-man's version of the Gibson ES-335, which, to his mind was "the best guitar of the day." But even with his new job working for his grandfather, he couldn't afford Gibson's £200 price tag. At ten pounds for the Kay, Eric's choice was simple. "Much as I loved this guitar, I soon found out that it wasn't that good," he said. "It was just as hard to play as the Hoyer, because again, the strings were too high off the fingerboard, and, because there was no truss rod, the neck was weak. So after a few months' hard playing, it began to bow, something I had to adapt to, not having a second instrument."

Yet Eric's experience with the Kay proved to be far more revealing than he realized at first. "Something more profound also happened when I got this guitar," he later wrote. "As soon as I got it, I suddenly didn't want it anymore. This phenomenon was to rear its head throughout my life and cause many difficulties." For the time being, the Kay would be, as a matter of necessity, Eric's go-to guitar. And it would shortly come in handy. At eighteen years old—and without the shackles of the Kingston School holding him back—Eric was ready to throw himself headlong into the blues. In January 1963, he met Tom McGuinness at the Prince of Wales pub, where the guitarist was playing in a blues outfit called the Roosters. The band had been founded by vocalist Paul Jones and guitarist Brian Jones. Brian had left the previous year to establish a new R&B group with Mick Jagger that would shortly become known as the Rolling Stones. Paul would shortly follow suit. With a vacancy in the Roosters' lineup, Eric was invited to take Brian Jones's place, joining McGuinness on guitar, alongside Ben Palmer on keyboards, Robin Mason on drums, and Terry Brennan on vocals.

As with McGuinness, Eric was mesmerized to be working with the likes of Brennan, who "was a fantastic guy, a genuine, full-blown Teddy Boy. He had a pompadour haircut with a quiff about six inches high in front, and wore a fingertip jacket with a velvet collar, drainpipe jeans, and 'brothel-creepers,' which were suede winkle-picker crepe-soled shoes. Unlike most Teds, however, who had a reputation for being hard men, and who only listened to Bill Haley and Jerry Lee Lewis, he was incredibly gentle, and he really loved the blues." For Eric, allegiance to the blues was an essential quality. Fortunately, Palmer also had the bug. "I knew Ben would be a big part of my life the minute I heard him play," Clapton recalled. "He was an absolute purist, with a love for the blues that more than matched my own." Still, life with the Roosters wouldn't be easy. The band possessed only a single amplifier with which to project their sound, and instead of a proper van, they had to stow all of their equipment in Mason's cozy convertible. They would rehearse in a room above a pub, where they began trying their hands at a raft of Chuck Berry and Muddy Waters songs.

In truth, the band only performed a handful of gigs—certainly, no more than a dozen—rehearsing far more often than they actually played on stage. The blues had very few adherents in Ripley, and the Trad Jazz boom that had begun in the 1950s seemed to be on the wane. "Pop was the order of the day, with the current craze being the Mersey sound," Clapton later wrote. "The Beatles were just starting to be popular, and once a week a radio show called *Pop Go the Beatles* came on, which consisted entirely of them playing their own songs and covers of other people's. They were taking off really quickly, and everybody wanted to be like them. It was the beginnings of Beatlemania. All over the country people were dressing like them, playing like them, sounding like them, and looking like them." While Clapton would later have occasion to see things differently, at the time he believed that Beatlemania "was despicable, probably because it showed how sheep-like people were, and how ready they were to elevate these players to the status of gods, when most of the artists I admired had died unheard of, sometimes penniless and alone." Worse yet, the overwhelming nature of Beatlemania left Eric feeling as though his pursuit of the blues was nothing short of a "lost cause." As the Mersey sound grew ever more popular, Eric and his fellow blues aficionados came to feel like refugees, forced to "go underground, as if we were anarchists, plotting to overthrow the music establishment."

But all was not lost. The world seemed to have changed for Eric after McGuinness played him a record by Freddie King. Entitled "Hideaway," it was an instrumental that would have a far-reaching influence on Clapton. "I'd never heard Freddy King [sic] before, and listening to him had an effect on me similar to what I might feel if I were to meet an alien from outer space," he remembered. "It simply blew my mind. On the B-side of 'Hideaway' was 'I Love the Woman,' which had a guitar solo in the middle of it that took my breath away. It was like listening to modern jazz, expressive and melodic, a unique kind of playing in which he bent the strings and produced sounds that gave me the shivers. It was absolutely earth-shattering for me, like a new light for me to move toward. Up until that moment, I had always thought of guitar playing as being little more than an accompaniment to the singing." While the Roosters still spent far more time sipping tea and talking about the irresistible pull of the blues, they began to expand their repertoire to include yet more blues tunes by John Lee Hooker, Muddy Waters, and Freddie King—songs like "Hoochie Coochie Man," "Boom Boom," "Slow Down," and "I Love the Woman." In the case of the latter song, Eric began to develop his own extended, melodic solos, like King, in order to find his particular niche in the ebb and flow of the music. It was an apprenticeship that would be the making of him.

Eric's life among the Roosters' ranks would be decidedly short-lived—no more than six months, all told—but his experience with his fellow blues disciples, especially McGuinness, led to his next group. Their salvation arrived in the form of Liverpudlian Brian Casser, who had previously fronted Cass and the Casanovas before moving to London, where he opened the Blue

Gardenia nightclub. With Clapton and McGuinness in tow, Casser founded Casey Jones and the Engineers. In total, Clapton's days with the band would be even shorter than his time as a member of the Roosters. After a mere six weeks, he and McGuinness called it quits. They had suffered through the same old problems—poor amplification and a paucity of gigs. As blues purists, Clapton and McGuinness could hardly stomach Casey Jones and the Engineers' repertoire, which consisted mostly of top-twenty cover songs. But what really rankled Clapton were the matching black outfits that Casser expected them to wear—topped off with Confederate army caps. The experience proved to be even less inspiring than Clapton's days among the Roosters.

By now, Clapton had become friendly with the Rolling Stones, who now included Mick Jagger, Brian Jones, and Keith Richards. Sometimes, Clapton would even perform in Jagger's stead when the singer suffered from throat problems. The Stones really took off after establishing their residency at Giorgio Gomelsky's Crawdaddy Club. Clapton would never forget the evening that the Beatles visited the Crawdaddy to see the Stones. As he later recalled, "They'd just released 'Please Please Me,' which was a huge hit. As they walked up and stood right in front of the stage, all of them were wearing long black leather overcoats and identical haircuts. Even then they had tremendous presence and charisma, but to me the weirdest thing was that they appeared to be wearing their stage outfits, and for some reason that bothered me. But they seemed friendly enough, and there was obviously a mutual admiration thing going on between them and the Stones, so I suppose it was only natural that I would be jealous and think of them as a bunch of wankers."

It was at the Crawdaddy, of course, that Clapton would come into the orbit of club owner and promoter Giorgio Gomelsky. By the autumn months of 1963, Clapton was not only a full-fledged member of Gomelsky's Yardbirds, but also the holder of an honest-to-goodness contract, complete with a regular weekly wage. With a new professional life seemingly splayed out before him, Clapton left his job with his grandfather, eventually moving out of his grand-parents' Ripley home altogether. Clapton had always reassured himself that the Yardbirds would only be a temporary gig, that there was a larger world of experience for him out there somewhere. And this point was hammered home for him as he came to realize his bandmates' lack of commitment to passionately pursuing life as bona fide bluesmen.

Things came to a head after Gomelsky landed the Yardbirds as the supporting act for blues legend Sonny Boy Williamson's British tour. "In my role as blues expert of Ripley," Clapton outed the headliner as not actually being the selfsame Sonny Boy Williamson, blues harp extraordinaire, who had composed "Good Morning Little Schoolgirl," "Sugar Mama," and "Early in the Morning." *That* Sonny Boy Williamson had met an early grave after being killed in a robbery, with an ice pick no less, at age thirty-four. Hoping to impress the faux Sonny Boy Williamson with his wide-ranging knowledge of the blues and its history, Clapton said, "isn't your real name Rice Miller?" Sonny Boy Williamson II, as he came to be known, revealed a penknife and began glaring at Eric. Not surprisingly, the bluesman barely tolerated the Yardbirds for the remainder of the tour. What really got to Clapton, though, was Williamson's (né Miller's) remark after the tour that "those English kids want to play the blues so bad—and they play the blues so bad."

4 | CLAPTON IS GOD

AFTER THE EPISODE INVOLVING "For Your Love" and Gomelsky's interpersonal shakeup and rebranding of the Yardbirds as a pop act, Clapton was done with pretending to be a bona fide bluesman. After he left the band—with nearly everyone he knew wondering aloud about how he quit the Yardbirds on the brink of serious fame—Clapton returned to Ripley, still distraught over the experience. He later wrote that he felt "shy, frightened, and disheartened by a business in which everyone seemed to be on the make and selling out rather than being in it for the music." Once again, it was Clapton who had effected an early exit—in this instance, using the pretext that the other Yardbirds didn't share his commitment to the high art of the blues. But to Clapton's mind, it was as if he had been abandoned, yet again, by people whom he trusted—beginning with his mother all those years ago—which left him wayward and distraught. It was a self-betrayal that Clapton repeated, time after time, with nearly every band who welcomed him into their ranks. In short, any time he began to feel settled and wanted, he would begin to get spooked and leave.

After the Yardbirds, Clapton's redemption as a bluesman came in the form of John Mayall. At age thirty-two, Mayall seemed like an elder statesman to Clapton. The younger guitarist was familiar with Mayall, a dyed-in-the-wool blues musician who led the Bluesbreakers, whom Clapton knew from the club circuit. After Mayall invited him to join the band, he knew that it was far from a perfect situation—after all, they had recorded two singles, "Crawling Up a Hill" and "Crocodile Walk," that sounded more pop than

R&B to his ears. Clapton also didn't necessarily care for Mayall's voice or his stage presence. What he did admire, though, was the value that the older man placed in Clapton's guitar work, as well as his interest in navigating the Bluesbreakers away from their current flirtation with jazz blues and toward a Chicago-blues-oriented style.

After joining the band in April 1965, Clapton took up residence in Mayall's home. For Clapton, Mayall acted as a mentor of sorts: "He had the air of a favorite schoolmaster who still manages to be cool," Clapton later wrote. "He didn't drink and was a health-food fanatic, the first proper vegetarian I had ever met. Trained as a graphic artist, John made a good living as an illustrator of things like science fiction books, and he worked as well for advertising agencies, but his real passion was music. He played piano, organ, and rhythm guitar, and he had the most incredible collection of records I had ever seen." Mayall's record collection exerted almost as powerful an influence on Clapton as did its owner. "I had a tiny little cupboard room at the top of John's house," he recalled, "barely big enough for a narrow single bed, and over the better part of a year, when I had any spare time, I would sit in this room listening to records and playing along with them, honing my craft. Modern Chicago blues became my new Mecca. It was a tough electric sound, spearheaded by people like Howlin' Wolf, Muddy Waters, and John Lee Hooker."

Things moved quickly in Mayall's world. Within a month, he asked Clapton to join him in the studio with none other than Bob Dylan, who had been excited to work with Mayall after listening to "Crawling Up a Hill." Of course, the chance to play a session with Dylan might have seemed like a once-in-a-lifetime opportunity. But the youngest Bluesbreaker didn't see it that way. As Clapton later wrote, "I hadn't really listened to any of Bob's stuff and was developing a healthy prejudice toward him, based, I suppose, on what I thought of the people who did like him. As far as I was concerned, Dylan was a folkie. I couldn't understand all the fuss, and it seemed like everyone around him was patronizing him to death." Once again, Clapton found himself unable to see beyond his youthful passions and biases. The Dylan session wasn't entirely a loss, though. While he didn't care much for the American folk hero, Clapton especially remembered meeting Bobby Neuwirth, an artist and member of Dylan's entourage. All in all, the experience typified Clapton's inflexible mindset about life in the music business, a place that he felt would never place as high a premium on the blues as he did.

Meanwhile, life in the Bluesbreakers was going full tilt. While the Roosters and the Engineers had never seemed to play enough gigs for Clapton's liking, Mayall's outfit performed somewhere in England seemingly every night. And while his experience with Dylan had been a bust, he leapt at the chance to play a session with Muddy Waters and Otis Spann, two of his all-time blues heroes. "I was absolutely terrified," Clapton remembered, "but not because I felt that I couldn't carry my weight musically. I just didn't know how to behave around these guys. They were incredible. They had these beautiful baggy silk suits on, and were so sharp. And, they were men. And here I was, a skinny young white boy. But it was fine. We cut a song called 'Pretty Girls Everywhere I Go,' and I played lead over Muddy's rhythm while Otis sang and played piano. I was in heaven, and they seemed pretty happy with what I did."

It was during this period—perhaps because of his nonstop barnstorming days with the Bluesbreakers or legendary studio sessions with the likes of Muddy Waters—that the graffiti began to appear. It all started on the walls of the Islington tube station, where someone had scrawled "Clapton Is God." Soon, the words began showing up all over the Underground and along the walls of Greater London. "I was a bit mystified by this, and part of me ran a mile from it," Clapton later wrote. "I didn't really want that kind of notoriety. I knew it would bring some kind of trouble. Another part of me really liked the idea, that what I had been fostering all these years was finally getting some recognition. The fact is, of course, that through my playing people were being exposed to a kind of music that was new to them, and I was getting all the credit for it, as if I had invented the blues."

This latter aspect simply didn't sit right with Clapton. For all of his youthful bluster and pigheadedness, he didn't believe that he was any kind of genius—much less a god. He knew that he was no match for the great blues players of the day. Plus, there were "tons of white American guitar players [who] were better than me. . . . Reggie Young, for example, a Memphis session player, was one of the best guitarists I had ever heard. I had seen him playing with the Bill Black Combo on the Ronettes package tour. Don Peake, who I saw play with the Everly Brothers, and James Burton, who played on Ricky Nelson's records, were two others. English guitarists I had seen who had knocked me out were

Bernie Watson and Albert Lee." Clapton also had to give Jeff Beck and Jimmy Page their props, although he felt their styles, originating in rockabilly, were very different from the blues that he adored. Ultimately, Clapton felt validated by the "Clapton Is God" episode. He had felt chagrinned by the Yardbirds' string of hits, and this unexpected bout of public adulation seemed to valorize his decision to pursue the higher art of the blues over what he perceived to be their pop self-exploitation. Besides, he reminded himself, "there's something about word-of-mouth that you cannot undo. In truth, I felt grateful about it because it gave me status, and, even better, it was the kind of status nobody could tamper with. After all, you can't muck around with graffiti. It comes from the street."

Although his experience with Muddy Waters in the studio had been a tonic, Clapton had long been concerned over his ability, or lack thereof, to translate his sound and passion onto record. That all changed with the production and release of *Blues Breakers: John Mayall with Eric Clapton*. While the "Clapton Is God" episode had afforded him with a welcome sense of mystique, the *Blues Breakers* LP offered audible proof of Clapton's sky-high potential. In order to capture the guitarist's on-stage prowess and sublime solos, Mayall had originally planned to record the album live at the Flamingo Club with Scottish musician Jack Bruce sitting in on bass. Dissatisfied with the poor quality of the Flamingo recordings, Mayall opted instead to take the Bluesbreakers, which included Mayall on vocals and keyboards, Clapton, bassist John McVie, and drummer Hughie Flint, into the studio. Working in Decca Studios in West Hampstead, London, Mayall and the band recorded *Blues Breakers* across three days in March and April 1966. The breakneck pace of the recording sessions mirrored the type of organic, near-spontaneous approach to music making that appealed to Clapton. With Mike Vernon in the producer's chair, Mayall led the band through several staples from their evolving repertoire. Mayall even hired a horn section, which included Alan Skidmore on tenor sax, Johnny Almond on baritone sax, and Derek Healey on trumpet, as accompaniment for some of the LP's tracks.

For the *Blues Breakers* LP, Clapton turned in a sizzling take on Freddie King's "Hideaway," one of the album's standout tracks and a longtime Clapton favorite. At one point, he reluctantly took the mic for a cover of Robert Johnson's "Ramblin' on My Mind." "John insisted I do vocals," Clapton recalled. "This was much against my better judgment, since most of the guys I longed to emulate were older and had deep voices, and I felt extremely uncomfortable singing in my high-pitched whine. Because the album was recorded so quickly, it had a raw, edgy quality that made it special. It was almost like a live performance." For listeners, the *Blues Breakers* LP would be a veritable showcase of Clapton's otherworldly guitar-playing skills. During the sessions, he played his prized 1960 sunburst Gibson Les Paul Standard—the Kay guitar had been long gone by this juncture, thanks to Clapton's regular paychecks as a member of the Bluesbreakers. At this relative early point in his career, he had already concocted a methodic, time-tested approach to working his gear. Whether on stage or in the studio, Clapton's setup allowed him to maximize the quality of his performance and lend it an aura of distinction. "What I would do was use the bridge pickup with all of the bass turned up, so the sound was very thick and on the edge of distortion," he later wrote. "I also always used amps that would overload. I would have the amp on full, with the volume on the guitar also turned up full, so everything was on full volume and overloading. I would hit a note, hold it, and give it some vibrato with my fingers, until it sustained, and then the distortion would turn into feedback. It was all of these things, plus the distortion, that created what I suppose you could call my sound."

For the musician who had been nicknamed Slowhand by Gomelsky only a few short years earlier, Clapton was quite suddenly known far and wide beyond London. *Blues Breakers* registered a number-six showing on the British charts, earning a gold record for Mayall and the band (technically, it wasn't Clapton's first, having participated in the accolades associated with "For Your Love"). Clapton even enjoyed a jolt of unexpected fame because of the album's cover photograph. Shot by David Wedgbury, the artwork featured the Bluesbreakers reclining on a bench along Old Kent Road. For his part, Clapton seemed intentionally distracted from the photo session. Reading *The Beano*, a British comic book that he had adored since childhood, he stood out from the group because of his nonchalance. Indeed, within days of the LP's release, it came to be known as the *Beano Album*.

The chart success of a blues album in the vein of the Bluesbreakers' new long-player was not entirely unexpected, given the tenor of the times. While Clapton himself had often taken the position that playing the blues was a dying art in an era when pop was king, the country was caught up in the throes of what came to be referred to as the British Blues Boom. And it wasn't just the musicians. As Mayall later recalled, "There was an underground feeling in the air. The people in the clubs were flocking to see us, regardless of what was happening in the record business or the pop charts. We were playing to capacity crowds, six or seven nights a week, everywhere we went. So we figured something was about to happen." Indeed, something was truly in the air. Only a year earlier, Mayall had recorded his first album, *John Mayall Plays John Mayall*, for Decca. After the LP sold a paltry one thousand copies, he had been dropped from the label. Thanks to Vernon, Decca had agreed to release *Blues Breakers*, and the label's gamble had paid off handsomely. Clapton's growing mystique certainly played a part in the album's success. "Eric's contribution was quite phenomenal," Mayall later recalled. "He was the best there was. He wanted to play the blues and I provided a platform on which he could develop that."

But it was more than that. For the past few years, the Rolling Stones had been making their name as an R&B act of the first caliber. Meanwhile, Alexis Korner had been leading the way with his formation, along with harmonica player Cyril Davies of Blues Incorporated. The supergroup's evolving lineup had included such luminaries as Mayall, Mick Jagger, bassist Jack Bruce, drummers Ginger Baker and Charlie Watts, and guitarist Jimmy Page. Their residencies at the Ealing Jazz Club since 1961 had become the stuff of legend. At the same time, numerous other blues aficionados had been making the mark in England, including Ten Years After, fronted by Alvin Lee, Chicken Shack, and a very talented newcomer named Peter Green. Sure, it was an increasingly crowded field—and by the end of the year, it would become more crowded still, in ways that nobody could have imagined. But as far as the British Blues Boom was concerned, Clapton was at the center of the whirlwind.

That spring, as the Bluesbreakers were performing in advance of their breakthrough LP's release, they played a gig in Oxford. Although he had met Clapton previously at the Marquee Club, and, more recently, at the Richmond Jazz Festival, Ginger Baker had come to the Oxford show with purpose in his step. A hard-driving drummer with an impressive pedigree as a former member of Blues Incorporated and, most recently, the Graham Bond Organization, Baker drove Clapton back to London. Along the way, he pitched the idea of forming a new group together. When it came to establishing new bands, Clapton had a well-honed sense of wanderlust, and even though the

Bluesbreakers seemed to be on the verge of something big, he entertained the notion. They would need a bassist, of course, to round out their power trio, and Jack Bruce would complement their musical triangle perfectly. Clapton shared this idea with Baker, knowing full well that Baker and Bruce had a history of personality clashes. At one point, Baker even threatened Bruce at knifepoint. Years later, Clapton would remember that Baker nearly crashed the car after he floated the idea of asking Bruce to join the band. Soon thereafter, though, the three men got together to explore the concept further, with Baker and Bruce agreeing to set aside their differences and concentrate, rightfully so, on making music. For a time, Clapton also proposed the idea of adding vocalist Steve Winwood to their lineup, but Baker and Bruce weren't having it; after all, they had enough trouble keeping themselves in line, much less adding yet another personality to the band.

And with that, rock's first supergroup was formed, with Clapton, Baker, and Bruce calling themselves Cream, underscoring their vaunted place as the cream of the music industry's crop. The group made their concert debut that July at the Windsor Jazz and Blues Festival. While Cream had been secretly rehearsing all spring, Clapton hadn't bothered to inform Mayall that he was leaving the Bluesbreakers until June—and scarcely a month before the release of the *Beano Album*. Worse yet, he only broached the subject after Baker had slipped the news about the band to a *Melody Maker* reporter, which led, almost predictably, to one of Baker and Bruce's patented dustups. In his mind, Clapton had already moved on, as he had been wont to do throughout his young career. And although he felt that Mayall had been "like a father to me," Clapton fell back on his standard behavior of making an early exit. Breaking the news to Mayall "was not a happy experience," Clapton recalled. "I told him I was leaving because I had come to a fork in the road and I wanted to form my own band. I was quite surprised by how upset he was, and though he wished me well, I was left in no doubt that he was pretty angry. I think he was sad, too, because I had helped take the Bluesbreakers to another level." Realizing that Clapton's decision was final, Mayall began making overtures to Peter Green to serve as a replacement. "It took me a while to talk him into it," Mayall said. "He'd been offered a job to tour America with the Animals. But in the end the music won out. He decided he'd rather play blues than go off to the States."

Even with the considerable wind of the British Blues Boom at their backs, Clapton recognized that debuting a power trio such as Cream was not without risk. By this time, he also knew that he would be playing the Windsor jazz festival without the benefit of his treasured Gibson Les Paul Standard, which had been stolen at some point after the conclusion of the *Beano* sessions. When it came to Cream, Clapton was excited about the notion of playing the blues in a three-man format, although he knew full well that Baker and Bruce were equally interested in exploring the vicissitudes of rock 'n' roll and nascent psychedelia. By the time they took the stage at the Windsor Racecourse, Cream had prepared a fairly limited repertoire that featured blues covers like "Spoonful," "Crossroads," and "I'm So Glad." During that first performance, they discovered that the audience was content to sit back and relish Cream's extensive jams. After Windsor, the band hit the ballroom and club circuit with a flourish, treating their viewers to still more longwinded jams and realizing they were sorely in need of original material.

That September, Cream went into London's Ryemuse Studio to cut their first single, "I Feel Free," which Bruce had cowritten with poet Pete Brown. A soaring *a cappella* number with a pop hook lost amid its blue palette, "I Feel Free" managed to land a respectable number-eleven showing on the British charts. The B-side, "N.S.U.," was a made-up jam that had been a staple of their rehearsals back in the spring. "It was like an early punk song," Bruce remembered. "N.S.U." stood for "non-specific urethritis," an inside joke among the group. "I used to say it was about a member of the band who had this venereal disease. I can't tell you which one," Bruce slyly added, "except he played guitar." The single's success demonstrated Cream's peculiar appeal to a music industry that wasn't quite ready for their hybrid sound. As Brown later recalled, "Luckily, they were all strong people and managed to motivate themselves. At first, people thought Cream were just going to be a Chicago-style blues band playing a few clubs. Indeed, the whole operation was initially club-oriented and based on percentages of the venue's door income. The British music business has always been terribly blinkered," he added. "Very few people could see that Cream were going to make it in America and around the world."

By this point, Clapton and the band were ensconced in recording sessions for their first album, which was to be entitled *Fresh Cream*. Working again in Ryemuse Studios with music impresario Robert Stigwood handling production duties, the LP was comprised of a raft of blues standards by the likes of Robert Johnson and Willie Dixon, along with an original composition from Bruce and "Toad," a rollicking instrumental credited to Baker. Released in December 1966, the album enjoyed strong reviews for Cream's innovative approach to blues and rock 'n' roll. Clapton could proudly point to *Fresh Cream* as the logical progression from his work on the *Beano* record.

But Cream's good tidings may not have been Clapton's most revelatory experience during that incredible year. That October, he found himself in the orbit of American guitar wizard Jimi Hendrix. Introduced by Chas Chandler of the Animals, Clapton and Hendrix met backstage at Central London Polytechnic, and the two men quickly realized that they shared a deep reverence for the blues. In short order, Hendrix asked if he could play a number with Cream. Along with Bruce, Clapton remembered being excited by the prospect, although Baker seemed "hostile" to the idea of playing with the American. As Clapton later recalled, "The song Jimi wanted to play was by Howlin' Wolf, entitled 'Killing Floor.' I thought it was incredible that he would know how to play this, as it was a tough one to get right. Of course Jimi played it exactly like it ought to be played, and he totally blew me away. When jamming with another band for the first time, most musicians will try to hold back, but Jimi just went for it. He played the guitar with his teeth, behind his head, lying on the floor, doing the splits, the whole business. It was amazing, and it was musically great, too, not just pyrotechnics." Seeing Hendrix perform live and up close was a moment of pure epiphany. Clapton recognized intuitively that he had witnessed the future of rock music unfolding right in front of him. "The audience was completely gobsmacked by what they saw and heard," he recalled. "They loved it, and I loved it, too, but I remember thinking that here was a force to be reckoned with. It scared me, because he was clearly going to be a huge star, and just as we were finding our own speed, here was the real thing." That December, as *Fresh Cream* debuted on the British charts, eventually earning yet another gold record for Clapton, the Jimi Hendrix Experience released their first single, a cover version of "Hey Joe," an old blues tune *cum* murder ballad that featured Hendrix's searing vocals arrayed against his smoldering guitar work.

For Cream, as well as for Hendrix, 1967 proved to be a banner year. Any anxiety that Clapton felt after coming face-to-face with a future rock 'n' roll megastar dissipated as Cream not only won over a slew of British fans, but also successfully exported their brand, as Brown had predicted, to the United States and the whole of the Western world. That May, Cream began recording their second LP, *Disraeli Gears*. During that same month, Clapton recalled lounging in the Speakeasy when the Beatles strolled in with an acetate of their unreleased album *Sgt. Pepper's Lonely Hearts Club Band*. "Even though I was not overawed in the least by the Beatles, I was aware that this was a very special moment in time for anyone that was there," Clapton later wrote. "Their music had been gradually evolving over the years, and this album was expected by everybody to be their masterpiece." At one point, Harrison handed the acetate to the club's DJ, and Clapton heard the LP for the first time under the influence of an acid trip. As the album emanated from the PA system, Clapton could tell that the Beatles had begun "to explore Indian mysticism, perhaps as a result of George's influence, and at some point the chanting of 'Hare Krishna, Hare Krishna, Krishna Krishna, Hare Hare' began to be heard in the club. The acid gradually took effect, and soon we were all dancing to the sounds of 'Lucy in the Sky' and 'A Day in the Life.' I have to admit I was pretty moved by the whole thing."

Cream's sophomore effort, *Disraeli Gears*, was recorded largely in New York City's Atlantic Studios, with American musician Felix Pappalardi handling production duties and Tom Dowd serving as engineer. By 1966, Dowd was already something of a legend in the recording industry. He represented an unusual amalgam of skills, having grown up with highly musical parents—his father was a concertmaster, and his mother was a renowned opera singer. Not surprisingly, by the time he graduated from high school, Dowd was a full-fledged multi-instrumentalist. During the Second World War, he was part of the Manhattan Project, given his studies at Columbia University in nuclear physics, where he also continued his musical pursuits. After the war, Dowd landed a job with Atlantic Records. In addition to scoring a number-one hit with Eileen Barton's "If I Knew You Were Comin' I'd've Baked a Cake," Dowd collaborated with a string of chart-topping artists, including Ray Charles, the Drifters, the Coasters, and Bobby Darin, among others. Given his wide-ranging tastes, Dowd was equally at home working with jazz musicians such as John Coltrane and Charlie Parker as with classical artists.

When it came to working with a band like Cream—with their own interpersonal turmoil and heightened musical passions—Dowd found it difficult, at least at first, to establish a routine in the studio. As Clapton later recalled, Dowd "was thoroughly confused by the way we approached it. We were used to making albums as if they were live and did not expect to play songs over and over again, or to have to play instruments separately on different tracks. He wasn't quite prepared for the noise levels, either, and I got word that we could be heard several blocks away." In contrast with other bands who frequented the studio with their relatively small-wattage amps, Cream had brought their concert-ready Marshall stacks, and the result was deafening.

Eventually, Dowd was able to establish a working routine with the band, and the results were magnificent, even eclipsing their work on *Fresh Cream*. Clapton was clearly becoming more confident in the studio, as evidenced by his work on such songs as "Tales of Brave Ulysses," which he co-wrote with Australian pop artist Martin Sharp, and "Strange Brew." For the latter song, Clapton took the lead vocals, singing in falsetto against a blues shuffle. The band was particularly excited to try out Bruce's "Sunshine of Your Love" in the studio. The bassist had written it back in January after attending a January 1967 performance by the Jimi Hendrix Experience at the Saville Theatre, operated, at the time, by Beatles manager Brian Epstein. Bruce had been so moved by the experience of seeing Hendrix that he went straight home and devised the central riff for "Sunshine of Your Love." As Clapton recalled, Hendrix's concert had been "blinding. I don't think Jack had really taken him in before." For his part, Clapton was already well attuned to Hendrix's musical gifts. "After the gig," Clapton continued, Bruce "went home and came up with the riff. It was strictly a dedication to Jimi. And then we wrote a song on top of it." For Dowd, Cream's performance on "Sunshine of Your Love" seemed unsteady, at first, in the studio. As Dowd later observed, "Where all the other songs that they played were prepared, this one song, they never found a pocket, they were never comfortable." To assist them in finding their footing, Dowd said, "You know, have you ever seen any American Westerns [with] the Indian beat, where the downbeat is the beat?" Dowd's allusion made the difference, and Baker began "playing it that way, all of the parts came together, and right away they were elated."

Released in November 1967, *Disraeli Gears* registered a top-five hit on the UK and US charts. Not surprisingly, "Sunshine of Your Love" emerged as one of the LP's standout tracks and one of Cream's most well-known songs. Sharp created the LP's striking cover art as a collage, which he assembled out of the band's press releases, along with photographs of Cream by Robert Whitaker, who had taken the infamous "butcher" photos that initially adorned the Beatles' American LP *Yesterday . . . and Today*. Any satisfaction Clapton may have felt over the band's recording sessions in New York City was quickly tempered, though. "I will never forget returning to London after recording *Disraeli Gears*," he later wrote, "with all of us excited by the fact that we had made what we considered to be a groundbreaking album, a magical combination of blues, rock, and jazz. Unfortunately for us, Jimi had just released *Are You Experienced?*, and that was all anyone wanted to listen to. He kicked everybody into touch, really, and was the flavor not just of the month but of the year. Everywhere you went it was wall-to-wall Jimi, and I felt really down. I thought we had made our definitive album, only to come home and find that nobody was interested."

To suggest that "nobody was interested" would seem to be an incredible exaggeration, given the impending success of *Disraeli Gears* and its near-immediate acceptance into rock's pantheon of great albums. Rather, Clapton's feelings of inadequacy—and, indeed, a sense that his current band had already reached its zenith—was very much in character with his earlier musical experiences. In 1968, Stigwood arranged for Cream to embark upon a seven-week US tour in support of *Disraeli Gears*. The group's first full-length American tour had met their every expectation. Cream was flying high, the audience response had been overwhelming, and by his own admission, Clapton had a wonderful time. But then he heard the Band's *Music from Big Pink*. Suddenly, his same old anxieties came back with a vengeance. "It stopped me in my tracks," he recalled, "and it also highlighted all of the problems I thought we had. Here was a band that was really doing it right, incorporating influences from country music, blues, jazz, and rock, and writing great songs. I couldn't help but compare them to us, which was stupid and futile, but I was frantically looking for a yardstick, and here it was. Listening to that album, as great as it was, just made me feel that we were stuck, and I wanted out." In many ways, this was Clapton's same old pattern. Feelings of musical inadequacy and the identification of a talented rival (in this instance, the Band) ignited his now-typical desire to make his escape, to make an early exit in order to forestall what he saw as inevitable failure and abandonment. But there was an additional, even more corrosive element that had come to the fore—namely, Baker's on-again, off-again dalliances with heroin, which exacerbated *everything*, as far as Clapton was concerned.

Back in England, Clapton finally resolved to settle down in a home of his own after years of living the transient life of a professional musician. Hoping to find his new place in the vicinity of Ripley, he flipped through the pages of *Country Life*, and he found himself drawn to a photograph of an Italianate villa. The property featured a tiled terrace and a balcony, along with lavish gardens and picturesque views in several directions. Known as Hurtwood Edge, the twenty-two-room house had been designed by Arthur Bolton, a celebrated Victorian architect and historian. For Clapton, it was the garden that sealed the deal. With its hillside views, redwoods, palm trees, and poplars, the garden entranced him with its natural beauty and "Mediterranean feel." Although the £30,000 price tag on the Hurtwood Edge seemed like a princely sum to Clapton, he determined to buy it during his very first tour of the property.

Living at Hurtwood Edge afforded Clapton easy access to George Harrison, who lived at his Kinfauns home in nearby Esher. Their proximity enabled the two guitarists to continue the friendship they had begun back at the Hammersmith Odeon in December 1964. By this point, the Beatles had scuttled their lives on the road to concentrate on their studio work, allowing Harrison the freedom for other pursuits and, in time, new collaborations. Almost immediately, Clapton found himself attracted to Harrison's wife, Pattie Boyd. As he later recalled, "I went to Esher several times, and every time I left, after a nice time with George and Pattie, I remember feeling a dreadful emptiness—because I was certain that I was never going to meet a woman quite that beautiful for myself. I knew that. I knew I was in love. I fell in love with her at first sight—and it got heavier and heavier with me." But Clapton also knew enough about himself to recognize the nature of his desire, that it had very much to do with her seeming unobtainability. Besides, he had come to realize that his elevation to rock 'n' roll royalty had created unreal expectations about women. "You come out of school, you know, and you get into a group and you've got thousands of chicks out there," he later observed. "I mean, you were at school and you were pimply and no one wanted to know you. And then there you are—on stage, with thousands of little girls screaming their heads off. Man, that's power!"

By the same token, Clapton also knew implicitly that his attraction to Boyd was rooted in his fractured childhood, an era when abandonment and neglect seemed to be around every corner. "I also coveted Pattie because she belonged to a powerful man who seemed to have everything I wanted—amazing cars, an incredible career, and a beautiful wife," Clapton wrote. "This emotion was not new to me. I remember that when my mum came home with her new family, I wanted my half-brother's toys because they seemed more expensive and better than mine. It was a feeling that had never gone away, and it was definitely part of the way I felt toward Pattie." Not surprisingly, Clapton's fawning attentions weren't lost on Boyd, who was used to having men stumble their way around her. After attending a Cream concert with Harrison at the Saville Theatre, she held vivid memories of the first time she saw Clapton performing live, later writing that "he looked wonderful on stage, very sexy, and played so beautifully. But when I met him afterward, he didn't behave like a rock star: he was surprisingly shy and reticent."

The moment left a deep impression on Clapton, who remembered being mesmerized by Boyd's unusual attractiveness, which wasn't merely physical, to his mind, but also very spiritual. As the months wore on, Boyd observed Clapton and Harrison becoming ever closer as friends, playing guitars, writing music, and, eventually, recording together. Still, she knew why Clapton had taken to visiting Kinfauns so often. "I was aware that he found me attractive—and I enjoyed the attention he paid me," she recalled. "It was hard not to be flattered when I caught him staring at me or when he chose to sit beside me or complimented me on what I was wearing or the food I had made, or when he said things he knew would make me laugh or engaged me in conversation. Those were all things that George no longer did." As for Clapton, understanding his own wide-ranging emotional state during this period was no easy feat. While he readily acknowledged the fact that he coveted both Harrison's life and wife, his was a personality in flux—as it had likely been since his early childhood, when he struggled to find and maintain his identity in the face of parental abandonment. At one point, his publicist may have unwittingly revealed this dichotomous aspect of Clapton's psyche as part of a PR blitz with *The Sunday Times*. "He *becomes* different people," the publicist observed. "When he was with [Harrison], he bought a big house like George's and a Mercedes." Yet later, "when he met Delaney and Bonnie, he gave up traveling first class and just climbed onto their bus."

That winter, Cream began recording their third album, *Wheels of Fire*. With Pappalardi and Dowd working in the control booth, the band prepared a slew of new original material, while also reimagining several blues classics for contemporary consumption. As with *Disraeli Gears*, the band recorded the lion's share of their new material at Atlantic Studios in New York City, while conducting additional tracking at London's IBC Studios. Given Cream's well-regarded prowess in concert, the LP was slated to be a double album that would include a special live disc. As one of the album's standout tracks, "White Room" offered another gem from the songwriting team of Bruce and Brown. Complete with Bruce's searing vocals, the song featured innovative deployment of feedback along with Pappalardi's viola. For the album, Clapton offered a powerful reinterpretation of Robert Johnson's classic "Cross Road Blues." Redeployed as "Crossroads," the Cream track showcased Clapton's talent for reinventing Robert Johnson in a rock 'n' roll context. According to Clapton, making the transformation from the blues into rock was all about the "riff, a form that could be interpreted, simply, in a band format. In 'Crossroads,' there was a very definite riff. He [Johnson] was playing it full-chorded with the slide as well. I just took it on a single string or two strings and embellished it. Out of all of the songs, it was the easiest for me to see as a rock and roll vehicle."

For the album's live disc, Pappalardi dispatched a mobile recording unit in Los Angeles for Cream's March 1968 concerts at the Fillmore Auditorium and the Winterland Ballroom. With Bill Halverson serving as engineer, Pappalardi captured six Cream concerts for consideration to make the final cut. As with *Disraeli Gears*, *Wheels of Fire* proved to be a spectacular success. Released in August 1968, the LP holds the distinction of being the first double album to earn platinum status. Although Cream had proven themselves to be consistent hitmakers, Clapton still resolved to leave the band at the first possible opportunity. By this point, Stigwood realized that Clapton was determined to begin his post-Cream professional life forthwith. Scant days before the release of *Wheels of Fire*, Stigwood announced that the group would be recording one more album for posterity before going their separate ways. That October, they would undertake their farewell tour, beginning with a show in Oakland, California, and concluding with a pair of concerts at London's Royal Albert Hall. As with *Wheels of Fire*, the band's upcoming album was slated to feature a selection of live cuts, which Pappalardi recorded at the Forum in Los Angeles later that same month.

Entitled *Goodbye*, the album's cover art featured the bandmates in tails and top hats as if they were, rather fittingly, taking a final curtain call. The album was set into production almost immediately in order to capitalize on Stigwood's announcement, the farewell tour, and Cream's highly public breakup. Pappalardi was on board as the album's producer, with Halverson sitting in the engineer's chair. Recorded at IBC Studios in October 1968, *Goodbye* was a hurried affair, to say the least. For the album, each member was left to his own devices to create new material. The latest Bruce-Brown composition arrived in the form of the whimsical, nostalgic "Doing That Scrapyard Thing," while Baker contributed "What a Bringdown," rife with allusions to Cream's disbandment. Clapton's contribution to the album was crafted in collaboration with George Harrison. Together, the two friends concocted "Badge" while lounging at Kinfauns with Ringo Starr. As Harrison later recalled, "That whole song was quite silly. Ringo was sitting around drinking, out of his brain, saying anything. The part about 'Our kid, now he's married to Mabel,' well, 'our kid' is a common Liverpool expression that usually means your younger brother. We were amusing ourselves." At one point, Starr referenced a bevy of swans living in a nearby park, which Harrison and Clapton dutifully appended to the lyrics. To top things off, the song earned its title over a simple misunderstanding when Eric confused the word "bridge" for "badge" on Harrison's handwritten lyric sheet.

In the liner notes for *Goodbye*, Harrison was credited, rather cryptically, as L'Angelo Misterioso. The song's rambling piano was played courtesy of Pappalardi. For the distinctive guitar effects on "Badge"—especially on the bridge from whence it took its unusual name—Harrison performed his guitar part by plugging his instrument into a Leslie speaker system, which was comprised of a large wooden box containing an amp and two sets of revolving speakers emitting bass and treble, respectively. Originally designed as the speaker component for the Hammond organ, the Leslie's revolving effect was known for creating a dramatic vibrato. By playing his guitar through the speaker system, Harrison was able to affect his guitar sound with an ear-catching, organ-like quality.

During that same year, Harrison had tapped Clapton to perform the distinctive guitar solo on "While My Guitar Gently Weeps," one of the standout cuts on *The Beatles* [popularized as *The White Album*]. For Harrison, the song had already changed the course of his place in the band's political pecking order—and with George Martin, no less. Inspired to compose the song after reading the *I Ching*, Harrison recorded a solo demo in the studio for "While My Guitar Gently Weeps" with Martin in July 1968. As always, Harrison was fully aware of the uphill battle that he faced in order to make his presence known among the Beatles. "I always had to do about 10 of Paul and John's songs before they'd give me the break." While the rest of the band, and indeed Martin, may have diminished Harrison's role in the group at times, the producer came to recognize something greater in the quiet Beatle on this July evening. With Harrison singing his lead vocal with his acoustic guitar as his sole accompaniment, the producer found himself enchanted by the new composition.

Originally, Clapton had been reluctant to perform on a Beatles record, arguing that, outside of inviting nameless studio players, the Fab Four weren't in the habit of populating their music with guest-starring musicians. According to Clapton, Harrison told him that "he wanted me to play the guitar on the air because he couldn't do it the way he wanted to hear it." Still, "I thought he should have played guitar on it," Clapton added, "but it was great for me to do it. We agreed that I wouldn't get paid for it or have my name mentioned." While Clapton's presence on Harrison's magisterial new song didn't seem to impress Lennon and McCartney at the time, "While My Guitar Gently Weeps" proved to be one of *The White Album*'s essential tracks. Producer Chris Thomas remembered that, at Clapton's request, the guitar solo was appropriately modulated to sound more "Beatley." "I was given the grand job of waggling the oscillator on the 'Gently Weeps' mixes," Thomas later recalled. "So we did this flanging thing, really wobbling the oscillator in the mix." More obliquely, Clapton's growing influence in Harrison's life would be referenced in *The White Album*'s "Savoy Truffle." Inspired by Clapton's notorious sweet tooth, the song found Harrison referencing his friend's over-developed fondness for Mackintosh's Good News Double Centre Chocolates, a candy assortment that featured such delectables as Creme Tangerine, Ginger Sling, and Coffee Dessert.

Cowriting "Badge" and performing on "While My Guitar Gently Weeps" had offered Clapton welcome distractions from the restlessness he experienced during the demise of Cream as he pondered the next step in his already legendary career—albeit, a career pocked by a seeming inability to stay put. As Stigwood had intended, Cream's *Goodbye* enjoyed bestseller status in the UK and US alike, and while the album had been gently maligned in the music press for its slightness of vision, it provided Clapton with a means of closing the door on that chapter of his life. When the next chapter unfolded, it featured whiz singer/keyboard player Steve Winwood in a starring role. Still smarting over Bruce and Baker's refusal to consider Winwood for membership in Cream, Clapton was determined to work with the twenty-year-old musician from Birmingham. As Clapton recalled, he had first seen Winwood perform at the Twisted Wheel, and he "had really impressed me with his singing and playing. Most of all, he seemed to know his way around the genre. I think he was only 15 at the time, but when he sang 'Georgia,' if you closed your eyes, you would swear it was Ray Charles. Musically, he was like an old man in a boy's skin."

After Cream broke up, Clapton began regularly jamming with Winwood, who had left Traffic, the quartet behind the critically acclaimed *Mr. Fantasy* LP. In addition to singing lead vocals for the Spencer Davis Group, Winwood had recently played organ on the epic "Voodoo Chile" for Hendrix's long-gestating album-in-progress *Electric Ladyland*, the follow-up to the guitarist's *Axis: Bold as Love*. Things got serious when Baker sought out Clapton and Winwood after learning about their secret jam sessions. Soon thereafter, they were joined by bassist Ric Grech, who had made his name during his years with Family. Indeed, he had left the band midway through their current American tour to work with the likes of Clapton, Baker, and Winwood. When Stigwood announced the band's formation in February 1969, the music press began referring to the new quartet as rock's latest supergroup, and a kind of ceaseless momentum took over. For Clapton, it was simply another example of his standard *modus operandi* when it came to leaving one band for another.

During this same period, the supergroup's name was revealed to be Blind Faith. Publicly, Clapton attributed the name's origin to the belief that, no matter what happened, their collective talent would see them through—that one could take it on blind faith alone that they would be successful. But privately, Clapton admitted to himself that he was engaged in a much more complicated, ambitious gamble to reinvent a British version of the Band. When it came to their eponymous debut album, Clapton and the other group members came up trumps. Recorded from February to June 1969, *Blind Faith* was helmed by Jimmy Miller, a former drummer *cum* record producer. When he joined the Blind Faith project, Miller was in the midst of recording one spectacular album after another with the Rolling Stones: *Beggars Banquet* (1968), *Let It Bleed* (1969), *Sticky Fingers* (1971), *Exile on Main St.* (1972), and *Goats Head Soup*. Miller's association with the band existed as the high-water mark in the Stones' career. Working with Blind Faith in Olympic and, later, Morgan Studios in London, Miller was presented with topflight material, including "Presence of the Lord" and "Can't Find My Way Home"—can't-miss songs that any band would have been thrilled to perform. "Presence of the Lord" held a special significance for Clapton. In addition to its spiritual explorations, the composition depicts Clapton's good fortune and thankfulness at having discovered Hurtwood Edge. "I have finally found a place to live," he wrote, "Just like I never could before."

For Blind Faith's upcoming tour, Stigwood pulled out all of the stops, including a mammoth open-air show to usher in the supergroup ahead of the release of *Blind Faith* that August. As it happened, the album would be greeted with considerable controversy over its cover art, which featured Bob Seidemann's photograph of a topless eleven-year-old girl holding a silver model airplane; for the US marketplace, Seidemann's cover art was replaced with a tour flier. But for Clapton, the most pressing issue—namely, Baker's on-again, off-again flirtation with heroin—became apparent during the band's inaugural show. As he later recalled, "We started our professional career on June 7, 1969, with a free concert in Hyde Park. This was the first ever rock show in the park, and an audience of over 100,000 people turned up. We all met at Stigwood's office before the show, and as soon as I saw Ginger, my heart sank." Realizing that Baker was back on heroin, he continued, "I felt that I was stepping back into the nightmare that had been part of Cream. We played in front of this vast crowd on a beautiful, sunny afternoon, and I wasn't really there. I had zoned out." In Clapton's mind, Blind Faith had already failed in their quest. And they still had a lengthy concert tour splayed out before them that would take the band from Scandinavia to the States, where they would conclude the leg with a late August gig in Hawaii. For the tour, they would be supported by a host of opening acts, including Free, Taste, and a rock 'n' soul ensemble that went by the name of Delaney & Bonnie and Friends. The husband-and-wife musical revue was backed by a slick Southern band that included Carl Radle on bass, Jim Gordon on drums, Bobby Whitlock on keyboards, trumpeter Jim Price, sax player Bobby Keys, and Rita Coolidge sharing vocals with Bonnie. Clapton had first encountered Delaney & Bonnie during his last tour of the US with Cream, and George Harrison had been so impressed by their LP *The Original Delaney & Bonnie: Accept No Substitute* that he had attempted to release it on Apple, even while the group were under contract with Elektra. While that deal fell through, Harrison remained no less a fan, and Clapton asked the Delaney & Bonnie crew to be one of the openers on the Blind Faith tour.

By the time that tour alighted in Honolulu, Clapton was fully smitten, spending most of his free time with the Delaney & Bonnie group, having shunted his latest band aside in favor of the hard-driving rhythm and soul revue. Although it may have remained unsaid at this point, Clapton had little interest in a follow-up project with Blind Faith. If anything, his feelings for the supergroup after the June 1969 Hyde Park concert had only deteriorated even further. Back in England, Clapton had set up a rehearsal space for Delaney and Bonnie's entourage at Hurtwood Edge; by October, he was telling *Melody Maker* that Delaney & Bonnie were "the best band in the world" and had arranged a European tour with them. He also told the paper that his next step would be a solo album, produced by Delaney & Bonnie, featuring "a lot of Buddy Holly songs that perhaps people haven't heard before—lots of old B sides that used to knock me out like 'Fools Paradise.'" He needed to prove himself, he admitted, and hoped the project would help him decide "whether I want to lead a group in the future." As he considered the factors that led to Blind Faith's dissolution—overpromotion, heightened audience expectations—he eyed anonymity, musing that if only the supergroup could "go out to a club in Haslemere or somewhere and go on as the Falcons, it would take all the pressure off us."

Meanwhile, Clapton had installed his sixteen-year-old girlfriend, model Alice Ormsby-Gore, the daughter of a prominent English diplomat, in his manor house. Clapton would later confess to being taken with the much younger woman, although their relationship was largely chaste during its earliest months. Given his ongoing infatuation with Pattie Boyd, he was never sure if he could admit to being in love with Alice. He also wondered if the attraction had more to do with the class dichotomy of a working-class

Ripley kid being associated with an upper-crust Ormsby-Gore, with her family's regal, "double-barreled" last name. As it happened, Alice held a fondness for dressing in Arab attire, which, to Clapton's mind, made her seem like a vision from a fairy tale. Their mutual friend Ian Dallas enjoyed the allusion, telling Clapton the story about Layla and Manjun, a Persian romance in which a younger man falls head over heels in love with the delectable Layla, whom he is forbidden to court by her father. As a result, Manjun becomes a hopeless romantic and loses his mind. The story had been captured by Nizami Ganjavi, a twelfth-century romantic poet. Written in Arabic and originally entitled *Leyli o Majnun*, the work was completed in 1192 and composed of 4,600 distichs, or verse couplets. Clapton would later admit to buying into Nizami's fantasy, which he likened to his attraction to Alice. But like Manjun, Clapton couldn't simply quell his passions and sate his misery. And before long, he would realize that Alice hadn't been his Layla after all.

In Harrison's world, tensions had been rising within the Beatles. After completing work on *The White Album* and taking an all too brief hiatus, the group had reconvened to begin production of a new project in January 1969, loosely known at the time as *Get Back*. They hoped it would enable them to rekindle—or "get back"—to their rock 'n' roll roots. At the project's onset, they considered performing a concert in an exotic locale—perhaps onboard a ship at sea or in the Sahara Desert—while director Michael Lindsay-Hogg filmed their rehearsals, which they conducted in massive, sterile Twickenham Film Studios. Harrison had spent the past few months producing an album by Apple recording artist Jackie Lomax, as well as hanging out with Dylan and the Band, who had developed enormous respect for Harrison's musicianship. It must have been understandably difficult to return to his largely subordinate role in the Beatles after his post-*White Album* bout of creative energy. But in spite of the increased friction, Harrison attempted to appease his elder bandmates during the *Get Back* sessions, at one point tenderly observing that "there's so much material for us to get out, and there's no one better to get it out with than us, for me, really. Heart of hearts." But he wasn't always so charitable. As a means of blowing off steam, Harrison took to singing impromptu Dylan tunes during the rehearsals, including the symbolic "I Shall Be Released" and "All Along the Watchtower," with its prophetic opening lyric, "There must be some way out of here."

Harrison's stellar work on the *White Album* had apparently turned the heads of everyone except for Lennon and McCartney, who continued to see him as a subordinate to their talents, and a distant second to their abilities as songwriters. Although there is ample evidence on the *Get Back* tapes of the pair encouraging and participating in the development of arrangements for Harrison's songs, there were also plenty of dismissals. During a rehearsal of his new song "I Me Mine," Lennon at one point joked "that a collection of freaks can dance along with George's waltz," before telling the guitarist "to get lost—that the Beatles only play rock 'n' roll and there's no place in the group's playlist for a Spanish waltz." As if on cue, McCartney took to singing "I Me Mine" in a feigned Spanish accent. Everything finally came to a head on January 10. After enduring a morning session in which McCartney goaded him about how to perform his guitar part, and following a heated argument with Lennon during lunch, Harrison quit the group, saying "See you 'round the clubs" as he left the soundstage. Reaching for a joke to break the tension of a very uncomfortable moment in front of the film crew, Lennon began improvising the Who's "A Quick One While He's Away" within minutes of Harrison's departure. As they pondered what to do in the wake of their lead guitarist's exit, Lennon suggested that the group replace him with Clapton, an obviously caustic suggestion, given Harrison's close friendship with the renowned guitarist: "The point is: if George leaves, do we want to carry on the Beatles? I do," Lennon told McCartney and Starr. "We should just get other members and carry on."

Harrison blew off steam by immediately putting his frustrations into the song "Wah Wah" (his shorthand for a "headache") and, once his temper had cooled, met with the rest of the band five days later to make a plan for moving forward. He insisted that they leave Twickenham and continue their work in Apple's basement studio on Savile Row. Further, he demanded that they dispense with the concept of a live performance, staging instead a concert for Lindsay-Hogg's cameras without the benefit of an audience. In other words, they would abandon their earlier pretensions and concentrate on making a new album, which was their musical superpower anyway. When Harrison returned to the fold on January 22, he performed a duet of "You Are My Sunshine" with Lennon in order to signify their renewed camaraderie. Later that day, Harrison decided to alter the band's chemistry, similarly to his effort back in September 1968 with Clapton, by inviting ace keyboard player Billy Preston to lend his talents to the Beatles. Harrison and Clapton had seen Preston performing in Ray Charles's band on January 19. The Beatles had first met Preston back in Hamburg in 1962 when he was a member of Little Richard's backup band. "I pulled in Billy Preston," Harrison later recalled. "It helped because the others would have to control themselves a bit more. John and Paul mainly, because they had to, you know, act more handsomely," he continued. "It's interesting to see how people behave nicely when you bring a guest in because they don't want everyone to know that they're so bitchy." Harrison's gambit worked, with Lennon lobbying hard for Preston to become a permanent member of the group. Although McCartney demurred at the thought of five Beatles—"It's bad enough with four!" he exclaimed—for the next several days, Lennon, McCartney, Harrison, Starr, and Preston rehearsed with a vengeance. Taking charge and righting what seemed a seriously adrift enterprise, Harrison ensured the Beatles ended that initially dour month with a spate of new classic songs recorded for posterity—"Let It Be," "The Long and Winding Road," "Get Back," and "Don't Let Me Down," to name but a few—and performed their famous rooftop concert on January 30.

With the *Get Back* project in their wake—and in the early stages of what would prove to be the band's lengthiest and most tendentious post-production process—the Beatles went their separate ways. In between a series of increasingly quarrelsome and troubling meetings regarding Apple's slipshod finances, Lennon, McCartney, and Harrison began working to assemble fresh material for a new, as of yet untitled album. For his part, Harrison had been working on a pair of blockbuster compositions. The first, a love song for Boyd entitled "Something," had seen its debut during the *Get Back* sessions. By that summer, as Harrison and his mates took a fresh pass at "Something," Martin especially began to hear the song in a starkly different light. "It took my breath away," the producer recalled, "mainly because I never thought that George could do it—it was a tremendous work and so simple." By this point, the other Beatles had become genuine converts to the quality of Harrison's "Something," a composition at which they had openly scoffed earlier in the year. McCartney recognized "Something" as one of the strongest cuts among their current spate of songs, but he also realized that his own controlling nature may have been working against him—and possibly for quite some time. As he later recalled, "George's 'Something' was out of left field. It was about Pattie, and it appealed to me because it has a very beautiful melody and is a really structured song. I thought it was great. I think George thought my bass-playing was a little bit busy. Again, from my side, I was trying to contribute the best I could, but maybe it was his turn to tell me I was too busy."

The group's affirmation had been long overdue, but even still, Harrison found it no less satisfying. Starr took special notice of Harrison's growing currency among the band's core creative team. "George was blossoming as a songwriter," he later recalled. "With 'Something' and 'While My Guitar Gently Weeps,' are you kidding me? Two of the finest love songs ever written, and they're really on a par with what John and Paul or anyone else of that time wrote. They're beautiful songs." Even Geoff Emerick took notice of the band's quickly shifting attitude about Harrison's work. "A lot of time and effort went into 'Something,'" he later recalled, "which was very unusual for a Harrison song, but everyone seemed aware of just how good a song it was, even though nobody went out of his way to say so. That's just the way the Beatles were: compliments were few and far between—you could always tell more about the way they were thinking by the expressions on their faces."

A lot of time and effort did indeed go into "Something." The Beatles had been recording on eight-track tape now since the previous summer, and after four and a half years of strategizing to fit their increasingly ambitious arrangements onto four-track, having twice as many tracks to work with had felt like a luxury—one they deserved. But Harrison's vision for "Something" would extend beyond even eight tracks. After recording and abandoning a first version of the song, George led the band through thirty-six takes of a second version. To this, McCartney overdubbed his melodic bassline and Harrison his lead vocals and guitar; then backing vocals and handclaps were added, filling the eight-track tape. Harrison requested an orchestral score from George Martin, which would require two more tracks, but with all tracks used, the only solution was a "reduction mix," a technique the Beatles had used many times with their four-track recordings. Simply put, this required dubbing from one eight track machine to another while mixing tracks together during the transfer, consequently "reducing" the number of tracks used on the second tape. The technical details aren't nearly as important as what they suggest: Harrison, as much as Lennon or

McCartney, continued to look past what the technology allowed and imagine ever grander productions.

Concurrent with the Abbey Road recording sessions, Harrison worked on two side projects of his own. A year after producing an album for Jackie Lomax, he not only produced and played on an album with Billy Preston, *That's the Way God Planned It*, but also oversaw a recording of the Hare Krishna mantra (more accurately, the *maha mantra*). He had initially encountered the Krishna sect of Hinduism during his first trip to India in 1966, where he had the "fantastic experience" of seeing "thousands of people chanting Hare Krishna." By the following year, the Beatles all had copies of *The Happening: Krishna Consciousness*, an album of chants and prayers sung by the leader of the modern Krishna movement, Srila Prabhupada. On one blissful adventure that summer, Harrison and Lennon sailed around the Greek Islands playing banjo-ukuleles and singing "Hare Krishna." "Like six hours we sang," Harrison recalled in 1982, "because you couldn't stop once you got going. You just couldn't stop. It was like as soon as you stop . . . the lights went out."

When the Krishnas arrived in London at the end of 1968 to establish a temple, these experiences had primed Harrison to meet them, and soon they were a part of the flow of traffic at Apple as well as a regular presence at Kinfauns. Although Eastern philosophy in general had resonated more with Harrison than his Catholic upbringing ever did, the Krishnas' approach of chanting and meditation as a means of achieving "direct God perception" spoke specifically to his growing belief that "If there's a God, we must see Him." He also began to see music as a way of manifesting his devotion, and after an evening of playing harmonium and singing Hindu songs at home with a group of his new Krishna friends, he decided to bring this atmosphere to the recording studio.

Harrison produced the recording at EMI studios in July 1969, early in the day before a Beatles session. Although he Westernized the *maha mantra* a little with overdubs of electric guitar and bass, he retained the hypnotic spirit of the chant with a group of devotees leading the vocals and chorus. As improbable as it seemed, the record—credited to the Radha Krishna Temple and titled simply "Hare Krishna Mantra"—reached number twelve in the UK charts, and Harrison secured the group an appearance on the *Top of the Pops* TV show.

During this period, Clapton continued to socialize with the Harrisons. He would later recall sitting in front of Harrison and Boyd's fireplace in their sprawling bungalow in Esher, whiling away the hours in conversation or simply strumming guitars in fellowship. They would share many similar convivial evenings at Hurtwood Edge, where Harrison and Boyd would have dinner with Clapton. On another occasion, Clapton recalled Harrison playing his acoustic guitar in the estate's ample garden. It was going on lunchtime when Harrison hit upon a certain pattern and began singing, "De da de de, it's been a long cold lonely winter." In Clapton's memory, it was "a beautiful spring morning" that was complemented perfectly by his friend's lovely tune. Harrison remembered this era with less sunny optimism than Clapton. "'Here Comes the Sun' was written at the time when Apple was getting like school, where we had to go and be businessmen: 'Sign this' and 'sign that,'" said Harrison. "Anyway, it seems as if winter in England goes on forever; by the time spring comes you really deserve it. So one day I decided I was going to sag off Apple and I went over to Eric Clapton's house. The relief of not having to go see all those dopey accountants was wonderful, and I walked around the garden with one of Eric's acoustic guitars and wrote 'Here Comes the Sun.'"

Harrison completed the song during his May vacation with Boyd in Sardinia, putting the finishing touches on the lyrics, which he had scrawled on his personal stationery, replete with a Hindu drawing and spiritual quotations. In order to provide a mnemonic device to remind him of his scat lyrics, he described his refrain as "scoobie doobie," while referring to his guitar part during the bridge as "son of 'Badge,'" in reference to the descending guitar figure in his Cream composition with Clapton. Harrison illustrated his lyrics with a sketch of a smiling, radiant sun. The Beatles—sans Lennon, who had been in a harrowing automobile accident with Yoko Ono up in Scotland—began recording "Here Comes the Sun" during an afternoon session at Abbey Road on July 7, where a genial atmosphere prevailed. When the first take resulted in a false start, Harrison playfully remarked, "One of me best beginnings that!" To untrained ears, "Here Comes the Sun" might sound deceptively easy, but it shifts across a complexity of different time signatures in quick succession, including 4/4 time during the verses that's punctuated by intricate 11/8 and 15/8 sequences. For the recording, the Beatles concocted a basic rhythm track that featured Harrison singing a guide vocal and playing the song's distinctive melody on his Gibson J-200 acoustic guitar, McCartney on bass, and Starr—who was celebrating his twenty-ninth birthday—on drums. After Martin and the Beatles selected take thirteen as the best of the lot, Harrison devoted the remainder of the session to rerecording his guitar part until he had rendered a performance of remarkable clarity and precision. Neither Lennon nor McCartney would have dreamed up a rhythm part so intricate and then labored so carefully over its perfection.

Martin couldn't fail to be affected by Harrison's remarkable development as a composer. "I think there was a great deal of invention," Martin later recalled. "I mean, George's 'Here Comes the Sun' was the first time he'd really come through with a brilliant composition, and musical ideas, you know, the multiple odd rhythms that came through. They really became commercial for the first time on that one." After ignoring Harrison's songwriting for so many years, Martin was now decidedly paying attention. Indeed, he would come to admit—along with Lennon and McCartney themselves—that Harrison had finally arrived as a composer, writing material on par with that of his much-vaunted mates.

Outside of the studio, though, the Beatles seemed headed toward a day of reckoning. Their fraught business affairs—profoundly impacted by the ascent of New York businessman Allen Klein in their world and the ever-weakening position of Apple Corps—had taken a toll on the group's interpersonal relationships and were threatening to infiltrate their work in the studio as well. After Lennon and Ono's return from convalescing in Scotland, the band steeled themselves in order to complete their *Abbey Road* album by late August. Working over the course of six weeks, the group delivered a raft of new material, while also completing work on the symphonic suite that would famously conclude the LP. Meanwhile, Lennon and Ono struggled with a protracted heroin addiction. As they attempted to break free from the drug, Lennon composed "Cold Turkey," a song that illustrated the excruciating throes of heroin withdrawal in brutal detail: "My feet are so heavy / So is my head / I wish I was a baby / I wish I was dead." Unable to muster any interest in recording the song among the other Beatles, Lennon "thought, 'Bugger you, I'll put it out myself.' So I did it as the Plastic Ono Band. I don't care what it goes out as, as long as it goes out."

At the same time, Lennon and Ono had accepted an invitation to perform at the one-day Toronto Rock 'n' Roll Revival festival, scheduled for

Saturday, September 13, at the University of Toronto's Varsity Stadium. For Lennon, it seemed like the perfect opportunity to stage the Plastic Ono Band's debut live performance. The festival featured a host of rock 'n' roll greats, including Chuck Berry, Jerry Lee Lewis, Gene Vincent, and Little Richard, with the Doors closing out the event as the headlining act. At Lennon's instruction, Beatles roadie Mal Evans hastily rounded up a backing band for Lennon and Ono, which included Eric Clapton on lead guitar, Beatles intimate and current Manfred Mann bassist Klaus Voormann, and drummer Alan White. Before settling on Clapton, Lennon had invited Harrison, who declined to join his mate on his surprise North American adventure, feeling that the Plastic Ono Band concept was too "avant-garde" for his taste.

While Lennon was thrilled with the opportunity to play live again, he was simultaneously overcome with dread at the thought of performing in front of twenty thousand people. By the time they arrived in Toronto, the hastily organized band had just enough time to make a single pass at their set backstage at the Varsity Stadium. Worse yet for Lennon, his cycle of heroin addiction and withdrawal had returned with a vengeance. He later recalled being "full of junk": "I just threw up for hours till I went on. I nearly threw up in 'Cold Turkey,'" he added. "And I was throwing up nearly in the number. I could hardly sing any of them. I was full of shit." But even still, Lennon was energized by the performance. "The buzz was incredible," he said at the time. "I never felt so good in my life. Everybody was with us and leaping up and down doing the peace sign, because they knew most of the numbers anyway." Quite naturally, the Plastic Ono Band's setlist included a bevy of cover versions—songs like "Blue Suede Shoes," "Money (That's What I Want)," and "Dizzy Miss Lizzy." In addition to playing "Give Peace a Chance" and the Beatles' "Yer Blues," for which Clapton contributed a superb solo, the group performed "Cold Turkey," which "we'd never done before," said Lennon, "and they dug it like mad." For Lennon, "Cold Turkey" was still so fresh that he didn't even know all of the words. Ono resorted to holding a clipboard in front of her husband so that he could properly belt out the tune's lyrics.

To Clapton, the concert was great fun, but in truth, it was nothing more than "a glorified jam session." The real story that day had occurred on the plane ride across the Atlantic, when Lennon, Clapton, and the others had congregated in the galley in a breakneck effort to put together their set. As Clapton later recalled, "We picked out chords on the guitar, which you couldn't hear because we had nowhere to plug in, and, of course, Alan didn't have his drums on the plane with him." Without ready access to another fix, Lennon was struggling with bouts of nausea. At some point during the flight, Lennon confided to his makeshift bandmates that he intended to quit the Beatles—and soon. He even went so far as to ask them to join him in forming a new group. For his part, Clapton didn't take his friend's invitation too seriously, chalking his revelation up to heroin and nerves.

Still consumed with the idea of releasing "Cold Turkey" as a single, Lennon hurried into EMI Studios on September 25 to capture the basic track. Just twelve days removed from their performance in Toronto, the Plastic Ono Band's personnel had already shifted ever so slightly. Along with Lennon and Ono, Clapton and Voormann were still onboard, but White was no longer involved with the project. For the "Cold Turkey" recording, Lennon found a drummer much closer to home in the form of Starr, who was only too happy to share his talents with Lennon. During the September 25 session, Clapton and the other members of the Plastic Ono Band recorded twenty-six takes of "Cold Turkey," and apparently to Lennon's liking. But only three days later, Lennon regrouped the makeshift band to take yet another shot at landing the song. Slated for a late-October release, "Cold Turkey" was a top-twenty hit in the UK, although for Clapton, it had merely been a lark. And besides, he was eager to rejoin Delaney & Bonnie and Friends. For Harrison, the future of the Beatles was becoming more uncertain by the day.

As they closed in on *Abbey Road*'s much-anticipated release, the Beatles attempted to find a more equitable balance that would enable them to move forward. During a September 1969 meeting, Lennon, McCartney, and Harrison agreed they would each get four songs on albums from now on, with two for Starr if he wanted. The deal suggested they all saw a hopeful future together, but there was no accounting for personal instability. At another meeting around the same time, Lennon asked his mates for a "divorce," and although they couldn't stop him, Klein and McCartney, in particular, demanded that he keep any notion of a breakup secret for the foreseeable future. After all, Klein's negotiating position would be significantly weakened if the world were to learn prematurely about a Beatles breakup. For his part, McCartney was still hoping that the group's demise simply wouldn't come to pass. Lennon may have been hoping the same thing after he got the dramatic declaration out of his system. In interviews over the next few months, he never alluded to a desire to leave the band, and even predicted at least once that they would all get together again eventually.

The Beatles remained unsatisfied with Glyn Johns and Martin's post-production efforts on the still unreleased *Get Back*, leaving the potential album and documentary in a state of limbo. When it hit the stores at the end of September, *Abbey Road* enjoyed a massive commercial success, spurred on by the single "Something" b/w "Come Together," which was a global smash hit. The impact of "Something" underscored to Harrison, in dramatic fashion, how far he had come as a songwriter in the six years since he had composed "Don't Bother Me." Frank Sinatra himself would introduce his live cover versions of "Something" as "the greatest love song of the past fifty years."

Taking the success in stride, Harrison scarcely allowed himself a break once *Abbey Road* was behind him. He continued producing and playing on albums for both Billy Preston and Doris Troy, but most importantly he became swept up in the whirlwind of excitement that Delaney & Bonnie had generated. After their British debut at the end of October, Clapton played a number of European shows with the American group in November before kicking off a proper twelve-date tour on December 1 at the Royal Albert Hall in London. Harrison attended that show and by the next night was onstage playing guitar with the band in Bristol. The ability to be anonymous among the raucous camaraderie of the group satisfied something in Harrison, just as it had for Clapton. Sensing this, Delaney Bramlett wasted no time in asking Harrison to join the tour. Clapton *and* a Beatle?—this could only be good for business. Eager to be part of a group again, and no doubt remembering the rapport he'd seen between Dylan and the Band the year before, Harrison was outside his home in Esher the next day, December 3, with guitar in hand, waiting for the tour bus to collect him.

Writer Philip Norman, who accompanied the group on this tour, described Bramlett as a man of "unquiet manners . . . who embraces or clouts his wife and roisters generally like Attila the Hun." Bramlett may have been unruly, outrageous, and possessed of a temper, but he was also unmistakably charismatic—so much so that he had drawn together a spirited group of musicians and fashioned a sound that seamlessly combined blues, Southern gospel, Stax-like soul, and rock 'n' roll. He also had a gift for attracting talent. Rita Coolidge, who sang backing vocals with the group, later recalled, "There was magic in the music. It was unlike anything I'd ever heard." Guitarist Dave Mason, who also fell in with Delaney & Bonnie for a time, remembered, "They blew me away the first time I heard them. There sure as hell wasn't anything in England like they were doing."

Harrison blended in easily with this barnstorming crew, cheerfully strumming guitar on the tour bus and reveling in the cheap roadside food stops. As always, he was soaking up whatever he could musically from the people around him, and Bramlett demonstrated a tendency to push the musicians in his orbit. Responding to Harrison's curiosity about slide guitar, Bramlett had him take the electric slide part for "Comin' Home" throughout the tour, which would be captured on tape for a live album, *On Tour with Eric Clapton,* released in June of 1970; to obscure his identity, the Beatle was billed as "Misterioso." It was a more purely blues slide part than Harrison would have necessarily done on his own, a testament to his desire to blend in fully with his hosts, but it nonetheless introduced him to a new guitar technique that he would make his own in the coming year.

Harrison skipped the tour's Newcastle upon Tyne show on December 5 to check on his ailing mother, but rejoined the next night in Liverpool, and after the remaining dates in the UK he continued with the group for a series of shows in Sweden and Denmark. Absorbing the spirit of the music around him each night, he wrote the bluesy "Woman Don't You Cry For Me" in Gothenburg and slipped away from a press conference in Copenhagen to begin work on what he initially conceived as a gospel song, one where "Hallelujah" and "Hare Krishna" were interchangeable.

Although Clapton also wanted to remain largely anonymous, Bramlett pushed him toward the spotlight and encouraged Clapton to find his voice as a singer. Putting the guitarist center-stage may not have been entirely altruistic—Bramlett knew people were showing up as much for Clapton as anything else, a fact made painfully clear at one of the European shows in November, where the crowd demanded the guitarist lead the performance. In spite of his reluctance to be the center of attention, Clapton sang lead on two songs throughout the tour, "I Don't Know Why" and a cover of the Spencer Davis Group's "Gimme Some Lovin'," where Bobby Whitlock, Carl Radle, and Jim Gordon provided the backing. Bramlett had already gotten Clapton into the studio in November for an abortive attempt at a first Clapton solo album, and these two live showcases were a further part of Bramlett's scheme not just to get the guitarist singing, but also to bring him into Delaney and Bonnie's "Friends" as a full-time member. Perhaps Bramlett had sensed a vulnerability in Clapton that he hoped he could use to his advantage. During that same tour, journalist Philip Norman astutely observed the ways in which Clapton "is so self-effacing as to appear to disguise himself in the company of the moment."

Harrison, while he had enjoyed the two-week break from his regular life, left the group after the tour's final show back in London on December 15. But after a brief rest back home at Hurtwood Edge, Clapton would soon be bound for Los Angeles to start anew on his solo album. The November sessions, which consisted of five songs recorded at Olympic Studios, were abandoned. As Bobby Whitlock remembered, "Our minds were on the tour, and there really was not enough time to devote to the project." Now, once again with Bramlett producing and the Friends crew backing, they settled in for a concentrated series of sessions from January 23 to 31 at Village Recorders.

Clapton debuted his Fender Stratocaster, which he nicknamed "Brownie," on his solo record. For the past several years, he had been playing a Gibson Les Paul, which he had seen on the cover of *Freddie King Sings the Blues*. "I went out after seeing that cover and scoured the guitar shops and found one," Clapton recalled. "That was my guitar from then on, and it sounded like Freddie King." He purchased Brownie in 1967 during his Cream days, having admired the sound of the Fender Strat on records by Buddy Guy and Otis Rush. Henceforth, Clapton and Brownie would be inseparable.

Whatever Bramlett's motives may have been—and whatever chaos was already brewing from his egotism—his efforts to get Clapton to step out as a solo artist began to unlock the guitarist's full potential. "My solo career really began there," Clapton wrote later. "I knew I had it in me really, but I had stuffed it down to the point that I had stopped believing in myself." Bramlett seemed to exude music, and his fluency and enthusiasm were inspiring. He introduced Clapton to the music of J. J. Cale, whose song "After Midnight" they would record at these sessions. After cutting rhythm tracks with the guitars, bass, drums, and Hammond organ, Bramlett would lead him through the vocals, steadily building his confidence in his singing. They'd finish off the recordings with minimal overdubs—just backing vocals and horns—a quick and satisfying process for each tune. "Delaney," said Clapton, "had brought something out in me that I didn't know I had."

He also got Clapton writing. The five songs from the December sessions bore Clapton's name as coauthor, and six of the eleven songs recorded at these sessions were likewise co-written by Clapton, typically sparked by a suggestion from either Bramlett or Leon Russell; a track taped later in London, "Easy Now," was fully a Clapton original. Although his idea for an album of Buddy Holly cover tunes never materialized, in between his own sessions, at the same Los Angeles studio, Clapton played on two tracks with Holly's old band, the Crickets, for their *Rockin' 50s Rock 'n' Roll* album, and on January 26, he sat in on R&B saxophonist King Curtis's recording of a Curtis-Bramlett instrumental called "Teasin'." With Bramlett producing and the Radle-Gordon rhythm section powering the song, Clapton found the session so rapturous that he later called it "an experience I wanted to go on forever."

Working in California afforded Clapton with much-needed distance from his unrequited love for Pattie Boyd, but when he returned to Hurtwood Edge that spring, Alice Ormsby-Gore departed almost immediately for Tel Aviv to begin rehearsals for an onstage role in an Israeli production of the musical *Hair*, which would debut in June and run through November. Seeking a distraction, Clapton began pursuing Pattie's sister Paula Boyd, who eagerly fell into a relationship with him. At one point, George Harrison—having grown wise to Clapton's infatuation with his wife—suggested they swap partners. "The suggestion didn't shock me," Clapton recalled, "because the prevailing morality of the time was that you just went for whatever you could get, but at the last moment, he lost his nerve and nothing happened."

In February 1970, with a new year still unfolding before him, Clapton took an interview with *Fusion* magazine's Keith Altham. For Clapton, it marked an opportunity to speak frankly about his abiding friendship with Harrison, as well as to contemplate what he had learned over the past several years as he barnstormed through life as a professional musician, traipsing from band to band and engaging in his enduring search for a pure, unmitigated, heartbreaking blues. The only thing that defeated him, by his own admission, originated in the seemingly unquenchable "restlessness" that lorded over his life:

Altham: It would appear that possibly your closest friend within the business is George Harrison. Can you explain what it is that has promoted that association?

Clapton: It's a question of mutual respect. I have a great deal of respect for him because there have probably been a thousand times when he wanted to quit the Beatles and do something on his own, but he never has. In fact, he is probably the one in the Beatles who has done most of the patching up—he is their mediator and his philosophical outlook has been one of the primary reasons that has kept them together. Paradoxically, he respects me for having the courage to walk out on groups because I don't like what I am doing. He has often said to me that he does not see me in any band for very long, and I think he has a strange regard for my facing up to impossible situations and just cutting out. I try to put my restlessness behind me when I get involved in a new group, but it always seems to reappear and defeat me in the end.

5 | THE PARTY'S OVER

BY THE EARLY MONTHS OF 1970, Harrison and Clapton found themselves in remarkably similar places in their lives, both emotionally and professionally. Like Clapton, Harrison was beginning to come to terms with the idea of a solo career and all the attendant responsibilities and expectations that would involve. Even though "Something" had been a massive success, certain insecurities lingered for him; the years of taking a back seat to Lennon and McCartney had imprinted upon him a kind of second-class mentality, and his interviews during this period revealed how he had internalized this self-image, even as his talent drove him. Also like Clapton, Harrison continued to dabble, playing producer on a variety of projects even as he felt the growing urge to record the backlog of material he had written over the last few years.

Adding to the mix was the *Get Back* project, which, after lying dormant for months, was now alive again. Allen Klein, surveying potential Beatles product, moved to have the documentary completed, prompting director Michael Lindsay-Hogg to return to his rough cut from July. While Lindsay-Hogg refined his edit with no shortage of notes from the Beatles, Klein began the necessary work to have a soundtrack album ready to accompany the film's release.

Since the Beatles made plain their disinterest in revisiting the project, Klein floated the idea of having Phil Spector come make an album from the recordings they had done. The Beatles were certainly fans of Spector's work—they'd covered "To Know Him Is to Love Him" both at their Decca audition and one of their performances for the BBC, and the Philles Records had never failed to impress. Harrison had even provided a testimonial for a sticker on the front cover of the US release of the producer's 1969 album with Ike and Tina Turner: "'River Deep, Mountain High' is a perfect record from start to finish. You couldn't improve on it." In the 1990s, he recalled that "Phil Spector approached Allen Klein, and was trying to get some work, or somehow he was hanging out with Klein—probably because he knew Klein was in with the Beatles. I think Klein suggested to us that we should get Phil Spector to come and listen to the tapes of *Let It Be.*"

Spector was looking to jump-start a second act of his career. After developing his high-drama production style over a string of chart hits from 1962 to 1965 (what he described as "little symphonies for the kids") and painting himself as a studio Svengali, the true auteur of his records, he became the first celebrity producer. While the hits were flowing, the press was largely happy to indulge his self-mythologizing hyperconfidence. Tom Wolfe's 1965 essay for the *New York Herald Tribune*, dubbing Spector "The First Tycoon of Teen," was both the most famous and the most egregious example, a self-consciously hip candy-floss confection that was as much about Wolfe's ability to fashion florid prose as it was about burnishing the producer's image. But the essay, which became a signpost of New Journalism, certainly reflected the Spector image and riffed off its subject's strutting bravado.

Beneath the glossy surface of Wolfe's portrait, however, lay a troubled man. The neuroses and obsessive, perfectionist tendencies that had driven Spector to success sprang, at least in part, from his father's suicide, when Phil was just nine years old. His mother's subsequent overprotectiveness and what the boy perceived as her dissatisfaction with everything he did were further fuel to Spector's compulsions. In the studio, though, that perfectionism produced hits—and the hits in turn reinforced the need for the perfectionism. Spector gave life to George Bernard Shaw's observation that "if you cannot get rid of the family skeleton, you may as well make it dance."

But how long could he keep it dancing? While Spector was a dedicated professional, his early traumas still haunted him. He wasn't grounded—although, with his $600-a-month analyst, he seemed to be trying—and by assuming the role of the sole visionary, he also assumed full responsibility for both success and failure. When he made the Righteous Brothers' "You've Lost That Lovin' Feeling," the record seemed the ultimate expression of his sonic style; gobsmacked Rolling Stones manager Andrew Loog-Oldham was such a fan that he ran ads with his own money in the UK music papers promoting the recording, christening the production "Phil Spector's Wall of Sound." The record was a smash, the moniker stuck and, recognizing a brilliant stroke of branding, the producer actually went to the trouble of trademarking the term. The myth had a name now, but Spector, ever restless, had to go further.

The then-outrageous $22,000 Spector poured into producing the "Lovin' Feeling" follow-up, "River Deep, Mountain High," matched the psychic energy he invested in the recording, but in spite of the painstaking rehearsals, the layered arrangement, and Tina Turner's fiery vocal, the record stalled at number eighty-eight on the *Billboard* charts. Although it reached number two on the British charts, Spector was devastated. One friend told author Mick Brown in 2003 that it was the only time she ever saw Spector "really depressed. He said, 'I was sure people would love it; I just don't understand it.' More than upset, he felt betrayed by the American public." Feeling defeated, Spector declared in June 1966 that he'd "lost interest" in the music industry. He subsequently dabbled in film production, which went nowhere, married Veronica Bennett from the Ronettes, adopted a son, and withdrew.

When he reemerged in early 1969, producing the top twenty hit "Black Pearl" by Sonny Charles and the Checkmates, Ltd., he downplayed the failure of "River Deep," asserting that it was "made as an experiment" and "not as a hit record." He cast it as an intentional, temporary swan song: "I was just sayin' goodbye, and I just wanted to go crazy.... I enjoyed making it, but I didn't really think there was anything for the public." He also assumed his old bravado again, at least for the press. In a discussion of how he would produce various major rock acts, including Bob Dylan, Spector told *Rolling Stone*'s Jann Wenner in April, "I would like to record [the Beatles] a certain way because, again, other than what they do themselves—there's nobody." He confessed he didn't know the impact of George Martin's influence on their recordings, adding, "I am sure they have a great deal of respect for him and he's the fifth Beatle and all that, but I don't think he thinks the way I would think. Their ideas are so overpowering that you just sort of just go along with them and you're gonna end up with somethin' groovy."

Now, less than a year later, Spector had a chance to prove himself. Before he took charge of the tapes, though, the Beatles themselves still had work to do. Two of Harrison's songs, "For You Blue" and "I Me Mine," were set for inclusion in the film, but the latter had only been rehearsed in January 1969. The Beatles had never actually recorded it in the studio. To rectify this problem, Harrison returned to Abbey Road on January 3, joining McCartney and Starr, with George Martin producing, to tape a proper version of "I Me Mine." Lennon was still on holiday in Denmark, leaving just three members of the group to play on what would ultimately be the final band recording by the Beatles. Appropriately, the session took place in Studio Two, where it had all begun seven and a half years before, and Harrison prefaced one of the takes with a cheeky acknowledgment of Mr. Lennon's absence: "You all will have heard that Dave Dee is no longer with us, but Micky and Tich and I would just like to carry on the good work that's always gone down in Number Two." They completed the entire recording, overdubs and all, in less than ten hours, from 2:30 PM to 12:15 AM.

All that remained now were a few stray overdubs. The next day, onto one of the recordings taken January 31, 1969, of "Let It Be," Harrison and Paul and Linda McCartney taped backing vocals. George Martin's score for horns and cellos followed, and then a new guitar solo by Harrison, extra drums by Starr, and maracas by McCartney. Glyn Johns used the new mixes for "Let It Be" and "I Me Mine" to compile a new version of Get Back—his fourth and final compilation. On January 8, Harrison decided to rerecord his vocal on "For You Blue," which Johns cut into his proposed album reel.

Back from Denmark only the day before, Lennon began tinkering early on January 27 and by that afternoon had a new song in "Instant Karma!" He wanted to record it immediately, so he booked studio time and called Harrison to ask if he wanted to play on the session. Grabbing his guitar, Harrison left his house in Esher and dropped by the Apple offices, where he ran into Phil Spector, who was in town to discuss working on the Get Back tapes. "And I said, 'Come on, let's go and do this song with John,'" Harrison recalled. "And he said, 'No, no, I can't go.' You know, 'I haven't been invited.' And I said, 'Don't worry, just come on.'"

Lennon had also invited Klaus Voormann, Billy Preston, and drummer Alan White, and by 7:00 PM they'd all shown up at EMI Studio Three to start rehearsing. When Lennon recalled the session at the end of the year, he characteristically made the recording process sound breezily matter of fact: "Phil came in and said, 'How do you want it?' and I said, you know, '1950s,' and he said 'Right,' and boom, I did it." According to Harrison, though, Spector was reticent at first, standing at the back of the control room in Studio Three, "and the engineer was getting all paranoid. Phil wouldn't say anything. And after about a couple of hours, I said, 'Come on, do something.'" Voormann remembered they were working away when "suddenly we heard a different voice in the control room. We had no idea who it was." Spector was talking over the intercom telling White to take the cymbals off his drums, and he'd gotten engineer Phil McDonald to rig the tape echo up in the control room. As Spector refined the sound during run-throughs, White improvised some energetic off-meter fills. "I kind of sprang it on John and Phil and they loved it," White said in 2009. "Alan, just keep doing that," Spector said. "It's making the whole song!"

Once proper recording began, "Instant Karma!" only took ten takes to master, with the basic rhythm track finished by midnight. For overdubs, Spector had all four musicians layer on extra keyboard parts: Lennon on grand piano, White and Harrison playing octaves apart on another piano, and Voormann on electric piano. He then invited them to listen to a playback. "When we went into the room and heard what he'd done to it," Lennon remembered, "it was fantastic. It sounded like there was fifty people playing." "It was ridiculously loud," Voormann told author Simon Leng, "but there was also the ringing of all these instruments and the way the song had such motion. As a first experience of the difference from the way you played it to the sound in the control room, it was overwhelming."

After collecting some people from a nearby dance club to sing on the choruses, they wrapped up the overdubs by 3:00 AM and the final mix by 4:00 AM. Spector wanted to add violins, but to Lennon, the record was finished. "He wanted to go on with it, putting more people on it," he said. "Now the only thing I ever do with Spector is stop him, because otherwise he'd go on and on and there'd be nothing left. That time I didn't let him. I knew that was it."

Harrison could not have missed the way Spector handled this session, but he had not yet invited the producer to oversee an album of Harrisongs—for the moment, he had not even decided to record such an album. Instead, Harrison spent the first half of 1970 consumed by his own production projects, where he was not only working behind the glass, but also playing on the sessions and contributing songs. In January, he continued work on a second album with keyboardist Billy Preston, *Encouraging Words*, which he had begun in

December. Sessions for the album resumed upon Harrison's return from touring with Delaney & Bonnie and Friends in December, and when he walked into the studio, he had a new song in the works.

Inspired by the Edwin Hawkins Singers' recording of "Oh Happy Day," a surprise top-ten international hit in 1969, Harrison had set out to write a gospel song while on tour with Delaney & Bonnie. Both Bobby Whitlock and Bobby Keys remembered hearing Harrison on the tour bus strumming the hypnotic E minor to A major chord vamp that would eventually introduce the song. Harrison himself later said he "slipped away" from a press conference while the tour was in Copenhagen (December 10 to 12); he had realized at some point that "Hallelujah" and "Hare Krishna" had the same number of syllables, and once he had found a quiet space away from the press conference, he began fitting the words over the two-chord vamp. Once he discovered a tune he liked, he took it to the Delaney & Bonnie entourage, who responded by putting the nascent melody into four-part harmony. In response to this, he began singing "my sweet lord" and "dear, dear lord," and over the next week started working on the rest of the lyrics.

Harrison's interest in gospel music was the next step in the spiritual exploration he had begun as he delved deeper into Indian music and culture. His writing had long had a philosophical edge, often mixed with social critiques. By the time of "Within You, Without You" and "The Inner Light," he was making those preoccupations explicit. Even "While My Guitar Gently Weeps" was written from the perspective of someone trying to rise above earthly attachment and see things from an outside perspective. If there was a thread of self-righteousness, Harrison tempered it with his adherence to the Eastern principles he continued to absorb from Buddhism, Taoism, and Hinduism. By January 1969, he had written "Hear Me Lord," which he described to the other Beatles as a "gospel song," and the following month co-authored "Sing One For the Lord" with Billy Preston. Harrison's embrace of the Hare Krishna movement took him one step further. "The names change: his is Krishna; mine is Christ," Preston observed in 1971. "The spiritual promotion praising God, chanting, spreading it, turning people onto it—these are the things we have in common."

At Olympic Studios in January 1970, Preston's recording of "My Sweet Lord" leaned into the song's gospel inspirations with a funky pulse, decidedly more "Hallelujah" than "Hare Krishna" at this point. By coincidence, the Edwin

Hawkins Singers happened to be in London, and Harrison invited them to add backing vocals to the song. In spite of the Christian direction Preston's recording took, Harrison asked the singers to throw in the occasional "Hare Krishna." He told Anne Nightingale in 1977, "And they said, 'What is that? Hare Krishna?' And luckily there was one young guy in there, and he said, 'You know, Hare Krishna, you've seen them out there dancing on the street.' So if you listen to that version, there's one place where they're going 'Hallelujah, Hare Krishna!' So I was happy. I got it in twice, actually."

As they were recording, Harrison and Preston finalized the verse melody and the chord structure. Author Simon Leng has observed, "The dominant-seventh chord that shifts the tension of the song on the line 'but it takes so long' was straight out of the Hawkins ['Oh Happy Day'] single." Anchored by Preston's ascending piano figure, the recording also included the bassist and drummer from the Temptations' touring band, who were also in town at the time. With no clear plans for a George Harrison album on the horizon, for the moment "My Sweet Lord" was simply destined for release on Preston's *Encouraging Words* album later in the year, a gospel song donated to another artist.

Having completed one spiritual production, Harrison turned the following month to another, for which he fashioned a lush, alluring sound. Following on the success of his production of the Radha Krishna Temple's recording of the "Hare Krishna Mantra" in 1969 (a worldwide hit), he suggested the group begin gathering material for an album. Conveniently, Mukunda Das Adhikary (later Mukunda Goswami), the American-born founder of the Temple in London, had been a trained jazz pianist before devoting himself to Krishna and arranged seven new pieces for the project. Among them was "Govinda," recorded at Trident Studios on February 7, with Ken Scott engineering. Harrison first laid down a backing track, which included Billy Preston on organ, Klaus Voormann on bass, and Alan White on drums. White, who had not only played on "Instant Karma" but had also worked with Harrison and Clapton in 1969 on a proposed solo album for bassist Ric Grech, reckoned he got the call from Harrison because "he liked me as a person and thought I was somebody who would be relatively easy to work with. It was a kind of a mutual respect for each other."

To this familiar rock backing, Harrison overdubbed temple members playing along on bells, flute, oud, and the esraj (a bowed Indian instrument), all centered around female singer Yamuna Devi, who had provided the assured lead vocal on the previous single. Temple members and others who were present at the session overdubbed a chorus of backing vocals. Harrison commissioned a string score from John Barham, who wrote for eight violins, three cellos, one double bass, and a harp.

Barham would play a significant role in the *All Things Must Pass* sessions, being present from the beginning and going on to write the orchestral scores for the album. He and Harrison had been introduced by Ravi Shankar in 1966, when Barham was studying with and acting as Shankar's assistant in London. Barham's background, as he describes it, was in "Jazz, Western Classical, and North Indian Classical music," and he had already achieved a certain amount of notoriety of his own, having written piano pieces based on Indian ragas. These pieces led Shankar to commission Barham to transcribe an Indian classical piece into Western notation for a duet between Shankar and violinist Yehudi Menuhin. "Before I began working with George, we became friends based on our passion for Indian music," said Barham, "and it must have been obvious to George that I wasn't into rock. Fifty years ago, Indian music was generally thought to be on the cultural fringe, similarly to Indian religion, which also interested both of us. The only other friend of George who seemed interested was Brian Jones of the Stones.

"Looking back," said Barham, "now it is clear to me that George was gradually introducing me to his musical world, which up to that time was very different from mine. After a mind-bending trip George played me various recordings including [Karlheinz] Stockhausen, [György] Ligeti, Bob Dylan, Phil [Spector]'s production of 'Proud Mary,' and Muddy Waters." Admittedly, Barham "had never heard raw Chicago Blues before, and I was amazed by Muddy Waters pianist Otis Spann. I was familiar with the playing of most of the great jazz pianists from Fats Waller, Art Tatum to Bud Powell and Oscar Peterson but I had never heard a jazz pianist get such a vocal quality from the piano as Otis Spann. By hearing the connection between jazz and rock, over time I was able to develop an appreciation and a feeling for rock. Over the next few months I collected more than thirty recordings featuring Otis Spann. So if that was George's intention, it worked."

Barham had already collaborated with Harrison on the *Wonderwall* soundtrack in 1968 and had worked on arrangements for Harrison's productions of Jackie Lomax and Billy Preston. "My first meeting with Billy

Preston was when I was asked to arrange strings for his recording of the W. C. Handy song 'Morning Star,'" Barham said. "The three of us met at my studio in Kensington Square. Billy suggested using the strings to create a piano concerto-like effect and he mentioned Gershwin's Piano Concerto. George left it completely up to Billy to explain what he wanted but at the same time giving me the freedom to do it in my way." For "Govinda," Harrison was more specific. "George's way of communicating what he wanted for the orchestral accompaniment," said Barham, "was usually by singing the top line. All the inner voice leading was left to me; George left the writing of the harp part totally to me."

Harrison invested considerable energy in producing the rest of the Radha Krishna Temple album, with recording continuing into the following month. Given his devotion to Hindu spirituality, the project was even more important to him than the Preston and Troy albums, at least on a personal level. In a conversation years later with Goswami about the first Radha Krishna single, Harrison said, "It's just all a part of service, isn't it? Spiritual service, in order to try to spread the mantra all over the world." The album was a continuation of that service, and it also stands as a vivid example of his versatility both as a producer and a musician. On two tracks, "Sri Gurvastakam" and "Sri Ishopanishad," Harrison added dobro parts, seamlessly blending Eastern and Western musical ideas. Just months after Delaney Bramlett had first encouraged him to play slide, Harrison had already begun to grasp the expressive possibilities of this style of playing and was already demonstrating the sensitivity and precision with this technique he would soon apply to his own recordings. His first recorded slide playing was on "Coming Home" on the Delaney & Bonnie and Friends live LP, recorded in December, but his work on the Radha Krishna Temple sessions pointed toward a distinctive touch that would become instantly recognizable.

The "Govinda" single was released in the United Kingdom on March 6, 1970, and on March 24 in the United States. It reached number twenty-three in the UK by the end of the month, but of greater significance to Harrison's intent, the leader of the modern Krishna movement, Swami Prabhupada, requested that the recording be used to herald the day at all the International Society for Krishna Consciousness (ISKCON) temples. Even now, Harrison's production of "Govinda" greets devotees each morning in over eight hundred temples around the world.

On February 18, eleven days after the "Govinda" session, Harrison was back at EMI. Starr was in the midst of recording his first solo album, *Sentimental Journey*, produced by George Martin, and Harrison had dropped in to play guitar and direct the other musicians in the studio—including Klaus Voormann on bass and Stephen Stills on piano—on the recording of a new song, "You Gotta Pay Your Dues." After Starr overdubbed vocals onto two songs for his album, Harrison led the band through twenty takes of what would eventually be renamed "It Don't Come Easy." Harrison's presence was more than just a show of support for his fellow Beatle; while Starr had begun writing the song, Harrison had helped him finish it, though he would later decline a coauthor credit. After completing the backing track, Harrison added two guitar parts, and Starr overdubbed his vocal.

Starr remade the song entirely the next day without Harrison's assistance, but abandoned both recordings for a third version begun on March 8 and overdubbed on March 11 at Trident Studios. With Harrison now producing, Voormann and Stills returned, adding Mal Evans on tambourine, and Ron Cattermole on trumpet and sax. Harrison recorded a rough guide vocal, with Tom Evans and Pete Ham of Badfinger and Doris Troy adding backing vocals, including another appearance of "Hare Krishna," at Harrison's direction. They left the song there, however, and would not return to it until October.

Meanwhile, Clapton had left the Delaney & Bonnie tour in America. After finishing sessions for his first solo album, he'd returned to the Friends entourage for a series of dates that started in Toronto on February 2. The atmosphere quickly soured, however, as Clapton began to feel caught in an unhealthy dynamic with the Bramletts. "Delaney became very possessive," Clapton recalled, "and kept talking about what we were going to do together in the future. He embellished the relationship with a brotherhood and per-manence that I really couldn't see in it myself. . . . I just enjoyed hanging out with them." Clapton recalled that Delaney & Bonnie "set up a kind of triangle situation. She'd say 'Oh, you have no idea how much Delaney loves you. If you leave him, I don't know what will happen to him.' And he'd say, 'Bonnie's a great singer but we need you Eric.'" As the pressure increased from both sides, he said, "it got very claustrophobic."

Following a show on February 22 at the Fillmore West in San Francisco, Clapton returned to Los Angeles to polish off his album with a few final over-dubs. The Bramletts accompanied him and added touches to the recordings before Clapton flew back to London, leaving Delaney Bramlett to mix the tracks. Various miscommunications ensued, leading Clapton to have the session tapes sent directly to him so he could do his own mix at Island Studios in early March.

Top-tier artists often run in the same circles, and as Harrison and Clapton continued working on their own projects, their worlds kept overlapping. While he waited for the tapes for his own album to arrive, Clapton played on a session with rock trio Ashton, Gardner, and Dyke for the song "I'm Your Spiritual Breadman," a cheeky riff on fly-by-night gurus that also featured Harrison on guitar. In addition to working on the Billy Preston and the Radha Krishna Temple albums, Harrison continued to work with Doris Troy on her LP, which they'd begun the previous year, and to which Clapton had already contributed guitar. In February, Stephen Stills, in town working on his own solo album, joined Harrison at Olympic Studios and played piano on Troy's soulful cover of his Buffalo Springfield song "Special Care."

Meanwhile, Clapton mixed tracks at Island Studios for the album he would simply call *Eric Clapton*. After he recorded one final song for the project, "Easy Now," completely solo, Stephen Stills added a guitar and vocal overdub onto "Let It Rain." Clapton returned the favor on two tracks that Stills was recording at the same studio, "Go Back Home" and "Fishes and Scorpions." Onto the former, he overdubbed a stinging guitar solo, demonstrating just how effortless these kinds of session dates were for him. "Actually, that's Eric warming up," Stills recalled later. "You know, he said, 'Let me practice a little' and Bill (Halverson, co-producer and engineer) would say 'sure'—click! And he'd take it."

As for Clapton's album, Atlantic Records would reject his mixes and ask Tom Dowd to remix the record, which would see release in August. But even with the album soon to be finished under Dowd's expert supervision, Clapton remained uncertain of his identity musically. As grateful as he may have been, he knew that *Eric Clapton* was as much a Delaney & Bonnie and Friends album as his own. Even though he had cheered Clapton on, encouraging him to find his voice and sing, Delaney Bramlett had ultimately been in charge. Still adrift, Clapton would spend much of the spring and summer sitting in on sessions for other artists.

In his official capacity as Apple's director, Harrison gave an interview on March 11 on BBC radio for a forty-five-minute program called *The Beatles Today*, where he essentially served as the voice of the company at a time when rumors about the band's dissolution were increasing. Beginning with a discussion of his songwriting, he described his very first composition, "Don't Bother Me," as "an *awful* song" and continued along a self-deprecating course, saying, "It was difficult for me to write some sort of crummy song and expect the Beatles to record it, [with Lennon and McCartney] already having such fine material." In the next breath, however, he revealed a sense that some of his songs were more nuanced and did not reveal themselves immediately. "To do a song with the Beatles," he said, "it was always a matter of trying to do the song you thought they'd understand quickest or the song you could get onto the tape the quickest, so not necessarily the song you thought was the best." McCartney's aggressiveness in getting his own songs recorded was also a factor in this. He acknowledged that his experience producing other artists over the past two years, beginning with Jackie Lomax in 1968, had broadened his perspective in the studio. "If I'm a part of a band that's recording, if I'm playing guitar, then you think so much about just that one part, whereas if you're producing you can tend to withdraw from *that* situation and see it as a whole; you can see the different parts that make up the record."

He discussed his work with both Billy Preston and Doris Troy, and looking ahead to further productions, he expressed a desire to have a "permanent backing band for Apple artists." In the same breath he mentioned the young guitarist Peter Frampton, whom he'd worked with the previous October on a Troy session, saying, "There's a mutual thing; there's a point where you don't really have to talk much about what the weather's like, because if you're playing together you transcend that. There's a mutual understanding." He previewed the forthcoming Beatles film as "just pure documentary of us slogging, working, on the album" and warned that "some people may be put off at first hearing. People may think we're not trying, because it's really like a demo record. But on the other hand, it's worth so much more than those other records, because you can actually get to know us a bit more. It's a bit more human than the average studio recording."

He then talked up the solo projects of the other Beatles, calling Starr's *Sentimental Journey* "a great album," saying that Lennon was already planning to work with Spector on an LP, and revealing that McCartney was playing all the instruments on his own album. Then, almost hesitantly, he added, "So maybe if I get a chance, I'd like to do an album as well, just to get rid of a lot of songs . . . a George album . . . sometime during the summer," by which point he believed "we should be ready to do a new Beatle album. I certainly don't want to see the end of the Beatles. And I know I'll do anything—whatever Paul, John, Ringo would like to do, I'll do it." The interview ended on a curiously resigned note: "I think that's just part of our life, is to be Beatles. And I'll play the game as long as the people want us to."

"Get rid of a lot of songs" was an odd way to refer to a backlog of compositions, indicating he was still thinking of himself primarily as a Beatle. He'd used this same language speaking to the *New Musical Express* the previous November about a possible solo project, where he said, "At the rate of doing two or three [songs] an album, I'm not even going to get the ones I've done out for three or four years." He prefaced this by revealing the plan the Beatles had discussed in their September meeting, allotting Lennon, McCartney, and Harrison three songs each (and two for Starr) moving forward. "In future we're going to get an equal rights thing, so we all have as much on the album." In light of this, he painted a "George album" simply as an outside project—like *Wonderwall* or *Electronic Sounds*, his two previous extracurricular efforts. He made a solo album sound almost like a vacation before going back to the real job of being in the band. These weren't the last remarks Harrison would make suggesting the Beatles had a future together, but events were already in motion that would soon make the situation much more fractious.

As far as recording his own songs, Harrison had mentioned in that same interview in November that "I suppose I'm waiting till I've got myself a proper studio at home. And then I can just knock 'em off when I feel like it." He'd already assembled a substantial amount of equipment for recording, but his house at Esher had proven too small to create a workable space. "It's a bit of a vicious circle," he admitted, "because I don't want to get a studio fitted up until I move, and I've been trying to move for a long time."

Although Harrison and Boyd had long outgrown the Kinfauns bungalow, space wasn't the only issue. The relative accessibility of the property had made security a problem, with fans regularly breaking in and even stealing things.

Harrison also had specific provisions for the grounds, including a large yard. "I also am insisting on a private lake," he told the *Daily Express*, "because water is very peaceful for the mind." Just as the idea of a solo album to "get rid of songs" would soon grow far beyond his original vision, so too would the site he would eventually purchase far exceed his original plans.

In late 1968 or early 1969, Boyd dutifully set out to find the right property, accompanied either by Harrison or, more often, longtime Beatles associate and Harrison's assistant at the time, Terry Doran. Early on, she thought she'd found the perfect location, an estate in East Sussex called Plumpton Place, but the owner ultimately declined to sell to the Harrisons because "she didn't want rock 'n' roll musicians buying her lovely house." Boyd later recalled, "For about a year I drove around the countryside, looking at one grand house after another." Finally, their estate agent found a place in Henley-on-Thames called Friar Park, about an hour west of London.

Begun in 1889 and developed and expanded over the next two decades, Friar Park was the idiosyncratic brainchild of Sir Frank Crisp, a man who, from the broad outline of the first half of his life, seemed to have little in common with George Harrison. But the world Crisp made for himself was to have a profound impact on the youngest Beatle and become one of the abiding passions of the rest of his life. Almost immediately, Harrison felt a kinship with Crisp that would only increase in the coming years.

Frank Crisp was born in London in 1843, and when he was three his mother died, leaving him to be raised by his father and his grandfather, publisher John Filby Childs. A radical nonconformist, Childs had been imprisoned for pushing back against the church's monopoly on Bible printing and was a pioneer advocate for "cheap and good literature for the millions." In light of his grandfather's nonconformist and democratic attitudes, Crisp developed a keen intellect and by age sixteen decided to study law. He joined a firm of solicitors and prepared privately for exams at the University of London, where he graduated in 1864. In 1867, he married Catherine Howes, with whom he would have four sons and two daughters. By 1869, he became a solicitor himself, with honors.

He established himself quickly. In 1871, he bought into the firm where he had first apprenticed, and six years later the firm added Crisp's name to its masthead. As he specialized in company law, representing such diverse entities as foreign railway companies and the Imperial Japanese Navy, his fortunes grew. Meanwhile, his intellectual curiosity led him to become an expert collector of microscopes and eventually spurred an interest in the natural sciences. He became an adherent of Spiritualism, a movement popular in the middle and upper classes that advanced the belief that spirits continue after death, and which counted Sir Arthur Conan Doyle among its members. Crisp also became treasurer and later vice president of the Linnean Society, the oldest active organization in the world for biological sciences, where a longtime friend observed, "His quick grasp of essentials and common sense enabled him repeatedly to brush aside legal cobwebs which would have hindered the work at hand."

This is all to say that Crisp was an erudite professional with a broad range of interests and a sharp mind. When he began building his estate in Henley, however, he would bring to bear on the project *all* his gifts and curiosities— the natural sciences, Spiritualism, and what turned out to be a wry sense of humor and a philosophical view of life. After purchasing two adjacent plots of land, Friar Park and Friar's Field, Crisp hired architect Robert Clarke Edwards with the initial goal of making the sixty-two-acre property into a "weekend retreat." Working from Crisp's own designs, for the main residence Edwards designed a thirty-room, two-story mansion, a "colorful and eccentric mélange of French Flamboyant Gothic in brick, stone and terracotta, incorporating towers, pinnacles, and large traceried windows." Several smaller lodges in the same style followed, built on different parts of the property, with all the buildings displaying intricate stone and wood carved ornamentation.

Although the original name of Friar Park had no religious connection, likely referring to "the surname of an unknown owner or farmer," Crisp's love of wordplay led him to have engravings of friars made in the house and lodges. One that many visitors remember features the visual pun of a monk holding a frying pan with two holes in it—"two holy [or holey] friars/fryers." They also recalled light switches with friar faceplates, where the noses were flipped to turn the lights off and on. Crisp, the microscopist, reveled in the details, including illustrations of cherubs on the ceilings and religious symbols on the walls and engravings all around the property of what Crisp called "perverted proverbs," such as "A rolling stone waits for no man" and Oscar Wilde's "Punctuality is the thief of time." He also had bits of poetry engraved, from Ovid to Tennyson, and pithy little phrases like those over two windows in the gardener's shed: "Yesterday—today—was tomorrow" and "Tomorrow—today—will be yesterday."

The grounds of Friar Park, however, were what would occupy much of Frank Crisp's imagination over the next twenty years. He designed and oversaw construction of numerous themed gardens, including a Japanese garden, an "Olde English garden," and a rose garden. "Ye Dial Garden" featured a vast array of sundials set amid topiaries "trained and cut into endless imitative and fantastic shapes," including peacocks, pyramids, sheep, and even an umbrella.

Not content with simply having an array of gardens, he also had five themed caves built, which featured man-made stalactites and stalagmites and various animal figures and included distorting mirrors along with what Crisp called "optical delusions" amid electric lights. Another such "delusion" featured prominently in the Japanese garden. "The Walk Through the Water," with two lakes at different levels, created the visual effect that, from a certain vantage point, made it appear as though anyone walking along the steppingstones were walking on water. There were also, positioned throughout the property, many, *many* garden gnomes, a reliable fixture of any nineteenth-century English garden. That one of the themed caves was a Gnome Cave was inevitable.

The crowning touch of the entire estate was the painstakingly detailed Alpine garden, dubbed by at least one source as the "largest artificial rock garden in Britain," and possibly inspired by a similar attraction on the estate of Sir Charles Isham (who is also credited with introducing the garden gnome to the UK from Austria). Frank Crisp had a miniature Swiss Alp constructed, standing forty feet high and composed of 23,000 tons of stones brought down from Yorkshire. Atop this carefully arranged structure, Crisp placed a scale model of the Matterhorn, beneath which lay a replica of the Ice Cave at Capri, "reproduced from a photograph of the cave in the Glacier du Geant, Chamonix" and "populated with stalactites and cavities of blue ice, and with water from an artificial glacier entering in a fall which made real icicles."

It was all colorful and imaginative, what may have seemed at casual glance to be a rich man's folly. But after two decades, Crisp had, in essence, created a Victorian theme park before the concept of a theme park existed. And while he entertained heads of state, he also opened Friar Park to the public. By the early twentieth century, he had written, printed, and several times revised a guidebook for visitors; the final edition in 1914 was filled with exhaustive and obsessive detail about the grounds, running to 198 pages and handsomely illustrated by Alan Tabor. It included a colorful map of the grounds marked by such whimsically named sites as "Where ye lover plucked ye rose" and "Ye Fountain of Perpetual Mirth."

Alongside the more fanciful work on Friar Park, Crisp had continued his legal endeavors and in 1907 was knighted in recognition of his work on the Companies (Consolidation) Act, an important piece of legislation regulating corporate practices in the UK. As legal advisor to the Liberal Party, in 1913 Crisp was made baronet, a rank above knighthood, and in 1919, in recognition of his gardens at Friar Park, he received the Royal Horticultural Society's Victoria Medal of Honour, its highest award.

On April 29 that same year, Crisp died at the age of seventy-five. Financier Percival David (Sir Percival after 1926), son of the founder of the Bank of India, bought Friar Park for £46,500, and though he maintained the grounds, there is no evidence he had anything of Crisp's desire to continue developing the gardens. Still, he kept Friar Park open to visitors throughout the decade. If the £457 he gave to charity in 1922 from garden entry fees is any indication, the site remained a popular attraction: that number reflects more than eighteen thousand visitors paying sixpence each.

George Harrison would eventually come to know all this and more, but Friar Park in its Victorian and early twentieth-century glory was not the property he saw when he first came to view it in 1969. After Percival David left Friar Park in 1953, when he and his wife divorced, the estate began a slow decline. While David's ex-wife stayed on in one of the smaller lodges at Friar Park, David donated the remainder of the estate to the Salesian Sisters of St. John Bosco, a Catholic teaching order, which used the main house as a school.

Maintaining the grounds turned out to be well beyond the Sisters' capabilities, and during the seventeen years the estate was in their possession, the lakes dried up and the gardens became hopelessly overgrown. As a modest means of income, the nuns allowed local builders to use part of the land as a dump. The Sisters also didn't appreciate Crisp's sense of humor or his taste in décor. They painted over some of the aphorisms Crisp had inscribed around the house and plastered over the penises of the "cherub-faced angels smiling down" from the walls. In general, they cared as little for the main house and lodges as they had cared for the gardens, with grass even growing up through the floorboards in some ground-floor rooms. By the late 1960s, the nuns proposed tearing down the buildings and selling the property to a housing developer, only to be blocked by the Oxford County Council. Friar Park was in a precarious state.

And yet, as wild and unloved and in desperate need of restoration as it was, Harrison felt a profound connection with Friar Park. There was certainly room for his recording studio, and he was charmed by the flashes of Frank Crisp's humor that still remained, such as a "Don't Keep Off the Grass" sign and the friar-nose light switches. The beautiful stained glass throughout the main house and lodges and a benign haunted-house feel fostered an alluring atmosphere. One of Crisp's aphorisms—"Scan not a friend with a microscopic glass / You know his faults, now let his foibles pass"—clearly struck a chord, given all the strife with his fellow Beatles, and would occasionally crop up in Harrison's subsequent interviews, eventually serving as the foundation of his 1975 song "The Answer's at the End." But the gardens would require years of work to return to something near their original state and would need a large team to maintain properly. Harrison was looking at a massive fixer upper.

In early March 1965, Derek Taylor had asked Harrison in a radio interview if he liked gardening. "Well, I like a nice sort of garden," he responded, "but it's too much trouble really." The difference between the twenty-two-year-old who saw gardening as "too much trouble" and the twenty-seven-year-old who was about to embark upon a lifelong gardening project was profound and closely tied to Harrison's spiritual development. His studies of Eastern philosophy had awakened him to the realization of how all things are connected, person to person, humans to nature. When he first saw the property, though, he was concerned he couldn't afford it. Harrison had initially visited Friar Park sometime in the first half of 1969, while the Beatles' finances were in disarray. By the end of the year, however, Allen Klein had taken over management of Apple and had increased all the Beatles' bank accounts considerably. Further, Harrison's songwriting royalties for "Something," a number-one record in the US from a number-one LP (plus a bona fide standard that already had covers by Peggy Lee and Tony Bennett), were only adding to his income. Finally, in January 1970, George returned to Friar Park with Derek Taylor. They walked to the lower garden, smoked a joint, and Taylor's always reliable counsel cut through whatever reservations remained. He said simply, "Go ahead and get it."

On January 14, Harrison purchased Friar Park for £140,000, and he initially planned to take the rest of the year off to tend to his country estate, once he had completed work on albums by Billy Preston and Doris Troy. By the time Harrison and Boyd moved in (with Terry Doran in tow) on March 12, he was already thinking more seriously about making a solo album, but he would soon realize that the condition of his new home precluded the construction of a recording studio for the moment. The main house needed to be completely renovated just to be livable; at the tail end of winter they could only heat two rooms, the kitchen and the hallway, the latter of which had a large fireplace beside which they bundled up at night to sleep. While work commenced on the middle lodge, where they would soon move temporarily to allow for the restoration of the main house, George Harrison, world-famous rock star, camped out.

On March 13, the day after moving into Friar Park, Harrison traveled to Paris to appear at Maxim's with a group of Krishnas to promote the "Govinda" single, which Apple had released a week earlier. The *New Musical Express* ran a piece the next day, March 14, based around a recent visit the paper had made to the Apple offices, during which Harrison and Starr played some of their new recordings, with Harrison running through "It Don't Come Easy" on guitar. On the subject of the state of the Beatles, the two men remained elusive. "Everything's fine," said Starr. "But I've got things to do, and George has things to do, and Paul has his solo album to come, and John has his peace thing. We can't do everything at once. Time will tell." "Say we've got unity in diversity," said Harrison, "because that's what it is—unity through diversity. We still see each other, still make contact. But we had to find ourselves, individually, one day. It was the natural course of events." Harrison gave this interview around the same time as the one for *The Beatles Today*, but his tone here about a prospective solo project was notably different, more upbeat, more enthusiastic. "Maybe I'll get round to doing something for myself! I'm almost a full-time Apple producer, but I'm going to stop. I don't want to die as 'George Harrison records producer,' or 'George Harrison lead guitarist' or even just a Beatle. They're all me, but they're not really me. I'm unlimited. We're all unlimited!"

After his return from Denmark and the recording of "Instant Karma!" Lennon had listened to Glyn Johns's most recent edition of *Get Back* and, along with the rest of the band, rejected this version as well. Like his previous attempts, the mixes were awash in a cavernous reverb and devoid of life. Johns was perhaps too close to the material, too close to the experience of recording the songs, to hear them with fresh ears, but whatever spark had been captured on tape during the sessions was absent from his mixes. For Lennon, the crackling energy of the "Instant Karma!" single confirmed that Spector was the man for the job. McCartney had been willfully avoiding the subject, keeping his head buried in work on his solo album, but eventually he agreed to let Spector take over the project.

On March 23, Spector set to work on the tapes for the *Get Back* album, henceforth to be known as *Let It Be*. The work primarily lay in remixing takes that Glyn Johns had already chosen for his own compilations, meaning that Spector had decided not to listen through all the session tapes; the takes at hand, he concluded, were all satisfactory enough to begin work. This first day, his most dramatic contributions came in the form of edits, removing a section at the beginning and end of "Dig a Pony" and, even more importantly, extending Harrison's "I Me Mine" from 1:34 to 2:25 with a clever edit. Harrison attended this day, as well as the six remaining sessions where Spector polished the tracks.

As Spector worked in Room Four, a mixing-only space at EMI, Paul McCartney was in the control room of Studio Three finishing the mastering of his own solo album. Whether they were aware of each other this day is unclear, but McCartney remained preoccupied with his own record, and he had, after all, been out of touch with the other Beatles, had been absent from the Apple offices, and hadn't spoken to Lennon in months. He had effectively cut himself from all things Beatles and Apple.

Peter Bown, one of the engineers who worked with Phil Spector on these sessions, told Mark Lewisohn in 1987, "I got on quite well with Spector except that he wanted tape echo on *everything*, seemed to take a different pill every half an hour and had his bodyguard with him." In addition to Harrison's attendance, Bown recalled that Allen Klein also came to the sessions, which continued on March 25, 26, 27, and 30, by which point nearly all the mixing was complete.

The *Let It Be* film was due to premier in the US on May 13 and a week later in the UK. Even before Spector began working on the tapes, Allen Klein—with the support of Lennon, Harrison, and Starr—had set the date of April 24 for the album (and accompanying book of photos) to hit the record shops. Along with the *Hey Jude* compilation LP (released February 26 worldwide, except in the UK) and Starr's *Sentimental Journey* (which was set for March 27), this meant a substantial but well-paced stream of Beatles-related product appearing in the first half of the year.

Unfortunately, McCartney and Neil Aspinall had long ago decided upon an April 17 release date for the *McCartney* album. With the rearranged release schedule for the Beatles' project, this was now just a week before the street date for *Let It Be*. With a potential oversaturation of Beatles products in mind, on March 20 Klein asked EMI to delay the release of *McCartney*—without informing McCartney. Klein reiterated this request to EMI in person on March 23, and the company agreed to delay the album. The math, to Klein, was simple: a multimedia project by the band promised a much greater financial return for Apple/EMI and should logically take precedence over any solo project. Whether Klein's failure to communicate with McCartney was just the result of a lack of consideration or an intentional dig at the Beatle who trusted him least, he could hardly have picked a more sensitive pressure point.

Realizing the news would be better coming from them than Klein, on March 31 Lennon and Harrison wrote McCartney a letter outlining the problem, saying they had decided to push the release of *McCartney* to June 4, which coincided with an Apple-Capitol record convention in Hawaii. "We thought you'd come 'round," the letter read, "when you realized that the Beatles album was coming out on April 24th. We're sorry it turned out like this—it's nothing personal. Love John George. Hare Krishna. A Mantra a Day Keeps MAYA! Away." Rather than have a courier deliver such an important message, Starr decided to bring McCartney the letter himself. As he read the note, with Starr saying he agreed with its contents, McCartney snapped. In an interview shortly afterward with the *Evening Standard*, McCartney said, "I called him everything under the sun," before throwing Starr out of the house. "I had to do something like that in order to assert myself," he said later, "because I was just sinking."

McCartney's behavior may have seemed villainous, but Lennon's unwillingness to consider anyone other than Allen Klein as their manager had set these events into motion. It was a corrosive play for dominance in the group over

McCartney, establishing an "are you with me or against me?" ultimatum that swept Harrison and Starr along in the ensuing chaos. By agreeing to hire Klein, Harrison had unwittingly sided with Lennon. But Harrison saw McCartney's hostility through his own lens and would soon put his feelings into song.

Oblivious to these internal Beatle affairs, Spector oversaw a session on April 1 that would inadvertently amplify these already rising tensions. For "Across the Universe," "The Long and Winding Road," and "I Me Mine," the producer had commissioned orchestrations requiring fifty musicians, including a choir on the first two songs, all to be recorded in EMI's massive Studio One. Technical engineer Brian Gibson remembered the session well because of the friction Spector engendered. Most producers at recording sessions, said Gibson, "would leave the tracks completely dry, perhaps with just a bit of monitor echo, but certainly without any of the effects added later." Spector, however, "wanted to hear it, while it was being recorded, exactly the way it would sound when finished: all the tape echo, plate echo, chamber echo, all the effects. This was horrendously difficult in Studio One which is, technically, quite primitive." Gibson thought Spector was "getting towards the end of his tether and was giving everybody a hard time," until Starr, who was there to play drums along with the orchestra, pulled the producer aside and defused the situation.

Another issue arose when Spector booked the instrumentalists for two songs but tried to get them to record the third ("I Me Mine") without discussing extra payment. "I warned Phil that he would never get away with it," said Gibson, "and of course the orchestra got up and walked out." Once the financial details were settled, the orchestra returned. All told, the day had cost more than £1,100 in musician fees alone. Spector mixed these three songs the next day, April 2, completing the album sixteen months after the *Get Back* sessions had begun. He had sample discs cut for all four members of the band for their approval and included a note that read, "If there's anything you'd like done to the album, let me know and I'll be glad to help. Naturally little things are easy to change, big things might be a problem. If you wish, please call me about anything regarding the album tonight." Although Spector's reputation suggested he would have overwhelmed these recordings with his "Wall of Sound," when compared with Glyn Johns's attempts, it becomes clear that Spector had instead polished these performances more effectively than perhaps anyone else could have. That he had assembled a commercial, cohesive album out of a collection of recordings made by a band on the verge of collapse seemed to justify Lennon and Harrison's faith in his abilities.

Even McCartney seemed to agree, at least initially. Starr would recall, "I spoke to Paul on the phone and said, 'Did you like it?', and he said, 'Yeah, it's OK.' He didn't put it down." The other three Beatles had relented to McCartney's desired album release date of April 17 and pushed the release of the *Let It Be* album package into May, which may have helped mollify the situation for the moment. On April 7, after McCartney's attorneys announced the formation of McCartney Productions Ltd. and the upcoming release of *McCartney*, McCartney indicated he would attend a board meeting of Apple Films scheduled for April 10, at which Harrison and Allen Klein would also be present.

What might have transpired at that meeting is impossible to know, because McCartney's next move changed everything. Declining to do interviews to promote *McCartney*, he instead composed a press release in the form of a four-page Q&A to go out with promotional copies of the album. Most of it was fairly straightforward, covering the making of the recordings, but about midway through, he dropped in a few impossible-to-ignore personal jabs:

> Q: "Is it true that neither Allen Klein nor ABKCO have been nor will be in any way involved with the production, manufacturing, distribution or promotion of this new album?"
> PAUL: "Not if I can help it."
> Q: "Did you miss the other Beatles and George Martin? Was there a moment when you thought, 'I wish Ringo were here for this break?'"
> PAUL: "No"

And then, a few questions later:

> Q: "Is your break with the Beatles temporary or permanent, due to personal differences or musical ones?"
> PAUL: "Personal differences, business differences, musical differences, but most of all because I have a better time with my family. Temporary or permanent? I don't really know."

While nowhere in this press release did McCartney explicitly say he was quitting the band, the phrase "break with the Beatles" was like blood in the water.

After months of breakup rumors, the press finally had something solid to sink its teeth into. Although McCartney later said Peter Brown had written the prompts, Brown averred in his own book that McCartney alone was completely responsible for the press release. Just a month later, Derek Taylor would support Brown's version of events: "He was only supposed to write out information explaining how he made his album. Instead, he hands us this interview with himself asking questions such as would he miss Ringo. It was entirely gratuitous. Nobody asked him that question. He asked that question of himself."

On April 8, McCartney had copies of the press release hand-delivered to the *Evening Standard* and the *Daily Mirror*, with instructions to hold publication for two days. The *Mirror* didn't wait, though, and had copies of its April 10 issue with the front-page headline "Paul Quits the Beatles" available the evening of April 9. McCartney phoned Lennon to let him know personally that he was leaving the band, to which Lennon responded, "Good, that makes two of us who have seen sense." Harrison found out via Mal Evans, who had heard a radio story reporting the news. The next day, as the rest of the press picked up on the *Mirror*'s scoop, the story went global. Unsurprisingly, McCartney pulled out of the Apple Films meeting. Lennon would later conclude that McCartney had used the breakup bombshell to help promote the release of *McCartney*, but even if that were the case, the majority of the press attention would now be directed toward the dissolution of the band, not the new album.

The same day the breakup story caught fire, April 10, Harrison did an interview in his office at Apple with BBC television for a series on religion, *Fact or Fantasy*, to be broadcast on April 26 in the episode, "Prayer and Meditation." At length, he articulated his experience with Eastern philosophy, speaking of his disillusionment with Catholicism at age thirteen, and his discovery of meditation through his interest in Indian music. He described the purpose of yoga and meditation as transcendence from "a relative state of consciousness to an absolute state of consciousness." Wisely connecting this line of thought back to Christian beliefs, he observed, "Basically, everybody is a spirit, which is really what Christ was here to tell everybody about."

He expressed what he saw as the need for these spiritual practices and how they were fundamental to all faiths. "Through many years of pollution of consciousness through material energy and disassociation we've all ended up in a fallen state, but really everybody is basically potentially divine. So yoga—all these methods are really ancient methods just to stop further pollution of your system and your consciousness and to cleanse the system. The whole thing of purity they talk about in religion is really a mental, physical, and spiritual purity, which is obtained through discipline and through practice." Citing the importance of remaining anchored to "that pure state of consciousness, that pure state of being," he likened it to the calm on the ocean floor while the waves above were constantly changing. "If you're not anchored to the bottom of the ocean," he observed, "you're at the mercy of whatever change goes on."

If anyone could have used a dose of that bottom-of-the-ocean calm at this moment, it was Paul McCartney. He later confessed that he was going through something of a "nervous breakdown" during this time, and while focus on his own album had no doubt initially distracted him from Beatles-related concerns, fallout from his press release was intense. At some point amid this drama, he reassessed his opinion of *Let It Be* and, ignoring all the other work Spector had done, zeroed in on the production of "The Long and Winding Road." On April 14, he dictated a message for Allen Klein over the phone to an Apple employee, stating that, "In the future no one will be able to add or subtract from a recording of one of my songs without my permission." Admitting he had considered adding an orchestral backing to his song but had changed his mind, he requested that the strings, horns, and voices be mixed down (although, curiously, not mixed out completely), that the Beatles be increased in volume, and that the harp be removed at the end and replaced by the piano notes from the original recording. He closed by saying, "Don't ever do it again."

He had waited too long, though. To meet the May 8 release date, the album was already being pressed. Had McCartney responded when he and the other Beatles received their test copies of Spector's mixes, there would have been time, but now it was impossible. When Klein attempted to get in touch to discuss the situation, he found that, in another effectively isolating gesture, McCartney had changed his phone number. Klein then sent him a telegram asking for him to call Klein or Spector, but instead received a message in return that "the letter spoke for itself."

Attempting to plead his case publicly, Paul consented to an interview several days later with Ray Connolly for the *Evening Standard*, which ran on April 22 and 23. "A few weeks ago," he said, "I was sent a re-mixed version of my song 'The Long and Winding Road' with harps, horns, an orchestra, and a women's choir added. No one had asked me what I thought. I couldn't believe it. I would never have female voices on a Beatles record. . . . I don't blame Phil Spector for doing it, but it just goes to show that it's no good me sitting here thinking I'm in control because obviously I'm not. Anyway, I've sent Klein a letter asking for some of the things to be altered, but I haven't received an answer yet." He must have known by then, however, that it was too late. Deflecting blame regarding the breakup story, he asserted that "the party's over, but none of us wants to admit it."

6 | HARRISON COMES ALIVE

AS THE SECOND HALF of McCartney's *Evening Standard* interview ran on April 23, Boyd and Harrison boarded a plane bound for America; Boyd headed to L.A. to attend an MGM auction in search of décor for Friar Park, while Harrison stayed in New York City for twelve days. He picked up his travel visa, met with Allen Klein, and said he would be looking into why the Doris Troy and Radha Krishna Temple records weren't selling well in the States. Derek Taylor joined him on the trip, and Harrison did two revealing interviews. The first was conducted by Al Aronowitz, with whom Harrison had remained friendly since 1964, when the writer introduced the Beatles to Bob Dylan. On the morning of January 24, Aronowitz showed up with a borrowed guitar at the Hotel Pickwick, and Harrison played "All Things Must Pass" for him. Along with Taylor, they headed out into the streets of the city, and Harrison talked of how Allen Klein was "the first to really take a personal interest in me" and expressed his wish that Klein had been the Beatles' manager nine years earlier. Harrison claimed that Apple lost more than $1 million in its first year, as McCartney "ran the company almost single-handedly." Aronowitz reported, "According to the figures in the press, the Beatles earned a total of $17 million in their first seven years. Since Allen Klein took over, the Beatles have earned $17 million in seven months."

The radioactive glow of McCartney's April 10 press release remained fresh and potent, and the last time they spoke Harrison recalled that he had to hold the phone away from his ear: "He came on like Attila the Hun." And yet, noted Aronowitz, when Harrison spoke of McCartney, there was "no bitterness . . .

only hurt," and when the journalist asked him if there was a group he would like to tour with, Harrison responded, "The Beatles." He also spoke enthusiastically about Friar Park and its myriad eccentricities: the Alpine garden, the grotto, the caves, the light switches with friar faceplates and, plucking a Dylan line from the air, "a thousand telephones that don't ring." He explained that the house was "like a horror movie but it doesn't really have bad vibes. . . . I thought after I moved into my new house, I'd take a year off and do nothing, but here I am getting ready to make my own album in two weeks. The point is that we're all of us writing too much now to put it all onto one Beatles record anyway."

In this last remark Harrison alluded once again to the Beatles' meeting in September 1969, where they laid out a plan for a potential next album. Even with three songs each, as proposed, they would all still have a backlog. He referred directly to this meeting again the next day in an interview with Howard Smith, where he repeated that they all have "so many songs," and by doing their own albums, "we don't have to compromise. I mean, we lose whatever we get from each other—we sacrifice that in order to do a total sort of thing, you know, because in a way, Paul wants to do his songs his way. He doesn't want to do his songs my way, and I don't wanna do my songs their way, really."

During the interview, Harrison downplayed McCartney's press release to Smith and spoke optimistically about the future of the Beatles. "I'm sure that after we've all completed an album or even two albums each, then that novelty will have worn off. . . . I'll certainly try my best to do something with them again, you know. I mean, it's only a matter of accepting that the situation is a compromise. In a way it's a compromise, and it's a sacrifice, you know, because we all have to sacrifice a little in order to gain something really big. And there is a big gain by recording together—I think musically, and financially and also spiritually, and for the rest of the world, you know, I think that Beatle music is such a big sort of scene—that I think it's the least we could do is to sacrifice three months of the year at least, you know, just to do an album or two. I think it's very selfish if the Beatles don't record together."

Harrison refused to characterize the tension between Lennon and McCartney as anger, instead calling it "childish" and "bitchy," and believed that it was "just a matter of time" before they all worked out their problems and went back into the studio together. "But if not, you know, it's still alright," he said. "Whatever happens, you know, it's gonna be okay. In fact, it's never looked better from my point of view." He anticipated his own upcoming album sessions and indicated that the arrangements would depend on how he felt the songs should be interpreted, but his discussions with Spector had already sprouted ideas. "I really want to use as much instrumentation as I think the songs need," he told Smith. "Some will have orchestras, and some will have rock and roll, and some will have trumpets . . . it'll be a production album." He revealed publicly here for the first time that he had "enough songs for about three or four albums, actually. But if I do one, that'll be good enough for me."

In addition to a bit of clothes shopping, Harrison rented a Fender Stratocaster and a practice amp from Manny's Music Shop while out with Aronowitz, and on April 30 spent time with Bob Dylan at his home on McDougal Street. The morning of May 1, Harrison stopped by the Beatles Fan Club office, where he mentioned to Sandi Morse, one of the employees, that he believed the Beatles breakup was "only temporary while they do their own albums." That afternoon (2:30–5:50 PM), Harrison stopped by Columbia Recording Studio B on East 52nd Street, where Dylan was running through material for what would be his next album, *New Morning*, with Charlie Daniels on bass, Russ Kunkel on drums, and producer Bob Johnston on piano.

Plugging in his rented Strat, Harrison sat in on electric guitar and vocals for what was essentially a demo session: the vibe on the tapes is very loose, just a day to test out new material, and consequently, nothing recorded here would make the final album. They gave five new songs the most attention, with several takes each, which took up the afternoon session. But then they kept going, and Dylan began pulling from his back catalog, including "Just Like Tom Thumb's Blues" and "One Too Many Mornings," where Harrison harmonized on the chorus. They mixed in several late '50s and early '60s songs, including "Cupid," "Da Doo Ron Ron," and "Your True Love" by Carl Perkins. There was even a charmingly sloppy version of "Yesterday," where Harrison sang a kind of lopsided harmony on the final line and afterward said drolly, "Dub some cellos on."

Harrison's role was in no way meant to be official, and the absence of his name on the recording contracts underlined the informal nature of his presence at the studio; when *Rolling Stone* ran a story on the session at the end of the month, Dylan's secretary and Bob Johnston both categorically denied Harrison's involvement, but the tapes reveal he had stayed until the end of recording at 1:30 AM. They ran through twenty-five different songs in those eleven hours, but the one that Harrison carried back with him to England came from earlier in the day. "If Not for You" was a new Dylan original, recorded for the first time on this date and worked out over the course of five takes. Harrison applied the newest technique he was learning, adding a clear and effective electric slide part over Dylan's simply strummed acoustic guitar as the bassist and drummer followed along. Even in its rough state, this four-piece arrangement stuck in Harrison's mind.

After the Dylan session, Harrison finished up his New York trip and headed back home on May 4, leaving behind, on three separate occasions, the message that the Beatles would eventually work together again after a short break. A cynical reading of this message might say it was damage control. Both the album and film of Let It Be were about to be released, and it made sense to keep McCartney's pronouncement from overshadowing those events; it also took back some of the power from McCartney in the breakup narrative. But Harrison's comments in New York were consistent with those to the BBC in March. His words carry a tone of reassurance in these interviews, too, revealing that he was sensitive to how much the Beatles meant to people.

He was also likely working through what he was experiencing personally by talking it out. Like the end of any deep, long-term relationship, sorting through the emotions sparked by such a separation would take time, and just as with everything else related to this band, the expectations and scrutiny of the public and press added extra weight. While the wounds were fresh, they nonetheless seemed capable of healing, and although Harrison had been frustrated by the band's constraints and now felt liberated to a degree, the Beatles had been the center of his life for so long that their nonexistence was unimaginable. After all, none of them *wanted* this conflict. "Part of me thinks that George was happy they were breaking up," Pattie Boyd said, "and then other times he was brokenhearted, and so it was very extreme, because you see they had been together since they were all quite young."

As Harrison finished up his New York trip, Eric Clapton was in Olympic Studios yet again. Earlier in the year during Delaney and Bonnie's US tour, Chicago producer Norman Dayron had approached Clapton about recording with Chester "Howlin' Wolf" Burnett in London and getting together a backing band for the sessions. Clapton recruited Ringo Starr and Klaus Voormann on drums and bass, but at the first session on May 2, "the Wolf" was in foul temper, at one point even grabbing Clapton by the wrist to show him how to play a song correctly. Dayron would tell the press that the day hadn't gone well because Starr and Voormann "didn't really grow up with the blues," but in truth the bassist and drummer bristled against the bad vibes and decided not to return. Clapton was petrified in the presence of the old bluesman, "because he wasn't saying anything to anyone—he just sat there in a corner and let this young white kid [Dayron] kinda run the show and tell everyone what to do! It was a bit strange . . . and when he finally did open up, he was great, but he was very intimidating to look at. We weren't sure what he was thinking." For the remaining dates on May 4, 6, and 7, Bill Wyman and Charlie Watts took over the rhythm section duties, with Mick Jagger sitting in on percussion at one point, and the rest of the sessions went more smoothly. The Wolf himself told *Melody Maker*, "The sessions over here so far have been really wonderful." In spite of having recorded his first solo album in January, Clapton was still trying to find a good fit for his talents. In the middle of these sessions, on May 5, he played with a re-formed Traffic at the Student Union, St. Catherine's College, Oxford University. He would tell *Melody Maker*, "I was hoping after that gig that I would be asked to join the group. If I had been, I would have joined. Just like that. But I wasn't asked, so it didn't happen."

The *Let It Be* album finally arrived in record stores on May 8, with the world premiere of the movie following in the US on May 13 and the UK on May 20. The project was now a year and a half old, and, given the band's current state and where each of them was in his own life, none of them wanted to revisit the inertia of January 1969. Sending a clear and unfortunate message regarding their feelings for the movie, not a single Beatle showed up at any of the screenings. Harrison certainly had other things on his mind: a week after the UK premiere, not only was he due to start work on his album, but he was also facing a serious medical crisis with his mother. Pattie Boyd remembered they discovered Louise Harrison was very ill in September 1969 and went to see her in Cheshire, finding she had in fact been sick for two months already but had kept the news from her famous son, "in case George was busy." After his brother Harry Harrison called and described Louise's condition, George and Pattie headed north, finding his mother "rambling about people in the room whom we couldn't see." When the doctor, who had only done a superficial examination, asked George for his autograph, they moved to find another physician.

"She'd got a tumor on the brain," Harrison recalled in 1987, "but the doctor was an idiot and he was saying, 'There's nothing wrong with her, she's having some psychological trouble.' When I went up to see her, she didn't even know who I was." Even looking back seventeen years later, Harrison became visibly angry at the memory of it all. He had to force the doctor to find a specialist in neurology, who told him, "'She could end up being a vegetable, but if it was my wife or my mother I'd do the operation'—which was a horrendous thing where they had to drill a hole in her skull." Louise had been George's greatest champion from the beginning, defending his decision to start slicking his hair back like a Teddy Boy ("There's more than enough sheep in this life. Let the boy be," she told her husband), buying him his first guitars, and having a young Paul McCartney and John Lennon over to the Harrison home to practice. George's sister, also named Louise, remembered her mother as "bright and funny and witty, vital, *alive*. I always imagine her like a firework on Bonfire Night." The frontal lobe tumor, though, sapped her of that vitality and brought on debilitating headaches, leaving George's father, Harold Harrison, as her caregiver. George left the Delaney & Bonnie tour on December 5 to visit her, and she recovered well enough by Christmas to join her family for a holiday dinner, but the improvement was only temporary.

In May 1970, Louise Harrison returned to the hospital for an examination, and the doctors discovered that the tumor was malignant and ultimately resistant to treatment. The family decided not to inform her of the grim prognosis, and she remained in hospital with only a short time to live. George recalled that his father "had suddenly exploded with ulcers and he was in the same hospital. So I was pretending to both of them that the other one was okay."

In the shadow of this impending tragedy, Harrison began sessions for his solo album. Given the scale of what he now envisioned, there was no way he could produce the project himself, even though he had certainly grown into a capable producer over the past year. "I needed somebody to help me," he said later, "because, you know . . . after being in a group all the time with a producer, suddenly to be a solo artist with no producer, and no *group*—so you know it's quite a big jump." Having seen how Spector had handled "Instant Karma!" and especially *Let It Be*, he felt the American producer would be ideal.

When he heard Harrison and Spector would be teaming up, John Lennon observed, "George likes to go on and on arranging things, and Phil likes to go on and on adding things, so they've got to watch that when they get together, because they'll just end up in. . . . I don't know." Lennon's comments were filtered through his own current desire to get a song down on tape as quickly as possible, valuing raw expression over slick production—"Instant Karma!" being the latest, most vivid example. He had vetoed Spector's desire to add strings to the "Karma" recording, after all, so while he knew whereof he spoke, there may have been a note of the dismissive-older-brother dynamic held over from the Beatles. But he also wasn't wrong.

Spector's reputation for perfectionism preceded him, but Harrison's attention to detail may not have been as widely known. When he had the rare opportunity to indulge himself with his own songs in the studio, he layered them carefully; "Blue Jay Way" was his own exploration of the same experimental impulse Lennon had satisfied with "Strawberry Fields Forever" or "I Am the Walrus." By the time of *Abbey Road,* he had become the full (though rarely acknowledged) equal of Lennon and McCartney, and not just as a songwriter. Harrison fine-tuned the recording of "Here Comes the Sun" to be as precise as any song in the Beatles' catalog, and he continued adding and redoing parts for "Something" so that even the relative luxury of eight-track recording proved inadequate to his needs, requiring a tape reduction to another eight-track tape to make room for more overdubs. There was certainly potential for a Harrison-Spector collaboration to go off the rails.

At some point after his New York trip, Harrison played Spector a number of the songs at Friar Park, looking ahead to the idea of recording. He had told Howard Smith in New York, "I knew I'd do one eventually, but I hadn't decided to do it this soon, and it was only after that I decided that I'd do it straight away, so now I've got to meet with Phil and decide really which tunes, you know. I've got an idea which ones I'd like to use." Spector would later recall that Harrison "had literally hundreds of songs, and each one was better than the rest. He had all this emotion built up when it was released to me. I don't think he had played them to anybody—maybe Pattie."

While Harrison was captured in a home recording at some point in early 1970 playing some songs and musing that he might record an album of his own in the near future, Spector was largely correct. Although the estimate of "hundreds" of tunes was hyperbole, by the time Harrison was ready to record he had somewhere in the neighborhood of thirty songs from which to choose. This didn't include pieces he'd cowritten with Ringo Starr ("It Don't Come Easy"), Billy Preston ("Sing One for the Lord"), Doris Troy ("Ain't That Cute"), or Eric Clapton ("Badge"), and while a handful were admittedly incomplete, the majority were ready to go, and he would write several more during the sessions. In spite of what had become almost reflexive dismissals of his compositions by Lennon, McCartney, and George Martin, Harrison was on a hot streak. He'd been squirreling away songs, and now that he had committed to the idea of making an album, they came pouring out.

"On one occasion," recalled John Barham, "George invited me to come over alone to join him and Pattie for dinner. We ate in the kitchen, and the food was delivered by an Indian takeaway service. Immediately after eating, without speaking, George picked up a guitar and began playing and singing one song after the other. I hadn't seen George do this before, so I found it unusual. . . . The songs he sang were those that he subsequently recorded in the *All Things Must Pass* albums. Looking back on that evening I guess George wanted to know how I would react to the songs as he may already have decided to ask me to do string arrangements."

Back in November 1969, when discussing the idea of recording a solo project, Harrison imagined working best in a home studio, which would allow for a more relaxed environment. "I know that if I were doing it like that, I'd probably do it more like the Plastic Ono Band, where you just bash away!" This was before Spector, the "Instant Karma!" session, and the work on *Let It Be*, all of which would lead him to consider different approaches for his songs. Although Harrison didn't have a specific plan in mind, his vision was now far more ambitious than just bashing away, and his ideas would continue to grow as recording progressed.

Phil McDonald, a veteran of Beatles recordings since 1965, would engineer all the sessions for Harrison's album at EMI, and assisting McDonald in the control room would be twenty-year-old John Leckie. *All Things Must Pass* would be particularly memorable for the young engineer because it was his first major assignment, and he would be present for all but one of the sessions. "I started actually February 15, 1970," recalled Leckie, "so I'd only been there a few months when this was done. And I came from college—I did a film and TV college—and I actually wrote a handwritten thesis on electronic music called 'The Art of Noises.' I still have it. Because I was into that, Stockhausen and the Moog synthesizer had just been invented, and I guess this is how I got the job at Abbey Road. I'd worked in the film company in the West End, and I went for interviews with the BBC and didn't really want to work for the BBC. And I guess through hearing the records at the time, 1968, '69, Pink Floyd and psychedelic music, I thought, 'I want to do this. If I can't be a film director,

I'll work in a studio and do film music.' Even though I'm not a musician—I've never been a musician even though for fifty years I've worked in the studio."

While EMI Studios had relaxed a bit since the notorious white lab coats of the 1950s and early '60s, it was still strictly compartmentalized. Leckie's official title was "second engineer," "which meant you didn't touch any of the equipment or the mixing desk, but you ran the tape. You were totally responsible for being there and in charge of the tape. No one touched the tape machine except you, really. Meaning if you want to go to the toilet you have to say, 'Excuse me can I go to the loo.' And the session would stop until you came back. You didn't set up microphones or fix equipment or make tea even. We had a tea lady, or we had NO tea."

Except for one session, all the band recordings for the album at Abbey Road took place in Studio Three, the smallest of the building's recording spaces. Measuring thirty-two feet by forty feet with a high ceiling, it was certainly by no means "small," but it was fittingly only a little larger than the twenty-three-by-thirty-five-foot studio at Gold Star in Los Angeles, where Spector had perfected his famous Wall of Sound. Unlike Studio Two, with its control room high above the studio floor, Number Three was laid out all on the same level, with a large window providing a clear eyeline from producer to artist. The size of the studios was where the similarity ended, however. Gold Star's recording space had a low ceiling and was full of reflective surfaces that colored the sound of any recording done there; EMI Studio Three in 1970 was a notably "dead" room, built to absorb sounds and render a flat recording that could be manipulated entirely in the mix.

One feature of some of the *All Things Must Pass* sessions that *did* follow Spector's Gold Star practices was the focus on live band performances, often featuring a large ensemble of players. Guests were not uncommon. "I went to a couple of sessions," recalls Alan Parsons, who was then still an EMI engineer, "and every time a musician came in, George would tell them to go find a guitar and join in." Fortunately, and presumably to make sure everyone got paid, Mal Evans scrupulously kept track of who played at each session (see appendix for the full list).

Additionally, by cross-referencing interviews and using known dates of different individuals' whereabouts, other details are clear:

- Starr was available at the start of the sessions but would be out of the country from June 22 to July 1 and would therefore not be present on recordings covered by those dates.
- Badfinger was unavailable from June 4 onward (with the exception of June 22 and 23).
- Carl Radle and Jim Gordon wouldn't arrive in the UK until around June 10.
- Derek and the Dominos did not appear on the sessions as a functioning four-piece band until June 22.
- Any track prior to June 10 featured Ringo Starr on drums and Alan White on percussion, except June 3, when White played drums due to Starr's absence.
- Klaus Voormann played bass on all sessions up until Radle's arrival; thereafter, Voormann occasionally played guitar or keyboards.
- Eric Clapton was available from the first session through to the last band recording, July 3, though he may be absent from recordings on June 7 through 11.

In addition, Phil Spector's letter to Harrison on August 19 (see chapter 8) provides further confirmation of the performers on certain songs. Sessions began with a core group of players: George Harrison himself on guitar, Klaus Voormann on bass, Eric Clapton on electric guitar, Alan White on drums, Billy Preston on piano, and Bobby Whitlock on Hammond organ. As a producer, Harrison had been gathering around him a group of musicians with whom he could communicate clearly and easily. If his intent initially was to create a "house band" for Apple artists, as he had mentioned in March, the result was instead a house band for his own album.

The Beatles had been a closed unit, typically with just the four of them recording the basic rhythm tracks of their songs, accompanied occasionally by George Martin. Two notable exceptions were Harrison's doing: Eric Clapton playing lead guitar on "While My Guitar Gently Weeps" and Billy Preston joining in on keyboards at the Get Back sessions. But for the recording of Harrison's own album, inclusiveness would be the rule, not the exception.

Clapton was certainly part of that. He had done plenty of session work on his own throughout the first half of 1970, and Harrison had employed him on sessions for Billy Preston and Doris Troy. Bobby Whitlock was living at Hurtwood with Clapton, and since Harrison was familiar with his Hammond playing from the Delaney & Bonnie dates, Whitlock became one of the key players on the album.

Youngest of all the musicians, at age twenty Alan White had already played with John Lennon on several occasions, beginning in September 1969 at the Toronto Rock 'n' Roll Revival festival as part of the Plastic Ono Band, and then on "Instant Karma!" White was accustomed to being the junior musician in the room. "The first band I was ever in," he said, "I was called the youngest drummer in England. When I was thirteen, I was playing stuff!" White's background on piano early on gave his drumming a musical quality, an attentiveness to each song's needs; the performances with Lennon proved he could handle the more propulsive rock songs, while White's playing on the "Govinda" single confirmed for Harrison that he would also have the sensitivity necessary to back the quieter tunes in the Harrison songbook. White recalled, "I think probably one of the initial things that struck me in first meeting George and striking up any relationship with him was realizing he was really one of the nicest guys I'd ever met in my life. So peaceful and at rest with himself, just one of those people that seemed so calm, and I guess the kind of religion he was into gave him a peace of mind like that. And it immediately struck me when I first met George. And when he asked me to be part of the album, it was a pleasure. I knew I was going to have a good time doing it."

Spector's occasional technique of using two drummers for certain effects in his Gold Star productions has long been assumed to have carried onto *All Things Must Pass*, and while several participants recalled two drummers on some of these sessions, White, who estimated he played on about "two thirds" of the album, insisted this wasn't the case. "There was never two drummers," said White. "I only remember one drum kit playing at that time. If there was anything else like that, the other drums would have been put on there later. But I don't hear anything like that. It was just one drum kit." The pre-overdubbed basic tracks of the songs confirm White's memory: only one drummer is audible, although in a number of instances one or two percussionists played live with the rest of the track—another common feature of Spector's earlier recordings. Likewise, though some who were present recalled two bassists, Klaus Voormann is clear that he never played bass at the same time as Carl Radle. Working in the service of Harrison and his moveable feast of musicians were Mal Evans, the Beatles' longtime equipment manager, and Kevin Harrington,

Evans's twenty-year-old assistant. Together, they made an unlikely pair, with Evans's towering height and Harrington's conspicuous shock of red hair.

Meanwhile, as with "Govinda" and other recordings that Harrison had produced, John Barham would be tasked with composing the orchestral scores, and even though these parts would be written and overdubbed well after basic tracks had been recorded, Harrison requested Barham's presence at sessions from the beginning. Barham believed this was a continuation of the process begun back when Harrison introduced him to Muddy Waters and Otis Spann records. "I think this was also part of George inviting me into his musical world," Barham said. "I had worked in studios before with George: Billy Preston, Rhadha Krishna, etc., but with the exception of a single track for Jackie Lomax where Eric Clapton used two fingers on a piano to teach me a basic rock riff, I was only there for overdubs, not backing tracks. *All Things Must Pass* was the first time I was present right from the beginning. This gave me the opportunity to see two masters creating from the ground up. Witnessing the exchange between George, Phil and the musicians was something I benefited from when I began producing."

Before proper band recording began, Harrison took two days to tape simple demos of many of his songs, both for Spector and for the musicians in the sessions ahead. On May 26, with Starr on drums and Voormann on bass, he recorded fifteen songs, ten of which would make it to the released album: "My Sweet Lord," "All Things Must Pass," "Behind That Locked Door," "Apple Scruffs," "What Is Life?" "Awaiting On You All," "Isn't It a Pity," "I'd Have You Anytime," "I Dig Love," and a version of "Let It Roll" with some lyrics that would change before the final recording; "I Live For You," also demoed here, would be recorded later during the sessions but wouldn't see release for thirty years. Four others also didn't make the cut: "Going Down to Golders Green," a lighthearted rockabilly tune based on Elvis Presley's "Baby Let's Play House," and "Gopala Krishna," based on Sanskrit mantras, as well as "Dehra Dun" and "Sour Milk Sea," which had been kicking around since 1968. On May 27, Harrison laid down at least fifteen more selections for consideration, performed solo on acoustic or electric guitar. Seven of these were finished or nearly finished and would be recorded in the weeks ahead. He began with a complete "Run of the Mill," followed by "Art of Dying," which dated from 1966 and contained the telling line, "There's nothing Mr. Epstein can do / to keep me here with you." The next song, "Everybody Nobody," contained elements of "Let It Roll," with the "Oh Sir Frankie Crisp" refrain still present. He switched to electric guitar with, fittingly, a wah-wah pedal effect for "Wah Wah," now accompanied by Voormann on bass. Back on acoustic guitar, he struggled to sing "Window Window," which he described as "a bit silly" to Spector in the control room; while he had aired this during the *Get Back* sessions, he never returned to it after this demo. "Beautiful Girl," which he'd begun in 1969, was unfinished and would remain so until 1976. "Beware of Darkness" he introduced as "the last one I wrote the other day, and it's a few words needed yet." In the verse about "soft shoe shufflers" he notably sang "beware of ABKCO," referring to Allen Klein's company, suggesting he already had suspicions about the ethics of Apple's manager.

After a confident performance of "Let It Down," Harrison played a tune called "Tell Me What Has Happened to You," which he would abandon after this. He switched again to electric guitar for "Hear Me Lord" and then back to acoustic for a trio of recordings he would never touch again: "Nowhere to Go," "Cosmic Empire," and "Mother Divine." He finished with a pair of Dylan compositions: "I Don't Want to Do It" (which would not surface again until the soundtrack for *Porky's Revenge* in 1995), and from the May 1 session in New York, "If Not for You," with presumably either Spector or Voormann feeling out the chords on piano in the background. Before the end of the day, Harrison finished mixes for Billy Preston's new album *Encouraging Words*, which included Preston's versions of "My Sweet Lord" and "All Things Must Pass." Apple would release the album later in the year, and although he still had to complete mixing for Doris Troy's album, Harrison could now devote most of his attention to his own recordings.

How much the growing drama within the now-split Beatles was on Harrison's mind throughout these sessions is unclear. For anyone with knowledge of the Fabs' dissolution, it's easy to hear many of the songs on *All Things Must Pass* with an extra layer of meaning, manifesting either as direct addresses to Lennon or McCartney (or both) or as world-weary, philosophical ruminations on the once world-dominating, now dissolving group. Harrison generally left that meaning ambiguous enough, but opening the first full day of band recordings for his new album with the song "Wah Wah"—written on January 10, 1969, the day he walked out of the *Get Back* sessions and effectively quit the Beatles for a few days—was not likely an accident.

Regardless, the *song* "Wah Wah" was also a good high-energy rave-up to break the players in, and it gave Spector an opportunity to apply his trademark production techniques to the arrangement. Central to achieving that sound was having a studio full of musicians playing together, and on this first full day of recording—Thursday, May 28—as many as twelve people may have been in Studio Three.

Harrison played the lead riff, followed by Clapton on wah-wah guitar, and then the rest of the band: electric piano, bass, drums, tambourine, congas, piano, and rhythm guitars. On paper and on the tape, "Wah Wah" looked like quick work, finished off in three recorded takes, but before Phil McDonald called "take one," the band rehearsed and rehearsed, and Spector built the sound of the record in the control room one element at a time. This mirrored his approach at Gold Star, where rehearsals could seem mind-numbingly repetitive; on "Be My Baby," he had reportedly run the musicians through forty-two rehearsal takes before he had the engineer roll tape. Billy Preston recalled, "He would use a lot of keyboards playing the same chord and make it big and strong. We would do it several times in different octaves, and it was monotonous as hell. But he was making it the Phil Spector sound."

"We worked over and over on the songs in the studio," Harrison would remember, "so that everybody got the right routine, and it was sounding really nice. And then in the control room, Phil was in there with the engineer, making it sound like, you know, this *noise*. . . . And it sounded really nice in the studio, all this nice acoustics and piano and no echo on anything. We did it for hours until he had it right in the control room."

Once they nailed the master take, Harrison, Clapton, and a few others walked around to the control room to hear the first song they'd put on tape. Much like on "Instant Karma!" in January, the playback was loud and overwhelming and saturated with reverb. "George wasn't that happy about it, I remember that," said Voormann. "I thought it was fantastic—a really tight sound." Preston agreed: "Myself, I never really was a fan of [Spector's] sound. I thought it worked on the Ronettes' stuff, it worked on certain things but not on others. But with George's stuff it was perfect."

"When we went in to listen to it," Harrison said years later, "I just thought, 'I hate it. It's just, it's so horrible!' Eric said, 'Oh, I love it.' So I said, 'Well, you can have it on your album, then.' But I grew to like it." He would indeed grow to like it, and whatever Harrison's reservations were at the moment, they could be sorted out in the mixing stage. But for the musicians, the playing was the thing. Alan White described it as "jumping in the deep end. . . . It was a great song and had Eric playing this *wah wah* through everything. . . . I loved the feeling and everybody was happy to play. . . . You know, once you had that one under your belt it made you feel good, you could move on." Satisfied, Harrison and company turned to the next recording.

For all its subsequent success, "My Sweet Lord" was not a tune Harrison immediately embraced for himself. He'd written it specifically as a gospel song and already had Billy Preston's recording in the can, so doing his own recording may have initially seemed redundant, unnecessary, but his hesitation was really more personal. "I thought a lot about whether to do 'My Sweet Lord' or not," Harrison wrote in *I Me Mine*, "because I would be committing myself publicly and I anticipated that a lot of people might get weird about it. Many people fear the words 'Lord' and 'God'—makes them angry for some reason." With such a potentially powerful song in his reserves, once he finally committed to his own solo project, Harrison had to confront his feelings about releasing a song under his own name with such bold spiritual yearning, putting his feelings so nakedly, openly, on the line. Seeing himself "on the chopping block" and knowing that now he "would have to live up to something," he felt "My Sweet Lord" was a risk, but ultimately he realized that "if you feel something strong enough then you should say it."

Although Alan White has a vivid memory of George asking him to play drums on "My Sweet Lord," Mal Evans's diary confirms that Starr was drummer for both songs recorded this first day. Harrison played a twelve-string acoustic guitar, while Clapton, Pete Ham, Joey Molland, and Mike Gibbons (from Badfinger) played six-string acoustics. The remaining personnel were Voormann on bass, Gary Brooker on piano, Alan White on tambourine, and Bobby Whitlock on harmonium.

Although "My Sweet Lord" would progressively grow to be one of the most elaborately produced recordings on the finished album, Harrison and Spector today concentrated on the underlying rhythm track. The take-one demo was a rough and ready run-through featuring only Harrison on vocals and acoustic guitar, accompanied by bass and drums. As Spector worked away on his side of the glass, Harrison focused on constructing the arrangement with the musicians, one critical element of which was the way it built momentum, with instruments entering at key points. "It did take a little more work [than

'Wah Wah']," recalled White, "because there was a lot of experimentation on where the drums come in and how things appeared.... [George] wanted to make sure it was really right, and he analyzed a lot of things and made sure everything happened at the right time ... because the drums kind of fade in on that song. Which they actually did in the studio when we played—they elaborated on that when they mixed it too. They made it smoother than it was in the studio."

Central to the overall effect of the arrangement was the big rhythmic acoustic guitar sound, which played off another key technique of Spector's classic production style: multiple acoustic rhythm guitars playing in unison. Producer and engineer Phil Chapman, who has studied and recreated Spector's techniques in the studio, discovered that in hits by the Ronettes and others, "The drone all the way through is usually the acoustic guitars—they throw up so much ... overtones ... and he balanced them with the bass so it just became one solid rhythm track, and the keyboards too. All the string writing was blended in. Cellos and acoustics blend really well together, and all the lower string parts were blended right into the acoustic sound, so it just became one powerful force."

These guitars wouldn't blend in, however, but would be the central component of the recording. Badfinger had recently finished their second tour of the UK, which had seen them play twenty-six shows from March 20 to April 18, and they would be off again on another tour soon. While they were available, Spector employed them as a supplemental rhythm section, usually with two or three members of the band strumming acoustic guitars in tight formation while another played percussion.

"We had to learn everything very quickly," recalled Joey Molland, "just sort of absorb the general texture of each song. But that's what he hired us for, really: to lay down this very uniform acoustic backing. Which meant we really had to concentrate on getting our strumming in sync.... They put the three of us inside this huge blue wooden box made out of plywood, with doors in the front of it. Every day we'd go in there, get on these tall stools, they'd mic us up, and we'd begin recording. That was the only separation they used for the whole album. Luckily they kept the doors open while we were working!" On "My Sweet Lord," Harrison played along with them on his own track as he sang a guide vocal. The harmonium entered in the middle of the first verse, and, other than the guitars, remained the sole instrumentation until "I really want to see you," when the two pianos, drums, tambourine, and bass came in, at which point the track took flight. By take sixteen, they had a master take.

Even in this relatively spare state, the recording had a *sound*. "The guitar rhythm of 'My Sweet Lord,'" recalled Leckie, "when you added the tape echo, the repeat—which is a tape delay, and it's tuned to the speed of the track—it reaches a sweet point, and I learned a lot by watching Phil Spector and Phil McDonald make lots of guitars sound like one big guitar. It was just a magic moment, and I learned a lot about the way he created the delays. It depends on what the people are playing. It's a *feel* thing, really; you tune it as a feel. You don't go by numbers. It's not mathematical. With a computer you have to enter a mathematical number according to the tempo. But there's a sweet point. Reggae dub people understand all that." Molland recalled that "it sounded great as it was going down. I remember listening to the rough-mix of 'My Sweet Lord'—the balance was all there, everything was so full-sounding. The acoustic guitars were just enormous—there wasn't any double-tracking or anything, just all of us going at once, straight on."

Spector knew very well how to achieve the effect he wanted, and at some point, after the recording of the basic track, he set out to test what he had in mind. John Kurlander, who had been at EMI since 1968 and had worked as a second engineer on the *Abbey Road* album, recalled being enlisted to help. "They were in Studio Three," said Kurlander, "and they called me in and said, 'We need you to do a rough mix of "My Sweet Lord," so go into Room Four'— which was right down the corridor, a little remix room—'Go and set up this list of equipment, and Phil Spector will be along in about fifteen minutes.' So I went in there and set it all up, and it had all the tape machines, like two or three tape loops [for tape echo]. I hadn't done any engineering at that point; I was still an assistant. And Phil Spector walked in, and he basically dictated the mix to me. He said, 'Raise this fader, now feed this through this delay and now add a bit more feedback on the delay—that's it, a little bit more. All right, now slow it down a bit, that's it.' The thing that I remember so clearly is that the whole thing took about fifteen minutes, and at the end of the fifteen minutes there was a rough mix of 'My Sweet Lord' that sounded exactly like the 'Phil Spector Sound' did. He'd made it his own, and without laying a finger on any of the buttons or controllers. He wasn't interested in actually hands-on, but it was like giving an assistant shorthand notes, dictating the thing one hundred percent. That was how well he knew his formula. . . . And I'm sitting there with him listening to this finished mix: 'Wow, I did that!' But I didn't do it, really [*laughs*]. So somewhere on a little piece of tape is my rough remix with Phil Spector."

Even if Harrison was not yet enamored of Spector's mixing technique, this first day was a successful launch to the sessions and a confident demonstration of the producer's skill in managing a large group of players. "The first day there were so many musicians," said Leckie, "and miraculously we set it all up and recorded two tracks, which ended up on the record." The large number of musicians also meant that they would have to use their multitrack tape economically. EMI Studios still only had eight-track recording and with as many as a dozen players in the studio, each individual track might contain two or three instruments. To allow room for even minimal overdubs of vocals, they typically recorded on only five or six tracks. "Even though you record on eight tracks," Leckie explained, "you don't record on eight tracks in one go, because you always leave two for backing vocals or to bounce. If you've only got one track left, you can't do much. But if you've got two tracks left, you can mix things together onto one and you can add things up—you can bounce from [track] one to [track] two. . . . If you've got two tracks free you can bounce around."

Spector would already begin testing these limits on the first day of recording. On "Wah Wah," at the end of the evening, said White, "after we'd done the song and went for a playback and everything on there and we had the tambourine on there, in true Phil Spector kind of production—Ringo had already gone to dinner or something—he asked me to put another fifteen tambourines on there! So I had to go through and play the tambourine part over and over again so we could come up with this huge wall of tambourine." To achieve this, Phil McDonald bounced from one free track to another, building up recording after recording of tambourine on a single track. "You couldn't go any further," noted Leckie, "unless you went to a sixteen-track studio."

That time would come eventually, but for now the focus lay in getting a solid rhythm track for each song. Harrison opened the second day of recording, May 29, with "I'd Have You Anytime," which he began writing during Thanksgiving 1968 in Woodstock, New York, while visiting Bob Dylan and the Band. After a grueling five months' work on the *White Album* and the completion of production and mixing on Jackie Lomax's *Is This What You Want?* LP, the bucolic atmosphere of upstate New York, with its fall colors in full splendor, had been a refreshing change of scenery and a welcome escape for Harrison from being a Beatle. Welcomed by the Band and Dylan as an equal, Harrison also got a taste of the kind of group dynamic he had been missing in the Beatles.

Although initially uneasy around each other in this setting, after a few days the two musicians picked up their guitars and began to relax. Harrison urged his host to "write me some words," to which Dylan responded, "Show me some chords, how do you get those tunes?" Obliging him, Harrison began playing different chords until he had worked out a progression and a melody. Onto a home tape recorder, he played through the chords while singing them out: "A flat minor to G, F sharp minor to A minor." Once they had a set of rough lyrics in place, they recorded a demo together, harmonizing on the vocals for "Nowhere to Go," one of the songs Harrison would play for Spector a year and a half later.

They repeated the process, with Harrison playing a series of major seventh, diminished, and augmented chords, "and the song appeared as I played the opening chord (G major 7th) and then moved the chord shape up the guitar neck (B flat major 7th)." Harrison sketched out lyrics for the verse, and Dylan the bridge/chorus, and they recorded another home demo, both harmonizing again, with the song's general melody and structure already in place.

Although "Nowhere to Go" didn't make the final cut, the second song, "I'd Have You Anytime," did, not least because of the song's cowriter. "Maybe subconsciously I needed a bit of support," Harrison would admit later. "I had Eric playing the solo, and Bob had helped write it." Even with a successful first day of recording behind him and a song cowritten with Bob Dylan in his hip pocket, Harrison's confidence remained shaky, and he had no set plan for what songs he was going to record from day to day. "Having this whole thing with the Beatles had left me really paranoid," he said. "I remember having those people in the studio [for *All Things Must Pass*] and thinking, 'God, these songs are so fruity! I can't think of which song to do.' Slowly I realized, 'We can do this one,' and I'd play it to them, and they'd say, 'Wow, yeah! Great song!' And I'd say, 'Really? Do you really like it?' I realized that it was okay, that they were sick of playing all that other stuff."

While Harrison still struggled with self-doubt regarding his songwriting, musically he continued to create the same kind of collaborative atmosphere he had fostered in his Apple productions. "George's way of dealing with musicians in the studio was . . . very different from John's," Klaus Voormann wrote in his memoir. "While John liked developing plans alone or together with Yoko, George always formed a real team with the band. We often worked out pieces together, and our opinion about it was important to George. . . . While John put his ideas to tape very quickly, 'patience' wasn't just a word with George." Although Harrison was patient, he also gave specific direction for certain parts. For the opening of "I'd Have You Anytime," Clapton remembered many years later that Harrison "told me what to play. He wanted me to bend this note like three times. It was really hard, but he just told me what to play."

Harrison's patience and the spirit of collaboration he cultivated in these sessions assured long hours in the studio building arrangements and rehearsing. Sessions were booked to start at 2:30 PM and could run until 5 or 6 AM. "We'd all turn up and have a coffee or whatever," said Alan White of how each day began, "and sit around and pick who was playing what on what song, on the song of the day. We'd listen to some kind of demo and then go out and just all get into it and record it." Leckie concurred, recalling that "it would be endless routining and doing takes once everyone was ready to record, but with a lot of rapport and guidance from Phil Spector. I can always remember Phil stopping takes—you know, it would be really good, and Phil would just go on the talk back and say, 'Stop stop stop!' and say, 'What are you playing on the Hammond?' and ask people what chords they were playing, and someone would have changed the rhythm or something. So he was quite strict on the arrangement, as it were. But George would be showing people the songs, the chords, and you know Badfinger, teaching them acoustic guitar [chords]. Badfinger of course would play on anything, any opportunity to play, they would be there."

The actual instrumentation for each song would come down to what Harrison wanted for that particular track, and as White said, Harrison would also choose who would play those instruments. But the arrangements themselves would develop organically. "George would play the part," recalled Voormann, "and then it would be, 'Oh yeah, what can we do with it?' Or we'd double it—somebody might have learned the same lick and played it an octave lower. Everybody did what they thought was best for the song. He did not come and say, 'you play this' and 'you play that.' Of course the choice of what instruments on what song, that might happen in the studio—'No organ on this one, just play the harmonium'—that sort of decision, yes. But from what we played we mostly found our own way. He depended on those people. It was not like lots of people now think an arranger has to write things down. We all found our own way."

Once the arrangement was set, they finished off "I'd Have You Anytime" in seven takes, with a fluid and confident lead by Clapton that at once supported and embellished Harrison's vocal line. This subtle musical interplay reflected an almost telepathic understanding between the two men. "[Eric] and George had a really great relationship," said Alan White. "It was evident every day. They didn't have to say much to each other, and they did the right thing." This live performance—with two tracks of acoustic guitars, bass, drums, harmonium, and Harrison's lead vocal—needed very little in the way of overdubs.

For the other recording done on this day, Harrison chose one of the songs he had demoed on acoustic guitar two days before. Like "My Sweet Lord," which mixed Western and Eastern concepts, "Art of Dying" drew on both Christian and Hindu ideas. Replacing "Mister Epstein" from the demo with "Sister Mary" explicitly added Catholic shading, emphasized years later by Harrison's quoting of a line from Galatians ("For whatsoever a man soweth, that shall he also reap") to describe in Western terms the idea of karma at the center of the lyrics. The song's title itself recalls a fifteenth-century Latin text, *Ars moriendi*—literally "art of dying"—which provides instructions on how to prepare for death. Whether Harrison knew of this book is unclear, but his lyrics are a meditation on the inevitability of death and the likelihood of reincarnation by the "desire to be the perfect entity."

Harrison would write later that, in order to break the karmic cycle, rather than passively accepting the end of life or even fighting it when it comes, one must learn *Maha-samadhi*, the act of consciously leaving the body at death. "The Yogi who does that," he said, "doesn't have to reincarnate again." Like any practitioner of Hinduism or Buddhism, Harrison was preoccupied with breaking this cycle of death and rebirth; what's most remarkable is that he addressed this in "Art of Dying," written in 1966. His first brush with Indian music had only come in April 1965 during the filming of *Help!*, and within a year he had begun studying sitar with Ravi Shankar and was incorporating ideas from Hindu philosophy into his lyrics.

This particular idea took hold early and stayed with him. In later interviews he spoke openly (and sometimes incongruously, given the context of the interviews) of wanting to leave his body consciously at the moment of death, and at the end of his life, with his family and two of his close Krishna friends present, he maintained this aspiration. In song, he would revisit the idea again a few years after "Art of Dying" with "Give Me Love (Give Me Peace on Earth)," but then as in 1970, it wasn't exactly natural subject matter for a pop song. Speaking of his songwriting in 1969 after his triumphs on *Abbey Road*, Harrison observed, "I just write a song, and it just comes out however it wants to. And some of them are catchy songs like 'Here Comes the Sun,' and some of them aren't, you know. But to me they're just songs and I just write them, and some will be considered as good by maybe the masses and some won't. But to me they're just songs, things that are there that have to be got out."

"Art of Dying" may not have been a song for the masses, but Spector did his best to make it more commercial while shaping it in his own image. Committing nine takes to tape this day, the producer began building a textbook Wall of Sound arrangement, starting with the Badfinger acoustic rhythm guitar section establishing the necessary background drone. He constructed the rest of the sound atop this foundation, with two pianos, maracas, bass, and drums, emphasizing the slap of Starr's snare with a dramatic dose of reverb. Just as he had done for "My Sweet Lord" and even "Instant Karma!" Spector also used a specific trick to keep the drummer's focus where he wanted it. "He would do things like take the cymbals off for the drummer," said Voormann. "It was really interesting, because suddenly you could see the drummer, because normally he's hidden behind cymbals and stuff." Once the desired amount of echo was applied, the rhythm track began to sound like nothing so much as a minor key variation of the Ronettes' "Be My Baby."

It was a remarkable adaptation of the quintessential Spector sound to a most unlikely George Harrison song, and even as a beginning backing track the resemblance to a Philles record was uncanny. Unfortunately, Spector would not have the opportunity to layer it any further. A little over a month later, Harrison would remake the song in a completely different style.

7 | ONE BIG SOUND

OF ALL THE BEATLES, Harrison had the most expansive vision for his first solo album. Held back for so long by the prioritization of Lennon and McCartney's songs in the studio, Harrison had only rarely gotten to indulge his production ideas on his own songs, and more often than not he was shut down completely. The first song he recorded on June 2, 1970, was a case in point.

As with "Art of Dying," Harrison wrote "Isn't It a Pity" in 1966, demonstrating just how far outside of the pop music curve he already stood. He would later suggest that he'd written the song as an attempt to compose within the expected boy-girl pop song template—"love lost and love gained between 16- and 20-year-olds" as he described it—but he was already thoughtful enough and compassionate enough as a writer that his ideas spilled well outside those narrow boundaries. He may have begun thinking about a teenage love song, but he ended up with "an observation of how society and myself were or are. We take each other for granted—and forget to give back."

Dirge-like and reflective, how might the Beatles have rendered "Isn't It a Pity" during their *Revolver* period? Could it have been a ballad with angelic backing vocals, like "Here, There, and Everywhere"? Would George Martin have suggested another string quartet like "Yesterday"? Or would they have tried something with Indian instruments such as "Love You To"? The answer would very likely have been none of the above, since the Beatles had already done those things and were by this point committed to finding a new sound for every recording. And besides, Harrison had an unprecedented three songs on the album; there wasn't room for another composition within the Lennon-McCartney hegemony.

Harrison aired the song again during the *Get Back* sessions in January 1969 but once more made little headway at getting Lennon engaged in developing an arrangement. Abandoning hope of the Beatles taking an interest, later that month on January 26, he arrived at the Apple studio early and recorded a solo demo of the song along with two others, "Let It Down" and "Window Window," accompanying himself simply on electric guitar. On "Isn't It a Pity," he vocalized a melody for the instrumental middle section of the song that would eventually see the light in 1970. Now, four years after its composition, with tensions between the individual Beatles at their worst, the song's lyrics rang with an even more affecting world-weariness. Like all great writing, it continued to resonate both personally and universally.

They had attempted the song at the end of the previous session, after the first version of "Art of Dying" and a solo Harrison acoustic recording of "Run of the Mill." This initial pass at "Isn't It a Pity" consisted of bass, drums, several guitars (as on "My Sweet Lord") combined into a stereo guitar mix, two pianos, Moog synthesizer, electric harpsichord, and percussion. Harrison and Spector were dissatisfied with this recording and returned to the song on June 2, when the producer expanded the number of musicians, once more employing his trademark of layering multiple instruments playing the same part, a technique Chris Thomas described as being "a large array of sounds to create one big sound." Thomas had been George Martin's assistant during sessions for *The White Album* and *Abbey Road* and had begun producing for Procol Harum while still working with Martin's company, AIR (Associated Independent Recording). He would eventually go on to a successful production career spanning six decades, but in 1970 he was also picking up session work playing and programming the Moog synthesizer. As one of a handful of people in London proficient on this relatively new instrument, and because of the rapport he'd developed with Harrison on Beatles sessions, he was the natural call for this gig. Thomas recalled that "[the Moog] was actually set up in the studio with everybody playing live, and Spector and George Harrison came out looking for a sound, and basically, I got a sound, and they said, 'That'll do.' And I said, 'What do you want me to play?' and they said, 'Play arpeggios,' and they gave me a chord chart." (Thomas's Moog part would eventually be taped over on the master take.)

As the session began, Harrison led the musicians through the song on acoustic guitar, running through the chords to familiarize everyone with the changes. Klaus Voormann played bass, while three members of Badfinger were again employed on acoustic guitar (Pete Ham and Joey Molland) and maracas (Mike Gibbons). John Barham was at the electric harpsichord, Alan White played tambourine, and session guitarists Martin Kershaw (electric) and Ray Galow (acoustic) rounded out the band for the moment, but Thomas remembered that other musicians gradually drifted in.

"I was sitting there playing," said Thomas, "and while I was playing, Ringo just sort of walked in and sat down at the drums in the middle of a song. And I thought, 'What? That's weird.' And the next minute Billy Preston walks in, and then the next minute Eric Clapton walked in. It was such a bizarre thing. It's not like we all turned up and ran a song down. These people were all coming in one by one. They're all turning up a bit late. It was almost like it was stage managed—every couple of minutes somebody *globally* famous walked in and joined the band. I imagined a queue of superstars out in the corridor waiting for their turn to walk in. I thought, Christ, this is like [the Bonzo Dog Doo Dah Band song] 'Intro and Outro,' where Vivian Stanshall says, 'and on vibes, Adolf Hitler!' and there'd be somebody playing the vibes. To me it was almost comical. It was absurd!"

Another late comer, though not quite as famous, only got word on the day of the session to show up at Abbey Road. Across town at Olympic Studios, Gary Wright, formerly of the band Spooky Tooth, was in a mixing session when he got a call from Klaus Voormann, who had recently played bass on Wright's solo album, *Extraction*. Wright remembered Voormann saying, "Phil Spector is producing George's new album and wants an additional keyboard player for the song they're working on. Can you come to Abbey Road Studios now, as George is keen to get started?"

Such was the power of a Beatle that he could summon a keyboard player at a moment's notice. Anxious at such an opportunity, Wright dropped what he was doing and headed to Abbey Road. After sitting down at the electric piano and scribbling out a chart as Harrison played through the chords on guitar, Wright remembered stumbling frequently as he worked to catch up with the rest of the band. When the red recording light came on, he still wasn't quite certain of the arrangement, and in the middle of a take, Spector interrupted: "Wait a minute, wait a minute; who's that on the Wurlitzer piano making all those mistakes?" As Wright later remembered, "Devastated and utterly embarrassed, I meekly raised my hand and said, 'Sorry it's me, Gary, and I'm still learning the structure of the song.' George immediately walked over to me and said consolingly, 'Take all the time you need, we're in no rush.'"

Harrison would eventually turn the coda of "Isn't It a Pity" into a long, hypnotic vamp reminiscent of the ending of "Hey Jude," embellished with overdubs of orchestra, slide guitar, and multiple tracks of vocals, but on this day the tail end of the song mainly featured a tentative solo from Eric Clapton. Once they'd recorded the master take, Harrison went into the control room to listen to playback, and Chris Thomas, eager to observe Spector at work, asked if he could come along. "This was seriously my hero as well," said Thomas. "'You've Lost That Loving Feeling' was [for me] like, 'this is the job I need to do.' Because that incredible sound that he created."

Just as the musicians playing on "Instant Karma!" were astounded by the first playback of that recording, Thomas remembered the playback of "Isn't It a Pity" sounding "absolutely enormous." Gary Brooker from Procol Harum, who played grand piano on one of the sessions early in the process of recording *All Things Must Pass*, told *Melody Maker* on June 13, "Spector was definitely in charge. . . . What you play in the studio and what you hear back in the control booth are like two different worlds. When he played it in the studio it was really rocking—but in the box afterward there was lots of echo and stuff, and we all fell over. But after a while we realized he's really got it, and he hasn't changed at all. It was like playing on 'Da Doo Ron Ron.'"

"All the time musicians were playing and they're doing takes," said John Leckie, "Phil [Spector] had to hear it with reverb on it, the Wall of Sound. Even though it was on the monitor and not being recorded, there was something about that, about the inspiration of hearing it with all that as close to the finished product. What I took away from those sessions and Phil Spector was that every time you play the track that you're working on, the music, in the studio, you want it to sound like the finished record. You want it to sound like it's on the radio. You want it to sound great all the time. And through my career I've carried that, and also from experience you never know when the A&R man's going to turn up and say, 'Let's see what you're doing.' It's got to sound great. They don't want to hear it all dry and unfinished. They want to be impressed with it. So every time you play the track, it's got to sound fucking *great*. It's got to sound *impressive*. Which is what Phil [Spector] did. Even though he may not have been doing a proper mix, he wanted to make sure he *could* do it, what was on the tape he could make a mix from it. Because you were very constricted, you only had eight tracks. It's not like today where you have computers or even twenty-four track. Something has got to come from the music, a bit of soul to it."

Beginning to reconsider Spector's approach, Harrison asked to hear a play-back of "Wah Wah" from May 28. Chris Thomas remembered, "And George said to Phil, 'Can you lift up Eric's guitar [in the mix]? and Phil said, 'No.' And he said, 'What do you mean 'no'? He said, 'Because I've recorded everything to two-track.' And there was a bit of a discussion, because George was kinda like, 'What are you talking about?' He'd actually mixed everything down to two track from the [multitrack] from what I can remember, so George was a bit upset about that. And Spector was basically saying, 'Well this is what I do.'" For Thomas, "that was actually a really pivotal moment in my career. 'Cause I suddenly realized that I had to start to, rather than just be a producer who goes like, 'Yep, try it again,' or 'Yep, the backing vocals are in tune,' or anything, if I wanted to get my ideas ahead I had to actually stick my head above the parapet and say, 'I'd like to try this, I'd like to try that.' So then when I went on to do *Broken Barricades* with Procol, I approached Gary [Brooker], and I said, 'I've got an idea for this song and an idea for that song,' and he gave me that freedom to start experimenting. So I was forever grateful to him for that. He really gave me a lot of leeway to come up with various ideas. But it was seeing Spector in motion—because what I'd seen before was George Martin, who was basically a bit of a diplomat, just gently guiding people along."

Despite all the effort and the studio full of musicians, Harrison wasn't satisfied. "After doing it for a few hours," he recalled in 2001, "I decided I didn't like it." Was he beginning to feel that the Wall of Sound was overwhelming the song? Was he still troubled by Spector's approach to mixing? These first few days of recording there were a *lot* of people in the studio—again as many as twelve musicians on "Isn't It a Pity"—and the openness of the sessions began to show its downside. "One time," said Voormann, "a crazy guy came in with a big robe on and started—I don't know how they all got in the studio—of course all the famous guys could walk in. But all of a sudden, this crazy guyed turned up like an Elvis fan *and* the Maharishi—he had all these things in his head, and he came into the studio, and somebody had to push him out!" And apparently, things proceeded at this pace with one strange happening after another. Voormann continued: "One day [guitarist] Dave Mason would come in, and this one would come in. . . . There were too many people coming in and out. It was a little overdone. But George noticed that and that's why some of the sessions get a little more calm—'Let's have this, this and this, and those guys, and that will do for the next day.' . . . So that of course came from George."

Harrison set aside "Isn't It a Pity" for the moment and thinned the players out for the next recording, which would be far more subdued. "I Dig Love," which the band mastered in twenty takes, prioritized the space between the instruments. Starr played drums here, according to John Leckie, who recalled, "I think when we recorded it, we had the delay effect on the drums. He would have heard that in the headphones when he recorded it." While "I Dig Love" notably features the least complex lyric of any song from these sessions, its *sound*—including a generous dose of tape delay that threatens to submerge Harrison's vocals—is more Beatlesque than Spectoresque. Harrison liked this scaled-back approach and continued with it at the next session. In spite of what Gary Wright considered his faux pas on "Isn't It a Pity," Harrison took a liking to him and asked him to return. "As time went on," Wright remembered, "the sessions became smaller and more intimate, moving away from the large production concept Phil had created for some of the earlier tracks we had recorded." For Wright, the result was that he began to feel like he was part of a band, rather than an anonymous face in an army of session players.

On June 3, Harrison had another run at "Isn't It a Pity." "[The second version] was very intimate," said Voormann. "It was not so many people in the studio. It was a calm session. I guess George knew that beforehand and it was arranged this way. It felt really good. It was a nice atmosphere." With Voormann on bass and Alan White on drums, they ran through thirty takes, though rerecording the song wasn't exactly planned. "One of the guys in the band just started playing it," Harrison said in 2001, "and we needed to get that slow version, and so then we did that." Alan White added that "'Isn't It a Pity' was pretty hard to play." He described it as "a very sensitive song. [It] was hard to record with a lot of people, but with a smaller group you could get the feel out of the song better. Because it needed a lot of very good eye contact and feel between each other in the studio on the basic track."

The well-established Beatle habit for altering the sounds of instruments had yet to find an outlet on these sessions, but on this remake of "Isn't It a

Pity," Harrison employed two techniques familiar from Beatles recordings. The first saw Eric Clapton's lead guitar run through a revolving Leslie speaker, a sound Harrison had used extensively throughout *Get Back* in January 1969 and then more sparingly on *Abbey Road* (the rhythm guitar on "Something," for example). The second technique altered the sound of the piano and organ to an extreme degree. Back in 1966, EMI engineer Ken Townsend had developed a recording technique called Automatic Double Tracking (ADT), and two by-products of this technique, varispeed and phasing, would color many of the Beatles' recordings for the rest of their career. ADT required a second tape machine, the speed of which was manipulated by turning a knob on an outboard device. This created a second delayed signal that could yield a variety of effects, from the illusion of doubling an instrument or voice to phasing, a kind of swishing, watery sound; "Itchycoo Park," a 1967 hit by the Small Faces, featured a famously extreme example of phasing.

"You always had it standing by," said John Leckie. "But you can kind of play it, you can move it in between beats, and you'd get exciting parts, and so you make a mark. And that's what that is on the piano [on "Isn't It a Pity"], probably because someone went too far. That may have been me actually, because we'd have two of these machines going, so the voice, the backing vocals . . . you'd move it and create a color with it with the phasing. Just fiddle around until something takes off and everyone goes, 'That's great, keep that.' And of course it's never the same twice because you never know where you are in the space of the phase when you do another take, because you're changing the repeats. So it's kind of a live performance very often when you do tape phasing, which is all the more exciting. On 'Isn't It a Pity,' on the piano and the organ, it almost goes out of tune. If you go right out, it's out of tune, and it spoils the illusion." The smaller scale approach to recording fit well with the relaxed atmosphere Harrison had created from the start. The practice of burning incense he'd started during Beatles sessions continued here, and he created what Gary Wright characterized as a "profoundly peaceful" environment. "He tried to get the atmosphere right," said Voormann, "and George actually bought these joss sticks. He'd light them up and give a nice smell to the studio, and he lit up a candle and made a little altar type of thing. He made it comfortable, dimmed the light; that was important to him."

Harrison would also very often sit in lotus position in the control room, chanting quietly on breaks or during playbacks. As he would explain in his book *I, Me, Mine*, the concept of "chanting the names of the Lord" that appears in "Awaiting on You All" derives from Japa Yoga meditation, which uses the *maha mantra*—"Hare Krishna, Hare Krishna / Krishna Krishna, Hare Hare / Hare Rama, Hare Rama / Rama Rama, Hare Hare"—an ancient "petition to God: 'O Krishna, O energy of Krishna, please engage me in Your service.'" As a means of focusing the mind, part of the Japa Yoga practice includes the use of a strand of 108 beads, typically held inside a bag while chanting. Everyone at the sessions would become accustomed to seeing Harrison reciting this mantra with his hand in his bead bag, cycling through the strand. Years later he would reveal, "Using the beads also helps me to release a lot of nervous energy."

As calming as this may have been for Harrison, chanting could also plug into his obsessive nature. Looking back in 1973, he observed, "There is one sort of problem in a way, that I found when chanting all the time, and that was that I start being able to relate less and less to all the people I know. . . . I suddenly found myself on such a different level. . . . You know, there's a point where suddenly I'm not going to be. . . . I'm not going to know them anymore." In 1970, this turn of events affected Pattie Boyd intensely. "He became increasingly obsessive about meditating and chanting," she recalled and said that she and Terry Doran, who continued living at Friar Park, developed a code. "To gauge his mood, we would ask whether his hands were 'in or out of the bag'—meaning his prayer bag. If they were in it, he was in spiritual mode and incommunicado; if they were out, there was a chance of talking to him." She realized, "We were living in a surreal world with a very creative and eccentric person."

———————

Longtime Beatles associate and Harrison's current assistant Terry Doran was sitting at a pub on Wardour Street in Soho with his friend, guitarist Peter Frampton, in the fall months of 1969, when Doran said, "Do you want to meet George?" Frampton, age nineteen, was lead guitarist in the band Humble Pie, which was currently on the UK charts with the song "Natural Born Bugie." Frampton, not immediately grasping who Doran meant, drew a blank. "George who?" Once Doran clarified he was talking about the Beatle, he explained that Harrison was recording just around the corner at Trident Studios in St Anne's

Court. Walking into the studio, Frampton was surprised when Harrison recognized him, saying "Hello, Pete," and asked if he wanted to play on the session. He was working on the recording of "Ain't That Cute" for Doris Troy, along with Ringo Starr, Billy Preston, and Klaus Voormann. "So he handed me the very famous reddish Les Paul," Frampton recalled, "and I started playing rhythm. He's the lead guitarist of the Beatles—you don't play *lead*. So underneath him I played some rhythm. We got halfway through, and he stopped, said, 'I'll play rhythm, you play lead.' I thought the floor was opening up and I was disappearing through it."

In his interview with the BBC back in March, Harrison mentioned Frampton specifically as he spoke of wanting to create "a permanent backing band for Apple artists" that could also "record their own songs, their own records." Although an Apple house band never really came to fruition, Frampton had made an impression. Eight months after "Ain't That Cute," while preparing for the next set of recordings for his own album, Harrison rang Frampton directly and asked the guitarist to join him at Abbey Road. Frampton got the call because Harrison was losing his guitar rhythm section. Badfinger had left for Hawaii on June 4 for an appearance at the Capitol Record Convention on June 8 and then began a tour of the UK and Europe on June 20 that would run through August. Eric Clapton would be occupied over the next week with two of his own projects—one of which was to bear remarkable fruit—and was likely absent on some, if not all, of these dates, and there's no evidence of his lead guitar on the undubbed tracks. He may have simply strummed an acoustic guitar, of course, as Dave Mason may also have done at this point. Instead of the acoustic overtones of the Wall of Sound, the aim was for a warm acoustic sound. During that same week, Clapton was the subject of a *Melody Maker* cover story that, once again, brought his penchant for self-betrayal to the fore. The banner headline "Clapton and Bruce to Join Miles!" suggested that Clapton was on the verge of performing with American jazz great Miles Davis at a New York festival in July. While the event never came to pass, the Miles Davis episode demonstrated Clapton's enduring need to effect his escape even as other, potentially more fulfilling projects were about to transpire.

Frampton recalled that his tenure on the sessions began with the recording of "If Not for You," on June 5. Bob Dylan himself would record several more versions of the song over the summer of 1970 before finally settling on an arrangement in August that bore little resemblance to the one on which Harrison had played. But it was that May 1 arrangement, slide guitar and all, on which Harrison had been ruminating. For the basic track of his own recording, he fleshed out the instrumentation with harmonium, brushed drums, acoustic and electric piano, and Hammond organ. The slide guitar, plucked acoustic guitars, and harmonica would be overdubbed later. Dylan's final version of "If Not for You" on *New Morning* seems deliberately roughshod, whereas the commercial precision forged within the Beatles informs Harrison's recording on *All Things Must Pass*. Like the crystalline acoustic glory of "Here Comes the Sun," every element here is in its place. And where Dylan's original reads as a straightforward romantic ballad, in the context of Harrison's spiritual preoccupations and the other material on these sessions, "If Not for You" doubles as a devotional text.

Recording the song took two days. On June 4, after two incomplete takes of "The Ballad of Sir Frankie Crisp (Let It Roll)," they laid down eight takes of "If Not For You," running at a faster tempo than the final version with the drummer using sticks to start, then moving to brushes. They picked up recording again the next day, slowing the pace, and then after take seventeen Harrison said, "Hang on. There's too many fiddlin' on the guitars. I think it should all be just straight." With this adjustment they laid down the master, take eighteen.

With the basic track of "If Not for You" on tape, Harrison returned to what he would later call "a piece of self-indulgence." "The Ballad of Sir Frankie Crisp (Let It Roll)" was an enigmatic tour of Friar Park, and like John Lennon's "Being for the Benefit of Mr. Kite!" Harrison drew many of the lyrics from an already existing text. In this case, the text was an illustrated map that Frank Crisp had commissioned for one of his guidebooks of the estate and its grounds, published in 1914. Harrison's handwritten lyrics (and the demo from May 26) show him trying to fit in different features of the house and gardens featured on the map—"leper's squint" and "abode of prancing steeds"—before settling on different phrases for the proper recording. The song begins as a literal tour, starting in the hall of the mansion and heading outside through the east entrance to the terrace gardens and the "Fountain of Perpetual Mirth." In the second and third verses the tour becomes more impressionistic, cleverly weaving together phrases from different parts of Crisp's map: "where ye echo lays," "a maze for losing ye bodies" (changed to "lose your bodies in the maze"), "ye long walk of coole and shade." Throughout "Let It Roll," Harrison plays off the Elizabethan affectations and spellings from the map, almost as if Crisp were speaking through the song or, perhaps more accurately, speaking through Harrison. The final verse returns to the present, immortalizing Harrison's own housekeepers at the time, Joan and Molly, and recalling the title of his 1967 song "The Inner Light." They mastered the tune by the eighth take, with the low "Oh, Sir Frankie Crisp" between the verses overdubbed onto the final recording later by Mal Evans. Spector believed that the song had potential as a single if the lyrics were different, but Harrison preferred to keep the words as written.

Having mastered two songs on June 5, Harrison moved to a third, "Behind That Locked Door," which had been inspired by his visit with Dylan and the Band before their Isle of Wight performance in August 1969. The band mastered the recording in thirteen takes, featuring Harrison on slide guitar and Alan White playing drums with a very light touch. "There are a couple of songs on the album," said White, "where you had to be very delicate on what you were doing and not to intrude on the song and just do what was necessary. And that was a bit of an anthem at the time for myself: only do what is necessary for the song. If you do anything else, you're overplaying, and you're trying to project yourself too much. Just do what is necessary to make it a group sound. That's the object."

By now, the sessions had fallen into a steady routine. "Drums were set up in the same place every day," said Alan White. "All of the musicians basically sat in the same seats every day, and it was kinda like going to work actually. You just took your place and got on with the daily task of recording what song George had that day." While the arrangement of the studio could change slightly depending on the number of players and the instrumentation of the session, generally speaking the layout remained fairly consistent. If you were to walk into the double doors of the studio space, you would see the grand piano and the drums, separated by sound-dampening screens, on the opposite wall facing the doors. Harrison would be standing with his guitar midway between the doors and the drums, with Clapton and Voormann near him. Hammond organ and other keyboard instruments would be farther down toward the middle of the studio. "Bobby Whitlock, as I looked out into the studio, was to my left," recalled White. When Badfinger had been present, their acoustic guitars were screened off farther back away from the other musicians. Despite the smaller number of players Harrison now had in the studio, he still relied on Spector to manage the sessions. Alan White remembered, "We'd do something, and once we got a version of it done, [George would] go in and confide in him and see if it was OK to do this and OK to do that. They'd talk about it, and then he'd come out and give us his input."

"George spent most of the time in the studio, and Phil was doing the recording," said Voormann, "which I found very helpful. George liked to play and liked to be with the musicians, and he was playing the song to us and had headphones on, but Phil was really in charge of the technique and the engineer. George, if he hadn't had Phil, he would have to do the producing *and* the playing *and* communicating with the musicians. In this case he had a partner. . . . It was more like a partner. It wasn't 'Oh Phil, you are the producer, and I am the musician.' That wasn't the case. It's more like a collaboration—that's what I would call it." Billy Preston added that "Phil didn't seek to overtake George or anything. He would hold court and all you could do was laugh 'cause he had the floor and Phil looked like a cartoon to me, a funny little guy with a funny little voice, loony but a lot of fun. And he was brilliant."

While Spector mostly stayed in the control room, he did venture out into the studio from time to time. "At one session in Abbey Road," said John Barham, "Phil and George were conversing, and I came into the studio at the end of the conversation. Phil picked up a guitar and started playing and singing a German folksong. The melody was identical to the Beatle song 'Ob-La-Di, Ob-La-Da.'" Voormann added that "he was really always part of the musicians, too. He was going around, playing a little piano. I remember at the sessions for *All Things Must Pass*, he went to the piano and played 'River Deep, Mountain High,' but slow, a really, really beautiful slow ballad. He played it so nice, with that little tiny voice he had. It was so moving."

Although Harrison fashioned the sound of each song's arrangement according to his own instincts, one of his continuing reference points was Dylan's recent work, both with the Band and in his incarnation as a country singer on the previous year's *Nashville Skyline*. Harrison's decision to call Pete Drake, the pedal steel player who appeared on *Nashville Skyline* and *John Wesley Harding*, only underlined this connection and suggests how in thrall to Dylan's country sound he was. It also indicates that he'd planned out the next week of sessions, at least to some degree, because Drake's sound perfectly fit the songs Harrison had lined up for recording. Drake had already been playing for over a decade when he crossed the threshold at Abbey Road. After a grueling period backing various country acts on the road, he settled in Nashville in 1959 to become a session musician, and while he struggled for the first year and a half, by the middle of 1960, following a notable appearance on the Grand Ole Opry, he started picking up session work, clocking twenty-four sessions the first month. Two of those sessions produced number one country hits, and the demand for Drake increased until he was voted Instrumentalist of the Year in 1964 by *Cash Box* magazine. Work with Elvis Presley followed in 1966, and by the late '60s, Drake was playing "fifteen sessions a week, usually three a day." He began diversifying too, starting a publishing company and becoming a producer himself. When in 1966 John Sebastian sang the praises of "Nashville Cats" who "play clean as country water" and "wild as mountain dew," he had people like Drake in mind. Playing on Dylan's albums expanded his reach even further. Drake told *Guitar Player* magazine in 1973, "Bob Dylan really helped me an awful lot. I mean, by having me play on those records he just opened the door for the pedal steel guitar, because then everybody wanted to use one. I was getting calls from all over the world."

While in New York in May, Harrison had met Charlie Daniels, who was playing bass on the Dylan session he attended, and who had also played on *Nashville Skyline*. A Nashville session musician himself, Daniels connected Harrison with Drake. "One day my secretary buzzed me and said, 'George Harrison wants you on the phone,'" Drake recalled. "And I said, 'Well, where's he from?' She said, 'London.' And I said, 'Well, what company's he with?' She said, 'The Beatles.' The name, you know, just didn't ring any bells—well, I'm just a hillbilly, you know (laughter). Anyway, I ended up going to London for a week where we did the album *All Things Must Pass*." Even before he arrived at Abbey Road, Drake sensed a certain kinship with the musicians he was about to meet. Learning that the pedal steel player needed a ride, Ringo Starr sent his driver to pick Drake up from the airport. On the trip to the studio, Drake saw a cache of country music cassettes in the drummer's car.

At thirty-seven, Drake was the oldest musician here by far, but despite the difference in age and his distinctly American "hillbilly" background, his aura of complete professionalism and the new sound he brought with him gave the other musicians a boost. He was a source of joy at these recordings, for Harrison in particular. One of the photos from the recording of the album, taken with Drake's camera, shows the pedal steel player in the foreground, while behind him Harrison gives a big grin as he poses with his Gibson acoustic guitar. In another shot, Harrison takes Drake's place at the pedal steel, with Starr joining them in the frame. "Pete Drake was incredible," said Voormann, "very, very natural. He had those great sounds, that jazzy stuff he could play, those bright, great chords. . . . We were dilettantes, I would say, in comparison to those cats from Nashville. How quick they were, and how fast, and they would never make a mistake. You know, like Billy [Preston] never made a mistake. And Pete Drake knew his sound and knew how to play. It was really incredible. I really enjoyed playing with him. So delicate and musical, really fantastic guy. Very, very straight, very American guy."

Drake's pedal steel and the smaller number of musicians seemed ideal for the next song. They began "I Live for You" on Friday, June 9, and like "My Sweet Lord," this composition was directly and unmistakably spiritual. But opening with "All alone in this world am I" and claiming to possess "only sadness from all that has grown," its lyrics read as despondent rather than celebratory, the shadowy twin of Harrison's song of praise. The band expended no small amount of energy recording it, dedicating all of June 9 to the song, with multiple breakdowns and false starts, leaving just eight of the sixteen takes this day complete. A couple of between-takes jams reveal the chemistry of the band, most notably an old Gene Vincent tune the Beatles played live from 1960 to 1961, "Wedding Bells (Are Breaking Up That Old Gang of Mine)," with Harrison in fine voice.

The next day, June 10, they began with what would become the title track of the album. Harrison had written "All Things Must Pass" during his visit with Bob Dylan in Woodstock on Thanksgiving 1968 and had attempted repeatedly and with little success to work up an arrangement of the song with the other Beatles during the January 1969 Get Back sessions. It was yet another dispiriting battle he could not win. The response the song would receive from the musicians he'd chosen for his own recording, however, stood in stark contrast. Harrison had borrowed from the Tao Te Ching before, after having been introduced by a fan to a passage from chapter forty-seven of the book for his song "The Inner Light" in 1967. For "All Things Must Pass" he returned once again to the ideas of Taoism, but this time via an interpretation by Timothy

Leary. His 1966 book, *Psychedelic Prayers After the Tao Te Ching*, much like his 1964 book, *The Psychedelic Experience* (which provided the inspiration for John Lennon's "Tomorrow Never Knows"), was intended as a series of guided meditations for "LSD sessions" (acid trips). Based on Book I of the *Tao Te Ching*, Leary's interpretations aren't radically different from other translations, but his overall intent was to "find this seed idea in each sutra and rewrite it in the lingua franca of psychedelia."

The plain, direct language of Leary's translations resonated with Harrison, who drew the first two lines for his song from the fifth poem in the book:

> All things pass
> A sunrise does not last all morning
> All things pass
> A cloudburst does not last all day

If a Taoist expression of the transitory nature of all things filtered through Timothy Leary's aspirations for LSD served as the lyrical inspiration, the *sound* Harrison imagined for the song originally came from a very different place. Attempting to give the Beatles some focus in working up an arrangement on January 3, 1969, he had said at one point, "We're pretending to be the Band on this one." Much later he recalled, "'The Weight' was the one I admired. It had a religious and a country feeling to it, and I wanted that. You absorb, then you interpret, and it comes out nothing like the thing you're imagining, but it gives you a starting point." In spite of numerous rehearsals of the song throughout the sessions as well as audible encouragement and attempts from both Lennon and McCartney to solve arranging problems, the Beatles never recorded a take of "All Things Must Pass" that satisfied its composer. Recalling Harrison's comment in March 1970 that "it was always a matter of trying to do the song you thought they'd understand quickest, or the song you could get onto the tape the quickest," perhaps "All Things Must Pass" was one of the songs he had in mind. After the band toiled over the track again on January 8, McCartney (with Lennon's agreement) suggested Harrison do the song alone on acoustic guitar as an introduction to their planned live performance; even though they would pull together a group performance by the end of the day, the Beatles didn't seem to "understand" the song. Rather than press forward and tempt his own frustration, after two more attempts on January 28 and 29, Harrison decided to abandon it for the moment.

Harrison *knew* the song was good, though. Almost a month after he had taped three solo studio demos at the Apple studio, he again entered Abbey Road alone on February 25, 1969, recording solo versions of "Something," "Old Brown Shoe," and "All Things Must Pass." Onto the last of these he overdubbed a second vocal and guitar track. Now, over a year later and deep into sessions for his own album, the musicians were far more receptive. "The mood in the room was really cool," said Alan White, "and I thought the lyrics were just wonderful. That was a great song . . . when something is that good of a song it tends to make it pretty easy to play. It kind of just flowed out of what people played." This time, Harrison did not attempt to channel the sound of the Band. Instead, the configuration of the basic rhythm track varied little from the previous day, composed of two acoustic guitars, bass, two pianos, and Drake's ghostly pedal steel part, with the addition of a harmonium. Eric Clapton and Bobby Whitlock overdubbed backing vocals on the bridge, which finished off the recording for the moment.

After recording the keeper take of "All Things Must Pass" (take eighteen), Harrison turned his attention once again to "I Live for You" this day. After sixteen more takes, they finally laid down a master at take thirty-two—notably without Drake's pedal steel guitar, which he would overdub later. The instrumentation at this point consisted of the Harrison/Frampton acoustic duo, two pianos, bass, and Starr on brushed drums. Harrison overdubbed a vocal to the final take, but getting the right feel had proven elusive. Alan White remembered that the song "wasn't working for most of the musicians." Harrison would say later, "Nobody had a feel for it except for the pedal steel guitar player and the rhythm guitarist. And so I didn't want to use it. I didn't think we got it and I think at the time I was thinking the song's a bit fruity anyway."

They then returned to "Art of Dying," attempting just a single take—take ten—of a completely different arrangement from the one on May 29. More in line with the sound of the recordings of the last few days, the instrumentation would be brushed drums, bass, acoustic guitars, harmonium, piano, vocals, and congas. The last of these instruments would feature a guest appearance from one Phil Collins, who was just nineteen at the time and still a little over two months away from joining a fledgling band called Genesis. Collins was at this point an unknown musician, between bands and looking for gigs. "I'm a jobbing drummer without a job," he wrote later, "and this is a job." Collins remembered being placed between Ringo Starr and Billy Preston, running through the song repeatedly to get the sound Spector wanted. As the producer called out from the control room to hear certain groups of instruments on take after take (unrecorded), Collins, a novice to studio work and eager to impress, played his heart out on each performance, his hands growing more raw with each take, unaware that Spector wasn't hearing him. Eventually, Collins got his turn: "Ok guys, congas can you play this time?" As Collins later wrote, "I don't even have a name. Worse, he's not even heard me. Not once." Pete Drake would add a steel-guitar overdub the next day, but Harrison ultimately rejected this arrangement.

During a break in recording, Drake decided to impress his hosts. "In a slow moment," recalled Peter Frampton, "they were changing [tape] reels. He said, 'Do you want to hear something,' so George and I said 'Yeah!' So he brings this black box, puts it by the side of his pedal steel, and he starts plugging things up, and then all of a sudden this plastic tube, he puts it in his mouth, starts playing the pedal steel, and it's singing to me. . . . But he was talking to us too, and everyone just freaked out. No one had ever heard that or seen anybody do that before. Of course, the first thing I said was, 'Where do I get one?' and he said, 'I made this one myself.'" Drake's "Talking Guitar," as it came to be known, dated to 1963, on the song "Lock, Stock, and Teardrops" by Roger Miller, followed in 1964 by an instrumental that sold millions called "Forever," under Drake's own name. The idea for this technique was born out of the pedal steel player's restless creativity. "Well, everybody wanted this style of mine," he recalled, "but I sort of got tired of it. I'd say, 'Hey, let me try and come up with something new,' and they'd say, 'Naw, I want you to do what you did on So-and-so's record.' Now, I'd been trying to make something for people who couldn't talk, who'd lost their voice. . . . So I saw this old Kay Kayser movie, and Alvino Rey was playing the talking guitar. I thought, 'Man, if he can make a guitar talk, surely I can make people talk.' So I worked on it for about five years, and it was so simple that I went all around it, you know, like we usually do."

"You play the notes on the guitar and it goes through the amplifier," Drake explained to *Guitar Player* magazine in 1973. "I have a driver system so that you disconnect the speakers and the sound goes through the driver into a plastic tube. You put the tube in the side of your mouth then form the words with your mouth as you play them. You don't actually say a word: The guitar is your vocal cords, and your mouth is the amplifier. It's amplified by a microphone." For Frampton, this was a profound moment. "It was just the coolest effect," he remembered in 2014. "It's like I think I've died and gone to heaven—this is the sound, and it's right in front of me." In 1974, he finally got one of his own, courtesy of inventor Bob Heil, who was manufacturing the device under the name "talk box." By then, guitar-centric rock artists had already absorbed the effect into their tool kits, with Joe Walsh, Aerosmith, Todd Rundgren, Rufus and Chaka Khan, and Steely Dan all employing the talk box on their own records. But when Frampton's live double LP, *Frampton Comes Alive*, became the bestselling album of 1976, driven by the massive popularity of "Do You Feel Like We Do" and "Show Me the Way"—both prominently featuring the talk box—Frampton's name became synonymous with the effect.

Harrison, always on the lookout for a new sound, was equally impressed. On June 11, he set aside time for a demonstration of the technique, and Drake ran through a variety of effects. Sitting near the steel player in the studio while Spector made comments from the control room, Harrison was particularly taken with an effect on one of the bass strings. After Drake played a few bluesy licks, Harrison remarked, "We should have done some blues tunes." Drake then performed a bit of "Danny Boy" and a haunting verse and chorus of "Bridge over Troubled Water," which had reached number one on *Billboard* in February. Ultimately, Drake overdubbed his talking guitar onto "Wah Wah," playing along with every appearance of the title, creating a crying, whining sound, and the added bass effect that Harrison liked during the song's bridge sections. At the start of the session, Drake overdubbed his pedal steel, minus the talking effect, onto several songs, including "I Live for You," as well as shimmering arpeggios onto "Let It Roll."

Drake later recalled, "[George's] album is fantastic—it's not country, but his songs are so good. He's a tough writer. I got on real well with Phil Spector; he's a hell of a producer and he's got a track record you can't question. But George knocked me out. He lives 40 miles outside of London, yet he came to the airport to see me off. It seemed that I could do no wrong and he's the kind of person I'd work my tail off for." This marked the end of Drake's work on *All Things Must Pass*, but he'd gotten on so well with Starr that they decided to record an album together. "Ringo Starr asked me to produce him," Drake recalled, "so I told him I would if he'd come to Nashville." Drake lured him with the promise that the album could be finished in a week, and given his publishing and recording connections, he could pull together all the necessary material and players easily. Starr flew to Nashville on June 22, recorded the album June 25–27, and returned on July 1.

─────────────

With his first solo album due for release in August, Eric Clapton felt the looming need to assemble a band to promote the record with live shows. When not attending sessions for Harrison's album, Clapton and Bobby Whitlock had been jamming and writing songs at Hurtwood Edge, and forming this band would give them the opportunity to record the new songs. Near the beginning of the month, the two musicians considered potential candidates for this prospective group and decided on Jim Keltner for drums and Carl Radle for bass. Feeling he couldn't play lead and rhythm guitar, Clapton also thought of Dave Mason, who had worked on Harrison's sessions. Whitlock knew both Keltner and Radle from the first Delaney & Bonnie album in 1968, *Accept No Substitute*. Radle was an easy choice: he had been a regular during Clapton's time with Delaney & Bonnie and a number of other recording sessions, including (most importantly) the guitarist's own album coming out in August.

Keltner would go on to become one of the most prolific session drummers in Los Angeles, and while Clapton hadn't worked with him before, he certainly knew his playing from *Accept No Substitute*. While Keltner was busy in L.A. recording an album with jazz guitarist Gabor Szabo, those sessions were set to wrap at the end of June; as soon as he was finished, Keltner said, he would be on the first plane to London, which seemed perfect timing for the August LP release. The decision to perform at the June 14 benefit, however, seems to have been a last-minute one, which changed the future of Clapton's new band dramatically. In the week leading up to the performance, apparently assuming the lineup would move ahead as planned, Clapton's management ran an announcement for the gig in *Melody Maker*: "Eric Clapton" in large typeface, with Whitlock, Keltner, and Radle listed beneath in a smaller font. Before he left for England, however, Carl Radle had mentioned to another Delaney & Bonnie alum, drummer Jim Gordon, that Clapton was putting together a new band, and Gordon saw an opportunity. Jim Gordon worked in many of the same L.A. circles as Keltner, but had established himself earlier, beginning his career at age seventeen backing the Everly Brothers in 1963. While he was undeniably talented, he was also volatile. In one notorious incident from Joe Cocker's Mad Dogs and Englishmen tour from the spring of 1970, Gordon unexpectedly struck then-girlfriend Rita Coolidge in front of a number of witnesses. Much to Clapton and Whitlock's surprise, Gordon showed up unannounced in London on June 10. Clapton and Whitlock discussed the situation: they wanted Keltner and were willing to wait for him, but according to Whitlock, Gordon "was there and the need was immediate." If Clapton had any reservations, he pushed them aside. Gordon was in the group. Fortuitously, Gordon's arrival coincided with a recording session, which may have helped secure his place in the new band. Clapton's manager, Robert Stigwood, had planned an entire album for soul singer P. P. Arnold with Barry Gibb producing, but the Bee Gees' own busy schedule meant Gibb couldn't finish the work. Remembering Arnold from Delaney & Bonnie dates in 1969, Clapton agreed to help complete the project.

On June 10, while Harrison was at Abbey Road recording "All Things Must Pass," Clapton was both producing and playing guitar on the recording for Arnold at IBC Studios in central London. Radle reportedly got lost on the way to the session, but once the recording was finished, all four men moved into Hurtwood Edge and, along with Dave Mason, began rehearsing and jamming. The rapport was immediate. "It wasn't a pressure situation at all," recalled Whitlock. "We had all been playing together for quite a while, so it was very casual in a get-it-done sort of way. We just let it flow as usual and we were very tight. We were just playing and enjoying life, being who and what we were at that time, young and full of it and ready to go play at the drop of a hat. As for our song selection, Eric had an infinite blues well from which to draw, as did we all. So when it came to material there was always an abundance of it. It would just depend on which direction we wanted to go and how we had approached rehearsing whichever particular song that we were going to be doing."

Whitlock's protracted stay at Hurtwood Edge afforded him with a vital window into Clapton's musical soul. As he later recalled, "Eric had this big chest at his house, four- or five-feet long, three feet deep and three- to four-feet high, filled with blues records—Robert Johnson, Bill Broonzy, Skip James, Muddy Waters, Ray Charles—some stuff I had never heard. He could tell you everybody on every record, who was playing on everything, who wrote what.

The only thing he couldn't tell you is if it was daylight or dark when it got recorded."

Clapton had been writing with Whitlock, and the most promising of the new songs was "Tell the Truth." Born of the daily schedule at Hurtwood Edge, free of obligations when not needed at Harrison's sessions, the song began as Whitlock put his guitar into an open E tuning he had learned from Duane Allman, the gifted young guitarist for the Allman Brothers Band. As he searched for a chord progression, Clapton, uninspired, headed to bed while Whitlock stayed up all night, chasing a creative spark with the aid of a little cocaine, and gradually worked out a song. By sunrise, Whitlock recalled, "It was all finished except the last verse. Eric came down that morning for breakfast, and I said, 'Hey, Eric, I wrote this great rock 'n' roll song last night!' He said wearily, 'I know, I know, I've got my part already written.' His bedroom was right above the living room and I had been up all night long high as a Georgia pine singing 'Tell the Truth' at the top of my voice and had kept him up all night as well! He had been up there listening to me and he wrote the last verse from listening through the floor."

The group's live debut on June 14 was a benefit at the Lyceum Theatre for Dr. Benjamin Spock's Civil Liberties Legal Defense Fund. Spock, a pediatrician who had come to prominence in the 1940s and '50s for *The Common Sense Book of Baby and Child Care*, had by the '60s become an outspoken critic of the Vietnam War, and the Defense Fund served "the relatively radical causes of relatively radical people," according to the doctor. The music—including R&B/jazz fusion group Ashton, Gardner and Dyke, blues artist Alexis Korner, prog rockers Noir, and American rock band Raven—was scheduled for 4:30 PM and 8:00 PM. The headliners were billed as "Eric Clapton and Friends."

Photos taken backstage show Clapton clean-shaven, neatly dressed in a tan silk shirt with matching striped vest and pants, warming up on a Martin acoustic guitar and conferring with the other members of the band. The scene seems relaxed, but at some point before going onstage they realized they had neglected to pick a name for the band. "Eric Clapton and Friends" would not do.

Several variant stories exist explaining how "Eric Clapton and Friends" became "Derek and the Dominos," but they all center around Tony Ashton's penchant for calling Clapton by the nickname "Del" or "Derek" (depending on the account), which had begun during 1969's Delaney & Bonnie tour. Backstage on June 14, casting about for a name, everyone in the group began calling out suggestions. Jim Gordon would tell the LA Times later in the year that Ashton suggested "Derek and the Dynamics." Jeff Dexter, a deejay and the announcer for the show, said he made the final revision: "Derek and the Dominos." Though the Americans in the room thought the name sounded a little too much like an old-fashioned doo-wop group, this very quality may have been a selling point for Clapton, who had suggested in October of the previous year that Blind Faith tour small clubs under the name "the Falcons." Whatever the case, Clapton, still wanting to obscure his identity, loved the name. Derek and the Dominos it was, but as band names go, it was perennially fraught with confusion. In early September, when the "Tell the Truth" b/w "Roll It Over" single was released in the UK, Stigwood famously gave away "Derek Is Eric" badges at the Polydor launch party. While Derek and the Dominos would come to adore the seeming anonymity of their mysterious moniker, by the same token, it would prove to be a title that served them poorly in terms of name recognition—most notably, that of Eric Clapton, whose very presence held the power to sell concert tickets and LP units.

For Whitlock, performing with Clapton in any configuration was a real kick. And it was exciting for the keyboard player and the other band members to perform with Clapton as genuine peers, as opposed to acting as his backing group. But still, there was no denying Clapton's stardom. "It wasn't going to be Eric Clapton and Friends, or anything to do with Eric," said Whitlock. "Eric wasn't ready to step out in the front, and we *were* a band. When we were together, we were all equals. When Tony went out to introduce us, he said, 'Ladies and gentlemen, Derek and the Dominos!' I immediately saw Eric, Jim, Carl, and me, all in matching zoot suits, with three-inch cuffs and long chains, only Eric's was a different color from the rest of us." Weary of the virtuosic pyrotechnics of Cream and the regrettable "supergroup" albatross that had been hung on Blind Faith, Clapton meant to subvert expectations in every way. "When we did the Lyceum gig, we had planned on doing a couple of acoustic numbers," recalled Whitlock. "It was just Eric and Dave and me playing acoustic guitars and singing. We were standing rather than seated. . . . We did several numbers and then Carl and Jim came on and we all plugged in and rocked the house. I recall we played "Easy Now" [from the *Eric Clapton* LP] in the acoustic set and it was absolutely beautiful. Our vocals blended so well together that it is a memory that will stay with me forever. We were a great band no matter the configuration because everyone was a great player and never got in each other's way."

One photo of the performance shows Clapton on acoustic guitar (miked, not amplified) with Radle and Gordon behind him and Whitlock on organ at stage left; Mason, out of the frame, stands to the right of the stage. Another shot of Clapton alone shows him playing his Stratocaster. In addition to "Easy Now," Clapton would later remember also playing "Blues Power" and "Bottle of Red Wine," both familiar to the band from their time playing with Delaney & Bonnie, and both recorded for his album back in January. They also included two blues numbers, "Crossroads" and "Spoonful," and "because Dave Mason had joined us," the Traffic song "Feelin' Alright." The show wasn't just the first appearance of a new band, but Eric Clapton's public debut, at last, as a front man. One review applauded his performance, saying "Eric leads and sings his heart out." Others were not so receptive, however. One critic called it "ordinary" and "dull," while fans who had attended the shows wrote the music papers expressing their disdain. "His concert at the Lyceum must rate as one of the most bitter disappointments of the year for ardent Clapton fans," read one letter printed in *Melody Maker*. "I, for one, feel that he has relinquished his status as the world's 'leading musician.' He must surely realize that people who go to see him play do not really want him to play the brand of music he is playing. Call it what you will. Surely his name and reputation cannot continue with performances like this, people will just not bother to go and see him at all."

For Clapton, the criticism had little impact and may have even satisfied him, if he'd bothered to read any of the reviews. He had successfully subverted the expectations of both the music journalists and the audience. He knew that *this*, finally, was the right band for him.

Sir Frank Crisp (1843–1919). The curious and whimsical Crisp, a successful attorney, began building his Friar Park estate in 1889. Over the next two decades, he spent a million dollars turning it into an eccentric proto–theme park with vast gardens and attractions.

Friar Park, 2019. In January 1970, Harrison purchased the property for £140,000 (about $340,000 at the exchange rate of the time). While the grounds and the house were in serious disrepair, what remained of Crisp's spirit charmed Harrison. Harrison would spend much of the rest of his life tending to the estate, and consequently came to see himself as a gardener more than anything else (courtesy of Ricardo Pacheco/Shutterstock.com).

February 1966: George Harrison and Pattie Boyd during their honeymoon in Barbados. The early years of their marriage had been a happy partnership, but by 1970 the couple was beginning to drift apart (courtesy of Pictorial Press, Ltd./Alamy Stock Photo).

December 4, 1969: Harrison and Eric Clapton performing with Delaney & Bonnie and Friends at Birmingham Town Hall. Harrison joined the tour on December 3 and would be encouraged to begin playing slide guitar by Delaney Bramlett while also beginning the composition of several new songs, including "My Sweet Lord." From left to right, Jim Price with trumpet, Jim Gordon on drums, Carl Radle bass, Bobby Keys sax, Bonnie Bramlett, Harrison at back, Delaney Bramlett, and Clapton (courtesy of Trinity Mirror/Mirrorpix/Alamy Stock Photo).

February 1970: Harrison at Trident Studios playing guitar during the session for the Radha Krishna Temple recording of "Govinda." At the piano is Mukunda Das Adhikary (later known as Mukunda Goswami), who arranged the songs on the album, and on the right is Shyamasundar Das. Both men would remain friends with Harrison to the very end of his life. On the wishes of the leader of the modern Krishna movement, Swami Prabhupada, "Govinda" greets devotees each morning in more than eight hundred temples around the world (courtesy of Gurudas [Roger Siegel]).

March 1970: George Harrison on the roof of Apple Records posing with a group of Hare Krishnas, including Mukunda Das Adhikary (face obscured), Gurudas (with head covering), and Shyamasundar Das (to Harrison's right). In addition to producing the Radha Krishna Temple album, Harrison would heavily promote the Krishna movement during this time and would remain devoted to Krishna consciousness and its underlying philosophy throughout the rest of his life (courtesy of Trinity Mirror/ Mirrorpix/Alamy Stock Photo).

LYCEUM, STRAND, W.C.2

SUNDAY, JUNE 14th

An evening with

ERIC CLAPTON

with BOBBY WHITLOCK, CARL RADLE, JIM KELTNER

ASHTON, GARDNER & DYKE
ALEXIS KORNER   JOHN PEEL

(In aid of the Civil Liberties Legal Defence Fund, U.S.A.)

TICKETS STILL AVAILABLE FROM:
LYCEUM, STRAND

First House Doors open 4.30 p.m.
Second House Doors open 8.00 p.m.

AN A.P.B. INTERNATIONAL U.K. LTD. PRESENTATION

June 1970: Trade paper notice for Clapton and company's June 14 show at the Lyceum. Because the band didn't have a name, the musicians are listed instead. Note that Jim Keltner is included, since Clapton and Whitlock had hoped to retain him as their drummer for the new group. They would officially be dubbed as Derek and the Dominos moments before going onstage.

June 14, 1970: Backstage at the Lyceum Theatre. From left to right: Bobby Whitlock, Carl Radle, Eric Clapton, Dave Mason. Drummer Jim Gordon has his back to the camera. Clapton, Whitlock, and Mason would open their performance with an acoustic set, including the Clapton original "Easy Now" (courtesy of Koh Hasebe/Shinko Music/Getty Images).

Multitrack tape boxes of the two songs that Phil Spector produced for Derek and the Dominos during the *All Things Must Pass* sessions. Harrison gave the band studio time in exchange for their work on his album. These two recordings were released briefly in September 1970 but later recalled after the group began recording in Miami and found a new sound (courtesy of Bill Levenson).

August 19, 1970

NOTES FOR GEORGE HARRISON

From: Phil Spector

Re: George Harrison LP

Dear George:

I have listed each tune and some opinions on each for you
to use, as I will not be in London for some time. In general,
I feel the remixing of the album requires a great deal of work
or at least a few hours on each number. Therefore, I feel it
would be best if we saved all remixing until I return as a
great deal of the mixes should be done with a fresh approach
and should all be good. Though the following looks like a
book, it is just because there are so many songs and opinions.

1. AWAITIN' ON YOU ALL:

The mixes I heard had the voice too buried, in my opinion.
I'm sure we could do better. The performance probably will
be okay, unless you really think you can do it better.
However, as I said above, I think a lot of it is in the
final mix when we do it.

2. IF NOT FOR YOU:

The mix I heard also had the voice too buried. Performance
was fine. It also should be remixed when the entire album
is remixed.

3. I'LL HAVE YOU ANYTIME:

Same comments as "IF NOT FOR YOU".

August 19, 1970: Phil Spector's complete notes, published here in their entirety for
the first time, regarding the rough mixes that Harrison had conducted at EMI with
engineer Phil McDonald, outlining the necessary remaining work to complete the
All Things Must Pass recordings. At Harrison's urging, Spector had returned to Los
Angeles to seek treatment for alcoholism (courtesy of Allen Goldstein).

4. ALL THINGS MUST PASS:

   I'm not sure if the performance is good or not. Even on
   that first mix you did which had the "original" voice,
   I'm sure is not the best you can do. But, perhaps you
   should concentrate on getting a good performance. I
   still prefer the horns out on the intro but that is a
   remix decision which should be done at that time. Also
   the voices in the bridge (Eric and Bobby) sound flat, and
   should be very low in the final mix. This particular song
   is so good that any honest performance by you will be
   acceptable as far as I'm concerned, but if you wish to
   concentrate on doing another, then you should do that.

5. BEWARE OF DARKNESS:

   The eight track I heard after it was bumped had the
   electric guitar you played bumped on with the rhythm
   guitars. I personally feel you can make a better bump
   with a bit more rhythm guitars. The electric guitar seems
   to drown them out. Perhaps you should do another bump with
   more rhythm guitars, or seriously consider taking this one
   to Trident Studios using the original eight track and
   avoiding bumping, as each track we used is important and
   vital to a good final mix.

6. ISN'T IT A PITY (NO. 1):

   Still needs full strings and horns. Naturally, performance
   is still needed by you. I think you should just concentrate
   on singing it and getting that out of the way.

7. ISN'T IT A PITY (NO. 2):

   Still needs full or some type of orchestration. Performance
   seemed okay, but needs to be listened to at the end.

8. I DIG LOVE:

   Performance seems okay. Needs a very good remix and
   synthesizer over the intro would be nice (making a wave
   sound). This can be put on the vocal track before your
   voice comes in or at Trident Studios, etc. Also, handclaps of some type would be nice on each intro riff.
   Just an idea. I can't explain that very good in print.

9. LET IT DOWN:

This side needs an excellent and very subtle remix which
I am positive can be gotten and it will become one of the
great highlights of the album. Believe me. In listening
I find it needs an answer vocal from you on "Let It Down"
parts. I'm not sure about this next point, but maybe a
better performance with better pronunciation of words
should be tried at Trident without erasing the original
which did have much warmth to it. Perhaps you could try
this at Trident. The vocal group (Eric and Bobby) on the
"Let It Down" parts sounded okay. The "Moonlight Bay"
horn parts should be out the first time and very, very low
the second time they play that riff, I think. Perhaps at
the end, near the fade, a wailing sax (old rock and roll
stype) played by Bobby Keyes would possibly add some
highlight to the ending and make it totally different
from the rest of the song. It's hard to explain, but some
kind of a screening saxaphone mixed in with all that madness at the end might be an idea. Anyhow, it's something
to think about. Even though everything is not exactly as
we had hoped (horns, etc.) I think it will be great when
it is finished. Everything on those eight tracks now is
important and vital to the final product. I know the
right mix and sounds even on the horns, can be obtained
in remix. The only other thing the horns could have done
is what they play originally on the "Let It Down" parts,
only more forcefully. However, I still think it's all
there and there's nothing to worry about on that number.

10. MY SWEET LORD:

This still needs background vocals and also an opening
lead vocal where you didn't come in on the original session.
The rest of the vocal should be checked out but a lot of
the original lead vocal is good. Also an acoustic guitar,
perhaps playing some fills, should be overdubbed or a solo
put in. Don't rush to erase the original vocal on this one
as it might be quite good. Since background voices will
have to be done at Trident Studios, any lead vocals perhaps
should be done there as well.

11. WAH WAH:

This still needs horns on bridge, and perhaps a Bobby
Keyes solo. Also needs lead vocal and background voices.

12. ART OF DYING:(TWO VERSIONS):

No vocal on either rendition of this one at present.
Orchestration will probably be required as well. Did
you listen to first version which Ringo played on?

13. WHAT IS LIFE:

The band track is fine. This needs a good performance
by you and proper background voices. It should be done
at Trident Studios if further tracks are necessary.

14. RUN OF THE MILL:

The mix I heard also did not have sufficient lead voice.
This is no problem as I feel we should remix it when we
remix the entire album. The performance seemed to be
okay.

15. HEAR ME LORD:

Still needs horns or other orchestration. The vocal should
be checked out to see if it is okay in performance and
level.

16. APPLE SCRUFFS:

This mix seems to be okay as is.

17. LET IT ROLL:

This still needs a good vocal performance and maybe some
sustaining type of background voices along the way, as each
chorus is the same at present. Perhaps you can do this at
Trident. However, the most important thing is to get a
good lead vocal.

18. BEHIND THAT LOCKED DOOR:

Maybe vocal performance can be better. I'm not sure. Also,
the mix may be able to better as well. The voice seems a
little down.

George, on all the 18 numbers I just mentioned, what I feel are
the most important items on each. Naturally, wherever possible,
of main importance is to get a good vocal performance by yourself.

Also, if you do any of the backgro-nd voices, you should spend
considerable time on them to make sure they are good. In
practically every case, I would recommend that you use Trident
Studios for overdubbing voices, lead or otherwise, so as not to
bump tracks or go eight-to-eight, and also to be able to do as
much as possible before reducing everything back to the original
eight track. This would probably be an easier way to do it and
would also insure the best type or protection for our original
eight tracks when it comes to remixing, as most of those tracks
are presently very good and I'd rather avoid going eight-to-eight
and further bumping. Also, in many cases one erases a performance before comparing it to the new performance, which would
not have to happen on a sixteen track.

I'm sure the album will be able to be remixed excellently. I
also feel that therein lies much of the album because many of
the tracks are really quite good and will reproduce on record
very wel. Therefore, I think you should spend whatever time
you are going to on performances so that they are the very best
you can do, and that will make the remixing of the album that
much easier. I really feel that your voice has got to be heard
throughout the album so that the greatness of the songs can
really come through. We can't cover you up too much (and there
really is no need to) although as I said, I'm sure excellent
mixes can be obtained with just the proper amount of time spent
on each one. It would be much better to spend an allotted amount
of time just on remixing rather than doing it in bits and pieces.
When the recording of the album is finished, I think we can get
into it better on a remix level if we just devote time to it
and thereby we will make a much better album since we will be
concentrating on one thing at a time.

George, thank you for all your understanding about what we discussed. I appreciate your concern very much and hope to see
you as soon as it is possible.

Much love. Regards to everyone.

Hare Krishna,

Phil Spector

PS/sjh

P.S. These notes were written just before I left for my treatment; I hope they make sense.

Tom Wilkes's proposed poster design for the *All Things Must Pass* package. Wilkes put in over one hundred hours of work on this watercolor, rendered in what he described as a "classic East Indian style." Wilkes sensed that Harrison was uncomfortable with the imagery and scrapped the idea. The poster in the final package used one of the photos Barry Feinstein shot of Harrison in the main house at Friar Park (courtesy of the collection of Bruce Spizer).

Duane Allman, summer 1971. With the Allman Brothers Band, Duane would launch the Southern Rock movement. Known as Skydog among his contemporaries, Duane died after a motorcycle crash in October 1971 at the age of twenty-four (courtesy of MirrorPunch/Alamy).

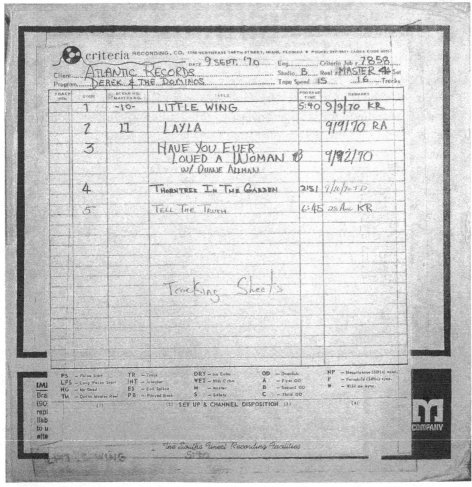

September 1970: Multi-track tape box from the *Layla* recording sessions. These five master takes were cut from their respective reels and edited together onto a single tape. The unused takes were scrapped (courtesy of Bill Levenson).

October 1970: From left to right, ABKCO record-promotions man Pete Bennett, Phil Spector, and Harrison in New York City listening to the master tape of *All Things Must Pass*. Harrison was very particular about the mastering of the album for vinyl and went to three different studios before he was satisfied with the results (courtesy of Bettmann/Getty Images).

Derek and the Dominos' official promo photo: from left to right, Jim Gordon, Carl Radle, Bobby Whitlock, Eric Clapton, and Jeep, Clapton's dog (courtesy of Michael Ochs Archives/Getty Images).

September 1970: An outtake from the *All Things Must Pass* album-cover shoot by Barry Feinstein at Friar Park. Harrison said in 2001, "Originally, when we took the photo, I had these old Bavarian gnomes which I thought I would put there, like, kinda John, Paul, George, and Ringo" (courtesy of Barry Feinstein Photography).

8 | DEREK IS ERIC

BECAUSE THE STORY of the making of *All Things Must Pass* has long been relayed through fuzzy memories with a lack of access to documentation, the conventional assumption has been that Derek and the Dominos were the core band for the album, augmented by other players as needed. While Clapton and Whitlock were present from the start, the late arrival of Radle and Gordon to the UK in June and the participation of three-fourths of the group in the P. P. Arnold session on June 10 rules out their presence as a *band* until after this date; Mal Evans's diary confirms this fact, first documenting Radle and Gordon's presence at Harrison's sessions on June 22. But the fundamental truth remains: the band that would become Derek and the Dominos came together as musicians during the production of *All Things Must Pass*. As Clapton has noted, "We made our bones, really, on that album with George."

Following the overdub session with Pete Drake on June 11, Harrison would take a break from his own album; his mother's health was declining quickly, and he may have traveled to Liverpool to spend time with her after the Dominos' Lyceum gig. With the backing tracks and a few overdubs of at least ten songs in the can, he'd earned a rest, but his songbook was far from exhausted. After a week away, Harrison returned to the studio for the next series of sessions, and it was here that Derek and the Dominos entered the picture as a fully formed group.

With Radle and Gordon installed at Hurtwood Edge, the band had set up instruments in one of the larger downstairs rooms before the Lyceum show. With their first gig now under their belt, they dug in. "All we did was jam and jam and jam," Clapton wrote in his autobiography, "and night would become day and day would become night, and it just felt good to me to stay that way. I had never felt so musically free before." The last week of June, they began channeling that energy into a final burst of recording that would see seven more basic tracks completed for Harrison's album, as well as the B-side of the first Derek and the Dominos single.

The recording session for that first single, on June 18, saw the start of work on "Tell the Truth" in EMI Studio Three, with Harrison sitting in on electric guitar along with Dave Mason, who was still considered part of the band. The jam energy that would soon come to define the band spilled over into two recordings, which Harrison would later dub "Thanks for the Pepperoni" (after a Lenny Bruce sketch) and "Plug Me In." Clapton has said that he asked Harrison for studio time for his new group in exchange for the work Clapton and Whitlock had done already, but a curious entry in Mal Evans's diary from June 17 suggests another possibility. After "Telegram to Eric," Evans writes, "'Could you, Jim, Carl, Bobby do session with George EMI Thursday' Love Mal," with "Talk to George. Phil Spector" written underneath. Evans by this point had ambitions of being far more than an assistant to the Beatles. He had discovered Badfinger already and was keen to impress Harrison. Did Mal Evans take the initiative to have Derek and the Dominos do their first recordings?

Whatever the case, this fruitful week and a half was also where Spector's big production aesthetic once again found an outlet. While the acoustic country tracks glowed under Harrison's meticulous touch, the next set of songs would all have a *big* sound and would benefit in different ways from Spector's production techniques. Returning to Studio Three on Monday, June 22, Harrison and company first tackled "What Is Life?" Written quickly—"15 minutes or half an hour maybe"—in 1969 while traveling to Olympic Studios for a Billy Preston session, "What Is Life?" features another lyric that deftly blurs the line between the religious and the romantic. As he had written it for Preston but withheld it, the song was an early step toward the kind of gospel-type writing that would begin to preoccupy Harrison later in the year.

"What Is Life?" was a good, energetic kickoff to the day, but it would not surrender easily. After initial work on the song, the musicians turned their attention to "Awaiting for You All," the initial inspiration for which had been a certain cadence. "I was just going to bed and I was cleaning me teeth," Harrison recalled, "and suddenly in me head came this, 'You don't need a *doon-doot da pum pum.'* All I had to do was pick up the guitar, find what key it was in, and fill in the missing words."

The words he found reflected some of the language he had been using for many months when discussing Eastern philosophy. The ideas of the "polluted" consciousness and the way to "get it clean" appeared in Harrison's introduction, written in March, for the book *Krishna: The Supreme Personality of Godhead,* the publication of which he also funded. He spoke of these concepts again in the *Fact or Fantasy* interview in April, describing meditation and yoga as "methods just to stop further pollution of your system and your consciousness and to cleanse the system. The whole thing of purity they talk about in religion is really a mental, physical, and spiritual purity, which is obtained through discipline and through practice." A month earlier, he spoke of the spiritual power of "chanting the names of the lord," through the Hare Krishna mantra: "The purpose is to give people a bit of relief from the normal pressures. . . . It's like anything, like singing 'Hallelujah, Hallelujah.' If you really sung that for an hour, you'd feel good." The overall concept of simplification that ran through the Krishna teachings gave Harrison a hook for the verses, a laundry list of things unnecessary for worship. Ironically, one of these was rosary beads, the use of which was very similar to the Japa Yoga technique he had adopted.

"Awaiting on You All" was another up-tempo rocker, and while the demo from May 26 had been an electric-guitar-bass-drums sketch, the arrangement grew to be one of the most Spectorized productions on the album, awash in reverb and packed with sounds all fighting for space. This arranging and mixing strategy ultimately worked to obscure the pointed—some would certainly say preachy—lyrics, including a final chorus (ultimately omitted from the album's printed lyrics) featuring a dig at Harrison's Catholic upbringing: "The Pope owns 51 percent of General Motors / And the stock exchange is the only thing he's qualified to quote us." For recording, the basic rhythm track would be comparatively simple, without effects, and with two slide guitars set against the bass and drums. Price and Keys, isolated in the back room of the studio to minimize bleed from the other instruments, would lay down their parts live. They would only begin work on "Awaiting on You All," though, before setting it aside as well and moving on to a third song for the session.

As with the previous composition, "Beware of Darkness" saw Harrison talking as much to himself as to his audience. The "falling swingers" and "soft shoe shufflers" could have referred to any of the insincere, unreliable characters he'd encountered throughout the Beatle years, but the "darkness" in the song was very much his own. Pattie Boyd had begun noticing the first appearance of her husband's depressive states after their return from Rishikesh in 1968. "This was new: he had never been depressed before," she wrote in her memoir, "but there was nothing I could do." He withdrew from her and became obsessive about meditation and chanting; in one dark mood before buying Friar Park, he decided he didn't want the estate anymore. Some of this was certainly in response to business tensions within the Beatles, with which he was coping the best he could, but he held it all in, telling his wife very little. When he sang of sadness in "Beware of Darkness" and concluded, "That is not what you are here for," he may well have been looking in the mirror.

He threaded other potentially self-soothing reminders throughout the lyrics, too. From the May 27 demo, he replaced "beware of ABKCO" with "beware of Maya," which Harrison would describe later as "the cosmic illusion (that which is not)." Perhaps more to the point of the song, the concept of Maya in Hindu philosophy refers to attachment to the temporary, physical world as opposed to spiritual transcendence. Or as Harrison was fond of saying in 1970, "We are not these bodies." The lyrics also hint again at how his surroundings at Friar Park had taken hold in his imagination. Juxtaposing the "greedy leaders" of the final verse against the "weeping Atlas cedars" that he observed on his property wanting to "grow and grow" suggests he was already beginning to understand a gardener's long view of the world. Years later, his sister-in-law Irene remembered, "He pointed out a group of blue firs saying, 'Do you realize that when Frank Crisp planted those, he was never going to see them. . . . He knew by the time he was an old gentleman he wasn't going to see this garden looking as he'd planned it.' And [George] felt the same way." That Harrison could distill all of these ideas into a four-minute song speaks to the complexity of his thought and writing, as well as his ability to express intensely personal feelings in a way that could resonate universally. If he came off as a little preachy, well, he was still only twenty-seven years old.

As Olivia Harrison later said, "[George] also wrote these things to remind himself. People sometimes accused him of preaching. But you know, he was really preaching to himself. He wasn't trying to say, 'You be like this because I'm already like this.' No, he was always trying to remind himself. And that's the reason he liked India so much, because he said that, 'Everywhere you went, there was a reminder.'" Phil Spector echoed these thoughts. "He just lived by his deeds," he recalled. "He was spiritual, and you knew it, and there was no salesmanship involved. It made you spiritual being around him." The master take of the song, recorded late in the night, featured nearly all the parts heard in the final mix: acoustic guitars, Clapton's lead guitar through a Leslie speaker, bass, drums, vocal, vibraphone, and piano, the last of which Bobby Whitlock said Harrison asked him to play with a "gospel feel." Even though Derek and the Dominos were on fire now, their presence didn't preclude the participation of other musicians. Klaus Voormann, who remembered playing on "Beware of Darkness," said, "I mean, I'm happy because the Delaney & Bonnie [guys] were so tight and so good, and some of the fast tracks when they're playing really fit so good together. I think it was great. I love Carl. He was a great bass player. There was no jealousy or anything like that, never. We could have swapped bass in the middle of a song!" Voormann added that "we never played together but . . . I remember looking at his fingers and seeing how he played that part and how I played. But we never played at the same time. It might even happen that he'd say, 'Come on, Klaus, you play,' or the other way around: 'Oh, Carl, you play on this song.'"

While "Beware of Darkness" may have sprung from Harrison's own experience, his skillful and sensitive writing couldn't help but resonate with the musicians playing on these songs. How open they were to hearing the ideas Harrison was trying to convey is impossible to know, but Bobby Whitlock sensed that Clapton may have been absorbing at least some of the messages in Harrison's lyrics. "Every song had meaning that was relevant to the climate of the room," Whitlock wrote in his autobiography. "Eric and George both knew, as did I, the deep nature of some of those songs. These were subliminal messages, going back and forth, between two good friends as a way of healing and setting each other free. Saying what they could not say any other way except through a song." There was potentially plenty of darkness to go around, but not from the places one might expect. Phil Spector certainly had demons lurking in him, but his reputation for eccentricity and outrageousness was, for the most part, in short supply during these sessions. "He talked a lot. He was in command," Leckie recalled. "You know, you'd often take half an hour off while he'd tell jokes—big storytelling."

One consistent target of Spector's "humor" was engineer Eddie Klein who, along with Phil McDonald and John Leckie, was part of the control room team assuring everything made it to tape as the producer wished. Klein was largely responsible for physically managing the machines that created the various effects Spector wanted, from tape echo to phasing to reverb. "Phil was on him all the time," Voormann said. "If Eddie did anything wrong, there'd be half an hour of jokes and laughing at his expense. Cruel for Eddie perhaps, but great fun for everybody else." Spector could take these jokes to absurd levels. At one session, he wound up signing Eddie Klein to a contract to make a *tap-dancing record*, with George Harrison, Billy Preston, Klaus Voormann, Gary Wright, and Ringo Starr as the backing band. To preserve the moment for posterity, they had a photo taken of the entire group in the studio, posing around Klein at the center holding his recording contract.

These kinds of antics had become commonplace at Gold Star sessions, where Spector knew all the musicians well, and the long hours in the studio necessitated a release of tension through practical jokes and other silliness. Here, with a revolving group of largely unfamiliar players, Spector may have used humor to break the ice while also easing his own anxieties. As a way of ingratiating himself with the musicians, from whom he was mostly separated behind the control room glass, these flashes of humor proved an effective gambit. "Lots of people say he was crazy," Voormann recalled, "and I never really thought he was crazy. He was not shouting at anybody, not being strange. He was very particular. . . . He was always very nice and talking to people and being very into the thing and very delicate and sensitive. Very, very funny man." Leckie's memories concurred with Voormann's. "Phil would talk a lot," said Leckie, "but I don't remember him falling over. I never saw any guns, never saw him drunk. George would sit in the corner chanting Hare Krishna a lot of the time with his hand in his little bead bag. And the band was just rock and roll, they just wanted to play, and everyone was positive, and Phil was running the show. Everyone was relaxed because Phil was in charge."

Although Harrison had done his share of acid and pot and would later in the '70s indulge in cocaine, "plus all the other naughty things that fly around," 1970 found him in a period of abstention. "What most people don't know," said Voormann, "is that George was very vulnerable. One day he's this, and then suddenly—like when I was at Friar Park, he would get up at five in the morning and meditate and see the sun coming up—and then suddenly there's a period where he's sniffing the coke. It's all mixed up! When he did the sessions for *All Things Must Pass,* he was very straight, I must admit."

In October 1969, Harrison told David Wigg that "as soon as I smoked pot, I gave up alcohol, because I realized the only reason I was drinking alcohol was to get high. So I got high much easier without any sickness after it. But the thing is now that to really have pure state of consciousness and good perception that is above the normal state of consciousness that we're aware of, then you must have a perfectly clear mind. So alcohol and any sort of drugs is out. But I haven't taken anything like that personally for a long time." Derek and the Dominos, however, were not abstaining. Clapton and Bobby Whitlock had both been using cocaine for some time, and joints were as commonplace as cigarettes and alcohol, but after Radle and Gordon had moved into Hurtwood Edge, the band's drug intake escalated. They combined either cocaine or alcohol with Mandrax, a powerful sedative, which together with the other drugs "would create a unique kind of high. . . . This became the chemistry of our lives, mixing all these things together. God knows how our bodies stood it."

This was also the period when Clapton began using heroin, introduced to him by a coke dealer who would insist "that you took a certain amount of smack at the same time." For a while, he let the packets of fine pink powder languish in a drawer at Hurtwood Edge, but according to Bobby Whitlock, one night after they'd finished recording at Abbey Road, Clapton decided to take the plunge. He was fully aware of the damage it could do, knowing well the stories of Charlie Parker and Ray Charles, but was convinced he could control his use. After snorting the first line, he told Whitlock he felt "warm all over, as if there was a cotton wool cushion under his head and soft pink cotton wool around him, and he felt very secure." The next night, Whitlock decided to do a couple of lines with him. In a moment of weakness and slavish immaturity, Clapton had once threatened Boyd that he'd begin using heroin if she didn't leave Harrison, which she wouldn't even contemplate at that point. And now he was doing just that. And he had gotten Whitlock hooked to boot.

Clapton and Whitlock's heroin use, at this point, was once "every two weeks," according to Clapton, but alcohol and pot were fixtures at the studio. Miraculously, none of this affected the recording sessions, and they managed to keep most of what they were doing under control; while it would ultimately be impossible to maintain the balance, the band continued for the moment to deliver. "We used to actually," recalled Leckie, "at the end of the sessions, go round the ashtrays because there were unsmoked spliffs and joints in the ashtrays, and bottles of tequila. And tequila, bourbon—it was American stuff. But tequila was priceless and a new thing to us in those days. And I lived in a house I shared with other people near Portobello Road in Notting Hill Gate, when I worked [at EMI], and we used to get drunk on Eric Clapton's tequila. I used to have this bottle of tequila on the table there and people would go, 'Hey can we have some of Eric's tequila?' There was a lot of drinking and smoking but I never saw anything else, and they kept playing."

On June 23, they returned to "What Is Life?," reaching take twenty-seven without getting a master yet, then turned to "Beware of Darkness," recording takes six to fourteen, with six marked best. Before finishing up at 2:00 AM, they committed three takes of "Hear Me Lord" to tape.

On June 24, they tackled two songs, both of which demonstrated the powerful interplay Derek and the Dominos had developed. "Let It Down" featured Clapton's crunchy electric guitar and Harrison's slide against the background of Whitlock's swirling Hammond organ, while Gordon's muscular drumming and Radle's bass work drove the rhythm; electric piano and grand piano filled out the rest of the basic track. "I think the intro on this song was a stroke of genius," said John Barham, citing the "extraordinary" dynamic shift from the explosive choruses to the hushed verses. This would be magnified with further production, but for now Harrison overdubbed his lead vocal, and Clapton and Whitlock added backing vocals. Rounding out the eight-track was session trombone player Roy Huckridge playing a part that John Barham would later transfer to the reeds for his own arrangement. The final mix would be edited down to five minutes, but today's master, take eight, ran to six minutes and forty seconds.

If Harrison was initially hesitant to wear his spirituality on his sleeve with "My Sweet Lord," he had nonetheless continued to record songs where he expressed his beliefs using language both veiled and forthright. "Hear Me Lord," an unambiguous and straightforward plea to God, was as direct as any sacred hymn, and as it predated "My Sweet Lord" by a year, it indicates how early he had been inspired to put these ideas to music. Writing the song over the weekend of January 4 and 5, 1969, Harrison first introduced it several times during the January 6 *Get Back* rehearsals, often strumming the distinctive chord progression with scant interest from the other Beatles. His studio demo for Spector, wherein he accompanied himself with a warmly distorted electric guitar, hinted at the compressed emotion in the tune. Now, eighteen months after he first composed it, Harrison had the confidence and the support to exhale, to release all he had held back, and dig into the song with the fervor it demanded.

Once again on the basic track—electric guitar, drums, bass, Hammond organ, grand piano, and Harrison's impassioned vocal—the sound of the song was already in place, only to be amplified by later overdubs. Picking up where they had left off the day before, the band recorded takes four through eight, with the last being chosen as best. Just like "Let It Down," "Hear Me Lord" ran considerably longer than the final mix, the master take clocking in after a long vamp at seven and a half minutes. Before the end of the session, Harrison also laid down a take of "Om Hare Om (Gopala Krishna)," sung entirely in Sanskrit, with an arrangement of electric guitar (played through a Leslie speaker), slide guitar, Hammond organ, bass, and congas.

Having finished basic tracks for four of his own songs since the beginning of the week, Harrison turned over another day of studio time to Derek and the Dominos on Thursday, June 25. They gave "Tell the Truth" another shot but the final take of the day, take twenty-nine, ran over eight minutes, unraveling at the end into a jam, a glimpse into what lay ahead for the band. They dropped the song for the moment and turned their attention to the tune that would occupy the B-side of the single, "Roll It Over," another new Clapton-Whitlock original. With Spector producing and Harrison again on rhythm guitar, they mastered the song in just two takes—three guitars, bass, drums, piano, and vocals, all cut live. Onto the only free track remaining, track seven, they added handclaps, harmony vocals, percussion, and Dave Mason's intense slide guitar solo through a wah-wah pedal—a very quick and effective piece of work.

For all the heavy, distorted guitars running throughout these sessions and the Derek and the Dominos recordings that would follow later in the year, both Harrison and Clapton's amplifier of choice was surprisingly modest in size. The year before, Delaney Bramlett had been using Fender Champs "souped up with Lansing speakers" and gave one each to Harrison and Clapton at the end of 1969. The Champ had just a single tube and only an eight-inch speaker, and even though the upgrade increased the volume, it was still small, even compared to a regular-sized guitar amp. But though they were little, they were fierce. EMI engineer Richard Lush, who would see a variation on this amp, the Fender Vibro Champ, in action later in the year during John Lennon's *Plastic Ono Band* sessions, called it, "a little portable amp, really—but you could really crank them up." Clapton found the amp's sound so effective that he continued to use it well beyond 1970, even as a preamp on stage.

On Friday, June 26, to finish off "Awaiting on You All," work moved to Studio Two at EMI, the only day of recording outside of Studio Three. "The equipment would be left out for a run of days," said Leckie, "but if there was a weekend or a week off then it would be cleared down. The reason for moving studios is because the other studio was booked. They would say, 'OK, you can have two weeks, but then the third week you have to move into Studio Two because someone else has booked [Number Three].' All the equipment would be left set up overnight if not for a whole week." After a three-day break, they returned to Studio Three on June 30 for what proved to be a long evening of work—from 9:30 PM to 5:00 AM—on just one song. So many of the lyrics Harrison had written in the last eighteen months reflected, either obliquely or directly, some aspect of his own experience, ultimately making this collection of songs as personal as anything John Lennon may have been writing at the time, though not nearly as raw or confrontational as the coming *Plastic Ono Band* LP. Harrison wasn't about to write a line as incendiary as "I don't believe in Beatles"; Lennon and McCartney would jab at each other in their lyrics the following year, and while Harrison points his finger a little sanctimoniously, his own breakup song is characterized more by sadness. He would later summarize "Run of the Mill" as "the problem with partnerships," and though he would admit it describes the unhappy atmosphere at Apple during this period, its lyrics allude to certain specific frustrations with Lennon, and especially McCartney.

The opening verse, with its reference to raised voices, echoes back to McCartney's rage-filled episode with Starr earlier in the year and to one instance when McCartney had shouted so loudly that Harrison had to hold the telephone away from his ear. The second verse is just as pointed: the chance to "realize me or send me down again" recalled any number of dismissals of his songs by Lennon and McCartney, including the recorded Apple meeting from September 1969, when McCartney blithely admitted he didn't think Harrison's songs had been good enough to merit equal space on Beatles albums. The next line, however, may be the sharpest and most mournful on the entire album: "You've got me wondering how I lost your friendship / But I see it in your eyes," reverberates with Al Aronowitz's observation from May that Harrison wasn't angry at McCartney, but deeply hurt. They had known each other since they were boys, aged thirteen and fourteen, they had conquered the world together, and they were each just one of four people who could understand the madness they had endured and the triumphs they had celebrated. How had it come to this?

As personal as this song may have been, Harrison was too private and too professional to state explicitly any of the real meaning behind these lyrics at the session. For the musicians, the main focus, as always, was getting the song arranged and down on tape, but it was not an easy song to master. Harrison had recorded two takes of the song accompanying himself on guitar back on May 29, then two incomplete takes with the band on June 24. The arrangement on June 30 featured a faster tempo than the final version, along with a tightly orchestrated lead line throughout, played in unison on electric guitars by Clapton and former Shadow Hank Marvin—very much the sound of Derek and the Dominos at this particular moment. Finishing up the session on take thirty-nine without settling on a keeper, they laid down a busk on Jimmie Rodgers's 1928 tune "Waiting for a Train" entitled "Going to the River," complete with Harrison yodeling rather unconvincingly. By that point, it was probably a good time to call it a night.

Picking up the next afternoon, July 1, with take forty, they exchanged electric guitars for acoustics, finally getting a master at take sixty-one. In contrast to the songs recorded during the last few sessions, which would all later be overdubbed to dramatic effect, "Run of the Mill" was complete as a live performance. With Harrison leading the way on twelve-string acoustic guitar, the piano, harmonium, drums, bass, trumpet, saxophone, and two more acoustic guitars (played by Clapton and Voormann) were all laid down live. After Harrison rerecorded his vocal, the song was complete. Between takes Harrison and the band ran through a less-than-serious take of "Get Back," with Clapton laying down some fleet-fingered acoustic lead work while Price and Keys punctuated the arrangement with a two-note hook.

Inspired, they forged ahead. Back on May 29, with Starr on drums and Voormann on bass, Harrison had led the band through nine takes of "Art of

Dying," but after finishing "Run of the Mill," he decided to take another pass at the song. Where the May recording adhered to Spector's massed instrumentation approach, this new version took flight powered by the combustible energy between the players. Now lowered a half step to the key of A, with Clapton's fiery wah-wah'd electric guitar opening the track and Radle and Gordon's thunderous pulse locked in with George's slashing electric rhythm guitar, the song was mastered in twenty-six takes. Electric piano (Gary Wright), electric guitar (Klaus Voormann), and Hammond organ (Bobby Whitlock) rounded out the rhythm track.

July 2 produced the longest and most dynamic of the released jams, "Out of the Blue," which builds and recedes with a compelling interplay of the musicians for twenty minutes, which would ultimately be edited down to just over eleven minutes for release. Clapton was not present, and Voormann was quick to point out that "I played guitar on 'Out of the Blue.' I played those kind of chops, and at the end I played this really fast guitar thing. And later on when George wrote the credits, he wrote in Eric Clapton, even though I was playing. Eric didn't even play on that track! I had that little Gretsch guitar. I brought it along—I don't know why I brought it along. George gave me that Gretsch guitar! And I started playing. Carl Radle had the bass, and I couldn't play the bass, so I picked up this guitar and just played along."

While the album credit for journalist Al Aronowitz on "unspecified instrument" on this track may have superficially read as tongue in cheek, it was actually a kind gesture from Harrison to his friend. Aronowitz had been present at many of these sessions, though he inexplicably never wrote about them at any length—he later claimed to have been "too close" to the project, and when asked what instrument he played, he would reply "typewriter." But credit on the album guaranteed Aronowitz a small royalty check twice a year. "To a deadbeat like me," Aronowitz later wrote, "those checks have come in handy at just the right times."

Regarding the jam energy of the previous day, the engineers were grateful for the breaks these kinds of performances afforded, said John Leckie, "because we could go off for an hour. So the tape would last—if I put it on seven and a half [inches per second], so they were recorded at slow speed—we had an hour and four minutes from when I pressed record to when the tape ran out. So within an hour and four minutes we had to run 'round to the pub, have Guinness and Turkish sandwiches and crisps, and run back. For days on end really, that was the routine, before the pub closed, before they finished doing food, which was seven o'clock, which was early, considering there was another twelve hours to go. There'd be no food unless you brought your own sandwiches. Sometimes there'd be curries brought in, but there were so many people it would get devoured."

On July 3, they returned to "What Is Life?" which now featured a fuzz guitar riff played by Harrison himself, making it difficult for him to sing at the same time. "So all I could do on the [initial] take," he recalled later, "was to give the band the cue line—the first line of each verse—and then go back to playing that riff." This riff is doubled on bass by Radle; in later overdubs the riff would be reinforced further, but for the backing track, Spector added yet another layer of rhythm to the arrangement, with Jim Price on trumpet and Bobby Keys on saxophone mostly playing a three-note descending riff against the main riff, while Voormann held down acoustic rhythm guitar duties in the background. The trick of introducing each element individually, suggesting a precision engine coming to life one piece at a time, recalled Beatles songs like "Day Tripper," which built their tension and momentum gradually with the addition of each instrument.

Work wrapped up at 4:30 in the morning, marking an end to band recordings for the album. Up in Liverpool, his mother was nearing the end, and he headed north to be with her. But while Harrison was attending to his family, Clapton and the band still had work to do.

On Monday, July 6, Derek and the Dominos returned to EMI studios to finish recording their first single. For the third time, they tackled "Tell the Truth," finally mastering the song on the thirty-seventh take. "One day we came in," said John Leckie, "all the equipment was out and the microphones, and George wasn't there, and I don't think Phil Spector was there—I think he came much later—and basically we were recording Derek and the Dominos. And they were called 'Derek and the Dominos,' that's what I was told to put on the recording sheet."

Spector may have been late, but he arrived in time for the recorded takes and left a peculiar stamp on the recordings. Typically, any effects like reverb or phasing/flanging would be added after initial recording, with the multitrack featuring "dry," unprocessed sounds. The benefit of this approach was that it delayed a wide variety of creative decisions until the mixing stage and allowed for experimentation and, possibly, a change of heart. If these effects were applied to tape during the session, they could not be changed or removed later. "I can remember Phil Spector getting angry at Phil McDonald," said Leckie, "because sometimes when you have reverb, you have it on monitor, so you're listening to the reverb, but you're not actually recording. You're not committing it to tape. Because you can always add reverb, but you can't take it off. So it's for safety, really."

In spite of Spector's protests, McDonald had mostly maintained this practice throughout Harrison's sessions, but on this date, he relented and, for reasons unknown, recorded the effects live to tape, specifically a peculiar phasing effect on the drums. This effect was audible in the final mix, done on July 31, for the single release. Bill Levenson, who remixed both "Roll It Over" and "Tell The Truth" for the Eric Clapton *Crossroads* box in 1988, recalled what he discovered when he pulled the multitrack tapes for that project: "The single—'Tell the Truth' b/w 'Roll It Over'—was difficult to work with. The English single, the final mixes were mono; the American single, the final mixes were stereo. None of it was very good sounding, so we pulled the multitracks. What I remember about 'Roll It Over' is that it was pretty dry. I don't think it was a difficult mix to do, so it was a pretty fun thing to discover." As it happened, "Tell the Truth" proved to be surprisingly problematic. As Levenson recalled, it "was a miserable track to mix, and it was diminishing returns as we did it—all that moosh was on tape. There was nowhere to go because all of the reverb, all of the swishing sounds—everything was on the tape. [The phasing] wavered in and out; everything was wrong with it. I have no idea what they were thinking."

As for the actual recording session, Dave Mason played slide again, and Bobby Whitlock switched from organ to electric guitar, playing a crunchy duet in octaves with Clapton throughout, all recorded live with Radle and Gordon. McDonald then bounced the drums to track eight while Jim Gordon simultaneously played a percussion overdub. They added piano and another guitar part together onto track two, and Clapton and Whitlock overdubbed their vocals to finish off the song. The odd phasing effect on the drums wasn't enough to diminish the overall impact, and the result was a supercharged, high-velocity record—a rousing, ear-grabbing way to introduce the band to the world.

The session ended up making waves within EMI, however, resulting in a headache for John Leckie. "I wrote on the recording sheet 'Derek and the Dominos.' But every job, every artist, whether it's an album, has a job number which it's charged to, so every session is charged to such-and-such a job number. And I didn't have a job number. And the next day when I came in after doing the session sheet, Vera Samwell—who did the bookings and was kind of my boss really, she organized all the sessions—she said, 'What's the George Harrison session without a job number—Derek and the Dominos?' And I said, 'I don't know, that's what the band's called.' It turned out that Derek and the Dominos was managed by Robert Stigwood, and Robert Stigwood was banned from the studio and not allowed to book time because he owed money. Vera: 'Who authorized these sessions? Who said these sessions could go ahead? Because if they're from Robert Stigwood, we're not allowed to accept bookings from him,' because he never paid his bills. I always remember that commotion going on and me getting the blame for it. If I'd written 'George Harrison' and charged it to George's job number—which is what George wanted, to give them some free time—instead, because I never put a job number, it got traced back to Robert Stigwood."

———————————

Louise Harrison passed away on July 7, 1970, at the age of fifty-nine, with George at her bedside. She was cremated, and her funeral was held on July 10. Even though the family had had months to prepare for this inevitability, George revealed later that he had felt utterly helpless throughout this time, witness to a drawn-out suffering he had no choice but to absorb. This period of helplessness spanned the entire process of recording the basic tracks for the album, and after one hospital visit, he had returned home and channeled his exhaustion and despair into a song, "Deep Blue." He later recalled, "It's filled with that frustration and gloom of going in these hospitals, and the feeling of disease—as the word's meaning truly is—that permeated the atmosphere. Not being able to do anything for suffering family or loved ones is an awful experience." When Harrison released the song the following year as a B-side, even critic Robert Christgau, who was generally dismissive of Harrison's solo work, called it "George's most affecting piece since 'Here Comes the Sun.'" From Los Angeles, where he was undergoing Primal Therapy with Arthur Janov, John Lennon sent a postcard on July 19 that read simply, "Sorry about your ma—Love John and Yoko."

Despite the stress he experienced due to concerns for his parents' health, Harrison never let these feelings show during recording sessions. Participants in these recordings consistently remember them fondly as a positive experience where Harrison created an atmosphere of calm. This was the "professional" way, of course. Voormann, who was going through a divorce and had moved into one of the lodges at Friar Park, saw Harrison every day, and even though they'd known each other since 1961, he says Harrison never discussed his mother's condition with him and never even let on that she was ill; this was a *very* private matter. While Pattie Boyd may have considered his meditation excessive at this stage of his life, it had become a way for Harrison to manage his feelings about his mother's illness while still getting through each day of recording, reckoning with his own insecurities about his songs, dealing with Apple-related matters, and processing the breakup of the Beatles. Later, when looking back and enumerating all the factors he had to contend with, he unsurprisingly referred to this period as a "bad time." His inner world was in turmoil, and emotionally he was facing the hardest challenges of his life. The pressure was immense, but he chose not to share very much of what he was feeling with his wife.

Harrison took a two-week break after his mother's funeral, and when he returned to the studio, he did so without Phil Spector. He had one more song he wanted to get down on tape, and he knew he wouldn't need a producer. In fact, he would perform nearly everything on the recording himself. For his inspiration, Harrison drew on his memories of the so-called Apple Scruffs. Beatles fans had been a familiar fixture outside EMI Studios at least as early as 1963, when some of them had stormed the entrance of the building during the recording of "She Loves You." Most conducted themselves respectfully, however, and were satisfied with simply seeing or briefly interacting with the members of the band in their comings and goings at the studio or, later, at the Apple building on Savile Row. By 1966, the Beatles were so used to their presence that they knew some of the girls by name. In February 1968, the Beatles even enlisted two of the fans, Lizzie Bravo and Gaylene Pease, to add backing vocals to the recording of "Across the Universe." By the end of 1969, the girls had given themselves a name: Apple Scruffs. Early in 1970 they began a magazine called *Apple Scruffs Monthly*, which included articles and comic illustrations of the Beatles. Derek Taylor recalled, "John used to disappear into his office when each issue came out and you'd hear him roaring with laughter, especially the stuff about him and Yoko."

The Scruffs were most certainly not groupies. There was a naïvety and innocence about their adoration that endeared them to the members of the band and their inner circle, and these qualities allowed them to get close the Beatles in a unique way. "Looking back, the Scruffs were very Zen," Taylor remembered. "I'd seen groupies with the Byrds, but these girls were different. They didn't want to sleep with the boys or attempt to get their psychic tentacles into them or invade their space." Taylor admitted he found this "bewildering but fascinating," and the Beatles too were charmed. Even Phil Spector had befriended them. Some of the girls would bundle up in their sleeping bags outside Abbey Road when sessions ran late into the night and would stay until morning sometimes. "Often we'd stay out all night, see the Beatles, go home, wash and then go off to work," one of the Scruffs, Gill Pritchard, said in 1996. One morning, after a long night of recording, she recalled, "Phil Spector comes toddling out and asks what we were doing. 'Breakfast,' we said. 'Can I have some?' So there we were, the dawn breaking over London, crouched under a tree with Phil Spector munching on cornflakes and he's really enjoying himself!" When the album was released, Pritchard recalled that Spector sent them a letter addressed to "The Apple Scruffs at 'The Steps,' 3 Savile Row."

Harrison certainly had his fans among the Scruffs, but during the recording of *All Things Must Pass*, three of the girls in particular—Cathy Sarver, Carol Bedford, and Lucy Rigor—stood vigil on Harrison's sessions, from Apple Studios to Abbey Road to Trident. Al Aronowitz would later write, "Outside the studio door, whether it rained or not, there was always a handful of Apple Scruffs, one of them a girl all the way from Texas." Bobby Keys noticed how Harrison "always took time to have a word with them, and I seem to remember him going out with tea for them sometimes when it was cold. I was impressed with how caring he was about these girls. I've been around a lot of other folks who have quite a different way of dealing with people, let's put it that way."

Harrison also looked out for them. "We were waiting at Trident Studios which wasn't in the best part of town," recalled Cathy Sarver. "A drunk guy came down the mews and stopped at us. He was interested in what a group of young girls were doing there, at night. It was no big deal, and we could handle ourselves, but in the middle of it, George arrived. He walked through us, turned to face the guy, and glared such an angry face the guy just took a couple steps backwards and then walked away. George went in without saying a thing. We were in shock that sweet George was able to look like that."

The girls had no way of knowing all that Harrison had been dealing with emotionally, but Sarver, Bedford, and Rigor's reliable enthusiasm and kindness had affected him deeply. Derek Taylor would recall in 1996, "George, in particular, always had a problem with the fans, being naturally shy and a bit diffident, but he grew very fond of them because he got to know them and they were there when he was going through some bad times [in 1970]." He repaid their kindness with the most gracious possible gesture. On Saturday, July 25, Harrison and Mal Evans returned to EMI, and beginning at 2:30 PM in Studio Three, he ran through eighteen takes of a new song he'd written for the girls, called simply "Apple Scruffs." Harrison sang while playing acoustic guitar and Dylanesque harmonica breaks. Only seven takes were completed, the rest being breakdowns or false starts. On a few that broke down he tried tapping his foot for accompaniment, before turning over percussion duties to Evans.

Harrison overdubbed his vocals onto take eighteen of "Apple Scruffs" numerous times, with Phil McDonald on each pass bouncing from one track to another so that, in the end, Harrison had as many as eight vocal parts (both harmony and backing) spread across four tracks, along with three tracks of slide guitar. Even with such a seemingly simple song, he had pushed the eight-track tape past its limit. At 6:00 AM the following morning, the song was complete—recorded, overdubbed, and mixed in a single session. When Phil McDonald had finished mixing the track, Harrison sent Mal Evans to bring the Apple Scruffs—including Sarver, Bedford, and Rigor—into the studio to hear the finished product. "Of course, we were dumbfounded," Sarver recalled in 2011, "because we were never asked to come in."

Pritchard recalled that Harrison "was very nervous, pacing up and down" as the song was playing. "I remember it as dark in the control room," said Sarver. "There were several girls there, not just the three George fans that were always with George. I just remember sitting next to my best friend and Mal. It was shocking hearing the song, especially the 'Apple Scruffs, how I love you!' It was hard to believe what I was hearing was true!" Another of the girls, Wendy Sutcliffe, said, "It was like he had seen it all, understood how we felt and, most of all, knew that we weren't just sad, stupid girlies." According to Pritchard, "It was the first time any of the Beatles had actually acknowledged the Scruffs by name publicly. He told us it was going to be on the album then slipped away in typical George fashion." But there was more to come. "Once we were back outside," said Sarver, "one of the girls said George was getting flowers tomorrow, because of the line [about] standing there with 'flowers in your hand.'" Pritchard remembered they made him a floral wreath. "When we gave it to him, he said, 'Well you have your own magazine, your own office on the steps, so why not your own song?'"

With all the backing tracks for the album now complete, Harrison moved ahead with overdubs, many of which he would do himself. Some parts, including percussion tracks, some vocals, and additional guitar, had been done the day of (or the day after) each session, but Harrison kept adding more. "George always came up with new ideas," said Voormann. "He had one line, and then he had another line. And then it got more and more. He didn't know how many lines to put on the record."

Peter Frampton remembered Harrison calling him back for a day just to add more acoustic guitar to some of the songs. Perched together on stools in front of the Studio Three control room window with Spector looking on, together they ran through song after song. "I don't know how many tracks I played on," Frampton said, "because they just kept adding acoustic guitars to anything with acoustics on it. . . . The most enjoyable part of that whole thing was in between, when they would change reels, because it was analog, obviously, George and I would start jamming. We were playing whatever; you name it, we were jamming on it. That was the highlight for me, to jam with George and just have fun."

Even though Spector has gotten credit (or blame, depending on who's speaking) for the production sound of the album, Harrison himself was just as responsible for piling on the overdubs. "George told me that he wasn't all that happy with it when he heard it years later," said Voormann. "He thought it was overproduced, he did much too much and it wasn't necessary. . . . At the time he was very much into overdubbing, doing another slide guitar and doing another vocal. I thought at the time it was too much, which I found really sad. So maybe he didn't know his plan, or he would have known his plan better. It was the first time he was recording by himself. But everybody loves it. I love it too, but he could have done it simpler. . . . Those early mixes, for example, of 'Wah Wah,' it was simpler. Some of the tracks were simpler before. The rough mixes that Spector did were very, very good."

"In the overdubbing," Spector said later, "he was in control of his parts. He wouldn't let anything go until it was right. . . . Perfectionist is not the word. Anyone can be a perfectionist. He was beyond that. He just had to have it so right. He would try and try and experiment upon experiment, to the point where I would leave the studio for several hours while he played different parts over and over with the engineer. Then I would come in and listen, and he would say, 'How does it sound? Are there too many parts? Too few parts?'"

While these multiple intricate overdubs reflected Harrison's ability to produce himself, they left no room for creative input from Spector. Working alone in the studio, Harrison now primarily needed a sounding board for his ideas, but Spector was no mere sounding board; he needed to direct. As the prior quote indicates, the producer would often leave while Harrison worked on his parts, and some days he simply wouldn't show up at all. With a studio full of musicians, he was engaged and stimulated—he had his army to command—but as Harrison worried over his guitar and vocal parts, Spector began to drift. For the first time in his life, he started drinking excessively. "What people couldn't understand was that just because there were drinking stories in the '70s they assumed that [I was drinking] in the '60s," Spector told the *Los Angeles Times* in 1991. "I ran a company all that time (in the '60s). I wouldn't drink, do drugs, nothing. I lived and died with every record. I felt invincible and scared at the same time. I was working 24 hours a day. I thought sleep was a waste of time. I didn't even think about drugs, and I never had alcohol (to any extent) until 1972 [*sic*], when I went to England to work with George Harrison on his album and I started getting bored."

The drinking, unfortunately, had a *very* adverse effect on his personality, a fact that had already been clear when he was younger. His teenage friend Michael Spencer recalled that when their band would play frat parties, if Spector got a look that he didn't like from someone, "He'd want to take on some of these guys, and you'd have to step in and quiet things down. . . . My guess is there was liquor in the formula, because at frat houses there was always a lot of liquor going on and Phil could never hold his drink." Another of Spector's later friends told author Mick Brown that alcohol was "poison to his system.

Phil would have two drinks and he'd become Mr. Hyde. It was like he'd taken some kind of potion. He would turn on people and be horrible."

Outrageous stories from later in the decade, which included pulling guns on artists, would come to define Spector's image, but at this point he was only just beginning to show signs of instability. This became another point of stress for Harrison, and he later recalled he kept trying to convince Spector to go into hospital, because he obviously wasn't well. At one studio date, however, he very clearly lost control. Klaus Voormann would often ride in from Friar Park with Harrison to attend overdub and mixing sessions; even though he no longer had any role to play himself, he enjoyed hearing the work Harrison was doing, and he loved the songs. One evening, Voormann recalled, as Harrison was refining another part, Spector fell and badly injured his arm. "He was very drunk. . . . George was doing all these overdubs and he [Phil] wasn't very interested. This is after we were in the studio [for basic tracks], and he didn't produce *that* part [the overdubs], so that was more George's thing."

Apple Scruff Gill Pritchard recalled, "You couldn't help but like Phil. He was in love with music like we were, but we knew he was on the edge emotionally. Once we were all outside Abbey Road and the doors opened, and George came out clutching Phil, he put him in a car, and it sped off. We asked George if Phil was OK. 'Yes,' he said. 'Well, actually, no. Phil's a bit destructive. Great producer and a really beautiful person but very self-destructive.'" With Harrison's encouragement, Spector returned to Los Angeles after his fall to seek treatment for his drinking. Harrison was now on his own for the foreseeable future, but the work continued. On August 2, 3, and 4, Harrison supervised the first session for orchestral recordings, most likely for "Beware of Darkness," "All Things Must Pass," and "Let It Down," all of which were conducted by John Barham from his own scores.

In total, Barham wrote scores for nine songs: "My Sweet Lord," "Isn't It a Pity" (version one), "Let It Down," "All Things Must Pass," "Awaiting on You All," "Art of Dying," "Hear Me Lord," and "What Is Life?" Although the orchestral backing was a feature of Spector's production work, it was again Harrison who gave Barham direction in what he wanted for these scores. Just as on the "Govinda" score, Harrison would sing or play lines on guitar to indicate what he wanted for the orchestral instruments, while Barham would work out the voicings of the instruments. "I worked with George in Friar Park shortly after he and Pattie moved in," said Barham. "At that time they both spent most of their time in the large kitchen, which doubled for dining room and sitting room. We went through the string arrangements in a large, poorly decorated room, which contained only an upright piano and two chairs. I slept in a room that contained only a single bed and a chair. Wandering around the place at night felt slightly eerie. If you have ever seen some of the English Hammer horror films of that period, it will give you an idea of the atmosphere at times."

By now, Harrison had filled all eight tracks on the tapes for many of the songs, and to move forward at EMI, which only had eight-track recording at this point, Phil McDonald would have to do tape reductions like he had done for "Beware of Darkness." While this would open up more tracks for further work, it would limit options for adjusting individual parts later on at the mixing stage; once tracks were combined, they were locked in together and couldn't be separated. But someone—possibly Harrison, or perhaps even McDonald—had an idea. Back in January 1967—when EMI was still only a four-track studio—EMI maintenance engineer Ken Townsend had worked out a way to synchronize two four-track machines so that George Martin could add multiple tracks of orchestral overdubs onto "A Day in the Life." Townsend recalled, "It was quite simple really. Putting a 50cps [cycles per second] tone on one track of the first machine and making that drive the capstan motor of the second machine." There was no reason it wouldn't work for eight-track machines as well. While John Leckie didn't remember being involved in this setup, he noted, "It's possible, but it's risky. You may start them together, but you never know *where* you're going to start. They're going to drift, and then the drift will multiply as time goes on."

In spite of the potential instability, McDonald apparently gave it a try anyway. According to another engineer, Nick Webb, who had recently begun working at EMI, McDonald called him into the control room to have a listen to what he'd rigged up. "I think the expectation was the more tracks you had, the bigger it would sound, but oddly it didn't seem the case," said Webb. McDonald, needing another fresh pair of ears, "played one, then both together with added tracks, [and] I told him the version with the two machines running sounded smaller. He was delighted, as it's what he was worried about."

Given his grand ambitions even before sessions began, Harrison must have suspected he would eventually need more than eight tracks, and the only facility in London with sixteen-track recording was Trident Studios. On August 12 at EMI, Harrison finished the last of the rough mixes—eighteen recordings in total, dropping "I Live for You" from consideration. Rather than pare the selection down to a single LP, he reflected later that, "I didn't really want to chuck any away at the time—although I'm sure lots of them in retrospect *could* have been chucked away. I wanted to get shut of them so I could catch up to myself." He sent copies of the mixes to Phil Spector, who was recuperating in Los Angeles, and a week later, on August 19, Spector sent back a detailed five-page letter with his thoughts on the mixes and the work he believed still needed to be done.

Overall, the tone of the letter is supportive and encouraging, and Spector repeatedly assures Harrison of the quality of the recordings. He cites "Let It Down" as a potential highlight, suggesting an "old rock and roll style" wailing sax solo by Bobby Keys "mixed in with all that madness at the end." He lists a number of overdubs yet to be done, both orchestral and vocal, indicating they've planned these parts already. Of "All Things Must Pass" he says, "This particular song is so good that any honest performance by you will be acceptable as far as I'm concerned, but if you wish to concentrate on doing another [vocal], then you should do that." The main thread that emerges here is Spector's encouragement of Harrison's singing. In many cases, he notes, Harrison has mixed his vocal too low: "I really feel that your voice has got to be heard throughout the album so that the greatness of the songs can really come through. We can't cover you up too much (and there really is no need to)." Spector also urges him not to do reduction mixes—or, as he phrases it, to "bump" from eight track to eight track—but instead utilize the sixteen track at Trident for further recording, because each individual track would be important to the final mix. And, in Spector's final estimation, it is in the mixing where the recordings will really blossom. Since he admits he won't be "in London for some time," he recommends concentrating on overdubs and doing the mixes in bulk when he returns, rather than one by one while still recording. He closes with, "George, thank you for all your understanding about what we discussed, I appreciate your concern very much and hope to see you as soon as it is possible." And then he adds a postscript: "These notes were written just before I left for my treatment; I hope they make sense."

Spector is famously known for his "Back to Mono" credo, and although in an interview in 1969 he continued to push the myth that "I don't believe in eight-tracks and 16-tracks and those machines. I like to record in one track in monaural," he is very clearly sensitive in this letter to the benefits of having all the original tracks available for mixing. That Spector took the time to listen carefully to each mix and dictate this long letter full of precise commentary and plans for his return indicates that he was still very much engaged in completing the album. Considering all the work he'd already done, his dedication would have been no surprise. But a more significant question still lingered: would Spector be capable of completing the task at hand?

9 | MIAMI

THAT AUGUST, WITH THE SESSIONS for *All Things Must Pass* having moved into the lengthy overdub phase, Derek and the Dominos undertook a three-week English tour, barnstorming across the nation's club scene, both provincial and urban alike. When they departed EMI Studios, they didn't go alone. They were joined by Kevin Harrington, who, along with Mal Evans, had served as Harrison's equipment manager for *All Things Must Pass*. For Harrington, it was a dream opportunity. After serving as Evans's assistant for the past few years, Harrington had heard hundreds of stories about the ramshackle, no-holds-barred life of a rock 'n' roll tour. By this point, Harrington didn't simply "want to go on the road," he recalled. "I *needed* to go on the road."

For Harrington, touring with Derek and the Dominos would be a trial by fire—one that would begin as a slow burn before cascading into banner headlines in the music press. As Clapton later recalled, "We did a club tour in England as Derek and the Dominos, which was funny because no one knew who we were. But the word spread quickly, and we had crowds most of the time." After making their London debut back in June, the band had continued jamming and rehearsing at Hurtwood Edge. For the UK tour, the Dominos opened at the Village Blues club in Dagenham Essex. In all, the group played nearly twenty gigs, including such venues as London's Speak-easy Club, Bexley, Kent's Black Prince Pub, and Scarborough's Penthouse in Yorkshire. At one point, they even played a gig in Biot across the English Channel in France.

179

Just as the band's debut in June had inspired disappointed fans to write into the music papers, this tour brought out similar reviews from ticket buyers. "If Clapton wants to lose his crown to another young guitarist, he only has to carry on what he's doing," wrote one correspondent. Another observed, "After seeing Clapton looking like a de-greased Elvis Presley and playing poorly disguised rock and roll, I came away feeling sick." In a particularly lengthy letter to the *New Musical Express* after the October 5 show in Birmingham, one reader praised the backing band but derided Clapton's vocals. "The experiment of Derek and the Dominos proves that he is at his best when allowed to just play, and not distracted by the necessity to sing."

By the end of the tour, the band was eager to reconnect with the incredible studio vibe that they had mustered during their sessions with Harrison. Determined to maximize their efforts together, Clapton tapped Tom Dowd for production duties. For Clapton, Dowd had been Cream's secret weapon in the studio. Years later, Clapton would recall that "Tom gave so much time to me, teaching me to recognize my individuality, to value myself, yet at the same time pushing me forward, encouraging me to try new methods and techniques. I owe him more than I can ever repay."

By this point, Dowd no longer considered Atlantic Studios in New York City to be his primary venue, instead working out of Miami, having relocated to oversee Atlantic's recording operations down south. In those days, Dowd had taken up residence at Criteria Studios. Where Abbey Road was austere and now, thanks to the Beatles, stood as a great monument to rock history, Criteria was free and easy, a relaxed studio environment where musicians came to play after a day at the beach. When he learned about Clapton's interest in his services, Dowd had been mixing the Allman Brothers Band's second album. "I'm doing *Idlewild South* in Miami, and I don't usually take calls during sessions," Dowd later recalled. "But this one I had to take because it's Stigwood, and he says, 'Eric has put a new band together and he'd like to record, and he's wondering if you have time.'" After readily agreeing to produce Clapton's new band, Dowd couldn't help thinking about the Cream sessions at Atlantic in New York City, where the power trio threatened to blow the doors off the studio. "I had alerted the staff at Criteria that this was going to be brutal," Dowd recalled. "Bring earmuffs because these guys would be showing up with double stacks of Marshalls and God-knows-what." After Dowd had concluded his phone call with Stigwood, Duane Allman strolled into the control room at Criteria Studios. "That was Eric Clapton's management talking about him coming here to record," Dowd announced to the guitarist. "You mean the guy from Cream?" Allman asked. "Man, are you going to record him? Oh, man, yeah, I gotta meet him. Do you think I could watch?"

While *All Things Must Pass* had taken months to perform and produce in the studio, the Dominos' debut record would be captured in a matter of days. Indeed, things happened quickly in the Dominos' universe, as events would shortly demonstrate. When Clapton and the group arrived at Criteria on August 26, Dowd was pleasantly surprised by their choice of gear, as well as their plans for enhancing their level of musical engagement in the studio. The producer would never forget the sight of Clapton walking into the studio with his Fender Champ and a small, battery-operated Pignose amp. He was followed by Radle, who had a piggyback Ampeg B-15. Dowd recalled thinking, "*Whoaaaaaah,* what the hell is going on here?" For his part, Whitlock wasn't worried, later recalling that they came to Miami in search of "a purist sound. There was no slapback echo, no fuzz tones. It was keeping it real simple and getting back to being pure. Eric had the ability to get great tone with just his Fender Strat and a tiny little tweed Champ or a battery-powered Pignose. It was just about making it simple."

After setting up their equipment at Criteria, Derek and the Dominos got right down to business during their very first session, taking a stab at "Anyday," one of the recent compositions by Clapton and Whitlock. Having whet their chops, the group performed a couple of extended jams in order to acquaint themselves with the studio before launching into their first take of "Have You Ever Loved a Woman," a blues number penned by Billy Myles and popularized by Freddie King. Clapton had first tried his hand at the tune back in 1965 in concert with the Bluesbreakers. As for Dowd, he quickly learned that the band wanted to continue some aspects of their recording sessions back in England with Harrison and Spector. Like George Martin back in the Beatles' studio heyday, the American producer had recorded with the tape running, in order to capture each and every nuance or stray musical idea as it unfolded. "That's the one thing we did get from Phil Spector," Whitlock recalled. "He got all those jams on *All Things Must Pass.* Eric and I discussed it, and decided to also keep the tape running on our sessions, no matter what happened and who came in. That's how we wound up with all those jams and alternate masters and stuff."

As Polygram's Bill Levenson pointed out, "Whenever there's an Eric Clapton album, there's going to be jams. It's the nature of the interaction of the musicians. They warm up to jams, they entertain themselves with jams and they develop songs as jams." Working in Studio A, Clapton and Radle set up their diminutive amps on chairs. Meanwhile, the Leslie speaker associated with Whitlock's Hammond organ was placed in a nearby sound room, and Gordon's drum kit was set up at a slight distance away from the other players. The grand piano in Studio A was covered with a canopy in order to control any unwanted reverberation. To Dowd's mind, it seemed that Clapton "had gotten more intimate with his technique, and he'd gone back the other way in terms of equipment." He admired the way in which they seemed to be stoking a sense of live interaction and natural acoustics over the blast of electric sound that he recalled from the Cream sessions. In order to avoid sound leakage, the musicians played their instruments at an incredibly low volume. As Whitlock recalled, "You could talk over the amplifiers, so we had to be particularly quiet when he did guitar overdub. Tom was very pleased that we recorded at low levels."

"As I think back on it," Dowd later remembered, "I made the comment that if anybody walked into that studio with squeaky shoes, we'd blow a take. That's how quiet they were. They weren't wearing headphones, so that everybody could hear each other. Jim Gordon could hear everything that everybody was playing in the room." For the Dominos, this unusually quiet, concentrated attempt at music making would characterize their days at Criteria. "That's the way it went," said Dowd. "I couldn't believe what I was listening to, and they completely relished it." But there was more to the story than that. The band's low-watt approach to the studio certainly afforded their recordings with a sense of intimacy, but as it happened, Clapton was desperate to preserve his hearing. As he told *Guitar Player*, his years of massive amplification with Cream had more than taken their toll. "I don't think I'll ever be the same. I think one ear is stronger than the other. One ear is at least half deaf—I don't know which one. When I'm on stage, I have to stand a certain way to be able to hear everything. Otherwise, I can only hear half of what's going on."

Dowd was clearly impressed with the Dominos' workmanlike approach and their obvious musical prowess, but he sensed that they didn't have enough material to fill out an album, much less a double LP. Would their sojourn at Criteria be nothing more than an extended walk down memory lane as Clapton and his mates waxed nostalgically over a slew of old blues riffs? At this juncture, Clapton was clearly playing things close to the vest. As for Derek and the Dominos, they were confident about what they wanted to accomplish in Miami. "We were fit," Clapton later recalled. "We would have sauna, go swimming during the day, and then go to the studios and get loaded. It didn't affect the playing or the sessions. But as is the way with drugs, it would catch up later." At first, Dowd attempted to intervene when it came to the bandmates using in the studio, cautioning Clapton that things could get out of hand. But as Whitlock recalled, it was too late for that. "If Tom had had any idea what we were doing in there," said Whitlock, "he would have shut the sessions down in an *instant*." In truth, Dowd was hardly a novice when it came to the music business. As he later remarked, "If I denied that they drank, that they used ups and downs, that they smoked, I'd be lying. But when I said, 'Two o'clock we're starting,' then at two o'clock I would have four, five, six, seven people walking in clear-eyed, fresh out of the shower, wanting coffee, and saying, 'What are we doing today?'"

For Clapton, illicit substances acted as a salve for his aching soul. While Paula Boyd had accompanied Clapton to Miami, she could sense that his heart wasn't in their relationship. Before long, she would fall into a relationship with Whitlock, which was fine with Clapton. By this point, Clapton and Pattie Boyd had taken up a clandestine affair. Things came to a head back in July at a party held by Stigwood, which the Harrisons had dutifully attended. The occasion was a gala event in honor of the West End premiere of Kenneth Tynan's bawdy *Oh! Calcutta!* It had been less than a month since the completion of the *All Things Must Pass* sessions and just twenty days since Harrison's mother had died. As if he could no longer contain himself, Clapton confessed his feelings about Boyd to Harrison. "I blurted the whole thing out to him: 'I'm in love with your wife.' The ensuing conversation bordered on the absurd. Although I think he was deeply hurt—I could see it in his eyes— he preferred to make light of it, almost turning it all into a Monty Python situation. I think he was relieved in some way, though, because I'm sure all the time he knew what had been going on, and now I was finally owning up to it." But even still, Boyd steadfastly refused to abandon her husband. Clapton could now sate himself with her love—but it would have to be on the margins of her life at Friar Park with Harrison. During this same period, Clapton left a cryptic note for Boyd, addressing it to "Dearest L." With Alice Ormsby-Gore having long departed from his life, was there a new Layla in Clapton's personal mythos?

And as it happened, Clapton actually had a spate of new songs to unveil for Dowd in Miami. But first, Derek and the Dominos' fate took an unexpected turn. On the same day that the band began working at Criteria, the Allman Brothers Band were in Miami to perform a benefit concert. Earlier that afternoon, Duane Allman had renewed his interest to Dowd about observing the Dominos' sessions in the studio. When the producer informed Clapton about Allman's plans to take in one of the sessions, Clapton answered, "You mean that guy who plays on the back of 'Hey Jude'?" in reference to Allman's soulful guitar solo on Wilson Pickett's hit cover version of the Beatles' classic song. During that same session with Pickett, Allman had apparently earned the nickname "Skydog," because of his soaring guitar work, although others would suggest that the name actually derived from his ability to become "sky-high" via his frequent drug usage.

In short order, Dowd arranged for Clapton and his mates to attend the Allman Brothers' August 26 show. The Coconut Grove benefit called for the group to perform on a flatbed truck with sandbags acting as a barrier against the crowd. After the concert began, Clapton and the other Dominos crawled in front of the stage, leaned back against the sandbags, and soaked up Allman's performance. "It was just really magical, you know," Clapton recalled later. "There was like the perfect kind of weather—it was dark, it was balmy and hot and there was a strong breeze. They all had really, really long hair—right down to their waists, almost—it was blowing back in the wind, and it was so picturesque." At one point, Allman caught a glimpse of old Slowhand himself sitting in front of the stage, and he could scarcely believe his eyes. For his part, Clapton was impressed with Allman's skillful and passionate approach to the guitar. Clapton admired his "air of complete conviction, and although he didn't sing, I felt sure he was the leader of the band, just by his body language."

Hours later, the Allman Brothers joined the Dominos at Criteria for a late-night jam session. For the occasion, Duane Allman played his gold-top 1957 Gibson Les Paul, while Clapton performed with "Brownie," his 1956 Fender

Stratocaster. Dowd was awestruck by the experience of watching Clapton and Allman become familiar with each other's playing style: "They were trading licks, they were swapping guitars. They were talking shop and information and having a ball—no holds barred, just admiration for each other's technique and facility." Even more astoundingly, the jam session stretched on for hours, captured for posterity by Dowd's team in the control room, who kept the tape running as they had been instructed by Clapton and Whitlock at the outset. "They went on for 15, 18 hours like that," Dowd recalled. "I went through two or three sets of engineers."

The August 27 recordings found a band—two *separate* bands, really—coming together and becoming lost in the thrall of music-making. Up first was the "Key of D Jam," in which the Dominos and the Allman Brothers Band joined forces. It was nothing short of an all-star rock 'n' roll revue, with the triple lead guitars of Clapton, Duane Allman, and Dickey Betts locking horns with Whitlock and Gregg Allman on keyboards, Berry Oakley on bass, and Butch Trucks on the drums. "We were invited to come jam, that was it," Trucks later recalled. "It was just loose and fun—like whoever felt like it would pick up an instrument and start playing—at one point, Jim Gordon got off the drums and I just went back there and started banging on them and we played a few shuffles. It was completely spontaneous—every once in a while we'd stop and talk, and they'd play us some of the songs they had recorded, then someone would pick up an instrument and start playing again."

By the time that the assembled musicians attempted a third jam during that incredible daylong session, the other members of the Allman Brothers Band had called it a night, leaving the Dominos in a five-piece lineup that included Clapton, Duane Allman, Whitlock, Radle, and Gordon. And the tunes kept on coming. For a time, the band settled into extended jams associated with "Tell the Truth," which still felt unfinished, at least as far as Clapton was concerned, before trying their hand at "Tender Love" and Tampa Red's old blues classic "(When Things Go Wrong) It Hurts Me Too." For the latter song, Clapton and Allman brought the day's whirlwind session to a close with a guitar duet.

To Clapton, the all-night session had been a revelation in more ways than one. Having lost the services of Dave Mason earlier in the summer, Clapton had been content to be the Dominos' lone guitarist. But quite suddenly, those plans were all for naught. According to Whitlock, Clapton could hardly contain his excitement about Allman's incredible talent, saying, "Let's get him to play on our record—do the whole thing." As with Whitlock, Trucks could tell that Clapton and Allman had fallen into sync right before their eyes. "They just went off like a firecracker—you could tell, it was like long-lost brothers had found each other. As soon as they met they sat down and started talking about Robert Johnson. At the time that they met, I don't think either had met another guitar player that was so immersed into Robert Johnson." Years later, Clapton remembered strategizing about how to rope Allman into the Dominos' project. "I kept thinking up ways to keep him in the room. 'We could do this. Do you know this one?' Of course, he knew everything that I would say, and we'd just do it—a lot of those things like 'Key to the Highway' and 'Nobody Knows You When You're Down and Out.'"

When Clapton finally got up the nerve to ask Allman if he would perform on the Dominos' album, Allman heartily accepted. Derek and the Dominos would have twin leads, after all. As Allman recalled, Clapton turned to him and said, "Okay, man. We're going to make us a record here." With Allman sitting in with the band, Clapton felt that the Dominos now enjoyed the right chemistry to produce what he considered, even while they were still working in Miami, to be his signature album—the blues effusion that he had always hoped to create. Indeed, Clapton had told Whitlock that the LP would be "the epitome" of his career. For his part, Whitlock was impressed with Clapton's candor, although he couldn't help thinking that "it's what you'd expect to hear a guy say when he's 70, not 25."

At just twenty-three years old, Allman was thrilled with the opportunity to cut some tracks in the studio with the Dominos, although his obligations to the Allman Brothers Band precluded any commitment beyond the current LP. Even still, when Clapton suggested something more long-term, Allman gave membership in Derek and the Dominos some thought. Allman Brothers drummer Butch Trucks remembered "a conversation or two with Duane because Eric offered him the job to come on the road and be a part of the Dominos, and Duane was considering it." But as Trucks was quick to note, "I said, 'Duane are you ready to go out and follow somebody else? We've worked hard—the Allman Brothers are really, really locking in.'"

When the Dominos got back to work on the afternoon of August 28, Allman's value to the band revealed itself almost immediately. Up first was "Tell the Truth." The group was still unsatisfied with Spector's version. With Dowd in the control room, they remade the song. With his trademark Coricidin bottle at the ready, Allman's slide-guitar playing afforded the song with previously unrealized textures. Clapton simply couldn't believe his ears. Allman's bottleneck style was so innovative that it took the entire slide-guitar genre "to another place" altogether. "There were few people playing electric slide that were doing anything new; it was just the Elmore James licks, and everyone knows those," Clapton recalled. "No one was opening it up until Duane showed up and played it a completely different way." That different way of playing struck Clapton, ardent traditionalist, at right angles, but even if he couldn't engage with Allman's approach, Clapton recognized immediately how the tension between their styles served as a catalyst for great music. "For a start," Clapton recalled, "he would play in straight tuning a lot of the time. I mean, I couldn't understand it. He would do—I really don't know how to describe it—but he would hit this seventh thing all the time, which I actually didn't approve of . . . every now and then we would argue about stuff like this because . . . I only believe that you should really play what had gone down before—which jived in a way with why I liked him, because I loved the fact that he was an improviser. He threw away any tradition a lot of the time, but for me that was really quite . . . sort of . . . inappropriate." During his early years, Allman played slide guitar with a water glass. That all changed in Muscle Shoals in 1968. Musician Johnny Wyker remembered casing "several drug stores with Duane in the Shoals, and we'd ask the pharmacist if Duane could look through his empty bottles." Afterward, "we'd sit on the floor and dig through the boxes, and Duane would try out different bottles as a slide. He finally settled on the Coricidin bottle."

Clapton had been so moved by Allman's performance on the revamped "Tell the Truth" that he telephoned Stigwood back in the UK and asked him to pull the "Tell the Truth" b/w "Roll It Over" single from distribution. The single was scheduled for release in the UK and US on September 4 and September 14, respectively. Not only was the new version of "Tell the Truth" clearly elevated by Allman's musicianship, but it also saw Clapton and the band altering the song's tempo dramatically from their speedier effort with Spector back in late June.

With Allman on board, Clapton wasted little time in taking advantage of his new recruit's talents, realizing full well that in a matter of days the Allman Brothers Band would be traveling hither and yon. Up first was a live master take of Clapton's old Big Bill Broonzy favorite "Key to the Highway," followed by a mammoth August 31 session, during which the Dominos knocked out three more cuts, including the Jimmy Cox blues classic "Nobody Knows You When You're Down and Out," the Clapton and Whitlock original "Why Does Love Got to Be So Sad," and "Have You Ever Loved a Woman," which Clapton had recorded with Mayall and the Bluesbreakers back in 1965. During the recording of "Nobody Knows You When You're Down and Out," Albhy Galuten sat in on piano while Whitlock played the organ. For Clapton, the track was a welcome opportunity to dive into the fingerpicking style that he had studied all those years ago during his apprenticeship with his Grundig tape recorder back in Ripley. With Allman in tow, the Dominos quickly discovered that their hard-living ways had nothing on the Allman Brothers' lead guitarist. Whitlock looked on with a certain kind of awe one evening as Allman picked up the telephone, businesslike, and began "scoring coke and hookers." And these were "not just any hookers either," Whitlock later recalled. "They had to be imports from Macon."

On September 1, the Allman-inflected Dominos tried their hand at a newly concocted Clapton and Whitlock original, "Keep On Growing," complete with Clapton and Whitlock's lead vocals and Clapton overdubbing a pair of lead-guitar tracks. Suddenly in need of lyrics, Whitlock slipped out of the session and hastily penned the words to "Keep On Growing." As he later recalled, "It was like I was expressing my relatively short, inexperienced life. And when I was through writing, I went back into the studio. Eric and Tom were in the control room, and I said, 'Hit record.' I got halfway through the first verse, and I said, 'Stop!' I said, 'Come out here and sing this with me, Eric. Let's do our Sam & Dave thing.' And he did, and it just happened like that. It's exactly what you hear on the recording." Meanwhile, Clapton superimposed additional slide-guitar tracks onto "Tell the Truth," which led Allman to quip that "Eric is coming along on his slide. He's doing okay." He added in jest, "He ain't no Duane Allman of the slide guitar, but he's doing all right!" Allman polished off the evening by overdubbing a new lead guitar part onto "Why Does Love Got to Be So Sad."

With Allman on the verge of having to take a hiatus from the sessions to hit the road with the Allman Brothers Band, the Dominos turned in a banner day on September 2. That afternoon, they engaged in a lengthy blues jam before turning to the Clapton and Whitlock tune "I Looked Away," one of Clapton's most pointed—and poignant—compositions about Pattie Boyd. Overbrimming with regret, Clapton sings, "She took my hand / And tried to make me understand / That she would always be there." But when he "looked away," Clapton laments, she made her escape, leaving him awash in his loneliness. After overdubbing congas and tambourine onto "Keep On Growing," the band turned to the standout Clapton and Whitlock tune "Bell Bottom Blues." The song's lyrics had also been inspired by Boyd, who had asked Clapton to bring her a pair of hip-hugging Landlubber bell-bottom blue jeans from the States. Arguably his most tortured song about Boyd, this song finds Clapton teetering with heartbreaking abandon, singing "I don't want to fade away" against a wall of mournful guitars. During the bridge, he exposes his aching heart, singing, "Do you want to see me crawl across the floor to you? / Do you want to hear me beg you to take me back?"

For Whitlock, the September 2 session had been a marvel. As he later recalled, "After recording 'I Looked Away' and 'Bell Bottom Blues,' we were jamming on this thing with a kind of Latin beat, and it was just really great. And when we were finished, Eric said, 'I want to put another guitar on this,' and he put on a second part without even listening to the first part he'd recorded." Whitlock realized that during the jam, all Clapton had been "listening to the whole time was bass, drums and organ. And when he was done with that, he did it again. And I'll be damned if he didn't do it again! And all he was doing was putting in sporadic notes here and there. And I was thinking, 'He's got something going on.'" And Clapton did, of course. "When he was done," Whitlock concluded, "I think there were five guitars on there in the end—everybody was like racehorses at the starting gate, just waiting to shove those faders up to see what this sounded like. And when they did—whoa, boy! It all fit together like cogs in a wheel. It was amazing."

On September 3, Allman rejoined the Dominos and they took up Clapton's "I Am Yours," which featured lyrics that Clapton had drawn verbatim from Nizami Ganjavi's poem about the legend of Layla and Majnun. In point of fact, the composition owed such a debt to the Persian writer that Clapton gave the twelfth-century poet cowriting credit:

There blows no wind, but wafts your scent to me
There sings no bird, but calls your name to me
Each memory that has left its trace with me
Lingers forever as a part of me

After recording the basic track for "I Am Yours," the Dominos recorded the Clapton and Whitlock original "Anyday," the first song that they had attempted after they arrived in Miami. After overdubbing tambourine and maracas to the song, the band rounded out the day with a stab at "It's Too Late," the Chuck Willis country blues classic. Dowd had engineered the song for Willis back in 1956, but it was Radle who suggested that they record a cover version of "It's Too Late." As Dowd later recalled, "Carl Radle was into Chuck Willis, so we dug out a bunch of Chuck Willis records which is how 'It's Too Late' made it onto *Layla*." But in Whitlock's memory, the Dominos had something up their sleeve when they recorded "It's Too Late." Years later, he recalled that "We wanted to do Johnny Cash's TV show and in order to get on it, it helped if you were a country act and definitely not a rock 'n' roll act. So we decided to do 'It's Too Late' just as a demonstration of this is who we are and what we can sound like, to get on the show." And the gambit succeeded. In November, the Dominos performed the song on *The Johnny Cash Show*, the popular weekly variety program that was recorded at Nashville's Ryman Auditorium. When he introduced the Dominos' cover version of "It's Too Late" during the November 5 episode of his show, Cash quipped that "if you detect some country blues pickin' in the song you're about to hear—you're right."

On September 4, Allman was forced to take yet another hiatus. That evening, the Allman Brothers performed a show in Milwaukee, Wisconsin, followed by a September 12 gig at the University of Texas at Austin. On September 20, the Allman Brothers Band were scheduled to resume their ongoing American tour with a date at RFK Stadium in Washington, DC, which meant a hard stop as far as Allman's work with the Dominos was concerned. But as events would shortly demonstrate, it left all the time the guitarist would need to leave an indelible impact on the album. As for Clapton, he understood Allman's dilemma, even though he sincerely wished that Allman could become a more permanent fixture in his universe. "I knew that sooner or later he was going to go back to the Allmans, but I wanted to steal him! I tried, and [later] he actually came on a few gigs, too. But then he had to say, almost like a woman, 'Well, you know, I am actually married to this band, and I can't stay with you.' I was really quite heartbroken! I'd got really used to him."

On September 4, the Dominos took advantage of Allman's absence to record a host of overdubs. After superimposing Whitlock's vocals onto "I Looked Away," Dowd supervised the doubling of Clapton and Whitlock's harmonies on "Bell Bottom Blues." For "I Am Yours," Whitlock recorded a third harmony vocal, while Gordon overdubbed a tabla part. Later that evening, Radle would add cowbell and toms to "Tell the Truth." But the session's clear highlight involved the superimposition of Clapton and Whitlock's new lead vocals for "Anyday" and "Why Does Love Got to Be So Sad," with the duo taking another stab at their Sam & Dave revue. The latter song, as Christopher Scapelliti has astutely observed, not only captured the essence of Clapton and Boyd's relationship, such as it was at the time, but also provided what might very well have been an apt subtitle for the album.

For the Dominos, the September 5 session was rather slight, with Clapton and Whitlock overdubbing new vocals onto "Keep On Growing." Criteria Studio would be dark until Wednesday, September 9, a day of work that would define the eventual album for all time. Allman had now rejoined the band, and Dowd and the Dominos took full advantage of his presence, returning to songs like "Keep On Growing" and "Bell Bottom Blues," both of which saw further refinements and superimpositions. For "Keep On Growing," Clapton recorded a new lead guitar track and Gordon added a host of percussion adornments. Meanwhile, Clapton tinkered with his lead vocals on "Bell Bottom Blues," particularly on the second verse, where he had flubbed a few words.

But the real action occurred later that evening, when Clapton and Allman engaged in some of the finest twin lead guitar work ever captured on record. As Dowd would later recall, "There had to be some sort of telepathy going on because I've never seen spontaneous inspiration happen at that rate and level. One of them would play something, and the other reacted instantaneously. Never once did either of them have to say, 'Could you play that again, please?' It was like two hands in a glove. And they got tremendously off on playing with each other."

Clapton would later describe his interplay with Allman in language that oddly mirrored the way he spoke of his own longings for Pattie Boyd, suggesting how diffuse the British guitarist's passions were. "I'd kind of fallen in love with Duane," Clapton recalled. "I mean, I was even ignoring my own band, you know. We were just kind of having this musical affair in front of everybody." Gregg Allman attended many of the sessions as an observer, no doubt wondering if he was witnessing his brother in the process of leaving one band and join another, but Clapton scarcely took notice of him.

Up first on September 9 was a cover version of Jimi Hendrix's dreamy "Little Wing," which the Dominos transformed into a sizzling blues anthem. For the song, Clapton and Whitlock provided passionate lead vocals arrayed against the searing guitar work of Clapton and Allman. The result was a wall of electric, hard-edge sound. Whitlock had known the legendary American guitar hero from his Delaney & Bonnie days, recalling that "Jimi Hendrix had sat in with us a couple of times when we were out playing, so I knew him and had met him. Eric wanted to do 'Little Wing' as a tribute, because he really revered Jimi Hendrix." While he was well acquainted with Hendrix, Whitlock wasn't very familiar with the intricacies of "Little Wing." "I was writing out the chord sheet and lyrics for myself when Eric and Duane were working out their parts," he recalled. "We played the song part way through to get the balance [levels], and then it was 'roll tape.' And it was first take. Done." As for the Dominos' version of "Little Wing," Allman fashioned a high-octane three-chord riff to launch the song, "a central memorable motif," in Scapelliti's words, "that was missing from Hendrix's recording, turning the gentle ballad into a mammoth blues-rocker that is among *Layla*'s most powerful cuts." For his part, Clapton couldn't wait to present Hendrix an acetate of the song as his greatest possible tribute to the sublime guitarist—the veritable "force to be reckoned with" that he had first met back in October 1966.

With "Little Wing" having been captured in an economic single take, the Dominos turned to the album's centerpiece. At this juncture, the Dominos were ready to take up the album's title track, which Clapton had begun back at Hurtwood Edge during the previous summer. As he later recalled, when the Dominos arrived in Miami, "Layla" was little more than a "framework." But even still, he knew that it "was the key song, a conscious attempt to speak to Pattie about the fact that she was holding off and wouldn't come and move in with me." In its original form, Clapton had composed "Layla" as a slow guitar ballad, the tender story of how the Layla of his life and song had rendered him impotent in the face of her otherworldly beauty:

> Layla, you've got me on my knees
> Layla, I'm begging, darling please
> Layla, darling won't you ease my worried mind

But all that changed on September 5, when Allman, after hearing Clapton's impassioned lyrics for the first time, began playing a lick from blues great Albert King's "As the Years Go Passing By." In particular, he highlighted the first seven notes associated with King's vocal introduction, "There is nothing I can do if you leave me here to cry." As Whitlock remembered, "Duane suggested it, and he came up with it. We already had the song together, but it just started out completely different when we worked it up in England. And Duane said, 'How about starting it this way?'" At this point, Clapton recommended that Allman try playing the seven-note lick in double time. The result was a fiery, arresting lick. In the space of a few minutes, "Layla" had shifted from a tender ballad into a rock 'n' roll anthem.

For the song's basic track, Dowd and the band selected take eleven as the best version of "Layla." The Dominos' standard lineup dominated the take, with Clapton playing rhythm guitar, Allman handling the guitar solos, Whitlock playing organ, Radle playing bass, and Gordon playing the drums. They began superimposing overdubs almost immediately, with Gordon adding tambourine, Clapton and Allman playing a fusillade of solos, and Clapton layering additional guitar harmonies into the mix. As Dowd later recalled, the interplay between Clapton and Allman on "Layla" was "sublime," a masterwork of passion and intensity. As it happened, the incredible session at Criteria wasn't yet completed. Before the night was out, Clapton overdubbed a new lead vocal onto "It's Too Late," along with Whitlock's lead and harmony vocals, while Gordon added a shaker to the percussion track for "I Am Yours."

The next day, Thursday, September 10, Dowd and the Dominos brought the principal recording work for Layla to an end scarcely two weeks after they had begun working together in Miami. As Whitlock later recalled, it was Clapton's idea to record one more song. It was in the wee hours of the morning after they had wrapped up the title track. "Afterward, we were in the foyer just having a drink," Whitlock later remarked, "and Eric said, 'We've got room for one more on this'—because it was going to be a double-album. 'Why don't you do 'Thorn Tree'?'" Whitlock had composed "Thorn Tree in the Garden," a heartbreaking tune about love and loss, during his years with Delaney & Bonnie. For a while, he had lived communally with the Bramletts and a host of others at "The Plantation." Things came to a head when Whitlock brought home a dog and cat to live with them. When his roommates demurred, feeling that the Bramlett house was already overcrowded as it was, Whitlock found a foster home for the cat, which he had named Peaches. But he was devastated to discover that, in his absence, his housemates had given away Bekka, the dog. To soothe his aching heart, Whitlock channeled his energies into composing a song about a lost lover, and "Thorn Tree in the Garden" was born.

For the band's first pass at the song, Dowd assembled the group "sitting in a circle with two omni-directional mikes in the center, and they sang and played the whole thing live." With Whitlock handling lead vocals, Clapton and Allman took up their acoustic guitars for the song's gentle, ethereal musical accompaniment, complete with harmonics. Gordon would later superimpose a triangle part onto the song, but it went unused. "Thorn Tree in the Garden" had been brought to fruition in a single, magnificent take. As Whitlock later recalled, "Tom said that this was the most perfect stereo recording he ever made. Just like the whole record." With "Thorn Tree in the Garden" in the can, the Dominos took their leave from Criteria and returned to England for a brief respite and a weeklong tour, having already made plans to return to Miami at the beginning of October to sew up any loose ends with Dowd.

Unbeknownst to the other members of the band, Clapton was already falling into a familiar pattern—if only in his mind. It was the same urge for self-abandonment that had plagued his stints with the Yardbirds, the Bluesbreakers, Cream, and, most recently, Blind Faith. Only this time, his yen for escape was exacerbated by heavy drug abuse. As Clapton later wrote, "By the time I got back to America, my heart was no longer in the Dominos. We had scored masses of coke and smack before we left Florida and took it on tour with us. With the amount of drugs we were taking every day, I really don't know how we got through that tour alive, and by the time we came back to England, we were all on the path to becoming full-blown addicts." Things went from bad to worse for Clapton later that month. He had been excited to share an acetate of the Dominos' cover version of "Little Wing" with Hendrix. On September 16, he had even found a present to go along with the recording: "One afternoon I was browsing through some instrument shops in the West End when I saw this white, left-handed Stratocaster, and I bought it on impulse to give to Jimi." At first, he planned to gift the guitar to Hendrix after a Sly and the Family Stone concert at the Lyceum, where he expected to see him. "But he never turned up," Clapton later wrote, and soon thereafter he received the awful news that Hendrix had died from an overdose. "It was the first time the death of another musician really affected me," said Clapton. "We had all felt obliterated when Buddy Holly died, but this was much more personal. I was incredibly upset and very angry, and was filled with a feeling of terrible loneliness."

Thunderstruck, Clapton and the Dominos made their return to Miami in time for the October 1 rendezvous with Dowd at Criterion. The band had just concluded a September 28 show at Manchester's Free Trade Hall, and they were due back in the UK for an October 3 gig in Norwich. Time was clearly of the essence, and for all of his despair over Hendrix's untimely death, Clapton was on a mission. To his mind, "Layla" still seemed unfinished. As it happened, the idea for bringing the song to a close arrived in the form of a piano riff that he had heard Gordon playing back in September on the Criteria studio grand. To Clapton's ears, the wistful piano tune seemed like the perfect means for providing "Layla" with a coda and resolving the tension inherent in the title track's *Sturm und Drang* in one fell swoop.

But Whitlock wasn't so sure. First, he felt that "Thorn Tree in the Garden" already fulfilled this purpose, given the gentle song's placement directly after the rock 'n' roll climax of "Layla" in its current form. Second, Whitlock was already familiar with Gordon's piano riff, having witnessed the drummer in the act of composing it in the company of his former girlfriend, singer-songwriter Rita Coolidge. Whitlock recalled Gordon and Coolidge playing a song "called 'Time,' back in the Delaney & Bonnie days." He said, "They wanted me to play piano on it, with Rita singing. But I told them, 'I don't feel this at all.'" Suddenly, Whitlock found himself at odds with the very same melody. "Eric wanted to add it to the end of what we'd recorded for 'Layla,'" he lamented, "and I was totally against it. It didn't seem like it was part of anything that we were doing." There was a third and final factor that influenced Whitlock's thinking vis-à-vis the piano melody associated with

"Time." When he heard Gordon performing the solo in Clapton's earshot, he knew that the song actually belonged to Coolidge. "The nature of its origin," Whitlock later wrote in defense of Coolidge, who didn't receive songwriting credit for her efforts, "taints the integrity of this beautiful song ['Layla'] that Eric wrote all by himself." As it happened, Coolidge didn't take the situation lightly. When she heard "Layla" and the "Piano Exit" for the first time in 1971, she recognized "Time" immediately. She contacted Stigwood, who bluntly responded by saying, "What are you gonna do? You're a girl. You don't have money to fight this."

But Whitlock was utterly devoted to Clapton, and he would do anything in his power to see the guitarist's vision for the album become reality, no matter how much he may have disagreed with the inclusion of "Time" as the coda for "Layla." In fact, Whitlock even performed a second keyboard track on the "Piano Exit," as it came to be known, in order to afford Gordon's melody with more grandiosity. "Gordon was playing these octaves that were just straight and hard-sounding," said Whitlock. "It needed feeling." The coda was highlighted by Clapton and Allman's dueling slide-guitar work, as well as layer upon layer of complementary guitar tracks. All told, the mix included six guitar tracks. According to Dowd, "There's an Eric rhythm part, three tracks of Eric playing harmony with himself on the main riff; one of Duane playing that beautiful bottleneck; and one of Duane and Eric locked up, playing countermelodies." The twin slide-guitar parts as performed by Clapton and Allman often leave listeners shaking their heads as they attempt to discern the difference between the two players. Fortunately, Allman saw fit to bring some clarity to the matter, pointing out that "Eric gets more of an open, slidey sound. But here's the way to really tell: He played the Fender, and I played the Gibson." The song finally reaches its conclusion as the guitarists' sweeping countermelodies coalesce into a moment of pure bliss. At this point, Allman brings the track to fruition with his trademark "bird call," which he performed on the slide with his trusty Coricidin bottle. As Dowd later recalled, Allman "brought his bottle down behind the bridge and then he hit a harmonic on it."

When it came time to append overdubs to the "Piano Exit," Clapton superimposed a Leslied guitar part while Gordon adorned the section with an array of percussion—most notably, a series of dramatic cymbal crashes and swells. At this juncture, Dowd was left with the task of editing the two sections of "Layla" together. As Dowd came to discover, this would be no easy feat, later explaining that "when they wanted to add on the finale, we had to go back and get as close as we could to the original mix up to the point they liked, then figure out how to cut in this other part. I think I wired two or three tapes together to get the transition the way it was supposed to go, then readjust[ed] the front end to fit the back end." To effect the edit, Dowd likely pitched the first half of the song slightly sharp in order to accommodate the shift into the "Piano Exit." As Scapelliti pointed out, "What's particularly evident is that Allman's slide guitar, which is in tune for the first half of the song, is decidedly flat for the piano coda." With Dowd having succeeded in editing the two sections together, "Layla" was once and truly complete.

On the same day that they recorded the "Piano Exit," Clapton overdubbed a new bridge vocal onto "It's Too Late." During this period of his career, Clapton was still very self-conscious about his singing abilities, a fact that was not lost on Dowd. In the waning hours of the album's production, Clapton had even exhorted the producer to quiet his lead vocals, which he believed to have been mixed too loud. Dowd retorted by saying, "You don't realize that your record is going to get played on the radio alongside Mick Jagger or whomever and the vocal has to be out in front. Eric's biggest problem was his insecurity about his singing, but he was a brilliant singer. I knew from *Disraeli*, where there were songs when he and Jack would alternate lines," the producer continued, and "you couldn't tell the difference." Dowd's opinion held sway, and the record was complete, save for an October 2 session in which the Dominos rehearsed a cover version of Walter Jacobs's "Mean Old World," which didn't make the LP's final cut.

By the time the Dominos winged their way back to the UK to complete the British leg of their ongoing tour, the sequencing and package design for *Layla* had already been settled. In point of fact, Clapton and Whitlock had made many of the decisions back at Hurtwood Edge before the band had first alighted in Miami. In later years, Whitlock liked to believe that "every song on the album is in the order that we recorded it," but the studio records at Criteria simply don't support such a conclusion. At one point, Galuten attempted to underscore Whitlock's belief, remarking that "the stuff was recorded in chronological order—the same as on the album. I remember it was kind of important to Eric that the album be in the order in which it was recorded. But if you're going by the dates on the track sheets, it may not look that way." The evolution of the album's title is far more certain. As Whitlock later recalled, "Eric and I we were sitting in a room at the Thunderbird, [and] we knew that *Layla* was the title. I had some chocolate 'All Sorts' in my lap. I looked at the box and said, 'what about "and other assorted love songs"?' He said, 'Sounds good to me.'" As for *Layla and Other Assorted Love Songs'* cover art, Clapton had had a painting in mind since the Dominos' early August visit to Biot, where they stayed in a home in the French countryside owned by the son of renowned painter Baron Théodore Émile Frandsen de Schoenberg. Entitled *La Fille au Bouquet,* the painting depicted an attractive, blonde-haired woman who, for Clapton and the bandmates alike, was the spitting image of Pattie Boyd. During that same visit, Clapton led the group in a high-spirited egg fight in Émile's kitchen. For Kevin Harrington, who had only notched a few dates on his maiden voyage as a professional roadie, it made for an incredible scene. Fueled by "general mayhem, drunkenness, and drugs," Clapton and the band engaged in a food fight of epic proportions. By the time that the culinary skirmish had abated, Harrington recalled, "the kitchen was left in a state of ruin." To commemorate the episode, the liner notes for *Layla* offer thanks to "Émile for the abuse of his house."

By the time the Dominos took the stage on October 3 at the Norwich Lads Club, a provincial boxing gymnasium, *Layla and Other Assorted Love Songs* was ready to go into production for a November 9 release date. All told, the album had taken slightly over two weeks to record, mix, and master for distribution. The same couldn't be said for Harrison's *All Things Must Pass,* which had begun production back in May and was still mired in a protracted postproduction phase. Harrison had his heart set on a late October release, but at the moment, there was no end in sight.

10 | LET IT ROLL

IN 1980, A JOURNALIST asked Dee Dee Kennibrew, former background singer in the Crystals (one of the girl groups Spector had produced), what she thought of the Wall of Sound. "The voices suffered a lot," said Kennibrew, "and it took away from our voices because they added in more music. If he wanted to make a Wall of Sound, why not make a Wall of Voices? He could have put in more voices instead of putting in four pianos."

On Wednesday, September 2, 1970, George Harrison returned to Trident Studios to begin the last leg of recording for his album. As he entered the home stretch with *All Things Must Pass*, the inevitable questions about a Beatles reunion were already beginning to plague the former bandmates. On August 29, *Melody Maker* published an open letter from McCartney in which he wrote, "Dear Mailbag, In order to put out of its misery the limping dog of a news story which has been dragging itself across your pages for the past year, my answer to the question, 'Will the Beatles get together again?' . . . is no." For Harrison, any potential work with his former mates was decidedly on the backburner. Once engineer Ken Scott transferred the necessary eight-track tapes from EMI to sixteen track, Harrison had eight more tracks at his disposal for overdubs. But even with all of this extra space, his vision was so expansive that he would still stretch this technology well past its limits. As he considered the work ahead on what would become the album's centerpiece, he may have wondered the same as Kennibrew: why not make a Wall of Voices?

Harrison hadn't touched "My Sweet Lord" since recording the basic rhythm track back in May, almost three and a half months earlier. While there's no indication of when he decided he wanted layers and layers of harmony back- ing vocals on the song, he'd already done a small-scale version of this on "Apple Scruffs" at the end of July, overdubbing his voice repeatedly as Phil McDonald bounced the recording from one track to another with each pass. Now he would take that technique and multiply it tenfold. Ken Scott recalled the process: "We'd do four or six tracks of him singing a line and I'd bounce all of those down to one track. Then he'd do a harmony several times and I'd bounce those to another track. Then we'd bounce those two together at the same time as we were doing yet another backing vocal. It was painstaking but it sounded amazing in the end."

In particular, "George's big thing was backing vocals," said Scott. "On 'My Sweet Lord,' all of the backing vocals were him. There are some, the really high ones, where we slowed the tape down so he could do it, then came back to normal speed. You hear them on their own and it's hysterical. It's Mickey Mouse. He was confident, but we still did take after take." As recording history demonstrates, the Beatles had always put a remarkable amount of effort into their vocal harmonies. As early as "I Saw Her Standing There" and "There's a Place," the push and pull of Lennon and McCartney's vocals often created a compelling tension at the heart of each song. The three-part harmonies, regu- larly overdubbed a second time once they had moved to four-track, provided a warmth to "In My Life," "Nowhere Man," "If I Needed Someone," and many others, which rivaled the harmonies of the Beach Boys. From 1965 onward, their vocal parts grew in complexity; on "Paperback Writer" in 1966, they triple-tracked the intro vocals, a technique they repeated to much different effect (though admittedly orchestrated by George Martin) on "Because" in 1969, for a lush nine-part harmony.

As Beatle Second Class during the Fab Four's studio years, Harrison had invested much more time and energy in Lennon and McCartney's songs than his own. As a result, he learned quickly how to blend in on three-part har- monies while adding his own distinctive colorations. It was Harrison, after all, who introduced the idea of ending "She Loves You" with the G-E-D harmony, bringing the curtain down on the exuberant little rocker with an unexpectedly satisfying sixth chord. Though he'd been pushed into the role of supporting player so often even as he yearned deep down to be given even a bit of the spotlight for his own songs, those supporting skills served him well now that he was on his own, meaning he could handle both lead and harmony vocals easily. And he really *was* on his own at this point; Spector still wasn't back, so Harrison was also now effectively producing himself. Even if Spector still had to encourage him to push his voice up in the mix, Harrison was nonetheless fully in control of his powers as a harmony singer.

"I went down to Trident studios one day to do some more Moog stuff," said Chris Thomas. "I can't remember what it was for at all, can't remember if I played it, or if George played it. All I did was turn up with it and set it up. And when I walked into the room, there were all these voices, sounded like hundreds of guitars, hundreds of voices—this was the chorus of 'My Sweet Lord,' and George was there on his own. I remember walking in and hearing that and going, 'Wow. Who's doing that?' and George going, 'That's all me.'"

Not only were these backing vocals an impressive display of virtuosity, they also recalled the vocal chorus of the "Govinda" recording from February. More importantly, the lyrics this "Wall of George" sings draw a line right back to the very day he began composing the song, when he realized that "Hallelujah" and "Hare Krishna" had the same number of syllables. Through most of the backing vocals, he sings "Hallelujah" until the final chorus, where he switches to "Hare Krishna," then back again to the Christian name. For the song's coda, Harrison sings two Sanskrit prayers. The first is the more familiar *maha mantra*, or Hare Krishna Mantra, which appeared on the Radha Krishna single the previous year and which he used when chanting with his prayer beads. The second is the "Guru Stotram":

> *gurur brahmā gurur viṣṇuḥ gururdevo maheśvaraḥ*
> *guruḥ sākṣāt parabrahma tasmai śrī gurave namaḥ*
> [Guru is Brahmā. Guru is Viṣṇu. Guru is the Supreme Lord Śiva.
> Guru is both manifest Reality and the Absolute. Salutations to that
> glorious Guru.]

Literally, *Stotram* translates as "chant of praise," and the *Guru Stotram* names the holy trinity of Hinduism: Brahma (the creator), Vishnu (the preserver), and Lord Shiva (the destroyer). Just as he had exhorted listeners to do in "Awaiting for You All," in the backing vocals to what would become his most popular solo recording, Harrison is quite literally chanting the names of the Lord.

Although none of the other recordings would feature quite such painstaking multiplicity, Harrison layered his backing vocals repeatedly on many of the songs, including both versions of "Isn't It a Pity," "What Is Life?" and "Behind That Locked Door." This culminated on "Hear Me Lord," where he created a heavenly choir on a scale to match the hymnlike tone of the lyrics. Although Clapton and Whitlock had sung backing vocals on a few songs and a certain "Betty and Cyril" also contributed, these overdubbed choruses on the album were mostly composed of Harrison himself. And yet, rather than specify parts, he obscured even his own efforts by christening all these voices as "The George O'Hara Smith Singers." And still there was more. Unlike Lennon or McCartney, Harrison had really pushed himself to develop as an instrumentalist, and the slide guitar technique he had teased on the "Govinda" recording in February now blossomed fully. Either on acoustic or electric guitar, he applied his slide playing to ten songs on the album, embroidering another level of detail into an already rich tapestry.

While he had originally begun experimenting with the open tuning blues styles of his contemporaries, writing "Woman Don't You Cry for Me" during the Delaney & Bonnie tour, he soon found ways to apply his training on the sitar and his experience of Indian music in general. "I started playing slide," he recalled, "thinking maybe this is how I can come up with something that's half-decent. I got into doing corresponding guitar harmonies to the bedrock slide parts, double-tracking them, like on 'My Sweet Lord' and other portions of the *All Things Must Pass* album."

In 1992, Harrison said that "I remember Ravi Shankar brought an Indian musician to my house who played classical Indian music on a slide guitar. It's played like a lap steel and set up like a regular guitar, but the nut and bridges are cranked up, and it even has sympathetic drone strings, like a sitar. He played runs that were so precise and in perfect pitch, but so quick! He was rocking along, doing these really fast runs, it was unbelievable how much precision was involved. So there were various influences. But it would be precocious to compare myself with incredible musicians like that." John Barham elaborated on how both East and West overlapped in Harrison's slide playing:

> To the western ear, the outstanding characteristic of Indian sitar playing is the connection of melodic notes by use of *gamak* (the Hindi word which can be translated as glissando, portamamento, sliding). The use of *gamak* is common to all Indian music regardless

of instrument (except the harmonium which is typically used to accompany Indian vocal music). The main difference between the Indian use of *gamak* and the Western use of slide is that in Indian music an instrumentalist will frequently play an entire phrase using *gamak* technique. This includes (for example, on a sitar) several ascending and descending slides from a note produced by only one pluck of the string. In Western classical music the use of slide [glissando] in string playing is usually one slide to a note below or a note above. Typical is the opening bars of Mahler's fourth symphony and the long descending slide towards the ending of the Adagietto of his fifth symphony. Western folk music string playing is another story of course. In Indian music the performer's skill in using *gamak* is rated more highly than virtuoso speed, basically because *gamak* is closer to the human voice. In some ways country style slide playing, particularly Hawaiian, is similar to Indian *gamak* playing. So George's slide playing was influenced by both Western and Indian music.

In his August 19 letter, Spector had suggested a guitar solo for "My Sweet Lord," and, as he fashioned the part, Harrison brought to bear his melodic precision, his sense of harmony, and his inspirations from Indian music. "As opposed to his friend Eric Clapton," Klaus Voormann recalled in his memoir, "he was not a great improviser. He worked everything out note for note and then developed a real little solo melody which he, no matter how often he played it, only changed minimally." Spector recalled that "'My Sweet Lord' must have taken about twelve hours to overdub the guitar solos. He must have had that in triplicate, six-part harmony before we decided on two-part harmony."

By the time that the orchestral overdubs commenced at Trident—written and conducted by John Barham—Spector had returned to supervise, with both his ego and his sarcasm intact. "During one session," recalled Barham, "Phil was unhappy with the way I was conducting the string players. To make his point he told me that he didn't want his mother to like the strings.

I didn't like his tone, so I told him that I didn't want his mother to like the strings either. At this point George started falling about laughing without saying anything. George's laughter lightened the atmosphere, and Phil went down to the studio floor and gave me a conducting lesson. Years later when I read a short bio of Phil, it crossed my mind that Phil's mother and my great grandmother, who were both Ukrainian, might have seen the humorous side of this." Moreover, "Phil didn't make any verbal suggestions for conducting, but he did physically demonstrate. Phil's conducting was very physical, he used more of his body than I did, and after that lesson I began to do the same."

By this juncture, Harrison and his team had recorded the strings for "Beware of Darkness" and at least the horns for "All Things Must Pass" at Abbey Road, leaving the rest for the sixteen-track facilities at Trident. For the remaining string overdubs, Barham used the same configuration as "Darkness"—sixteen players—and in contrast to the loose sessions for the backing tracks, the orchestral recordings were necessarily organized and efficient. The brass and reeds would be overdubbed separately from the strings and would vary only slightly on each song. For "Art of Dying" and "Awaiting on You All," Barham wrote for two tenor saxes, a baritone sax, two trumpets, and a trombone. On "All Things Must Pass," he replaced the trumpets with two flügelhorns, giving the arrangement a more mellow sound. Greatest of all was the September 18 orchestral session for "Isn't It a Pity," which Barham scored for flute, oboe, two tenor saxes, two trumpets, two trombones, tuba, timpani, and a string ensemble of twenty-two players—thirty-two musicians in all. Later that day, Barham used the same number of string players for "My Sweet Lord."

Some other scoring ideas didn't make the final cut. On "Let It Down," Harrison asked for high-energy strings playing a descending part during the intro and choruses, but ultimately mixed them out. "The energetic strings were meant to reflect and add to the energy of the basic backing track," recalled Barham of this part. "I think George and Phil's decision to leave them out was right, as, if mixed in, the track could have sounded chaotic and they might have obscured the melodic line."

The distinctive glissandi parts on the strings in the verses of "Let It Down" reveal how Harrison and John Barham worked on the orchestrations. "In preparing the string arrangements," Barham said, "George would sing and play ideas on the guitar. I can't remember the exact details about how these slides [glissandi] came about, but for me the string line was asking for it." Barham would give his own suggestions for the string and horn arrangements, but Harrison had many ideas himself. According to Barham, it was Harrison's suggestion to use the strings to play the riff, along with the guitar and bass, on "What Is Life?" This tripling of the part was a classic Spector touch.

On September 18, the same date as the orchestral recording for "Isn't It a Pity," Harrison attempted to add unusual brass and woodwind parts on "What Is Life?" He told *Billboard* in 2001, "I tried having this piccolo trumpet player like the guy who played on 'Penny Lane.' It wasn't actually the same bloke, but I wanted that sound. So I had an oboe and a piccolo trumpet, and I had this part for them all written out, but they couldn't play it the same; they couldn't do this kind of 'hush' phrase, and they played it very staccato like a classical player." John Barham had no memory of scoring these parts, meaning Harrison likely had Jim Price write them. Dissatisfied with the result, however, he decided not to use the overdub.

Although Spector had returned, he was not nearly as engaged as before. "When it came time to mix," Ken Scott recalled, "Phil had come back to England by then, but he would come in [late to the studio]. . . . George and I would start a mix about two o'clock in the afternoon. Around seven, say, when we'd got it fairly close to what we thought it should be, Phil would come in, we'd play it for him, he'd make some comments. Some we'd go along with, some we wouldn't. He'd eventually go, we'd finish the mix. George would go, I'd set up for the next day. We'd come in, two o'clock, start the next mix. And it was like that every day. So working with Phil on *All Things Must Pass*—very little."

Harrison's final embellishments to "My Sweet Lord" were a few strums across the strings of an autoharp. In mixing the song, he decided he wanted a longer, slower fade; the original performance had run to about the four-minute mark. "The conclusion," Ken Scott recalled, "was that I did a fade of the song that was about halfway finished when the song ended, then went back to the beginning of the ending section and continued the fade from the lower level to the end, finally editing the two together." Scott's fix extended the song to 4:39. While working on the final mixes with Scott and Spector, Harrison played the jams back and decided they were worthy of release. "I listened to that stuff," Harrison said in 2001, "and I thought, 'It's got some fire in it,' particularly Eric. He plays some hot stuff on there!" Even before mixing, Harrison had already begun considering what to do with the jams that had broken out during the recording sessions; according to a note in Mal Evans's diary, as early as July 1970 Harrison had pulled the tape for "Jam Peace," recorded at Apple Studios on March 29, 1969, during a session for Billy Preston, featuring Harrison, Clapton, Preston, Ginger Baker, and Klaus Voormann. Harrison added Moog overdubs during mixing, and while John Lennon and Yoko Ono had written "Plastic Ono Band" on the tape box, intending to use it themselves, Harrison now reclaimed the recording for himself, naming it "I Remember Jeep" after Clapton's dog, Jeep. Along with "Out of the Blue," "Thanks for the Pepperoni," and "Plug Me In," this would constitute another full disc of music. But a two-disc set for the album would be costly enough. Could he dare include a *third* LP?

Not surprisingly, EMI pushed back. Recording engineer Betty Cantor-Jackson, who was working on an album at Trident at the time for a band called Stoneground, remembered Harrison saying the record company wouldn't let him do a three-record set because "the price will be too high. People won't buy it." Cantor-Jackson responded in Harrison's favor, countering that "well, Jesus, you've got enough money. Why don't you put out three and charge for two then? What the hell. You can afford it."

On September 19—one day removed from the Dominos' completion of the first leg of production for *Layla* down in Florida—Harrison appeared with Ravi Shankar at the Festival of Arts of India concert. Determined to win acceptance for Eastern music, Harrison was in attendance to lend his celebrity to promote the festival, which was held at London's Royal Festival Hall. During this same period, he met with Apple Creative Director Allan Steckler in order to play a preliminary mix of *All Things Must Pass* for his consideration. Steckler would never forget the experience, recalling that "I listened to it, and I was stunned. It was awesome." Meanwhile, "George sat shyly alongside him, almost frightened to meet his gaze. When it was over, Steckler said, 'George, that's the most amazing album I've heard.'" For his part, Harrison seemed skeptical about Steckler's response. He "looked startled, then bemused, then finally suspicious, as if he might be the subject of an elaborate joke. 'Really?' he muttered at last."

With all the tracks now mixed, Harrison began final work on the album at Abbey Road with an October release date in mind. The folks at the studio where the Beatles made their start were only too happy to see Harrison's return to St. John's Wood. As Ken Townsend, who had been promoted to Manager of Recording Operations and Deputy General Manager at Abbey Road, recalled, "George Harrison used to pop into my office upstairs quite frequently when recording for a chat and a cuppa. Lovely guy." On October 7, in the midst of the mastering process for the album, Harrison recorded a song for a reel of greetings from a variety of artists—including Janis Joplin, Ringo Starr, and Blossom Dearie—solicited by Yoko Ono to mark John Lennon's thirtieth birthday on October 9. While doing further work on the album at EMI (possibly editing the jam recordings), Harrison saw the cover of an album entitled *The Mighty Marenghi Fair Ground Organ* in the studio corridor. Using the recording of "Congratulations"—a 1968 hit by Cliff Richard—from the LP as a foundation, he wrote new lyrics appropriate for the occasion (the composers of the tune would be credited in the album packaging). With John Leckie engineering, Harrison added slide guitar with Mal Evans and Eddie Klein joining in the vocals. Leckie remembered, "Eddie had a fine baritone voice and can be heard up front on 'It's Johnny's Birthday,' which we put together with fairground organ tapes and us singing and wobbling the mix." Two days later, on Lennon's birthday, Harrison walked into Studio Three, where Lennon was recording "Remember" for his own album, with Phil Spector producing. With Starr at the drums, Lennon exclaimed, "*Geoooorge!*"—a happy, momentary reunion of three-fourths of the Beatles.

A perfectionist to the end, Harrison was unsatisfied with the mastering at Abbey Road, and on October 15, he and Spector went to a studio near Marylebone Station to continue work. The three loyal Apple Scruffs had once again picked up his trail and were waiting when he arrived at the studio. Inside the studio, Harrison penned a letter, which he handed to them later that day:

> Dear Carol, Cathy, and Lucy,
> Now as it's finished—and off to the factory. I thought I'd tell you that I haven't a clue whether it's good or bad as I've heard it too much now! During the making of this epic album (most expensive album

EMI ever had to pay for) I have felt positive and negative—pleased and displeased, and all the other opposites expected to be found in this material world. However, the one thing that didn't waver, seems to me, to be 'you three' and Mal, always there as my sole supporters, and even during my worst moments I always felt the encouragement from you was sufficient to make me finish the thing. Thanks a lot, I am really overwhelmed by your apparent undying love, and I don't understand it at all!

Love from George

(P.S. Don't hold this evidence against me.)

P.P.S. Phil Spector loves you too!

In truth, the album still wasn't *completely* finished; soon afterward, Harrison rejected the mastering job from this second studio as well. Spector later concluded that Harrison "never knew if he wanted the album to come out. So the longer it took to make, the happier George was." Meanwhile, production on the package design was already well under way. To shoot the album cover and promotional images, Harrison chose Barry Feinstein, a Hollywood-based celebrity photographer who had accompanied Bob Dylan on his tour of England in 1966 and had become known for his work with rock musicians. Feinstein photographed Harrison inside the mansion at Friar Park and at several different locations on the grounds, including a handful of shots in the garden with Boyd wearing a white coat, looking rather lost in the background. For the setting that would become the cover, Feinstein devoted twenty-eight frames shot on the east lawn, with four of the estate's garden gnomes arranged around Harrison, who was seated on a low stool and dressed in a blue denim jacket, brown trousers, and wellingtons, as if he had just come in from gardening. In eleven of the photos, Harrison held an umbrella enigmatically over his head, and in a few he was even smiling.

"Originally, when we took the photo," Harrison said in 2001, "I had these old Bavarian gnomes which I thought I would put there, like, kinda John, Paul, George, and Ringo." One can read this playful Beatles-as-gnomes tableau, with the four of them surrounding Harrison, as casting the band in stone, already an artifact of history of which Harrison is both a part and not. With his long hair and beard and his disheveled camouflage hat, he resembled nothing so much as one of the stone figures just come to life. For his part, Feinstein had recently established a design company called Camouflage Productions with artist Tom Wilkes, who had been the art director for the Monterey Pop Festival in 1967 and had already designed over forty album covers himself, including *Beggars Banquet* by the Rolling Stones. Closer to Harrison's immediate circle, Wilkes had done work for Delaney & Bonnie, as well as Eric Clapton's first solo album, released in August, and the last LP Phil Spector had produced, *Love Is All We Have to Give* by the Checkmates. He would go on to design the package for *The Concert for Bangladesh* and would win a Grammy for the album design of the London Symphony Orchestra's 1972 take on the Who's *Tommy*.

On October 5, Harrison wrote Feinstein and Wilkes indicating the release would "definitely [be] a double" album and sent along a mock-up of an idea for the paper sleeves that would hold each disc: a painting of Krishna with text on either side of the image reading, "Don't miss the Radha-Krishna Temple album produced by George Harrison coming soon! on Apple Records." Harrison suggested this be printed full size (12 inches by 12 inches) on the sleeves for "both records, i.e. 4 times . . . as an advertisement and excuse to use Krishna within the whole album idea." To accommodate the two (or possibly three) records, photographer and designer decided on a hinged box for the package. In a letter to Harrison dated October 17, Wilkes proposed a black and white cover with a photograph of Harrison with the gnomes and the album title in black; he wanted the back cover of the box to be "a black and white photo of you and the girl [Boyd] in the garden," with the Apple logo and song titles. Regarding Harrison's proposed Krishna illustration, Wilkes took the idea considerably further, writing, "Upon opening the box there will be an explosion of color." The record sleeves for each disc would simply be different colored paper, and the "explosion" would come in the form of a vivid painting Wilkes had done, which he described as "a surrealistic fantasy done in a *classic* East Indian style; very stylized with the accent on detail and the delicate execution of the watercolor. The poster will be an integration of color photographs and a piece of fine art."

The East Indian style that Wilkes used as the basis for his poster was not arbitrary. Traditionally known as *Pattachitra*, these myth-based narrative paintings often depict an incarnation of Krishna, but in adapting the elements of this style to Harrison's own life, Wilkes may have read his client a little too closely. The top of the poster features a photo of the spires and central tower of the Friar Park mansion with Harrison playing guitar in the middle window. This rests on a painted dark cloud in the sky with cranes flying past. Beneath this scene, across the middle of the poster, lies a terrestrial layer, beginning on the right with ten nude, dark-haired maidens and one blonde (depicting Boyd) moving toward the center of the piece, where Krishna, in a tree, has taken the maidens' clothing; three more maidens are pictured beneath him. At the left is a shadowy photo of Harrison alongside two painted cows walking toward the center. The bottom layer shows a male (Terry Doran) and female figure beneath a painted tree, next to a photo of Harrison in one of the Friar Park catacombs. Along with his letter and design sketch, Wilkes included a print of the poster with the photographs yet to be added, noting he had already spent over one hundred hours on the piece.

As brilliant as the draftsmanship was, the symbolism proved excessive, with the illustration of the maidens possibly suggesting something uncomfortably private. Boyd recalled that Harrison had returned from Rishikesh in 1968 "wanting to be some kind of Krishna figure, a spiritual being with lots of concubines. He actually said so." Harrison would be known for his dalliances with many women before and after this period, but given his intense focus on meditation and Krishna consciousness throughout the year, the desire for "concubines" seemed to have receded. When David Wigg had asked him in October 1969 about the "rules" of the Krishna movement regarding sex, Harrison responded, "No illicit sex. There are members of this Radha Krishna Temple who are married and now have children. So all that means, you know, not raving around and knocking off everybody. You know, because that then becomes a bit undisciplined. Because all those emotions like that lust and greed are emotions that have got to be curbed." Even if the maidens weren't the issue, seeing himself floating above everything else, including Krishna, may have made him balk. When Wilkes sensed Harrison's hesitation, he suggested they scrap the idea and just go with one of Feinstein's photos for the poster instead.

Harrison at last decided to add a bonus disc of the jams to the package, with "It's Johnny's Birthday" thrown into the mix. He even had a special label made for the third disc, adorned with a picture of a jar of "Apple jam." On October 23, after much hesitation, he announced that the first single from the album would be "My Sweet Lord." Phil Spector later said, "I picked 'My

Sweet Lord' of all the songs 'cause I told him 'That's the hit.' And everybody fought me on that 'cause they said it had religious overtones in it. I just said it didn't matter. It's the most commercial song in it. . . . It's a hit record." Just days later, though, Harrison changed his mind about releasing the song as a single, saying, "I don't want to detract from the impact of the *All Things Must Pass* triple album."

With the tapes of the mixed songs in his possession, Harrison flew with Boyd to New York, and on October 30, he met with Phil Spector to complete—*finally*—the mastering of the album at Mediasound Studios. On November 12, Apple announced that the album would be released on November 27. Harrison and Boyd flew to Florida for a well-deserved vacation, where they mostly managed to avoid the press, leaving the record company to do its thing. Riding months of buzz, from rumors of the Dylan session in May to scraps of information about recording sessions that had made it into the music papers, the critics unpacked their adjectives, often in what seemed an attempt to match the album's own grand ambitions. Most writers felt Harrison had delivered on the promise of "Something," offering "a new stroke of light and leadership for the scattered Beatles and their fans." Richard Williams in *Melody Maker* famously likened the album to Greta Garbo's first spoken lines in a sound movie: "Garbo talks!—Harrison is free!"

Rolling Stone's Ben Gerson recognized the album as "both an intensely personal statement and a grandiose gesture, a triumph over artistic modesty, even frustration." Even though Gerson's overall assessment was measured, and he detected a troubling thread of self-righteousness, he suggested it might be "the *War and Peace* of rock and roll," characterizing the production as "Wagnerian, Brucknerian, the music of mountain tops and vast horizons. The sound is often so glossy and dramatic it is difficult not to be seduced by it." Elsewhere in his review, he called the songs themselves "a mixed lot" and was the first writer to note that "My Sweet Lord" was "an obvious re-write of 'He's So Fine.'" Not all reviews were positive. While Alan Smith in the *New Musical Express* praised individual songs, he concluded that "somewhere along the line someone fell in love with the idea of releasing a massive album. Often its brilliance is overshadowed by its averageness." Robert Christgau of the *Village Voice* simply said he didn't like the album and declined to review it at the time of release (he also skipped reviewing the new Dylan and Lennon albums, opting instead to give column space to what he considered less heavyweight but worthwhile albums—including a rave for *Layla*). Look-ing back a few months later, he called the album "overblown" and said it sounded "more like Muzak" than McCartney's *Ram*.

The most dismissive review came from the closest source. John Lennon dropped by Friar Park one day just after the album was finished, Harrison remembered, "and there was a friend of mine living there who was a friend of John's. He saw the album cover and said, 'He must be fucking mad, put-ting three records out. And look at the picture on the front, he looks like an asthmatic Leon Russell,' there was a lot of negativity going down." Publicly, Lennon was only marginally less critical, saying in December 1970, "Well, it's better than Paul's, but it's not something I'd listen to," followed by the slightest backpedaling: "The reason I wouldn't listen to it is because I have weird tastes in music." The older brother struck again.

In spite of Harrison's reservations, he allowed Capitol to release "My Sweet Lord" b/w "Isn't It a Pity" in America on November 23, and any concerns about sales or controversy soon vanished. By December 14, the single had sold a million copies, and on January 2, 1971, "My Sweet Lord" reached number one on the *Billboard* singles chart, while *All Things Must Pass* was the number one album. Consequently, Harrison assented to Apple releasing "My Sweet Lord" in the UK on January 15, and by February the single and album would repeat the tandem number-one performance on the British charts. Even priced at $13.98—a princely sum at the time—*All Things Must Pass* was certified gold (five hundred thousand sales) by December 17, 1970, just three weeks after release, and remained number one in the UK for eight weeks. The *McCartney* and *Plastic Ono Band* LPs would peak at numbers two and eight, respectively.

To Harrison's great relief, there was no significant backlash from hav-ing "Hallelujah" and "Hare Krishna" rubbing shoulders in the same song, signaling a successful bit of subversion that delighted him. "My idea in 'My Sweet Lord,' because it sounded like a 'pop song,' was to sneak up on them a bit," he said. "The point was to have the people not offended by 'Hallelu-jah,' and by the time it gets to 'Hare Krishna,' they're already hooked, and their foot's tapping, and they're already singing along 'Hallelujah,' to kind of lull them into a sense of false security. And then suddenly it turns into 'Hare Krishna,' and they will all be singing that before they know what's happened, and they will think, 'Hey, I thought I wasn't supposed to like Hare

Krishna!'" Harrison released a "What Is Life" b/w "Apple Scruffs" single on the heels of the "My Sweet Lord" chart-topper, notching a top-ten showing on the US charts.

By the end of 1971, twenty different artists had recorded covers of "My Sweet Lord," including two straight gospel arrangements based on Billy Preston's original, Nina Simone's alchemical eighteen-minute live recording, an easy listening version by Andy Williams, and even a reggae version that injected a couple of shouts of "Irie, Irie" between the Hallelujahs. Most covers, however, noticeably dispensed with the Hare Krishna part, but it was the original that made the biggest impact. Even John Lennon quipped, "Every time I put the radio on, it's 'Oh my Lord.' I'm beginning to think there must be a God." "My Sweet Lord" would be nominated for Record of the Year by the Grammys, and *All Things Must Pass* for Album of the Year, and Harrison would collect two Ivor Novello writing awards for the song itself.

By contrast, *Layla and Other Assorted Love Songs* enjoyed a very different sort of coming-out party. The double album was issued in November by Atco in the USA and in early December by Polydor in the UK. For the latter release, Stigwood marked the occasion, as he had done with the withdrawn "Tell the Truth" single several months earlier, by distributing "Derek Is Eric" badges at the release party. Realizing that consumer confusion over the bandleader's identity continued to manifest itself in sluggish sales, Stigwood instigated a campaign in record stores by having "Derek Is Eric" stickers printed and affixed to the album; Atco would replicate the practice in the North American marketplace. But for all of Stigwood's efforts, it didn't seem to make any difference—particularly in Clapton's homeland.

In the States, where Clapton and Cream had always seemed to fare better than they had on the British charts, *Layla* notched an impressive showing at number sixteen. Even still, Dowd would later complain that the album might have done even better had the record enjoyed more extensive airplay on American radio. The album's first single, "Bell Bottom Blues" b/w "Keep On Growing," failed to make a dent in the hit parade in spite of being named by *Billboard* as one of the trade magazine's "recommended" record choices.

214 | ALL THINGS MUST PASS AWAY

In March 1971, the LP received a much-needed jolt when Atco released
the "Layla" b/w "I Am Yours" single. The A-side featured a radio-friendly
edit of the title track, sans the "Piano Exit," clocking in at a modest 2:43.
While the "Layla" single notched a disappointing number fifty-one showing,
the bump in airplay no doubt assisted the LP in cracking the top twenty.
Thanks to the well-timed release of the edited "Layla" single, the album had
achieved gold-record status by the end of 1971. In Dowd's estimation, the
single saved the project, sales wise. Originally, *Layla* "was like a dead dog.
Thank God Atlantic [Atco] had the patience and the perseverance to stick
with it, because it could have fallen by the wayside. But they stuck with it for
a year, and a year later, after 'Layla' hit, it became the national anthem." By
contrast, *Layla*'s UK release was an unmitigated disaster, not even making
so much as a ripple on the British album charts.

In the intervening years, critics have pondered the album's lackluster
UK debut. Perhaps the lack of a single had led to the LP's sluggish opening. Or could it be attributed to the lack of name recognition that Stigwood
had lamented? Harry Shapiro would chalk up the album's lifeless release to
a kind of "unrelenting and monotonous press litany of a post-Cream withdrawal syndrome." Whatever the reason, *Layla* was poorly served by the chat-
tering class—especially in the contemporary pop music pages, where the LP
received an odd array of competing notices. In his review for *Melody Maker*,
Roy Hollingworth described the album's contents as vacillating "from the magnificent to a few lengths of complete boredom." While he derided the LP's
"pretty atrocious vocal work," Hollingworth praised "Layla" as "by far the
busiest screaming item, which burns to nearly eight minutes of brilliance, with
rogue playing from all and some of the best Clapton you could ever wish to
hear. One thing is certain—these are assorted love songs. Eric is into the love-
licks, and you don't have to give this much of a hearing to know that he loves
every damned minute of it." Elsewhere, Hollingworth lauded "Little Wing,"
which was "played with such spreading beauty that Jimi would surely have
clapped till his hands bled, and then we have 'I Am Yours,' a *bossa* that *novas*
in pitiful directions." Ultimately, "Clapton and the Dominos have laid down
an assortment of patterns so varied that it would easily take a small pamphlet
to write an account of what has happened." In his assessment, Hollingworth
observed that, to his ears, *Layla* was "far more musical" than Clapton's recent

debut solo LP, while taking special note that Clapton and Allman offered a "superb essay on the playing of the electric guitar."

While the album registered eminently stronger sales in the US, *Layla* took a beating from a vast number of Stateside critics, save for a few bright lights. In the *Saturday Review*, Ellen Sander didn't pull any punches, writing that *Layla* was "pointless and boring" and "a basket case of an album," concluding that Clapton had "all but blown his musical credibility." Writing in *Rolling Stone*, Ed Leimbacher praised "Eric's developing style, the Delaney and Bonnie-styled rhythm section, and the strengths of 'Skydog' Allman's session abilities." Although he disparaged "Bell Bottom Blues" as "filler," he couldn't help raving that *Layla* was "one hell of an album." In the *Village Voice*, Christgau awarded the Dominos' LP with an unremittingly positive review—at least as far as the renowned, albeit cranky critic was concerned—writing that "even though this one has the look of a greedy, lazy, slapdash studio session, I think it may be Eric Clapton's most consistent recording," adding that the album was "one of those rare instances when musicians join together for profit and a lark and come up with a mature and original sound."

Meanwhile, as *All Things Must Pass* held dominion over the global record charts, Clapton and his drug-fueled Dominos barnstormed American cities during the latter months of the year, well aware of Harrison's chart-topping success. As always, Whitlock had plenty to say about the matter. "I remember George had a number 1 record while we were touring, and we were the band that was on it," he recalled. "We were driving down the road in some cold place like Minneapolis from the airport, and we're listening to the radio, 'My Sweet Lord,' then we look up and it's 'Eric Clapton and his Band' on the billboard, tonight at whatever stadium. Eric had Bruce McCaskill, our tour manager, pull over and call the office and tell them if they didn't change the sign we were not playing. It was changed within the hour." For his part, Whitlock wasn't surprised about the album's negative reviews. "Everybody wanted Eric to play with abandon, like he had with Cream," Whitlock observed. "Everybody wanted that flurry of guitar activity. What we were doing was so far from that. He wanted to get away from that himself because he was a blues purist, and his roots are in the blues."

As if things couldn't get any worse after Hendrix's death and the LP's lackluster debut, Clapton received the awful news that his grandfather had died back in England. As he later remembered, "I had a call from Stigwood telling me that my grandfather had been taken into the hospital in Guildford with suspected cancer. I flew home to see him. He was a sad figure in his hospital bed, diminished both by his illness and by a stroke he had suffered the previous year, which had left him paralyzed down one side. I felt stricken with guilt." Reflecting back on the experience, Clapton realized that he still had a lot of growing up to do. "In my arrogance, I believed that I had somehow contributed to his decline by having bought him a house and given him enough money to take early retirement," he wrote. "I felt that I had offended his pride by depriving him of his way of life. Of course, in reality, I was just doing what any grateful child would do, trying to pay back the love and support I had always received from him. But nevertheless, I couldn't help feeling that I was to blame for it all. It never occurred to me that perhaps I wasn't responsible for everything that happened in the world." After a short respite, the Dominos returned to the road. They were even joined by Allman on a couple of dates in early December in Tampa, Florida, and Syracuse, New York. The band finally concluded their American tour on December 6, somewhat inauspiciously, at Suffolk County Community College in Selden, New York. Looking back, the records from that evening indicate a fairly perfunctory nine-song set, although it was likely permeated by the extended jams for which the Dominos had become known. Neither "Bell Bottom Blues" nor "Layla" received any play that evening, although they performed "Little Wing" and, in what was to become a concert staple for Clapton over the years, "Blues Power" from his solo LP.

Inexplicably, the Dominos closed out their set—and the tour—that night at Suffolk County Community College with "Got to Get Better in a Little While," an original Clapton number that they planned to include on their next album. As it turned out, the gospel-tinged song actually predated the recording sessions for *Layla*. "It's one of my favorites," Whitlock recalled, although he couldn't explain why it wasn't recorded at Criteria with Dowd. "I really don't know," he admitted, "because we were playing that song before we went down to Miami, and I seem to remember us doing that on the road too."

In May 1971, the Dominos assembled at London's Olympic Studios to begin producing their sophomore effort with engineer Andy Johns, the talented younger brother of Glyn Johns, who had worked with such rock luminaries as the Beatles, the Who, and the Rolling Stones. As Whitlock recalled, the sessions were doomed from the start. "Paranoia was getting pretty heavy," he said, and "Eric was totally frustrated with Jim Gordon, who was making things pretty difficult. It was an ego thing. Jim was steady wanting something that he didn't have and was not going to get—and that was Eric's notoriety and fame. He wasn't content in being the greatest drummer on the planet." Things came to a head on May 9, when the band assembled to work on "Got to Get Better in a Little While." As it happened, Gordon had ordered a new drum kit, which required a three-hour setup time. As Whitlock recalled, "Each drum was tuned to the piano. Jim was a very musical drummer. All the while Eric was quietly re-stringing his guitar. When Jim was finally finished, Eric started to tune his guitar. Jim said something to the effect of 'Do you want me to tune that thing for you?!' Eric put his guitar down in the corner and said that he would never play with him again."

For Whitlock, the Dominos' disbandment wasn't entirely a surprise. "Jim and Eric weren't talking to each other," he remembered, and "Carl stayed out of the way. Sometimes it felt like Eric and I were the only band members. We might as well have been called Derek and the Domino." As for Clapton, he had predicted the group's dissolution after the Dominos' first stint in Miami. "Drugs were the beginning of the end for the band," he later wrote. "We couldn't do anything. We couldn't work. We couldn't agree. We were paralyzed, and this led to hostility growing among us. We attempted to make another album, but it just fell to pieces. The final straw came when Jim Gordon and I had a huge row and I stormed out of the studio in a rage. The band never played together again. Disillusioned, I retired to Hurtwood." He was joined at his estate by Whitlock, who longed to work with Clapton again, with or without the band that recorded *Layla*. As he recalled, "Jim had plans to play with Traffic after our second, failed attempt in the studio. Carl was going back with Leon [Russell]. It was just me and Eric, and I was just trying to wait it out."

In the intervening months since his return to the UK, Clapton had, not surprisingly, devoted much of his time to thinking wistfully about Boyd, as opposed to caring very much at all about the Dominos' future. Looking back, Clapton remarked that "I was a bachelor when I made that album, really. I had various optimisms about becoming embroiled with Pattie, but we weren't at that moment in a relationship. It was just something I was trying to write on the wall. And so *Layla* was that—a proclamation. But it was as anonymous as can be." Worse yet, Clapton had succeeded in convincing himself that when Boyd heard the LP—with its deep longing and sentiment—she would be over-whelmed with love for him. One day, he invited her over to Hurtwood Edge for tea and a private listening party. "I think she was deeply touched by the fact that I had written all these songs about her," he recalled, "but at the same time the intensity of it all probably scared the living daylights out of her. Needless to say, it didn't work, and I was back at square one."

By this juncture, Clapton was beginning to understand the futility of his quest to win her love away from Harrison. At one point, he penned a letter to her, writing that "I don't think, even if we were the last ones left alive, that you could be happy with me, and as for me I think I am content to remain alone until someday I am free to be discovered." He signed off with "I love you, even though you're chicken." Still, Clapton didn't give up so easily. As the months wore on, he continued to entreat her to leave Friar Park and live with him at Hurtwood Edge. But she simply wouldn't budge. "One day," Clapton wrote, after "another session of fruitless pleading, I told her that if she didn't leave him, I would start taking heroin full-time." In his desperation, he was renewing his threat from the previous year. His gambit hadn't worked back then, and it was surely destined to fail in 1971. Besides, Clapton admitted, "I had been taking it almost full-time for quite a while." In the end, Pattie Boyd "smiled sadly at me, and I knew the game was over. Apart from one brief meeting at the London airport, that was the last time I saw her for several years."

As it happened, Clapton managed to be in Boyd's orbit on one more occa-sion in 1971, although it was largely a wordless encounter—and it's doubtful if he even remembered it. But first, he had to make his way out of Hurtwood Edge. Awash in depression and a roiling heroin addiction, Clapton would only leave his estate sporadically over the next few years. Eventually, even Whit-lock, loyal to a fault, couldn't hold out any longer and was ultimately forced to save himself. "I waited two years for him to come out of isolation, and it wasn't happening," he recalled, "so that's when I said, 'Oh hell, I'm just get-ting out of here. I'm going back to the United States.' Sitting there waiting on Eric Clapton to come out of his heroin haze wasn't very productive for me. I started going downhill." Clapton's respite from seclusion, brief as it was, came at the behest of Harrison, who, in spite of everything, remained his steadfast and loving friend. Harrison's effort to wrest Clapton from Hurtwood Edge was occasioned by a pair of upcoming benefit concerts that he would be staging with Ravi Shankar at New York City's Madison Square Garden. Harrison and Shankar had organized the concerts in order to raise awareness and relief funds following the 1970 Bhola cyclone and Bangladeshi civil war atrocities. The events were scheduled for Sunday, August 1, 1971, and Harrison's guest list featured such rock luminaries as Ringo Starr, Bob Dylan, Billy Preston, Leon Russell, and Badfinger. Hoping to add Clapton to the marquee, Harrison began attempting to coax him out of his estate.

As Boyd observed, however, tempting Clapton to leave his home and appear on a stage in faraway New York City would be no easy achievement, although she admired her husband's goodhearted sense of pluck. "George knew that Eric was in a bad way but his addiction was unspoken," she later wrote. "He thought that if he got him onstage, even propped up with drugs, it would become an open secret and maybe he would open the door a little to his friends, who might be able to help. But everyone knew that if Eric was to have a chance of getting through two performances, one in the afternoon and another that evening, he would need a supply of heroin when he arrived in New York—obviously he couldn't travel with it." Working with Alice Ormsby-Gore, who had moved back into Hurtwood Edge to share in Clapton's addiction, Harrison was able to secure enough heroin to enable Clapton to make the trip. On the day of the concerts, Boyd recalled that Clapton "was surrounded by people, then onstage, and he was very out of it; I am not sure he really saw me. It was a shock to think that he had done this to himself because of me," she added. "At first I felt guilty, then my feelings would swing violently the other way, and I was angry that he should have put me in the impossible position where I had to choose between him and my husband." As for Clapton, the Madison Square Garden concerts proved to be one of the lowest points of an otherwise stellar career. He later recalled that "I got to the sound check and quickly ran through some of the things I was supposed to do, and although I have a vague memory of this, and then of playing the show, the truth is I wasn't really there, and I felt ashamed. No matter how I've tried to rationalize it to myself over the years, I let a lot of people down that night, most of all myself. I've seen the concert only once on film, but if I ever want a reminder of what I might be missing from the 'good old days,' this would be the film to watch." In addition to performing in Harrison's star-studded band, Clapton and the former Beatle performed "While My Guitar Gently Weeps," complete with dueling guitar solos.

Incredibly, 1971 would succeed in providing a new personal low for Clapton on October 29, when he learned of Duane Allman's untimely death at age twenty-four after a motorcycle accident in Macon, Georgia. The man whom Clapton had described as "my musical brother"—the guitarist who had joined with him to create his most lasting, pure blues statement with *Layla*—was gone, plunging Clapton into an even deeper depression. As for Harrison, the Concert for Bangladesh had delivered a veritable triumph in the wake of *All Things Must Pass*. At his press conference for the event, Harrison had lauded the power of music as a means for creating community in the wake of international disaster. "Music should be used to attain a spiritual realization," he remarked, highlighting the ways in which musicians can come together on behalf of humankind and not merely to line their pocketbooks. Over the years, the concerts would result in a best-selling live album and concert film. By the mid-1980s, more than $12 million had been raised through Harrison and Shankar's efforts. In 1973, *The Concert for Bangladesh* earned a Grammy Award for Album of the Year at the fifteenth Grammy Awards.

By the end of 1971, with the twin achievements of *All Things Must Pass* and *The Concert for Bangladesh* under his belt, Harrison had emerged from the ashes of the Fab Four as the reigning solo Beatle, both critically and commercially. But as he so presciently reminded us with his album's most heartfelt song, "all things must pass."

EPILOGUE

Royal Albert Hall, November 2002

IN ONE OF HIS LAST INTERVIEWS, John Lennon reflected on the similarities between Harrison's "My Sweet Lord" and the Chiffons' early 1960s recording of "He's So Fine"—the happenstance that preceded one of the darkest chapters in Harrison's solo career. When it came to his former bandmate, Lennon concluded that "he must have known, you know. He's smarter than that. It's irrelevant, actually—only on a monetary level does it matter. In the early years, I'd often carry around someone else's song in my head, and only when I'd put it down on tape—because I can't write music—would I consciously change it to my own melody because I knew that otherwise somebody would sue me. George could have changed a few bars in that song and nobody could have ever touched him, but he just let it go and paid the price. Maybe he thought God would just sort of let him off."

Before it became the subject of one of rock 'n' roll's most notorious lawsuits, "My Sweet Lord" had inadvertently become part of a brief wave in the pop music firmament that saw frankly religious music appear on the mainstream charts between 1969 and 1972. "Jesus rock" or "Jesus music," as it would come to be known, initially grew out of West Coast Evangelical Christian circles, and while the term would encompass artists from the so-called Jesus Movement, it would also be used to describe recordings with Jesus-themed lyrics produced by pop artists outside of those circles. Norman Greenbaum's "Spirit in the Sky" may be the most enduring song to fall under the Jesus Rock moniker, reaching number three in *Billboard* in 1970 and becoming a radio staple for years to come. The 1971 rock opera *Jesus Christ Superstar* by Andrew Lloyd Webber (which yielded two top-twenty chart hits) and the musical *Godspell* were also

221

part of this trend. More broadly speaking, Judy Collins's 1970 a capella recording of the traditional hymn "Amazing Grace" struck such a similar spiritual chord in the midst of the Vietnam War and became a top-twenty hit in the US and a top five in the UK, reentering the British charts *seven* times over the next two years. Something was in the air, and if "My Sweet Lord" had no connection to these other recordings aside from a coincidental religious theme, to casual listeners the song's content seemed a part of the zeitgeist, another exemplary song of spiritual yearning dominating the airwaves.

But for Harrison, the saga involving "My Sweet Lord" began to manifest only a few weeks after the single's release. On February 10, 1971, while "My Sweet Lord" was riding high in the charts, music publisher Bright Tunes filed suit against Harrison, his publishing company, Harrisongs, and Apple Records and BMI, for copyright infringement of the song "He's So Fine." Recorded in 1963 by the girl group the Chiffons and reaching number one in America and number sixteen in the UK, "He's So Fine" had been written by Ronnie Mack, who had died while the song was still making its way up the pop charts. Bright Tunes had been formed by the Tokens, a group most famous for the 1961 song "The Lion Sleeps Tonight," as a means of publishing their own compositions and those written by others, and it counted "He's So Fine" on their roster. Tokens lead singer and Bright Tunes co-owner Jay Siegel remembered that when "My Sweet Lord" became a hit, "radio stations all over the country would play half of that record and segue into 'He's So Fine.' The songs had practically the same melody." In May 1971, country singer Jody Miller released a cover of "He's So Fine" that used in its arrangement some of the chords and one of Harrison's slide guitar lines from "My Sweet Lord," making the connection between the two songs explicit.

Allen Klein minimized the suit initially, but in 1972 he played Miller's record for Harrison and said, "Those bastards . . . have really made it sound like 'My Sweet Lord.'" Harrison asked about settling the suit or even possibly buying the rights to "He's So Fine," but the publisher had gone into receivership. Miller's record wasn't the problem, of course; Klein had fatally underestimated Bright Tunes' case. By the time he gave a deposition on the matter in July of 1973, Harrison, along with Lennon and Starr, had fired Klein as their manager for a variety of reasons, and attorney Joseph Santora took over the case and attempted to settle out of court. In January 1976, Harrison had Santora make a settlement offer to Bright Tunes of $148,000, half the earnings to date of "My Sweet Lord" in Canada and the US. The publisher declined, however, and the suit headed to trial.

Bright Tunes v. Harrisongs landed in New York federal courthouse on February 23, 1976, presided over by Judge Richard Owen. Musicologists testified on both sides, those for the defense claiming that similarities in the songs came down to "traditional gospel-composing techniques," while the plaintiff's side cited "strikingly similar" groups of notes common to both tunes. Harrison took the stand on the second day, playing guitar to demonstrate what he believed were the differences between his song and "He's So Fine" and the ways the Miller recording had combined the two; he also explained his actual inspiration came from "Oh Happy Day." He denied "ripping off" anything, though, and while he may have been aware of "He's So Fine" as a song, he asserted that the arrangement and production of "My Sweet Lord" were more responsible for the record's success than anything else.

John Barham would later recall that Tony Ashton, one of the keyboardists on the recording session back in May 1970, noted the similarity between the two songs as they were building the arrangement of "My Sweet Lord." "So George was aware of the resemblances," said Barham. But he also agreed with Harrison that "the way the music was presented in 'My Sweet Lord' is more powerful than the song itself. It's like a painter; it's about technique." There is certainly plenty of evidence to support this stance. The history of popular music is littered with cover versions more successful than the original recordings due to arrangement and performance: Fats Domino's "Blueberry Hill," the Righteous Brothers' "Unchained Melody," and the Beatles' "Twist and Shout" have all comfortably eclipsed the original versions of those songs in the popular imagination. Of course, sometimes the dynamic is reversed, with Harrison's "Something" a vivid example. Joe Cocker's recording of the song in early 1969 was not released as a single and remains relatively obscure, while the Beatles' arrangement from later in the year was a worldwide success that became a beloved classic. More to the point, if Harrison had simply put the lyrics of "My Sweet Lord" to the arrangement of "He's So Fine," would it have been a hit?

In September 1976, Judge Owen handed down his verdict: Harrison had "unintentionally" infringed upon the copyright of "He's So Fine." Owen wrote, "It is clear that 'My Sweet Lord' is the very same song as 'He's So Fine' with different words. . . . This is, under the law, infringement of copyright, and is no less so even though subconsciously accomplished." The next phase would normally have been to award damages, but Allen Klein had already complicated the situation immeasurably. After his termination as the Beatles' manager, Klein had begun negotiating to purchase Bright Tunes—for himself. Recognizing Klein's insider knowledge regarding the earnings of "My Sweet Lord," the publisher realized that Harrison's original settlement offer was likely lower than the successful outcome of a court case. Klein's interference, then, led directly to the trial, and in 1978 he finally purchased "He's So Fine" for $587,000 from Bright Tunes, seeking to increase the potential award from damages now that he would be the beneficiary.

Ultimately, Judge Owen saw that Klein's intrusion had "irreparably destroyed" any chance of a pretrial settlement and ruled that once Harrison paid Klein the exact amount Klein had paid Bright Tunes—$587,000—Harrison would own "He's So Fine." Incredibly, because of various accounting entanglements and Klein's ruthlessness, litigation dragged on between Harrison and his former manager until 1998, when all disputes were finally settled, making it one of the longest-running cases in US legal history. In 1980, Harrison wrote, "I don't feel guilty or bad about it, in fact it saved many a heroin addict's life. I know the *motive* behind writing the song in the first place, and its effect far exceeded the legal hassle."

For both Harrison and Clapton, the *All Things Must Pass* and *Layla* albums proved to be nearly impossible acts to follow. While he had enjoyed a slew of accolades for *The Concert for Bangladesh*, Harrison soon learned that recording a studio collection of comparable scope and quality to *All Things Must Pass* would be daunting. Produced as they were within the complex tensions that characterized the last half of the Beatles' career, Harrison's songs had been shaped by the heat and pressure around him. When he wasn't directly responding to factors within the band, his desire to be a songwriter was sparked by the example set by Lennon and McCartney. The sheer volume of material Harrison produced from 1968 to 1970 is a testament to how much being in the Beatles drove him creatively. Once liberated from the expectations of that band, he became progressively less motivated to write and record with anything resembling urgency, choosing instead to put his energies into other pursuits. There would be high points and hits again—including a chart-topping single from 1987's *Cloud Nine* in "Got My Mind Set on You"—but nothing of the magnitude of his first true solo album.

As for *All Things Must Pass,* the album's reputation would wane precipitously as the 1970s wore on. Technology gave artists many more tracks for recording, and production consequently became cleaner and more compartmentalized. Disco dominated briefly and evolved into dance music, punk burned a bright, angry strip across the landscape, discarding all convention, and the sound of synthesizers and drum machines became ascendant. By the 1980s, the album sounded positively passé. When Harrison returned to the tapes in 1999 to prepare a thirtieth-anniversary edition of the album, he found he disliked all the reverb. "It was difficult to resist re-mixing every track," he admitted. "All these years later I would like to liberate some of the songs from the big production that seemed appropriate at the time, but now seem a bit over the top with the reverb in the wall of sound." Ken Scott, who worked on the rerelease with Harrison, recalled, "So we're sitting there, and we're listening, and we just look at each other and burst out laughing. And it was for two reasons: one, here we are, 30 years on, doing exactly the same as we did 30 years ago; it just didn't make any sense to us. The other thing was . . . how much we hated the sound. It was—we had both moved on, we loved all of the reverb and all that thirty years ago, but now we'd like things a lot drier, a lot cleaner. And so hearing it, it was just we wanted to remix it again."

While they did indeed avoid remixing anything, Harrison decided to finish off one of the unused band recordings from the original sessions, "I Live for You." To the basic track of acoustic guitars, bass, drums, pedal steel, and piano, Harrison added numerous subtle overdubs: more acoustic guitars, backing vocals (including his son Dhani), and Ray Cooper playing various percussion parts. "I didn't include it because I never finished it," Harrison told *Billboard* in 2001. "But coming back to it, I fixed the drums up very simply. But the main thing about it for me is the Pete Drake solo on pedal steel guitar. He died [in 1988], and I often thought if his family is still around, then suddenly they'll be hearing him playing this thing that they've never heard before. I really loved his pedal steel guitar—the bagpipes of country and western music."

Revisiting the tapes also allowed Harrison to play an elaborate prank on drummer Phil Collins. Back in 1970, when he bought a copy of the album,

Collins had been dismayed to find no trace of his name in the credits and no evidence of his impassioned conga playing on the recordings. Even though he had subsequently become a superstar both with Genesis and as a solo artist, denial of recognition on such a major work by one of his musical idols remained a sensitive point.

When the two saw each other in a recording studio in 1982, Collins reminded Harrison that they had in fact already met and told him the story of the 1970 recording session. Harrison responded, "Really, Phil? I don't remember that at all." Collins, who has confessed to a deep insecurity about his work, continued to nurse this particular wound, and though the two crossed paths periodically over the years, Collins didn't bring the subject up again until they ran into each other at a motor racing event in 1999. Again, Harrison had no memory of Collins playing on the album. Cut to the following year, another racing event, when journalist Matt Cooper approached Collins out of the blue and said, "Phil, you were on *All Things Must Pass*, weren't you?" Cooper, who had been attending the playback sessions at the Friar Park studio, graciously offered to see if Harrison could—at last—find evidence of Collins on the tapes. The following week, Collins received a package including a cassette and a handwritten note: "Dear Phil. Could this be you? Love, George."

Thirty years of anticipation came rushing up for Collins, who brought the tape to his home studio thinking he would finally get the closure he desired. He pressed play, heard the music start, and then heard the congas enter: rhythmically challenged, overly complicated, terrible. In shock, Collins wondered how he could have played *that* badly. As the recording finished, Harrison's voice appeared, addressing Spector: "Phil? Do you think we can try it one more time, but without the conga player?" "I rewind it four or five times," said Collins, "until I'm sure I heard it correctly—Harrison shouting to Spector, confining me to the dustbin, my worst fears realized."

Harrison waited a few days for the recording to sink in before phoning Collins and revealing the truth: while working with the session tapes, Harrison had asked percussionist Ray Cooper to "play congas badly over 'Art of Dying' so we could record a special take just for you!"

Harrison was never able to recall Collins's participation in the recording session, but in the 2001 reissue of the album, he wrote, "A lot of people new to me came into the sessions, I know not how; the most famous being Phil Collins. During one such session, Phil allegedly played congas on the 'Art of

Dying', and although it's taken me 30 years, I would like to thank him for his participation."

_____

Since its original release, *All Things Must Pass* has sold over six million copies and has grown to become one of the most beloved of all Beatles solo albums, while "My Sweet Lord" had sold ten million copies alone by 2010. *Rolling Stone* would place the LP at number 433 of its "500 Greatest Albums of All Time," and in 2014, *All Things Must Pass* would be inducted into the Grammy Hall of Fame. Had he lived to see the advent of such accolades, Harrison might have responded to these figures and achievements with bemusement, choosing instead to direct attention to the impact of the album's spiritual message. "I felt that there were a lot of people out there who would be reached," he said in 1982. "I still get letters from people saying, 'I have been in the Krsna temple for three years, and I would never have known about Krsna unless you recorded the *All Things Must Pass* album.' So I know, by the Lord's grace, I am a small part in the cosmic play."

Over the years, Harrison would repay many of the artists who participated in the production of *All Things Must Pass* by sharing his talents on their records, including works by Bobby Whitlock, Badfinger, Footprint (Gary Wright), and Bobby Keys, among others. Harrison had always made a point of surrounding himself with artists whom he could trust musically, and this practice became the prevailing standard throughout his career. From *Living in the Material World* (1973) through *Brainwashed* (2002), Harrison would regularly call on various musicians from the *All Things Must Pass* recordings, including in particular the drummer who would have performed on the album—Jim Keltner—if not for Jim Gordon's power move.

_____

In contrast with the release and reception of *All Things Must Pass*, *Layla* quite literally had nowhere to go but up. Almost from the beginning, Derek and the Dominos' debut album had been ripe for reassessment and, as it turned out, would undergo decades of reappraisal. Music critics and historians often trace *Layla*'s reconsideration to the 1972 release of *The History of Eric Clapton*, a retrospective double album released during the artist's protracted absence from the music scene. The compilation featured the full-length version of "Layla," complete with the "Piano Exit," and music lovers began to listen to the Dominos' anthem with new ears. That year, *Layla* made its bravura return to the US album charts, with Ed Naha of *Circus* lauding the LP as an "amazing collection of Clapton tumblers," while describing Clapton as "the high priest of rock guitar." Capitalizing on a growing interest in Derek and the Dominos, Polydor released *In Concert* (1973), a live double album recorded in October 1970 at New York City's Fillmore East, the storied venue operated by rock promoter Bill Graham. As the 1970s wore on, *Layla* continued its slow resurgence, returning to the US charts in 1974 and 1977, eventually earning a platinum disc to commemorate sales of more than a million units.

By the 1980s, *Layla* had fully taken its place as one of rock 'n' roll's premier albums, assisted, no doubt, by a series of deluxe remastered editions. In 1990, the album was feted with a twentieth-anniversary compilation entitled *The Layla Sessions*, which featured a host of outtakes and instrumental jams. In his review of the deluxe edition, the *Chicago Tribune*'s Greg Kot lauded the album as Clapton's "blues-rock guitar masterpiece," an accolade that surely must have pleased Clapton, who had originally undertaken *Layla* with such grandiose pretensions. But it was Christgau, of all critics, who took issue with the twentieth-anniversary compilation. It was a strange turn of events after Christgau had been one of the album's staunchest adherents. Rather than perceiving the new release as the product of the LP's decades-long reappraisal, the critic saw it as a gauche commercial move by Polydor with Clapton's "finest pickup band" as the record company's victim. Christgau even doubted if Derek and the Dominos merited "the kind of genius treatment that's dubious even with great jazz improvisors. And since it unearths not much Duane Allman (no surprise, since he barely met the band), it cheats on the dueling-guitars fireworks that made *Layla* explode. This is pop, gang—arrangements matter. Outtakes are outtakes because the keepers are better. Jams take too long to get anywhere worth going. And when a mix trades raunch for definition, the exchange is usually moot."

But nothing, it seemed—not even the "Dean of Rock Critics" himself—could derail *Layla*'s long journey toward consensus rock-blues superstardom. By the new century, *Layla*, as with *All Things Must Pass*, had been inducted into the Grammy Hall of Fame. During this same period, *Rolling Stone*'s Anthony DeCurtis branded the LP as "a masterpiece," taking particular note of the album's raw qualities and the way in which "the playing on the album, too, teeters on the edge of chaos but never tips." And when it came to the magazine's venerated "500 Greatest Albums of All Time," *Layla* clocked in at 117—several hundred places above *All Things Must Pass*. In 2012, the Super Deluxe Edition of the album, supervised by Bill Levenson, earned a Grammy Award for Best Surround Sound Album. And in 2011, *Layla* finally made the UK album charts, notching a number sixty-eight showing forty-one years after its original release.

By the 1980s, "Layla"—with its piano coda present and intact—had emerged as a regular concert staple on Clapton's setlists. On July 13, 1985, he even performed the song on the occasion of Live Aid, the global relief benefit that was broadcast to more than 1.5 billion people. That same year, he paused to reflect on his life with the Dominos, whom he described as "a make-believe band. We were all hiding inside it: Derek and the Dominos—the whole thing. I had to come out and admit that I was being me. Being Derek was a cover for the fact that I was trying to steal someone else's wife. That was one of the reasons for doing it, so that I could write the song, and even use another name for Pattie. So Derek and Layla—it wasn't real at all." He had been so chuffed by his experience at Live Aid, and much later, while recording *The Road to Escondido* (2006) with J. J. Cale and latter-day Allman Brothers guitarist Derek Trucks, that he invited Trucks to serve as a member of his backup band for his latest tour. In many ways, it seemed like a match made in heaven. According to Trucks, his parents chose his name in honor of Clapton's "make-believe band" of yesteryear. As the tour proceeded, Clapton and Trucks took to performing a clutch of songs from the *Layla* LP as the first half of their show. For a time, Clapton admitted, playing the album with the younger guitarist left him feeling nostalgic, as if he were back in Derek and the Dominos all over again.

In 1992, "Layla" notched one of the most unusual—and certainly unexpected—of milestones associated with the album. In January of that year, Clapton recorded an installment for the MTV Network's popular *Unplugged* series. Clapton included "Layla" on his all-acoustic setlist after Welsh guitarist Andy Fairweather Low suggested that he consider a new arrangement for the classic song. Working together, the two men transformed the fiery rocker into an easygoing, jazzy shuffle. At first, the idea of transforming "Layla" mystified

Clapton, who remarked that "I have done it the same all these years and never, ever considered trying to revamp it. And a lot of artists do that, you know? Bob Dylan for instance changes everything every time he plays it, and I thought this was another great opportunity to just take it off on a different path, to put it to a shuffle, and for a start, making it acoustic denied all the riffs, really. They would have sounded a bit weak, I think, on the acoustic guitar, so it just seemed to become jazzier somehow. And of course, I'm singing it a whole octave down. So it gives it a nice kind of atmosphere." When it came to performing the song for *MTV Unplugged*'s live studio audience, Clapton couldn't help but quip "see if you can spot this one" as he kicked the song into gear. Having enjoyed an unexpectedly new life, Clapton's subsequent "Layla" acoustic single notched a top-twenty showing on the *Billboard* charts, later earning a Grammy Award for Best Rock Song in 1993.

During the press blitz for the revamped "Layla," Clapton came to realize how different he felt about the album that he had recorded all those years ago with the Dominos, an album that was destined by design to become the purest distillation of his passion and performance of the blues. And when it came to the title trick, Clapton observed that "I'm very proud of it. I love to hear it. It's almost like it's not me. It's like I'm listening to someone that I really like." Indeed, "Derek and the Dominos was a band I really liked," he continued, "and it's almost like I wasn't in that band. It's just a band that I'm a fan of. Sometimes, my own music can be like that. When it's served its purpose to being good music, I don't associate myself with it anymore. It's like someone else."

———————

Perhaps Clapton had been right all along. Could it be that he had been someone else, for all intents and purposes, back in the days when he recorded his most profound blues effusion with the Dominos? Perhaps they had been a "make-believe band," after all.

As it happened, the Who's Pete Townshend had succeeded where George Harrison and Pattie Boyd had failed via the Bangladesh concerts back in 1971. In January 1973, Townshend determined to wrest Clapton out of his drug-induced stupor—and Hurtwood Edge—by organizing a benefit concert at London's Rainbow Theatre. Townshend had originally devised the plan with

Alice Ormsby-Gore's father, Member of Parliament and onetime US ambassador David Ormsby-Gore, the fifth Baron Harlech. Like Townshend, Lord Harlech was desperate to see his daughter and Clapton triumph over their longstanding heroin and alcohol addictions. The Rainbow Concert proved to be a star-studded affair, with Townshend, Steve Winwood, and the Rolling Stones' Ron Wood among the players in Clapton's backup band. For the show, Clapton managed to perform a slew of his standout cuts from his Cream, Blind Faith, and Derek and the Dominos days, but sadly, Townshend's effort had proven largely ineffective. In the months after the concert, Clapton and Alice Ormsby-Gore reached new lows, with Clapton eventually becoming listless and overweight. Their wake-up call, when it finally came, was twofold. Robert Stigwood's office had alerted Clapton that his £1,000-per-week heroin habit had nearly bankrupted him. In fact, he would shortly need to begin selling off his furniture in order to nurse his addiction. Second, Lord Harlech had reached his wit's end, threatening to turn in Clapton and his daughter to the authorities if they didn't attempt to change their corrosive ways.

At this juncture, Clapton contacted Scottish neurosurgeon Meg Patterson, who had pioneered neuro-electric therapy as a means for treating heroin withdrawal. As part of her treatment program, Patterson required Clapton and Ormsby-Gore to dispense with heroin immediately. But the most successful aspect of his treatment emerged in early 1974, when Clapton went to live and work on a Welsh border farm while Ormsby-Gore convalesced at a London nursing home. That spring, the pair briefly reunited, mutually agreeing to end their relationship, especially after Clapton admitted that his infatuation with Boyd still consumed him. For the first time in four years, he was free and clear of his heroin addiction. He had even begun composing new material during his stint at the border farm. Sadly, Ormsby-Gore would not be so fortunate, succumbing to a heroin overdose in 1995, when she was only a fortnight away from celebrating her forty-third birthday. As for Clapton, he simply couldn't stay away from Boyd, often visiting Friar Park on a whim, including a notorious occasion in 1974 when Harrison and Clapton engaged in an impromptu guitar duel. As actor John Hurt looked on, Harrison emerged with "two guitars and two small amplifiers, laying them down in the hall, then pacing restlessly until Eric arrived—full of brandy, as usual. As Eric walked through the door, George handed him a guitar and amp—as an eighteenth-century man might have handed his rival a sword—and for two hours, without a word, they dueled.

The air was electric and the music exciting. At the end, nothing was said, but the general feeling was that Eric had won. He hadn't allowed himself to get riled or to go in for instrumental gymnastics as George had. Even when he was drunk, his guitar-playing was unbeatable," Boyd recalled.

With a clarity of mind that he had not fully experienced since at least the late 1960s, Clapton set about recording his first album of new material since *Layla* back in 1970. Entitled *461 Ocean Boulevard*, the album proved to be a comeback record in every sense of the word. Named after the oceanside studio in Florida where Clapton recorded the album with Tom Dowd, the LP was released in July 1974, scoring a number-one hit on the album and singles charts thanks to Clapton's cover version of Bob Marley's reggae classic "I Shot the Sheriff." By the time that Stigwood had arranged for Clapton's first North American stadium tour, the guitarist had fallen off the wagon, drinking his way from one US city to the next. It was during this period that Boyd finally left Harrison, having left Friar Park to be with her sister Jenny Boyd, who was married at the time to Fleetwood Mac founder and drummer Mick Fleetwood and living in Los Angeles. Boyd and Harrison's relationship had deteriorated in recent years. In retrospect, Boyd would chalk up the demise of their relationship to cocaine binges and, ultimately, Harrison's affair with Maureen Starr, Ringo Starr's wife. For Boyd, it was the last straw.

Having roused the courage to telephone Pattie Boyd in Los Angeles, Clapton invited her to join him on the tour. To his delight, she finally came into his life unbeholden to her famous husband. Clapton soon discovered that the fantasy that he had concocted over life with Boyd—that he had nursed in his head and heart for so very long—had been lost to the mists of a very different time. They were both very different people from the man and woman who had carried on a shameless flirtation back in the late 1960s. The eminent literary critic Harold Bloom once observed that the great tragedy of human romance is not that we fall in love with each other, but rather, that we often do so at different intervals. For Clapton and Boyd, the interval between falling in love and their mutual willingness to enter into a relationship spanned across five years—a daunting arc, if ever there were one.

By the end of 1974, Boyd had come to live with Clapton, who was now a full-blown alcoholic, at Hurtwood Edge. In 1977, he even managed to score a top-twenty hit in her honor with "Wonderful Tonight." To Clapton's great surprise and relief, Harrison proceeded with their friendship like days of old, often popping over to visit with Clapton and with his estranged wife. "One Christmas Eve," Clapton recalled, Harrison "came over, and when I answered the door, he squirted a water pistol in my mouth, and it was full of brandy. For some time, we had this edgy relationship going on between us, and he'd often make sarcastic little remarks referring to Pattie's leaving. He wouldn't hide it under the carpet. Sometimes we'd laugh, and at times it would be uncomfortable, but it was the only way we could go on. One night we were sitting in the great room at Hurtwood when he said, 'Well, I suppose I'd better divorce her,' to which I replied, 'Well, if you divorce her, then that means I've got to marry her!'"

In May 1979, Clapton did just that. With Hurtwood Edge decked out for the occasion, rock 'n' roll's glitterati arrived in droves. The couple shared their nuptials in the very same garden where Harrison had composed "Here Comes the Sun" more than a decade earlier. At one point, Harrison, McCartney, and Starr provided a mini-Beatles reunion, climbing up on a makeshift stage and performing "Sgt. Pepper's Lonely Hearts Club Band," "Get Back," and "Lawdy Miss Clawdy" for Clapton and Boyd's guests. By this point, Harrison had entered into a second marriage of his own with Olivia Arias, whom he had met at A&M Records during the founding of his Dark Horse Records. In August 1978, their son Dhani was born, and they got married the following month in a private ceremony. By this point, Harrison had good-naturedly taken to calling Clapton his "husband-in-law."

In truth, Clapton and Boyd's marriage—for all of the mystery and romance associated with their love affair—never really stood a chance. Clapton's alcoholism continued unabated for years, leading to angry and, at times, abusive outbursts. In addition to his drinking problem, he was, by his own admission, an inveterate womanizer. Worse yet, the couple had been determined to have children, but to no avail, eventually engaging in *in vitro* fertilization treatment in the mid-1980s, which led to a series of miscarriages. At the same time, Clapton had entered into an affair with Italian model Lory Del Santo, who gave birth to Eric's son Conor in August 1986. For Boyd, it was a double blow, and by April 1987, she simply couldn't stomach life with Clapton anymore. Over the coming months and years, she came to realize the difference between what she felt for Harrison and the reality of her life with Clapton: "Eric and I were playmates," she reasoned, "but George and I were soulmates, and I had let something special go without analyzing what was happening between us." At a certain level, she also realized that Clapton's infatuation had been born out of envy, just as she had reckoned back in the late 1960s, when she concluded that he hadn't really wanted her, but instead Harrison's life and all that it entailed.

In many ways, Clapton and Boyd had been doomed from the start—since childhood, even. Clapton was a tortured man. By his own admission, his life had been driven by a lingering fear of abandonment that was rooted in his mother's early absence from his life and, later, in the pretense that she was his sister, created in order to protect the family's reputation in Ripley. His mother and grandparents had forced him to betray what he knew to be true early on; traumatized, he repeated that self-betrayal as an adult. As Clapton traipsed from one band to another during the 1960s, he experienced a sense of massive emotional upheaval that resulted, in every instance, with him disbanding his current project before it had run its course, recreating the instability so familiar from childhood. His ensuing obsession with Boyd was part and parcel of a larger self-destructive urge that was exacerbated by heavy alcohol and drug abuse. For her part, Boyd's childhood was strikingly similar in terms of family dysfunction and her abuse at the hands of her stepfather. In one sense, their romance may have been founded in physical attraction, but in yet another, it had been hardwired via the trauma-bonding that characterized their life together, such as it was.

Clapton's despair over losing Boyd once and for all was tempered by the joys of fatherhood. Having hit rock bottom after Boyd divorced him in 1989, Clapton finally began taking the steps to ensure his sobriety in the long term. His triumph over alcohol would serve him well in March 1991 when he faced the most harrowing challenge of his life. That month, four-year-old Conor had plunged to his death after falling out of a window in the Manhattan apartment building where he lived with Del Santo, Clapton's now long-estranged girlfriend. Clapton would famously express his unimaginable grief with "Tears in Heaven," which he had included in his *Unplugged* set along with "Layla." On the strength of "Tears in Heaven," the *Unplugged* LP had sold an astonishing ten million copies, which provided little solace for Clapton's aching heart.

It was at this improbable moment that Clapton reached out to his cherished friend Harrison to broach the notion of touring Japan in December 1991. In recent years, Harrison had enjoyed a string of successes with his *Cloud Nine* LP and the Traveling Wilburys supergroup, which also included Bob Dylan, Jeff Lynne, Roy Orbison, and Tom Petty. The idea to take Harrison out on the road had actually been Olivia Del Santo's. In the years since Lennon's senseless murder in December 1980, Harrison had become increasingly reclusive. And when it came to live performance, Harrison still smarted over what he perceived to be his mistreatment at the hands of the rock press during his 1974 North American "Dark Horse" tour. In spite of his gnawing grief, Clapton took up the assignment on behalf of his old friend. In short order, he put together a band, led a series of rehearsals that November, and accompanied Harrison on a twelve-day swing across Japan the following month.

At Clapton's urging, Harrison had assembled a twenty-five-song set with generous helpings from his Beatles and solo careers. They closed each show with thunderous takes on "While My Guitar Gently Weeps" and the Chuck Berry classic "Roll Over Beethoven." At one point, Harrison even had an opportunity to provide support for Clapton, when Del Santo arrived out of the blue, hoping to rekindle her relationship with Clapton in the wake of their son's death. As Clapton later recalled, "Lory showed up out of the blue and just checked into our hotel. I couldn't handle it. Curiously enough, George stepped in and took control. They travelled around together and he seemed to have a calming influence on her." But ultimately, Clapton realized that Harrison simply couldn't find his comfort level on stage, Clapton's presence notwithstanding. "It was a fine program, well-rehearsed with great songs and tremendous musicianship," Clapton later wrote, "but I knew his heart wasn't in it. He didn't really seem to like playing live, so it did nothing for him, except maybe give him a chance to see how much he was loved, both by his fans and by us."

Clapton would be there for Harrison, too, in December 1999, after the Harrisons were attacked at Friar Park by a madman bent on killing the former Beatle. It had been a gruesome scene, to be sure, and Harrison only managed to survive that attack after Arias subdued the intruder and called the police. Clapton would never forget sitting in the kitchen at Friar Park with Arias and family friend Brian Roylance as Harrison "relived the night that that crazy guy, Michael Abram, had come after him with a knife, believing himself to be on a 'mission from God' to kill him." In the media, Harrison had attempted to downplay the situation with his well-known sense of humor, saying that his attempted murderer "wasn't a burglar, and he certainly wasn't auditioning for the Traveling Wilburys." But Clapton could tell that his friend had been genuinely traumatized. Only later would Clapton realize that that was the last time he would ever see Harrison alive.

On November 29, 2001, Clapton learned that Harrison had died at age fifty-eight after a lengthy battle with cancer. Roylance had kept Clapton abreast of their friend's condition throughout the ordeal. At Olivia Arias and Dhani Harrison's request, Clapton agreed to serve as the musical director for a memorial concert to be held on the first anniversary of Harrison's death. So it came to be that Clapton assembled a band in Harrison's service for one last time. The other Dominos may not have been present on stage, but there were plenty of veteran musicians from the *All Things Must Pass* sessions, and, more recently, from the Japanese tour back in 1991. For Clapton, it was a genuine honor to provide his oldest rock 'n' roll friend with a first-class rock 'n' roll send-off. On November 29, 2002, the Concert for George commenced in London's Royal Albert Hall, with all proceeds going to the Harrisons' Material World Charitable Foundation. To his credit, Clapton had drawn participants from all walks of Harrison's life, including McCartney and Starr; Ravi Shankar and his daughter Anoushka; members of the Monty Python comedy troupe; and such rock stalwarts as Tom Petty, Jeff Lynne, Gary Brooker, Klaus Voormann, Billy Preston, and Jim Keltner, among a host of others. For his part, Clapton was never far from the stage, singing the *Rubber Soul*-era "If I Needed Someone," backing up Preston on "Isn't It a Pity," singing a pair of stirring duets with McCartney on "Something" and "While My Guitar Gently Weeps," and lending spirited guitar backing to such classic Harrison tunes as "All Things Must Pass," "My Sweet Lord," and "Wah Wah."

But buried deep in the set was the concert's emotional highlight. When Clapton took the stage to sing "Beware of Darkness" from *All Things Must Pass*, he turned in the event's most moving performance, a knowing take on Harrison's cautionary tale about the danger of cleaving too dearly to our illusions. Having reached age fifty-six—with plenty of scars, both emotional and physical, to show for it—Clapton knew a thing or two about suffering in the service of his illusions. But at the same time, he could surely take solace, like all of us, from George Harrison's kindly admonition that we should "beware of sadness / It can hit you / It can hurt you." But mostly, living in despair is simply "not what you are here for." It's tempting to draw a line from this performance straight back to the day Clapton had first played the song while making Harrison's album, at a time when Clapton was beginning the most self-destructive phase of his life while nonetheless holding himself together enough to make great music. But the line goes back further still, to that night in 1966 when Harrison saw the Cream guitarist backstage, and the young Beatle's natural kindness and generosity compelled him to take notice of Clapton and make a connection, which he would maintain for the rest of his life. At the Concert for George, as Clapton roared to life in the crescendo of "Beware of Darkness," the message was clear: now that the interpersonal strife, the insecurities, and the crippling self-sabotage had abated, what remained was a legacy of transcendent music and the memory of a deep and unshakeable friendship.

ACKNOWLEDGMENTS

A PROJECT OF THIS MAGNITUDE could not possibly come to fruition without the encouragement and support of a host of friends and colleagues. We owe special debts of thanks to the community of music historians and specialists, including Jim Berkenstadt, Allen Goldstein, Matt Hurwitz, Ashley Kahn, Mark Lewisohn, Dan Matovina, Joe Montague, Tim Riley, Marc Roberty, Sara Schmidt, and Bruce Spizer. We are grateful to Chip Madinger, for patiently answering numerous questions and providing valuable details about the EMI recording sessions, and to Andrea Robbins, whose unofficial @ theharrisonarchive on Instagram is an essential resource for George Harrison fans that consistently suggests new insights and avenues for research. Special thanks are due to Gary Evans and Julie Evans for permission to cite vital session data from the Malcolm Frederick Evans Archives. For their eyewitness accounts regarding the making of these landmark albums, tremendous gratitude goes to John Barham, Ray Connolly, Brian Gibson, Kevin Harrington, John Kurlander, John Leckie, Bill Levenson, Alan Parsons, Cathy Sarver, Phil Spector, Allan Steckler, Chris Thomas, Ken Townsend, Klaus Voormann, Nick Webb, and Alan White. Although we weren't able to speak to him due to a timing issue, we would like to thank Bobby Whitlock for his consideration. We are especially thankful for the support of the folks at Chicago Review Press, particularly Kara Rota and Ben Krapohl, as well as for the indefatigable efforts of our publicist Nicole Michael.

APPENDIX
Sessionographies

All Things Must Pass Sessionography

In his diary, Mal Evans kept detailed notes on who played at each session for *All Things Must Pass*, and then later he documented the postproduction process. He accompanied Badfinger to Hawaii for a Capitol Records conference on June 4, 1970, and his diary is blank for June 7–12. Information for those dates as well as other details have been filled in using data included in the *All Things Must Pass* thirtieth-anniversary remaster and the fiftieth-anniversary Uber Box Set. All 1970 EMI sessions were engineered by Phil McDonald and John Leckie, except for the July 25 session for "Apple Scruffs," which was engineered by Phil McDonald and John Barrett.

Saturday, March 29, 1969
Apple Studios
"Jam Peace"

This jam was recorded during a preliminary session for Billy Preston's album *That's the Way God Planned It*. The recording features George Harrison and Eric Clapton on electric guitar, Klaus Voormann on bass, Billy Preston on piano, and Ginger Baker on drums. At EMI Studios on May 12, 1969, with Phil McDonald and Alan Parsons engineering, Harrison added various Moog synthesizer effects during the mix, because the eight-track tape was full, leaving no room for overdubs. John Lennon dubbed the recording "Jam Peace" and inscribed "Plastic Ono Band" on the mix tape box, marking the first instance of that band name's usage on a recording. Lennon had intended to use the

241

recording himself, but in July 1970 Harrison pulled the tape and eventually claimed it for the Apple Jam disc of *All Things Must Pass*, giving it the title "I Remember Jeep" after Eric Clapton's dog, an "orangy-brown" Weimaraner named Jeep.

Tuesday, May 26, 1970
EMI Studio 3

The first of two days of studio demos recorded for the benefit of Phil Spector and the musicians who would play on the upcoming sessions. In this first session, Harrison taped fifteen songs, joined on most by Ringo Starr on drums and Klaus Voormann on bass. All spellings are as inscribed on the tape boxes: "All Things Must Pass" (2 takes), "Behind That Locked Door," "Dera Dera Duhn," "I Live For You," "Apple Scruffs," "What Is Life?" (3 takes, including a track with piano, with the third marked best; guitar overdubs by Klaus and George plus harmony vocal overdubs), "Awaiting for You All," "Isn't It a Pity" (2 takes), "I'll Have You Anytime," "I Dig Love," "Going Down to Golders Green" (3 takes), "Behind That Locked Door" (take 2), "All Things Must Pass" (take 3), "Derra Derra Doon" (take 2), "Om Hare Om (Gopala Krishna)," "Ballad of Sir Frankie Crisp (Let It Roll)" (2 takes, with vocal refrain by Mal Evans), "My Sweet Lord," "Apple Scruffs" (takes 2–4, guitar and vocal only), "Sour Milk Sea" (guitar and vocal only).

Wednesday, May 27, 1970
EMI Studio 3

The second day sees George demo another fifteen tunes, accompanying himself only on electric or acoustic guitar, except for "Wah Wah," which has a bass part most likely played by Klaus Voormann.

"Run of the Mill," "Art of Dying," "Everybody Nobody," "Wah Wah," "Window Window," Untitled ("Never Seen Such a Beautiful Girl"), "Beware of Darkness," "Let It Down," "Tell Me What Has Happened to You," Untitled 2 ("Hear Me Lord"), "No Where to Go," "Cosmic Empire," "Mother Divine," "I Don't Wanna Do It," "If Not For You."

Thursday, May 28, 1970
EMI Studio 3

"Wah Wah" (takes 1–3, take 3 marked best)

George Harrison (electric guitar), Eric Clapton (electric guitar), Ringo Starr (drums), Klaus Voormann (bass), Pete Ham (acoustic guitar), Joey Molland (acoustic guitar), Mike Gibbons (acoustic guitar), Gary Brooker (piano), Alan White (congas), Mal Evans (maracas), Bobby Whitlock (electric piano).

"My Sweet Lord" (takes 1–16, take 16 marked best)

George Harrison (vocal and acoustic guitar), Eric Clapton (acoustic guitar), Ringo Starr (drums), Klaus Voormann (bass), Pete Ham (acoustic guitar), Joey Molland (acoustic guitar), Mike Gibbons (acoustic guitar), Gary Brooker (piano), Alan White (tambourine), Bobby Whitlock (harmonium).

"I'd Have You Anytime" (takes 1–6)

George Harrison (vocal and acoustic guitar), Eric Clapton (electric guitar), Ringo Starr (drums), Klaus Voormann (bass), Pete Ham (acoustic guitar), Joey Molland (acoustic guitar), Mike Gibbons (acoustic guitar), Alan White (vibraphone), Bobby Whitlock (harmonium).

Friday, May 29, 1970
EMI Studio 3, 3:30 PM–2:00 AM

"I'd Have You Anytime" (takes 7–13, take 7 marked best)

George Harrison (vocal and acoustic guitar), Eric Clapton (electric guitar), Ringo Starr (drums), Klaus Voormann (bass), Badfinger (acoustic guitars), Bobby Whitlock (harmonium), Tony Ashton (vibraphone).

"Art of Dying" (takes 1–9, take 9 marked best)

George Harrison (vocal and guitar), Eric Clapton (electric guitar [takes 1–5 only]), Badfinger (acoustic guitars), Ringo Starr (drums), Klaus Voormann (bass), Bobby Whitlock (harmonium [takes 1–5], piano [takes 6–9]), Tony Ashton (piano), Alan White (percussion [takes 8 & 9]).

"Run of the Mill" (takes 1 & 2)

George Harrison (vocal and acoustic guitar)

"Isn't It a Pity" (take 1)

George Harrison (vocal and guitar), Eric Clapton (guitar), Ringo Starr (drums), Klaus Voormann (bass), Badfinger (guitars), Chris Thomas (Moog synthesizer), Tony Ashton (piano), unknown—possibly Bobby Whitlock (piano), John Barham (electric harpsichord), Alan White (percussion).

Tuesday, June 2, 1970
EMI Studio 3, 2:30 PM–1:30 AM

"Isn't It a Pity" (takes 2–19, take 19 marked best); this will be labeled VERSION ONE

George Harrison (acoustic guitar), Ringo Starr (drums), Klaus Voormann (bass), Mike Gibbons (maracas), Pete Ham (acoustic guitar), Joey Molland (acoustic guitar), Gary Wright (electric piano), Billy Preston (grand piano), Martin Kershaw (electric guitar [2:30 PM–7:00 PM]), Ray Galow (acoustic guitar [2:30–7:00 PM]), Chris Thomas (Moog synthesizer), John Barham (electric harpsichord), Alan White (tambourine).

"I Dig Love" (takes 1–31, take 20 marked best)

George Harrison (electric guitar [steel]), Eric Clapton (electric guitar [steel]), Ringo Starr (drums), Klaus Voormann (bass), Bobby Whitlock (organ), Mike Gibbons (tambourine), Alan White (congas), Gary Wright (piano), Billy Preston (electric piano).

Wednesday, June 3, 1970
EMI Studio 3, 5:00 PM–12:00 AM

"Isn't It a Pity" (takes 20–30, take 30 marked best); this will be labeled VERSION TWO

George Harrison (guitar), Eric Clapton (Leslie guitar), Klaus Voormann (bass), Alan White (drums [8:00 PM–12:00 AM]), Mike Gibbons (unknown, probably percussion), Joey Molland (unknown, probably guitar), Pete Ham (unknown, probably guitar), Bobby Whitlock (harmonium), Billy Preston (piano), Gary Wright (unknown keyboard).

Thursday, June 4, 1970
EMI Studio 3

"The Ballad of Sir Frankie Crisp (Let It Roll)" (takes 1–2)

George Harrison (acoustic guitar), Peter Frampton (acoustic guitar), Gary Wright (piano); other personnel unknown.

"If Not for You" (takes 1–8)

George Harrison (acoustic guitar), Peter Frampton (acoustic guitar), Klaus Voormann (bass); organ, piano, drums—personnel unknown.

Friday, June 5, 1970
EMI Studio 3

"If Not for You" (takes 9–18, take 18 marked best)

George Harrison (acoustic guitar), Peter Frampton (acoustic guitar), Klaus Voormann (bass); organ, piano, drums—personnel unknown.

"The Ballad of Sir Frankie Crisp (Let It Roll)" (takes 3–8, take 8 marked best)

George Harrison (acoustic guitar), Peter Frampton (acoustic guitar), Klaus Voormann (bass), Pete Drake (pedal steel guitar); organ, piano, drums—personnel unknown. Mal Evans will overdub his "Oh Sir Frankie Crisp" backing vocals on July 26.

"Behind That Locked Door" (takes 1–13, take 13 marked best)

George Harrison (guitar), Peter Frampton (acoustic guitar), Klaus Voormann (bass), Pete Drake (pedal steel guitar); drums, electric guitar, piano, organ—personnel unknown.

Tuesday, June 9, 1970
EMI Studio 3

"I Live for You" (takes 1–16)

George Harrison (acoustic guitar), Klaus Voormann (bass), Ringo Starr (drums), Peter Frampton (acoustic guitar), Pete Drake (pedal steel guitar); electric guitar (with vibrato) and two pianos—personnel unknown.

Wednesday, June 10, 1970
EMI Studio 3

"All Things Must Pass" (takes 1–19, take 18 marked best)

George Harrison (acoustic guitar), Klaus Voormann (bass), Ringo Starr (drums), Peter Frampton (acoustic guitar), Pete Drake (pedal steel guitar), Eric Clapton (backing vocals—overdubbed), Bobby Whitlock (backing vocals—overdubbed); piano, harmonium—personnel unknown.

"I Live for You" (takes 17–32, take 32 marked best)

George Harrison (acoustic guitar), Klaus Voormann (bass), Ringo Starr (drums), Peter Frampton (acoustic guitar), Pete Drake (pedal steel guitar); electric guitar (with vibrato) and two pianos—personnel unknown.

"Art of Dying" (take 10)

George Harrison (acoustic guitar), Ringo Starr (drums), Klaus Voormann (bass), Peter Frampton (acoustic guitar), Pete Drake (pedal steel guitar), Billy Preston (piano), Phil Collins (congas); harmonium—personnel unknown.

Thursday, June 11, 1970
EMI Studio 3

Pete Drake overdubs pedal steel onto "Ballad of Sir Frankie Crisp (Let It Roll)" and "Behind That Locked Door."

"Woman Don't You Cry for Me" (takes 1–3)

George Harrison (acoustic guitar, foot taps [take 3 only], harmonica [take 3 only]).

Friday, June 12, 1970
EMI Studio 3

Pete Drake demonstrates his "Talking Steel Guitar."

Thursday, June 18, 1970
EMI Studio 3

Derek and the Dominos: "Tell the Truth" (takes 1–??)

Jams: "Thanks for the Pepperoni" and "Plug Me In"

Eric Clapton (electric guitar), Bobby Whitlock (organ), Carl Radle (bass), Jim Gordon (drums), George Harrison (electric guitar), Dave Mason (electric guitar).

Monday, June 22, 1970
EMI Studio 3, 7:00 PM–1:00 AM

"What Is Life?" (takes 1–4)

George Harrison (electric guitar), Eric Clapton (electric guitar), Carl Radle (bass), Jim Gordon (drums), Tom Evans (acoustic guitar), Pete Ham (acoustic guitar), Dave Mason (acoustic guitar), Gary Wright (piano), Bobby Whitlock (piano), Alan White (percussion).

"Awaiting on You All" (take 1 & 2)

George Harrison (electric guitar), Eric Clapton (electric guitar), Carl Radle (bass), Jim Gordon (drums), Tom Evans (acoustic guitar), Pete Ham (acoustic guitar), Dave Mason (acoustic guitar), Gary Wright (piano), Bobby Whitlock (organ), Alan White (percussion).

"Beware of Darkness" (takes 1–5)

George Harrison (electric guitar), Eric Clapton (electric guitar), Carl Radle (bass), Jim Gordon (drums), Tom Evans (acoustic guitar), Pete Ham (acoustic guitar), Dave Mason (acoustic guitar), Gary Wright (piano), Bobby Whitlock (organ), Alan White (vibraphone).

"What Is Life?" (takes 5–11)

George Harrison (electric guitar), Eric Clapton (electric guitar), Carl Radle (bass), Jim Gordon (drums), Tom Evans (acoustic guitar), Pete Ham (acoustic guitar), Dave Mason (acoustic guitar), Gary Wright (piano), Bobby Whitlock (piano), Alan White (percussion).

Tuesday, June 23, 1970
EMI Studio 3, 2:30 PM–2:00 AM

"What Is Life?" (takes 12–27)

George Harrison (electric guitar), Eric Clapton (electric guitar), Carl Radle (bass), Jim Gordon (drums), Tom Evans (acoustic guitar), Pete Ham (acoustic guitar), Dave Mason (acoustic guitar), Gary Wright (unknown keyboard), Bobby Whitlock (unknown keyboard), Alan White (percussion).

"Beware of Darkness" (takes 6–14, take 6 marked best)

George Harrison (electric guitar), Eric Clapton (electric guitar [through Leslie speaker on take 8]), Carl Radle (bass), Jim Gordon (drums), Tom Evans (acoustic guitar), Pete Ham (acoustic guitar), Dave Mason (acoustic guitar), Gary Wright (piano), Bobby Whitlock (organ), Alan White (vibraphone).

"Hear Me Lord" (takes 1–3)

George Harrison (electric guitar), Eric Clapton (electric guitar [through Leslie speaker on take 8]), Carl Radle (bass), Jim Gordon (drums), Tom Evans (acoustic guitar), Pete Ham (acoustic guitar), Gary Wright (piano), Bobby Whitlock (organ), Alan White (percussion).

Wednesday, June 24, 1970
EMI Studio 3, 2:30 PM–2:30 AM

"Hear Me Lord" (takes 4–8, take 8 marked best)

George Harrison (electric guitar), Eric Clapton (electric guitar [through Leslie speaker on take 8]), Bobby Whitlock (organ), Carl Radle (bass), Jim Gordon (drums), Gary Wright (piano).

"Let It Down" (takes 1–8, take 8 marked best)

George Harrison (electric guitar), Eric Clapton (electric guitar), Bobby Whitlock (organ), Carl Radle (bass), Jim Gordon (drums), Gary Wright (piano).

"Gopala Krishna" (takes 1–3)

Personnel unknown but likely with same musicians as above.

"Run of the Mill" (takes 3 & 4, both incomplete run-throughs)

Full band recording, personnel unknown but likely with same musicians as above.

Thursday, June 25, 1970
EMI Studio 3

Derek and the Dominos: "Tell the Truth" (takes ??—28)

"Roll It Over" (takes 1–2, take 2 marked best)

Eric Clapton (electric guitar), Bobby Whitlock (piano), Carl Radle (bass), Jim Gordon (drums), George Harrison (electric guitar), Dave Mason (electric guitar); with overdubs of harmony vocals, slide guitar, and percussion onto take 2 of "Roll It Over."

Friday, June 26, 1970
EMI Studio 2, 7:00 PM–2:00 AM

"Awaiting on You All" (takes 3–25, take 25 marked best)

They try several different arrangements before reaching the master. George Harrison (fuzz guitar), Eric Clapton (electric guitar), Bobby Whitlock (organ), Carl Radle (bass), Jim Gordon (drums), Klaus Voormann (guitar, bass [from 8:00 PM on]). The brass—consisting of two trumpets, two tenor saxes, two baritone saxes, one alto saxophone, one trombone, and one bass trombone—are all recorded live onto track 7 of the eight-track tape.

Tuesday, June 30, 1970
EMI Studio 3, 2:30 PM–8:30 PM

Derek and the Dominos Session

Further work on "Tell the Truth."

EMI Studio 3, 9:30 PM–5:00 PM

"Run of the Mill" (takes 5–39)

George Harrison (Leslied acoustic), Eric Clapton (electric guitar), Bobby Whitlock (organ), Carl Radle (bass), Jim Gordon (drums), Bobby Keys (saxophone),

Jim Price (trumpet), Gary Wright (piano), Klaus Voormann (electric piano), Hank Marvin (electric guitar).

Wednesday, July 1, 1970
EMI Studio 3, 5:00 PM-??

"Run of the Mill" (takes 40–61, take 61 marked best)

George Harrison (acoustic guitar), Eric Clapton (acoustic guitar), Bobby Whitlock (harmonium), Carl Radle (bass), Jim Gordon (drums), Bobby Keys (saxophone), Jim Price (trumpet), Gary Wright (piano), Klaus Voormann (acoustic guitar).

"Art of Dying" (takes 11–26, take 26 marked best)

George Harrison (electric guitar), Eric Clapton (electric guitar), Bobby Whitlock (organ), Carl Radle (bass), Jim Gordon (drums), Bobby Keys (saxophone), Jim Price (trumpet), Gary Wright (electric piano), Klaus Voormann (electric guitar).

Thursday, July 2, 1970
EMI Studio 3, 5:00 PM-1:00 AM

"Out of the Blue"

The only recording from this date is this twenty-minute jam, edited down to 11:13 for the Apple Jam disc. Note that Eric Clapton is not present on this recording. George Harrison (electric guitar), Klaus Voormann (electric guitar), Bobby Whitlock (organ), Carl Radle (bass), Jim Gordon (drums), Bobby Keys (saxophone), Jim Price (trumpet), Gary Wright (electric piano [5:00 PM–1:00 AM]).

Friday, July 3, 1970
EMI Studio 3, 6:30 PM-4:30 AM

"What Is Life?" (takes 28–42, take 42 marked best)

George Harrison (fuzz guitar), Eric Clapton (electric guitar), Bobby Whitlock (piano), Carl Radle (bass), Jim Gordon (drums), Bobby Keys (saxophone), Jim Price (trumpet), Klaus Voormann (acoustic guitar).

Monday, July 6, 1970
EMI Studio 3, 7:00 PM–??

Derek and the Dominos: "Tell the Truth" (takes 34–37, take 37 marked best)

Eric Clapton (electric guitar), Bobby Whitlock (guitar + piano overdub), Carl Radle (bass), Jim Gordon (drums), Dave Mason (electric guitar).

George's mother passed away on July 7 and her funeral would be held on July 10.

Monday, July 20, 1970
EMI Studios, 2:30 PM–??

Work begins on overdubs for *All Things Must Pass*. Ringo attends this session but nothing else is known about the work done this day. Phil Spector is not in the UK at this point and no further work is done this week.

Saturday, July 25, 1970
EMI Studio 3, 2:30 PM–7:00 AM

"Apple Scruffs" (takes 1–18, take 18 marked best)

George Harrison (acoustic guitar, harmonica, vocals), Mal Evans (percussion).

Sunday, July 26, 1970
EMI Studios, 7:30 PM–5:00 AM

Mal Evans overdubs his "Oh Sir Frankie Crisp" backing vocals onto "Let It Roll"; the other work done this day is unknown.

July 27–August 12, 1970

Two weeks of steady work on many of the songs by George alone, including overdubs of slide guitar and backing vocals, plus acoustic guitars with Peter Frampton. Some orchestral overdubs are done at EMI as well.

Monday, July 27, 1970
EMI Studio 2, 4:00 PM–1:30 AM

Phil McDonald does eight-track-to-eight-track reduction mixes to make space for further overdubs at EMI. Songs include "Awaiting On You All," "What Is

Life?" "Let It Down," and "Art of Dying," though all of these will see work at Trident Studios as well.

Tuesday, July 28, 1970
EMI Studios, 3:00 PM–3:30 AM

George pulls the "Jam Peace" tape, indicating he is already considering releasing the jams from his sessions.

Sunday, August 2, 1970
EMI Studios, 10:00 PM–12:00 AM

An overdub session for six violins, six violas, four cellos, and "flute doubling on alto."

Monday, August 3, 1970
EMI Studios, 2:30 PM–1:00 AM

Overdubs of one baritone saxophone, two tenor saxophones, two trumpets (doubling on flügelhorns), one trombone, plus Bobby Keys and Jim Price. This is probably for "All Things Must Pass."

Tuesday, August 4, 1970
EMI Studio 1 with No. 2 Control Room, 10:00 AM–5:00 AM

A long day of string and brass overdubs for songs unknown. Phil Spector leaves at midnight after four hours of brass recording, with George Harrison playing guitar with the musicians in the studio. George works until 5:00 AM with Jim Price and Bobby Keys.

Wednesday, August 5, 1970
EMI Studios, 7:00 PM–5:00 AM

George Harrison arrives at 6:35 PM, followed by Mal Evans at 6:45, Phil Spector at 8:30. Work with Jim Price and Bobby Keys from 9:00 PM to 5:00 AM.

Thursday, August 6, 1970

There is an EMI session this evening, but Mal Evans notes that not much is accomplished.

Friday, August 7–Wednesday, August 12, 1970

No details available.

Tuesday, August 18, 1970

Driver Alf Bicknell picks up John Barham at 1:00 PM to go to Friar Park, presumably to work on scores for the rest of the songs.

Wednesday, September 2, 1970
Trident Studios, 10:00 AM–5:00 PM

With Ken Scott engineering, George Harrison adds layers and layers of backing vocals first to "My Sweet Lord" and then to "Wah Wah."

Thursday, September 3, 1970
Trident Studios, 10:00 AM–5:00 PM

Unspecified work on "Art of Dying"

Friday, September 4, 1970
Trident Studios, 10:00 AM–5:00 PM

George Harrison multiplies himself into another chorus, adding backing vocals onto "Hear Me Lord," which will have as many as twenty-two voices.

Saturday, September 5, 1970
Trident Studios, 2:30 PM–??

Sunday, September 6, 1970
Trident Studios, 2:30 PM–??

Thursday, September 10, 1970
Trident Studios, 2:30 PM–??

Overdubs of brass onto "Hear Me Lord": four tenor saxophones, four trumpets, one trombone, and one baritone saxophone. Saxophones: Dave Brooks, Stan Suzlmann, Geoff Driscoll, and Phil Kenzie, Dave Coxhill (baritone saxophone). Trumpets: Terry Noonan, Bud Parks, Bob Thompson, Mike Davies. Trombone: Derek Wadsworth.

Friday, September 11, 1970
Trident Studios, 2:30 PM-??

Saturday, September 12, 1970
Trident Studios, 2:30 PM-???

Work on "Isn't It a Pity" version 2. From 2:30 PM to 4:30 PM, George Harrison supervises orchestral overdubs. The instrumentation is: two flutes, two clarinets (one to double bass clarinet), two oboes (one to double English horn), and one bassoon (also to double contrabassoon). Mal Evans also picks up Chris Thomas with Moog synthesizer at AIR Studios, 214 Oxford Street, and brings him to Trident for an overdub of the Moog onto the song.

Friday, September 18, 1970
Trident Studios, 2:30 PM-??

A full day of orchestral overdubs for three songs. First up, from 2:30 to 5:30 PM, "Isn't It a Pity" version 1, which sees overdubs of eight violins, eight violas, four cellos, two double basses, timpani, flute, oboe, two tenor saxes, two trumpets, trombone, tuba, and baritone saxophone.

Next, from 6:30 to 9:30 PM, the addition of eight violins, eight violas, four cellos, and two double basses onto "My Sweet Lord."

Finally, from 9:30 to 11:30 PM, George Harrison experiments with a high-energy overdub of oboe and piccolo trumpet onto "What Is Life?" Oboist Léon Goossens, who received an OBE in 1950 and commissioned works from Edward Elgar and Ralph Vaughan Williams, was offered the gig but declined because "I don't like that sort of music."

September 19–24 & 26–28, 1970

Work at Trident Studios, most likely sixteen track mixes.

Friday, October 2, 1970
Olympic Studios, 6:00 PM-8:00 PM

George Harrison does rough mixes of the tapes for the Radha Krishna Temple album, which will be released in May 1971.

Tuesday, October 6, 1970
EMI Studios, Remix Room, 2:30 PM-??

Wednesday, October 7, 1970
EMI Studios, Remix Room, 2:30 PM-??

Further work on the album at EMI, and recording "It's Johnny's Birthday."

This same date, George Harrison also tapes a slide guitar part for a novelty recording by producer (and former Beatles engineer) Norman Smith. The record is issued by Smith using the pseudonym Amos Gherkin Quartet.

Thursday, October 8, 1970

Remix work at Trident.

Friday, October 9, 1970

Remix work at EMI.

October 10–13, 17–18 & 21, 1970

Remix work at Trident.

Thursday, October 22, 1970
Apple Studios, 4:00 PM-??

Engineer George Peckham masters *All Things Must Pass.*

Layla and Other Assorted Love Songs Sessionography

Derek and the Dominos session data has been compiled from the twentieth- and fortieth-anniversary editions of *Layla and Other Assorted Love Songs* as well as additional session sheets and tape boxes provided by Bill Levenson, producer of those box sets. Only the master takes and a few alternates of each song were kept, along with some of the jams; session tapes were destroyed. All sessions were recorded at Atlantic South–Criteria Studios, Miami, Florida. Recording engineers: Ron Albert, Chuck Kirkpatrick, Howie Albert, Karl Richardson, and Mac Emerman. Executive producer: Tom Dowd. Produced and arranged by the Dominos.

Wednesday, August 26, 1970

"Anyday" (unreleased)

Jam 2: Eric Clapton, Bobby Whitlock, Carl Radle, Jim Gordon.

Jam 3: Eric Clapton, Bobby Whitlock, Carl Radle, Jim Gordon.

"Have You Ever Loved a Woman" (alternate take 1)

Thursday, August 27, 1970

"Key of D Jam": Eric Clapton, Duane Allman, Dickey Betts, Bobby Whitlock, Gregg Allman, Berry Oakley, Butch Trucks.

Jam 4: Eric Clapton, Duane Allman, Dickey Betts, Bobby Whitlock, Gregg Allman, Berry Oakley, Butch Trucks.

Jam 5: Eric Clapton, Duane Allman, Bobby Whitlock, Carl Radle, Jim Gordon.

"Tell the Truth" (Jam 1): Eric Clapton, Bobby Whitlock, Carl Radle, Jim Gordon.

"Tell the Truth" (Jam 2): Eric Clapton, Bobby Whitlock, Carl Radle, Jim Gordon.

"Tender Love" ("double time drums" on tape box, unreleased)

"Tender Love" ("2/4 drums—Best version" on tape box, unreleased)

"Tender Love" (2:45): Eric Clapton, Bobby Whitlock, Carl Radle, Jim Gordon.

"(When Things Go Wrong) It Hurts Me Too": Eric Clapton, Duane Allman.

Friday, August 28, 1970

"Tell the Truth" (Basic Track): Eric Clapton, Bobby Whitlock, Carl Radle, Jim Gordon.

Sunday, August 30, 1970

"Key to the Highway" (live master take, no overdubs): Eric Clapton, Duane Allman, Bobby Whitlock, Carl Radle, Jim Gordon.

Monday, August 31, 1970

"Nobody Knows You When You're Down and Out" (live master take, no overdubs): Eric Clapton, Duane Allman, Bobby Whitlock, Carl Radle, Jim Gordon, Albhy Galuten (piano).

"Why Does Love Got to Be So Sad" (basic track + overdub: Clapton, lead guitar): Eric Clapton, Duane Allman, Bobby Whitlock, Carl Radle, Jim Gordon.

"Have You Ever Loved a Woman" (alternate take 2): Eric Clapton, Bobby Whitlock, Carl Radle, Jim Gordon.

Tuesday, September 1, 1970

"Keep On Growing" (basic track + overdubs: Clapton, two lead guitar tracks; Whitlock, lead vocal): Eric Clapton, Duane Allman, Bobby Whitlock, Carl Radle, Jim Gordon.

"Tell the Truth" (overdub: Clapton, slide guitar, tracks 15 & 16): Eric Clapton, Duane Allman, Bobby Whitlock, Carl Radle, Jim Gordon.

"Why Does Love Got to Be So Sad" (overdub: Duane Allman, lead guitar)

Wednesday, September 2, 1970

Jam 1: Eric Clapton, Bobby Whitlock, Carl Radle, Jim Gordon.

"I Looked Away" (basic track + overdubs: Clapton and Whitlock, vocals; Clapton, two tracks of lead guitar; percussion): Eric Clapton, Bobby Whitlock, Carl Radle, Jim Gordon.

"Keep On Growing" (overdubs: congas, tambourine)

"Bell Bottom Blues" (basic track + overdubs: Clapton, two tracks of lead guitar): Eric Clapton, Bobby Whitlock, Carl Radle, Jim Gordon.

"Have You Ever Loved a Woman" (master take live, no overdubs): Eric Clapton, Duane Allman, Bobby Whitlock, Carl Radle, Jim Gordon.

Thursday, September 3, 1970

"I Am Yours" (basic track): Eric Clapton, Duane Allman, Bobby Whitlock, Carl Radle, Jim Gordon.

"Anyday" (basic track + overdubs: tambourine and maracas): Eric Clapton, Duane Allman, Bobby Whitlock, Carl Radle, Jim Gordon.

"It's Too Late" (basic track): Eric Clapton, Duane Allman, Bobby Whitlock, Carl Radle, Jim Gordon.

Friday, September 4, 1970

"I Looked Away" (overdub: Whitlock, vocal)

"Bell Bottom Blues" (overdub: Clapton and Whitlock, vocals, both doubled on chorus)

"I Am Yours" (overdub: Whitlock, third harmony vocal; tabla)

"Anyday" (overdubs: Clapton and Whitlock, vocals)

"Why Does Love Got to Be So Sad" (overdubs: Clapton and Whitlock, vocals; tambourine)

"Tell the Truth" (overdubs: cowbell and toms)

Saturday, September 5, 1970

"Keep On Growing" (overdub: Clapton and Whitlock, vocals)

Wednesday, September 9, 1970

"Keep On Growing" (overdubs: Clapton, new lead guitar track 2, replacing Duane's lead; Clapton and Whitlock, new vocal tracks; cowbell/maracas, track 15; tunable toms & cymbals, track 16)

"Bell Bottom Blues" (overdub: Clapton fixes his vocal in verse 2, bars 5–8)

"Little Wing" (complete live take, no overdubs): Eric Clapton, Duane Allman, Bobby Whitlock, Carl Radle, Jim Gordon.

"Layla" (section 1, take 11, basic track): Bobby Whitlock (organ), Jim Gordon (drums), Eric Clapton (rhythm guitar), Carl Radle (bass), Duane Allman (solos).

"Layla" (section 1, overdubs: tambourine; Clapton/Duane Allman, duplicate solos; Clapton, guitar harmony, 3 tracks)

"Layla" (section 2, basic track): Jim Gordon (piano).

"Layla" (section 2, overdubs: percussion; Clapton, Leslie guitar; Duane Allman, bottleneck, two tracks; bass; cymbals)

"It's Too Late" (overdubs: Clapton, lead vocal; Whitlock, lead and harmony vocals)

"It's Too Late" (alternate master)

"I Am Yours" (overdub: shaker)

Thursday, September 10, 1970

"Thorn Tree in the Garden" (complete live take, no overdubs): Eric Clapton, Duane Allman, Bobby Whitlock, Carl Radle, Jim Gordon.

"Thorn Tree in the Garden" (with triangle, unreleased): Eric Clapton, Duane Allman, Bobby Whitlock, Carl Radle, Jim Gordon.

Thursday, October 1, 1970

"Layla" (overdub, section 1: Clapton, guitar)

"Layla" (overdubs, section 2: Clapton, box guitar reinforcement of lead; Whitlock, piano reinforcement of lead)

"It's Too Late" (overdub: Clapton, bridge vocal)

Friday, October 2, 1970

"Mean Old World" (rehearsals + take 1, 14:59)

"Mean Old World" (band version, master take, 3:39)

"Mean Old World" (duet version, master take, 3:54)

Five takes total were recorded; only these three have been released.

Eric Clapton, Duane Allman, Bobby Whitlock, Carl Radle, Jim Gordon.

NOTES

Prologue: Hammersmith Odeon, December 1964

"Hanging out backstage" through *"The Beatles were then"*: Eric Clapton, *Clapton: The Autobiography* (New York: Three Rivers, 2007), 51.

"They were playing good" through *"for the first time"*: Clapton, 46.

"What I immediately liked": Clapton, 45.

"While most other bands": Clapton, 49.

"Sam did his first": Michael Schumacher, *Crossroads: The Life and Music of Eric Clapton* (Boston: Little, Brown, 2020), 44.

"Who, in their right mind": Peter E. Meltzer, *So You Think You Know Rock and Roll?: An In-Depth Q&A Tour of the Revolutionary Decade, 1965–1975* (New York: Sky-horse, 2017), 297.

"told me that it was quite": Clapton, *Clapton: The Autobiography*, 54.

"I was developing" and *"In truth"*: Clapton, *Clapton: The Autobiography*, 48.

"The truth is": Clapton, 53.

"I just met him then": Ashley Kahn, ed., *George Harrison on George Harrison: Interviews and Encounters* (Chicago: Chicago Review Press, 2020), 225.

"He seemed to like what I did": Clapton, *Clapton: The Autobiography*, 51.

"like looking at myself" through *"It's the same with me"*: Kahn, 51; Joshua M. Greene, *Here Comes the Sun: The Spiritual and Musical Journey of George Harrison* (New York: Wiley, 2007), 291.

Chapter 1. The Quiet Beatle

"priests used to come round": The Beatles, *The Beatles Anthology* (San Francisco: Chronicle Books, 2000), 26.

"Before that" through *"confirm it later for myself"*: The Beatles, 26.

"From then on" through *"another church or pub"*: The Beatles, 26.

"was very pleasant": Graeme Thomson, *George Harrison: Behind the Locked Door* (London: Omnibus, 2013), 29–30.

262 | NOTES TO PAGES 3–15

"I had a happy childhood": The Beatles, *The Beatles Anthology*, 26.

"jolly, very friendly and outgoing" through *"She'd always tell you how she felt, Louise"*: Thomson, *George Harrison*, 24–25.

"In those days": The Beatles, *The Beatles Anthology*, 26.

"He taught us a few basic root chords straightaway": Bob Spitz, *The Beatles: The Biography* (Boston: Little, Brown, 2005), 122.

"funny break in-between songs": The Beatles, *The Beatles Anthology*, 28. With its powerful transmitter located in the tiny European nation of Luxembourg, Radio Luxembourg began offering French and English broadcasts in 1933 and was a forerunner of the pirate radio stations that broadcast across England and Europe via ships. Radio Luxembourg reached its influential peak in the 1950s, when it contributed to the popularization of rock 'n' roll in Great Britain.

"We asked George": The Beatles, 12.

"The Quarry Men": The Beatles, 30.

"When George was a kid": Keith Badman, *The Beatles Off the Record: Outrageous Opinions and Unrehearsed Interviews* (London: Omnibus, 2001), 19.

"It was difficult to play": Andy Babiuk, *Beatles Gear: All the Fab Four's Instruments, from Stage to Studio* (San Francisco: Backbeat, 2001), 27.

"That was our first professional gig": The Beatles, *The Beatles Anthology*, 44.

"Sieg heil!": Mark Lewisohn, *The Beatles Live!* (London: Pavilion, 1986), 39.

"In the Kaiserkeller": The Beatles, *The Beatles Anthology*, 49.

"booted out of town": The Beatles, 55.

"Everyone—the whole lot": Philip Norman, *Shout!: The Beatles in Their Generation* (New York: Simon and Schuster, 1981), 106.

"It was that evening": Badman, *The Beatles Off the Record*, 29.

"We probably looked German": The Beatles, *The Beatles Anthology*, 59.

"Tony Sheridan had an up-side": The Beatles, *The Beatles Anthology*, 62.

"I doubt I would have" and *"looking out the window"*: Mark Lewisohn, *Tune In: The Beatles—All These Years* (New York: Crown, 2013), 137, 444.

"Paul came with me": The Beatles, *The Beatles Anthology*, 65.

"I saved up for years": Lewisohn, *Tune In*, 465.

"The name 'Beatle' meant nothing": Brian Epstein, *A Cellarful of Noise: The Autobiography of the Man Who Made the Beatles* (New York: Pocket, 1998), 94–95.

"Hello there": Epstein, 98–99.

"we've got to have them down": Spitz, *The Beatles: The Biography*, 274, 285.

Chapter 2. Abbey Road

"*I remember when*": John C. Winn, *Way Beyond Compare: The Beatles' Recorded Legacy, Volume One: 1957–1965* (Sharon, VT: Multiplus, 2003), 6–7; Spitz, *The Beatles: The Biography*, 28.

"*groups with guitars*" through "*Stick to that*": Spitz, *The Beatles: The Biography*, 28.

"*It's* interesting": Spitz, 301.

"*We didn't go to the funeral*": The Beatles, *The Beatles Anthology*, 69.

"CONGRATULATIONS, BOYS": Lewisohn, *Tune In*, 624.

"*Well, I don't like your tie*": Spitz, *The Beatles: The Biography*, 318.

"*The first gig*" and "*Some of the fans*": The Beatles, *The Beatles Anthology*, 77.

"*much too dreary*": Geoff Emerick and Howard Massey, *Here, There, and Everywhere: My Life Recording the Music of the Beatles* (New York: Gotham, 2006), 44–45.

"*Gentlemen, you've just made*": Lewisohn, *Tune In*, 773.

"*While we were staying at the Plaza*": The Beatles, *The Beatles Anthology*, 77.

"*Brian Epstein and I worked out a plan*": Lewisohn, *The Complete Beatles Recording Sessions: The Official Abbey Road Studio Session Notes, 1962–1970* (New York: Harmony, 1988), 28.

"*The train took us to Cornwall*": Pattie Boyd and Penny Junor, *Wonderful Tonight: George Harrison, Eric Clapton, and Me* (New York: Three Rivers, 2007), 60–61.

"*as the train neared London*": Boyd and Junor, 60–61.

"*There was a press photo call*": Boyd and Junor, 62–63.

"*I had never felt so miserable*": Boyd and Junor, 12–15.

"*I felt as though my world had ended*": Boyd and Junor, 17, 23.

"*London belonged to the young*": Boyd and Junor, 47.

"*I took him home*": Boyd and Junor, 62–63, 66, 90.

"*serious*" through "*new music*": William Mann, "What Songs the Beatles Sang," *Times*, December 27, 1963, www.jolomo.net/music/william_mann.html; William J. Dowlding, *Beatlesongs* (New York: Simon and Schuster, 1989), 57; Deryck Cooke, "The Lennon-McCartney Songs," *Vindications: Essays on Romantic Music* (Cambridge: Cambridge University Press, 1982), 196–200.

"*Songwriting for me*" and "*John and I had really*": The Beatles, *The Beatles Anthology*, 96, 194.

"*written for George*": David Sheff, *All We Are Saying: The Last Major Interview with John Lennon and Yoko Ono*, ed. G. Barry Golson (New York: Griffin, 2000), 165–166.

"*I was sick in bed*": The Beatles, *The Beatles Anthology*, 96.

"*I knew a little bit*": The Beatles, 96.

"*I had bought a very cheap sitar*": Badman, *The Beatles Off the Record*, 190.

"*spirit guide*": Thomson, *George Harrison*, 11.

"Nobody I know": The Beatles, *The Beatles Anthology*, 263.

"been awfully poor": George Martin, "Listen to My Story: George Martin Interview with *Melody Maker*," interview by Richard Williams, *Melody Maker*, August 21, 1971.

"there is no doubt in my mind": George Martin and Jeremy Hornsby. *All You Need Is Ears* (New York: St. Martin's, 1994), 259.

"Religion, inevitably, played": Boyd and Junor, *Wonderful Tonight*, 27–28.

"Maharishi used to say": The Beatles, *The Beatles Anthology*, 263.

Chapter 3. Little Bastard

"was divided into" through "One day I heard": Clapton, *Clapton: The Autobiography*, 5.

"Ours was run": Clapton, 8.

"that would single me out": Clapton, 12

"which was permanently switched on": Clapton, 17; Schumacher, *Crossroads*, 11.

"Music became a healer": Clapton, *Clapton: The Autobiography*, 18.

"One evening": Clapton, 10.

"There was something": Clapton, 20.

"One night they had Buddy Holly": Clapton, 21.

"The instrument I had": Clapton, 23.

"I learned it totally" and "Though I still hadn't": Clapton, 25.

"Guitar playing": Clapton, 25; See Bruce M. Conforth, *Up Jumped the Devil: The Real Life of Robert Johnson* (Chicago: Chicago Review Press, 2019).

"It was almost like": Schumacher, *Crossroads*, 34.

"it was almost as if": Schumacher, *Crossroads*, 145.

"following this man's example": Clapton, *Clapton: The Autobiography*, 40.

"I saw a very odd-looking guitar": Clapton, 25.

"tremendous sense of belonging": Clapton, 25.

"which was to accompany yourself": Clapton, 29; see Bob Riesman, *I Feel So Good: The Life and Times of Big Bill Broonzy* (Chicago: University of Chicago Press, 2011).

"star-struck": Clapton, *Clapton: The Autobiography*, 30.

"all the students": Clapton, 36.

"I knew my portfolio": Clapton, 36.

"You've had your chance": Clapton, 37.

"Almost as soon as I arrived": Clapton, 38.

"the best guitar of the day": Clapton, 39.

"Something more profound": Clapton, 39.

"was a fantastic guy": Clapton, 41.

"Pop was the order of the day": Clapton, 42.

"I'd never heard": Clapton, 43.

"They'd just released": Clapton, 45.
"In my role": Clapton, 48.

Chapter 4. Clapton Is God

"shy, frightened, and disheartened": Clapton, *Clapton: The Autobiography*, 56.
"He had the air": Clapton, 58.
"I hadn't really listened": Clapton, 60.
"I was absolutely terrified": Clapton, 64.
"I was a bit mystified": Clapton, 64.
"tons of white American": Clapton, 64–65.
"John insisted I do vocals" and *"What I would do"*: Clapton, 72.
"There was an underground feeling": David Sinclair, "1966 – The Year That Built Rock: The Brit Blues Boom," *Louder*, January 22, 2016, www.loudersound.com /features/1966-the-year-that-built-rock-the-british-blues-boom.
"like a father to me": Clapton, *Clapton: The Autobiography*, 80; see Sinclair, "1966."
"was not a happy experience": Clapton, 80.
"It was like an early punk song": Chris Welch, *Cream: The Legendary Sixties Supergroup* (San Francisco: Backbeat, 2000), chapter 2.
"The song Jimi wanted to play": Clapton, *Clapton: The Autobiography*, 80.
"Even though I was not overawed": Clapton, 84.
"was thoroughly confused": Clapton, 86.
"blinding. I don't think": Jon Brewer, dir., *Cream: Their Fully Authorized Story* (Image Entertainment, 2005).
"Where all the other songs": Harry Shapiro and Cesar Glebbeek, *Jimi Hendrix: Electric Gypsy* (New York: St. Martin's Press, 1990), 137.
"I will never forget": Clapton, *Clapton: The Autobiography*, 87.
"It stopped me": Clapton, 96.
"Mediterranean feel": Clapton, 103.
"I went to Esher": Jan Reid, *Layla and Other Assorted Love Songs by Derek and the Dominos* (New York: Rodale, 2006), viii, ix.
"I also coveted": Clapton, *Clapton: The Autobiography*, 173.
"I was aware": Boyd and Junor, *Wonderful Tonight*, 141.
"He becomes different people": Reid, *Layla and Other Assorted*, 102.
"riff, a form": Dave Headlam, "Blues Transformations in the Music of Cream," *Understanding Rock: Essays in Musical Analysis* (Oxford: Oxford University Press, 1997), 69.
"That whole song": Schumacher, *Crossroads*, 114.
"I always had to do": Elliot J. Huntley, *Mystical One: George Harrison after the Breakup of the Beatles* (Toronto: Guernica Editions, 2004), 26.

"he wanted me to play": Schumacher, *Crossroads*, 111.

"I was given the grand job": Lewisohn, *Complete Beatles Recording Sessions*, 162.

"had really impressed me": Clapton, *Clapton: The Autobiography*, 75.

"We started our professional career": Clapton, 111.

"the best band": Chris Welch, "Delaney & Bonnie: Out of the South Comes 'The Best Band in the World.'" Melody Maker, October 18, 1969.

"there's so much material": Peter Doggett, *Abbey Road/Let It Be: The Beatles* (New York: Schirmer, 1998), 12.

"that a collection of freaks" through *"See you 'round the clubs"*: Doug Sulpy and Ray Schweighardt, *Get Back: The Unauthorized Chronicle of the Beatles' Let It Be Disaster* (New York: Griffin, 1997), 170.

"I pulled in Billy Preston": Doggett, *Abbey Road/Let It Be*, 33, 38.

"It's bad enough with four": Sulpy and Schweighardt, *Get Back*, 124, 232; see Kevin Ryan and Brian Kehew, *Recording the Beatles: The Studio Equipment and Techniques Used to Create Their Classic Albums* (Houston: Curvebender, 2006), 506.

"It took my breath away" and *"George's 'Something' was"*: The Beatles, *The Beatles Anthology*, 266.

"George was blossoming": The Beatles, 403.

"A lot of time and effort": Emerick and Massey, *Here, There, and Everywhere*, 282.

"fantastic experience" through *"Like six hours"*: Kahn, *George Harrison on George Harrison*, 291, 307.

"If there's a God": Kahn, 188.

"De da de de" and *"a beautiful spring morning"*: Clapton, *Clapton: The Autobiography*, 106.

"'Here Comes the Sun' was written": The Beatles, *The Beatles Anthology*, 339.

"One of me best beginnings": Lewisohn, *Complete Beatles Recording Sessions*, 178.

"I think there was a great deal": George Martin, "The Producer Series, Part 1," interview by Ralph Denver, *Studio Sound*, January 1985, 58–59.

"thought, 'Bugger you'": Badman, *The Beatles Off the Record*, 477.

"avant-garde": Badman, 462; The Beatles, *The Beatles Anthology*, 347.

"full of junk": Badman, *The Beatles Off the Record*, 464–465.

"a glorified jam session": Badman, 464; see John C. Winn, *That Magic Feeling: The Beatles' Recorded Legacy, Volume Two: 1966–1970* (Sharon, VT: Multiplus, 2003), 267.

"the greatest love song": Ian MacDonald, *Revolution in the Head: The Beatles' Records and the Sixties* (New York: Holt, 1994), 305–306.

"unquiet manners": Philip Norman, "The Great God Clapton," *Sunday Times Magazine*, March 1, 1970.

"There was magic" and *"They blew me away"*: Jim Fusilli, "Clapton, Harrison, on the Bus," *Wall Street Journal*, August 14, 2010.

"is so self-effacing": Norman, "The Great God Clapton."

"Our minds were on the tour": Bobby Whitlock and Marc Roberty, *Bobby Whitlock: A Rock 'n' Roll Autobiography* (Jefferson City, NC: McFarland, 2011), 52.

"I went out after": Christopher Scapelliti, "An Oral History of Derek and the Dominos' Layla," *Guitar Player*, July 2, 2020, www.guitarplayer.com/players/an-oral-history-of-derek-and-the-dominos-layla.

"My solo career really began": Clapton, *Clapton: The Autobiography*, 120.

"an experience": Clapton, 120.

Ormsby-Gore departed almost immediately: Robert Mcg. Thomas Jr., "She Follows a Life Style All Her Own," *New York Times*, May 14, 1972.

"The suggestion didn't shock me": Clapton, 122.

"It would appear" through *"in the end"*: Keith Altham, "Eric Clapton: Another Crossroad," *Fusion*, February 6, 1970, www.rocksbackpages.com.

Chapter 5. The Party's Over

"'River Deep, Mountain High'": Richard Williams, *Phil Spector: Out of His Head* (London: Omnibus, 2009), 137.

"Phil Spector approached": The Beatles, *The Beatles Anthology*, 323.

"The First Tycoon of Teen": Williams, 77.

"if you cannot get rid": George Bernard Shaw, *Immaturity* (London: Constable, 1921), xxiv.

"Phil Spector's Wall of Sound": Mark Ribowsky, *He's a Rebel: Phil Spector—Rock and Roll's Legendary Producer* (New York: Cooper Square, 2000), 401; see Mick Brown, *Tearing Down the Wall of Sound* (New York: Knopf, 2007), 174.

"really depressed": Brown, 205, 208.

"made as an experiment" through *"I was just sayin' goodbye"*: Pete Senoff, "Spector on Pop Today," *Melody Maker*, October 11, 1969.

"I would like to record": *Rolling Stone*, November 1, 1969.

"You all will have heard": The remark jokingly references the departure in September 1969 of David John Harman (nicknamed Dave Dee) from the British rock group Dave Dee, Dozy, Beaky, Mick and Tich.

"And I said": Martin Scorsese, dir., *George Harrison: Living in the Material World* (HBO, 2011).

"Phil came in and said": Jann S. Wenner, *Lennon Remembers: The Full Rolling Stone Interviews from 1970* (New York: Verso, 2000), 16.

"and the engineer was getting" through *"It's making the whole song"*: Alan White, interview by Jason Kruppa, June 1, 2020.

"When we went into the room": Simon Leng, *While My Guitar Gently Weeps: The Music of George Harrison* (Milwaukee: Hal Leonard, 2006), 70.

"It was ridiculously loud": Williams, *Out of His Head*, 143.

"He wanted to go on with it": Williams, *Out of His Head*, 144; see Chip Madinger and Scott Raile, *Lennonology: Strange Days Indeed—A Scrapbook of Madness* (Springfield, MO: Open Your Books, 2015).

"slipped away": Stan Soocher, *Baby You're a Rich Man: Suing the Beatles for Fun and Profit* (Lebanon, NH: ForeEdge, 2015), 179; see *Bright Tunes Music Corp. v. Harrisongs Music Ltd.* 42 Federal Supplement 177 (1976).

"gospel song": Andy Davis, liner notes for *Encouraging Words*, by Billy Preston (Apple, 2010).

"And they said": Anne Nightingale, "Pop Profile—George Harrison," BBC Radio 1, February 1977.

"The dominant-seventh": Leng, *While My Guitar*, 71.

"he liked me as a person": White, interview by Jason Kruppa, June 1, 2020.

"Jazz, Western Classical": John Barham, interview by Jason Kruppa, August 12, 2020.

"Looking back": Barham, interview.

"My first meeting": Barham, interview.

"It's just all": Kahn, *George Harrison on George Harrison*, 296.

"Delaney became very possessive": Marc Roberty, *Eric Clapton: Day by Day* (Milwaukee: Backbeat, 2013), 152.

"Actually, that's Eric": Roberty, 153.

"an awful song" through *"If I'm a part"*: Johnny Moran, *The Beatles Today*, BBC Radio 1, March 11, 1970.

"permanent backing band": Moran, *The Beatles Today*.

"a great album": Moran, *The Beatles Today*.

"At the rate of doing": Alan Smith, "Beatle Single—By George!" *New Musical Express*, November 1, 1969, www.rocksbackpages.com/Library/Article/beatle-single-by-george.

"I suppose I'm waiting": Smith, "Beatle Single—By George!"

"I also am insisting": Thomson, *George Harrison*, 236.

"she didn't want": Boyd and Junor, *Wonderful Tonight*, 148.

"cheap and good": Anita McConnell, "Crisp, Sir Frank, First Baronet (1843–1919)," *Oxford Dictionary of National Biography* (Oxford: Oxford University Press, 2007), www.oxforddnb.com.

"His quick grasp": "Sir Frank Crisp, Bt.," *Proceedings of the Linnean Society of London, 1918–1919* (London: Burlington House, 1919).

thirty-room: Some latter-day sources have stated incorrectly that the mansion at Friar Park has 120 rooms.

"colorful and eccentric" and *Several smaller lodges*: "Friar Park, Henley," Victoria County History, accessed February 19, 2021, www.victoriacountyhistory.ac.uk/explore/items/friar-park-henley.

"the surname of an unknown": "Friar Park, Henley."

"*perverted proverbs*": "Home of the 'Sleeping Friars' to Be Bulldozed?" *Reading Evening Post*, February 9, 1967.

"*Yesterday—today—was tomorrow*": Harrison, *I, Me, Mine*, 280.

"*trained and cut*": "Friar Park, Henley: The Residence of Frank Crisp, Esq.," *Gardener's Chronicle*, October 28, 1899.

"*largest artificial rock garden*": "Friar Park, Henley: The Residence of Frank Crisp, Esq."

Crisp had continued: McConnell, "Crisp, Sir Frank, First Baronet (1843–1919)."

While David's ex-wife: Gerhard Bohrer, digital correspondence with Jason Kruppa, March 15, 2021.

"*cherub-faced angels*": "Home of the 'Sleeping Friars' to Be Bulldozed?"; "Henley Houses Plan Rejected," *Reading Evening Post*, October 4, 1968; see Klaus Voormann, *Warum spielst du Imagine nicht auf dem weißen Klavier, John?* (Munich: Heyne Verlag, 2003).

"*Well, I like a nice sort of garden*": Kahn, *George Harrison on George Harrison*, 44.

"*Go ahead and get it*": Timothy White, "A New *Yellow Submarine Songtrack* Due in September," *Billboard*, June 19, 1999.

"*Everything's fine*" through "*We're all unlimited!*": "The Beatles Have Unity through Diversity and Are Unlimited," *New Musical Express*, March 14, 1970, 3.

"*I got on quite well with Spector*": Lewisohn, *Complete Beatles Recording Sessions*, 197.

"*We thought you'd come 'round*" through "*I was just sinking*": Barry Miles, *The Beatles Diary, Volume 1: The Beatles Years* (London: Omnibus, 2007), 572.

"*would leave the tracks*" through "*I warned Phil*": John Kurlander, interview by Jason Kruppa, August 31, 2009.

"*If there's anything you'd like done*": Peter Doggett, *You Never Give Me Your Money: The Beatles after the Breakup* (New York: HarperCollins, 2009), 123.

"*I spoke to Paul*": Doggett, 123.

"*Is it true that neither*" through "*He asked that question of himself*": Doggett, 124.

"*Paul Quits the Beatles*": Doggett, 126.

"*a relative state of consciousness*": *Fact or Fantasy*, "Prayer and Meditation," BBC Television, April 26, 1970.

"*Through many years of pollution*": *Fact or Fantasy*, "Prayer and Meditation," BBC Television, April 26, 1970.

"*nervous breakdown*" through "*Don't ever do it again*": Doggett, *You Never Give Me*, 131.

"*the letter spoke for itself*": Doggett, 131.

"*A few weeks ago*": Doggett, 132.

Chapter 6. Harrison Comes Alive

"the first to really take": Al Aronowitz, "Staring Down Death: George Harrison and Me," *The Blacklisted Journalist*, August 1, 2001, www.blacklistedjournalist.com /column62.html.

"He came on like Attila the Hun": Al Aronowitz, "George Harrison: Why Is George in New York?" *Rolling Stone*, June 11, 1970.

"so many songs": George Harrison, interview by Howard Smith, New York City, April 25, 1970.

"I'm sure that after": Harrison, interview.

"childish": Harrison, interview.

"only temporary": *Harrison Herald*, July 1970.

Rolling Stone *ran a story*: "Bob Dylan's Secret Recording Session with George Harrison and Friends," *Rolling Stone*, May 28, 1970.

"Part of me thinks that George was happy": "Pattie Boyd Exhibits Pictures from Life with George Harrison," Sveriges Radio, September 16, 2014, sverigesradio.se/sida /artikel.aspx?programid=109&artikel=5966879.

"didn't really grow up": Jerry Gilbert, "Wolf Gathers His Flock in London," *Melody Maker*, May 16, 1970.

"The sessions over here": Roberty, *Eric Clapton: Day by Day*, 155–159.

"in case George was busy": Boyd and Junor, *Wonderful Tonight*, 136.

"She'd got a tumor on the brain": Timothy White, *George Harrison Reconsidered* (London: Larchwood and Weir, 2013).

"There's more than enough sheep": *Harrison Herald*, September 1970.

"bright and funny and witty": Lewisohn, *Tune In*, 44.

"had suddenly exploded": Lewisohn, *Tune In*, 44.

"I needed somebody to help me": Scorsese, dir., *George Harrison*.

"George likes to go": Williams, *Out of His Head*, 152.

"I knew I'd do one eventually": Harrison, interview by Smith, April 25, 1970.

"had literally hundreds of songs": Scorsese, dir., *George Harrison*.

thirty songs from which: Olivia Harrison, interview with Dark Horse Radio, November 2018.

"On one occasion": Barham, interview by Kruppa, August 12, 2020.

"I know that if I were doing": Smith, "Beatle Single—By George!"

"I started actually": John Leckie, interview by Jason Kruppa, December 2, 2019.

"second engineer": Leckie, interview.

Studio Three: See David N. Howard, *Sonic Alchemy: Visionary Music Producers and Their Maverick Recordings* (Milwaukee: Hal Leonard, 2004).

"I went to a couple of sessions": Alan Parsons, interview by Kenneth Womack, September 17, 2019.

"The first band" through *"There was never two"*: White, interview by Kruppa, June 1, 2020.

"I think this was also": Barham, interview by Kruppa, August 12, 2020.

"He would use a lot of keyboards": Ribowsky, *He's a Rebel*, 255; see also Richard Buskin, "Classic Tracks: The Ronettes' 'Be My Baby,'" *Sound on Sound*, April 2007, www .soundonsound.com/techniques/classic-tracks-ronettes-be-my-baby.

"We worked over and over": Ribowsky, 255.

"George wasn't that happy": Ribowsky, *He's a Rebel*, 255.

"When we went in to listen to it": Ribowsky, 255.

"jumping in the deep end": White, interview by Kruppa, June 1, 2020.

"I thought a lot": Harrison, *I, Me, Mine*, 176.

White has a vivid memory: White, interview by Kruppa, June 1, 2020.

"It did take a little more work": White, interview.

"The drone all the way through": Kingsley Abbott, ed., *Little Symphonies: A Phil Spector Reader* (London: Helter Skelter Publishing, 2011), 60.

"We had to learn everything very quickly": Soocher, *Baby You're a Rich Man*, 192. Eric Clapton may also be on acoustic guitar. Harrison would recall in court during the 1976 infringement case over "My Sweet Lord" that the configuration of the basic rhythm track included "five acoustic guitars, two drummers, and a tambourine player and two pianos, maybe even a harmonium, a pedal harmonium, all playing live in the studio together."

By take sixteen: Dave Simons, "Tales from the Top: George Harrison's *All Things Must Pass*," *Songwriter 101*, December 21, 2007, www.bmi.com/news/entry/Tales_From _the_Top_George_Harrisons_All_Things_Must_Pass.

"The guitar rhythm": Leckie, interview by Kruppa, December 2, 2019; see Simons, "Tales from the Top."

"They were in Studio Three": Kurlander, interview by Kruppa, August 31, 2009.

"The first day there were so many musicians": Leckie, interview by Kruppa, December 2, 2019.

"after we'd done the song": Leckie, interview by Kruppa, December 2, 2019.

"write me some words" through *"and the song appeared"*: Harrison, *I, Me, Mine*, 164.

"Maybe subconsciously": Timothy White, "*All Things* in Good Time," *Billboard*, January 8, 2001, www.billboard.com.

"Having this whole thing": Harrison, *Crawdaddy*, February 1977, www.beatlesinterviews .org.

"George's way of dealing": Voormann, *Warum spielst du Imagine*.

"told me what to play": Tim Grieving, "The Unmaking of a Beatle," *Los Angeles Times*, August 3, 2021.

"We'd all turn up": Leckie, interview by Kruppa, December 2, 2019.

"it would be endless routining": White, interview by Kruppa, June 1, 2020.

"George would play the part": Klaus Voormann, interview by Jason Kruppa, December 5, 2019.

"[Eric] and George had a really great relationship": White, interview by Kruppa, June 1, 2020.

"The Yogi who does that": Harrison, *I, Me, Mine*, 180.

"I just write a song": George Harrison, interview by David Wigg, *Scene and Heard*, BBC Radio 1, October 8, 1969, www.beatlesinterviews.org.

"He would do things": Voormann, interview by Kruppa, December 5, 2019.

Chapter 7. One Big Sound

"love lost and love gained": White, *"All Things* in Good Time."

"a large array of sounds": Chris Thomas, interview by Jason Kruppa, November 29, 2019.

"I was sitting there playing": Thomas, interview.

"Phil Spector is producing": Gary Wright, *Dreamweaver: A Memoir—Music, Meditation, and My Friendship with George Harrison* (New York: Penguin, 2014), 79.

"Wait a minute": Wright, 80–81.

"This was seriously my hero": Thomas, interview by Kruppa, November 29, 2019.

"absolutely enormous": "Harrison in Supersession," *Melody Maker*, June 13, 1970.

"All the time": Leckie, interview by Kruppa, December 2, 2019.

"And George said to Phil": Thomas, interview by Kruppa, November 29, 2019.

"After doing it for a few hours": Chris Carter, *A Conversation with George Harrison* (Capitol Records, 2001).

"One time": Voormann, interview by Kruppa, December 5, 2019.

"I think when we recorded it": Leckie, interview by Kruppa, December 2, 2019.

"As time went on": Wright, *Dreamweaver: A Memoir*, 85–86.

"[The second version] was very intimate": Voormann, interview by Kruppa, December 5, 2019.

"One of the guys in the band": Carter, *A Conversation with George*.

"'Isn't It a Pity' was pretty hard to play": White, interview by Kruppa, June 1, 2020.

"You always had it standing by": Leckie, interview by Kruppa, December 2, 2019.

"profoundly peaceful": Wright, *Dreamweaver: A Memoir*, 107–109.

"He tried to get": Voormann, interview by Kruppa, December 5, 2019.

"chanting the names": Kahn, *George Harrison on George Harrison*, 293; see Krishna.com.

"There is one sort": George Harrison in conversation with Srila Prabhupada, August 22, 1973.

"He became increasingly obsessive": Boyd and Junor, *Wonderful Tonight*, 169.

    "Do you want to meet George?": Peter Frampton, "'Nothing's Gonna Keep Me from Playing' Peter Frampton on Preparing for His Farewell Tour," interview by Tom Power, *Q*, Canadian Broadcasting Corporation, April 29, 2019, www.cbc.ca/radio/q/monday -april-29-2019-peter-frampton-rowley-irlam-and-more-1.5112767/nothing-s -gonna-keep-me-from-playing-peter-frampton-on-preparing-for-his-farewell -tour-1.5112895.

"a permanent backing band": Keith Badman, *The Beatles Diary, Volume 2: After the Break-Up, 1970–2001* (London: Omnibus, 2009).

"Clapton and Bruce to Join Miles!": "Clapton and Bruce to Join Miles!" *Melody Maker*, June 5, 1970, 1; see concerts.fandom.com/wiki/Badfinger.

"Hang on": Don Fleming and Richard Radford, archival notes for *All Things Must Pass: 50th-Anniversary Uber Box Set*, by George Harrison (Apple, 2021).

"a piece of self-indulgence": Harrison, *I, Me, Mine*, 118.

"There are a couple of songs": White, interview by Kruppa, June 1, 2020.

"Drums were set up": White, interview by Kruppa, June 1, 2020.

"George spent most of the time": Voormann, interview by Kruppa, December 5, 2019.

"Phil didn't seek": Ribowsky, *He's a Rebel*, 255.

"At one session": Barham, interview by Kruppa, August 12, 2020.

"he was really always": Voormann, interview by Kruppa, December 5, 2019.

"fifteen sessions a week" through *"wild as mountain dew"*: Douglas Green, "Pete Drake: Everyone's Favorite," *Guitar Player*, September 1973; see also petedrake.net/bio.

"One day my secretary": Tim Ghianni, "Nashville Starr: When Ringo Came to Town," *Nashville Scene*, July 3, 2008, web.archive.org/web/20080710100158/http://www .nashvillescene.com/Stories/Cover_Story/2008/07/03/Nashville_Starr/#; Green, "Pete Drake: Everyone's Favorite."

"Pete Drake was incredible": Voormann, interview by Kruppa, December 5, 2019.

"find this seed idea": Timothy Leary, *Psychedelic Prayers and Other Meditations* (Berkeley, CA: Ronin Publishing, 1997).

"We're pretending to be": White, *George Harrison Reconsidered*.

the musicians were far more receptive: Starr may be playing drums on the final take of this track. Notes Joe Montague, who makes a living studying Starr's drum style for the live show of Beatlemania: "On 'All Things Must Pass,' there is a few things. The way the hi hat very slightly opens with every backbeat. All of the fills end on crotchets (quarter notes), which Ringo did ninety-five percent of the time, as he finished the fills with the wrong hand and needed to get back to the hi hat. The overall feel is Ringo's to me, very laid back, not as smooth and 'professional' sounding as some of the other tracks. Particularly the little fill at around 2:05; it's not a smooth feel, it's got a little bump in it, which feels very much like Ringo. The fill at 2:58 ends on the high tom, another classic Ringo-ism."

"The mood in the room": White, interview by Kruppa, June 1, 2020.

"wasn't working for most of the musicians": White, interview by Kruppa, June 1, 2020.

"Nobody had a feel": Carter, *A Conversation with George*.

"I'm a jobbing drummer": Phil Collins, *Not Dead Yet: The Memoir* (New York: Crown, 2016), 64–68.

"In a slow moment": Frampton, "'Nothing's Gonna Keep Me from Playing,'" interview by Power.

"Well, everybody wanted this style" and *"You play the notes"*: Douglas Green, "Pete Drake: Everyone's Favorite," *Guitar Player*, September 1973.

"It was just the coolest effect": Peter Frampton, "Peter Frampton Talks Talk Boxes and Recording *All Things Must Pass*," interview by Damian Fanelli, *Guitar World*, 2013, www.guitarworld.com/artists/interview-peter-frampton-talks-talk-boxes -and-recording-george-harrison-all-things-must-pass; see Jeff Giles, "How Peter Frampton Met the Talk Box," *Ultimate Classic Rock*, September 9, 2014, ultimateclassicrock.com/peter-frampton-talk-box/.

"We should have done some blues": Green, "Pete Drake."

"[George's] album is fantastic": Green. See Chip Madinger and Mark Easter, *Eight Arms to Hold You: The Solo Beatles Compendium* (Springfield, MO: Open Your Books, 2018), 496; see Richard Williams, "Ringo and the Nashville Cat," *New Musical Express*, August 29, 1970.

"was there and the need was immediate": The unforeseen formation of Derek and the Dominos left Arnold's album abandoned after three more sessions in July; it remained unreleased until 2017; see Reid, *Layla and Other Assorted* and www .udiscovermusic.com/stories/derek-and-the-dominos-take-a-bow/.

Clapton was both producing and playing guitar: Clapton and Whitlock may have dropped in on Harrison's session later, since they're present on backing vocals on "All Things Must Pass."

"It wasn't a pressure situation": Roberty, *Eric Clapton: Day by Day*.

"Eric had this big chest": Ashley Kahn, essay and liner notes for *Layla and Other Assorted Love Songs: 40th-Anniversary Super Deluxe Edition*, by Derek and the Dominos (Polydor, 2011), 6.

"It was all finished": Whitlock and Roberty, *Bobby Whitlock*, 84.

"the relatively radical causes": Clapton, *Clapton: The Autobiography*, 124.

billed as "Eric Clapton and Friends": The British music papers—dated Saturday, June 13, but on newsstands as early as Wednesday, June 10—indicate just how last-minute Gordon's admission into the group had been. Based on information almost cer- tainly filed prior to Gordon's arrival in London on the tenth, *Disc and Music Echo* reported, "Eric Clapton's backing group at the two Lyceum charity concerts this

Sunday is now set. It features Bobby Whitlock on organ, Jim Keltner on drums and bassist Carl Radle." See *Disc and Music Echo*, June 13, 1970, 4.

Photos taken backstage: See www.thecrimson.com/article/1971/4/26/the-radical-consciousness-of-dr-spock/]; *Guardian*, June 4, 1970; *Observer*, June 7, 1970; Roberty, *Eric Clapton: Day by Day*.

"Del" or "Derek": Possibly an elision of "Delaney" and "Eric."

"Derek and the Dynamics": See Robert Hilburn, "Clapton Finds the Right Combination," *Los Angeles Times*, November 17, 1970.

the final revision: Roberty, *Eric Clapton: Day by Day*.

"It wasn't going to be": Whitlock and Roberty, *Bobby Whitlock*, 84–85.

"When we did the Lyceum gig": Kahn, essay and liner notes for *Layla*, 8.

"because Dave Mason had joined us": Clapton, *Clapton: The Autobiography*, 125.

"Eric leads and sings his heart out": Reid, *Layla and Other Assorted*, 104–105.

"His concert at the Lyceum": *Melody Maker*, June 27, 1970.

Chapter 8. Derek Is Eric

"We made our bones": Reid, *Layla and Other Assorted*, xiii.

"All we did was jam": Clapton, *Clapton: The Autobiography*, 123.

"Telegram to Eric": Mal Evans, Diaries, June 17, 1970, Malcolm Frederick Evans Archives.

"15 minutes": Harrison, *I, Me, Mine*, 162.

"I was just going to bed": Scorsese, dir., *George Harrison*.

"methods just to stop": Moran, *The Beatles Today*.

"The purpose is to give people": *Fact or Fantasy*, "Prayer and Meditation," BBC Television, April 26, 1970.

"This was new": Boyd and Junor, *Wonderful Tonight*, 122, 160.

"the cosmic illusion" through *"He pointed out a group of blue firs"*: Scorsese, dir., *George Harrison*.

"[George] also wrote these things": Olivia Harrison, interview on KSHE-95, December 26, 2018.

"He just lived by his deeds": Scorsese, dir., *George Harrison*.

"gospel feel": Whitlock and Roberty, *Bobby Whitlock*.

"I mean, I'm happy": Voormann, interview by Kruppa, December 5, 2019.

"Every song had meaning": Whitlock and Roberty, *Bobby Whitlock*, 77.

"He talked a lot": Leckie, interview by Kruppa, December 2, 2019.

"Phil was on him all the time": Brown, *Tearing Down the Wall of Sound*, 147. See Brian Southall, *Abbey Road: The Story of the World's Most Famous Studios* (Wellingborough: Patrick Stephens, 1982), 116.

"Lots of people say he was crazy": Voormann, interview by Kruppa, December 5, 2019.

"Phil would talk a lot": Leckie, interview by Kruppa, December 2, 2019.

"plus all the other naughty things": George Harrison, "A Conversation with George Harrison," interview by Mick Brown, *Rolling Stone*, April 19, 1979.

"What most people don't know": Voormann, interview by Kruppa, December 5, 2019.

"as soon as I smoked pot": Wigg, *Scene and Heard.*

"would create a unique kind of high": Clapton, *Clapton: The Autobiography*, 123.

"that you took a certain amount": Clapton, 125.

"warm all over": Whitlock and Roberty, *Bobby Whitlock*, 78.

In a moment of weakness: See Scapelliti, "An Oral History."

"We used to actually": Leckie, interview by Kruppa, December 2, 2019.

"I think the intro" and *"extraordinary"*: Barham, interview by Kruppa, July 11, 2020.

"souped up with Lansing speakers": Roberty, *Eric Clapton*, 146.

"a little portable amp": Matthew Longfellow, dir., *Classic Albums: John Lennon, Plastic Ono Band* (Eagle Rock Entertainment, 2008).

"The equipment would be left out": Leckie, interview by Kruppa, December 2, 2019.

"the problem with partnerships": Harrison, *I, Me, Mine*, 188.

"I played guitar": Voormann, interview by Kruppa, December 5, 2019.

"too close": Al Aronowitz, "Georgemania!" *Blacklisted Journalist*, July 1, 2001, www
.blacklistedjournalist.com/column61a.html.

"because we could go off": Leckie, interview by Kruppa, December 2, 2019.

"So all I could do": White, *"All Things* in Good Time."

"One day we came in": Leckie, interview by Kruppa, December 2, 2019.

"I can remember Phil Spector": Leckie, interview.

"The single" through *"what they were thinking"*: Bill Levenson, interview by Jason Kruppa, June 18, 2020.

"I wrote on the recording sheet": Leckie, interview by Kruppa, December 2, 2019.

"It's filled with that frustration": White, *George Harrison Reconsidered.*

"George's most affecting piece": Robert Christgau, "I.P.M.C.," *Village Voice*, September 1971.

"Sorry about your ma": Scorsese, dir., *George Harrison.*

Harrison never discussed: Voormann, interview by Kruppa, December 5, 2019.

"bad time": White, *George Harrison Reconsidered.*

he chose not to share very much: Boyd and Junor, *Wonderful Tonight.*

"John used to disappear": Cliff Jones, "We're Waiting for the Beatles," *MOJO*, October 1996, www.rocksbackpages.com.

"Looking back": Jones, "We're Waiting for the Beatles."

"Outside the studio door": Jones.

"always took time": Thomson, *George Harrison*, 245.

"We were waiting": Cathy Sarver, interview by Jason Kruppa, June 7, 2020.

"George, in particular": Jones, "We're Waiting for the Beatles."

"Of course, we were dumbfounded": Seth Swirsky, dir., *Beatles Stories* (Cinema Libre, 2011).

"I remember it as dark": Jones, "We're Waiting for the Beatles."

"Once we were back outside": Sarver, interview by Kruppa, June 7, 2020.

"George always came up": Voormann, interview by Kruppa, December 5, 2019.

"I don't know": Frampton, "Peter Frampton Talks Talk Boxes," interview by Fanelli.

"George told me": Voormann, interview by Kruppa, December 5, 2019.

"In the overdubbing": Scorsese, dir., *George Harrison.*

"What people couldn't understand": Robert Hilburn, "Tearing Down the Wall of Silence: Pop Legend Phil Spector Is Talking Comeback a Decade after Drawing the Curtain on His Life," *Los Angeles Times,* November 10, 1991.

"He'd want to take": Brown, *Tearing Down the Wall of Sound,* 247.

"He was very drunk": Voormann, interview by Kruppa, December 5, 2019.

"You couldn't help but like Phil": Jones, "We're Waiting for the Beatles."

"I worked with George": Barham, interview by Kruppa, August 12, 2020.

"It was quite simple really": Ken Townsend, interview by Kenneth Womack, December 4, 2019.

"It's possible, but it's risky": Leckie, interview by Kruppa, December 2, 2019.

"I think the expectation": Nick Webb, interview by Jason Kruppa, November 6, 2019.

only facility in London with sixteen-track recording: George Martin's AIR Studios in Oxford Circus, which would also have sixteen-track recording, wouldn't open for business until October 1970.

"I didn't really want": White, *George Harrison Reconsidered.*

"old rock and roll style" through *"I hope they make sense"*: Phil Spector, August 19, 1970, letter to Harrison. Special thanks are due to Allen Goldstein for sharing his transcription.

"I don't believe in eight-tracks": Smith, "Beatle Single—By George!"

Chapter 9. Miami

"want to go on the road": Kevin Harrington, interview by Kenneth Womack, February 3, 2021.

"We did a club tour": Richard Havers, "Derek and the Dominos' Historic First Gig in London," udiscovermusic, June 14, 2019, www.udiscovermusic.com/stories/derek-and-the-dominos-take-a-bow/.

"If Clapton wants to lose": Christopher Sandford, *Clapton: Edge of Darkness* (London: Da Capo, 1994), 116.

"The experiment of Derek": Roberty, *Eric Clapton: Day by Day,* 164.

"Tom gave so much time to me": Kahn, essay and liner notes for *Layla,* 10.

"I'm doing Idlewild South": Reid, *Layla and Other Assorted*, 115.

"I had alerted the staff": Kahn, essay and liner notes for *Layla*, 11.

"Whoaaaaaah, what the hell": Scapelliti, "An Oral History."

"a purist sound": Reid, *Layla and Other Assorted*, 115–116.

"That's the one thing": Kahn, essay and liner notes for *Layla*, 12.

"whenever there's an Eric": Bill Levenson, *"Layla's* 40th: The *Where's Eric!* Interview with Bill Levenson," *Where's Eric!*, March 19, 2011, www.whereseric.com/eric-clapton -news/303-laylas-40th-wheres-eric-interview-bill-levenson.

"had gotten more intimate" through *"low levels"*: Kahn, essay and liner notes for *Layla*, 11.

"As I think back on it": Reid, *Layla and Other Assorted*, 116–117.

"We were fit": Reid, 116–117.

"I blurted the whole thing out": Clapton, *Clapton: The Autobiography*, 187.

"You mean that guy": Reid, *Layla and Other Assorted*, 120.

"It was just really magical": Sam Hare, "Slowhand Remembers Skydog: Eric Clapton Comments on Duane Allman," *Hittin' the Note* 26 (2000), https://duaneallman .info/slowhandremembersskydog.htm.

"air of complete conviction": Clapton, *Clapton: The Autobiography*, 128.

"They were trading licks": Reid, *Layla and Other Assorted*, 121–122.

"We were invited": Kahn, essay and liner notes for *Layla*, 13.

"Let's get him to play": Kahn, 13.

"Okay, man": Reid, *Layla and Other Assorted*, 122.

"a conversation or two": Kahn, essay and liner notes for *Layla*, 15.

"to another place": Reid, *Layla and Other Assorted*, 122.

"For a start": Hare, "Slowhand Remembers Skydog."

"several drug stores": "Duane Allman's Coricidin Bottle (Slide)," *Ground Guitar*, 2005, www.groundguitar.com/duane-allman-guitars-and-gear/duane-allmans-coricidin -bottle-slide/.

"scoring coke and hookers": Reid, *Layla and Other Assorted*, 124.

"It was like I was expressing": Scapelliti, "An Oral History."

"Eric is coming along": Reid, *Layla and Other Assorted*, 123.

"After recording": Scapelliti, "An Oral History."

"Carl Radle was into Chuck Willis": Kahn, essay and liner notes for *Layla*, 20.

"I knew that sooner or later": Kahn, 15.

not only captured the essence: Scapelliti,, "An Oral History."

"There had to be some sort of telepathy": "100 Greatest Guitar Solos," *Guitar World*, October 28, 2008, web.archive.org/web/20090831061616/http:/www.guitarworld .com/article/100_greatest_guitar_solos_14_quotlaylaquot_eric_clapton_duane _allman.

"*I'd kind of fallen in love with Duane*": Hare, "Slowhand Remembers Skydog."

"*Jimi Hendrix had sat in with us*": Scapelliti, "An Oral History"

"*framework*": Clapton, *Clapton: The Autobiography*, 127.

"*Duane suggested it*": Scapelliti, "An Oral History."

"*sublime*": Kahn, essay and liner notes for *Layla*, 20.

"*Afterward, we were in the foyer*": Scapelliti, "An Oral History."

"*sitting in a circle*": Kahn, essay and liner notes for *Layla*, 21.

"*By the time I got back to America*": Clapton, *Clapton: The Autobiography*, 239.

"*called 'Time'*": Scapelliti, "An Oral History."

"*The nature of its origin*": Whitlock and Roberty, *Bobby Whitlock*, 97.

"*What are you gonna do?*": Coolidge's sister Priscilla would record a version of "Time" with Booker T. Jones in 1973. See Dean Budnick, "Delta Spirit: Rita Coolidge Reflects on Delaney & Bonnie, Mad Dogs & Englishmen, 'Layla,' and More," *Relix Media*, October 25, 2016, relix.com/articles/detail/delta_spirit_rita_coolidge _reflects_on_delaney_bonnie_mad_dogs_englishmen_layla_and_more/.

"*Gordon was playing these octaves*": Scapelliti, "An Oral History."

"*Eric gets more of an open*": Kahn, essay and liner notes for *Layla*, 20–21.

"*when they wanted to add on the finale*": Scapelliti, "An Oral History."

"*You don't realize*" through "*the stuff was recorded*": Kahn, essay and liner notes for *Layla*, 16.

"*general mayhem, drunkenness, and drugs*": Harrington, interview by Womack, February 3, 2021.

Chapter 10. Let It Roll

"*The voices suffered*": Abbott, *Little Symphonies*, 146.

"*Dear Mailbag*": Davis, liner notes for *Encouraging Words*.

"*We'd do four or six tracks*": Ken Scott, *Abbey Road to Ziggy Stardust: Off the Record with the Beatles, Bowie, Elton, and So Much More* (Los Angeles: Alfred Music, 2012), 102–103.

"*George's big thing*": Tom Doyle, "Let It Roll," *MOJO*, June 2020, www.rocksbackpages .com.

"*I went down to Trident*": Thomas, interview by Kruppa, November 29, 2019.

"*Betty and Cyril*" and "*The George O'Hara Smith Singers*": *All Things Must Pass* liner notes.

"*I started playing slide*": White, *George Harrison Reconsidered*.

"*I remember Ravi*": George Harrison, "George Harrison Interviewed," interview by Timothy White, *Goldmine*, November 27, 1992.

"*To the western ear*": John Barham, interview by Jason Kruppa, July 11, 2020.

"As opposed to his friend Eric": See Voormann, *Warum spielst du Imagine.*

"'My Sweet Lord' must have taken": Scorsese, dir., George Harrison.

"During one session": John Barham, interview by Jason Kruppa, June 16, 2020.

"The energetic strings": Barham, interview with Kruppa, July 11, 2020.

"In preparing the string arrangements": Barham, interview.

"I tried having this piccolo trumpet player": White, *"All Things* in Good Time."

"When it came time to mix": Tris Penna, "The Beatles Solo: *All Things Must Pass,"* BBC
    Radio 2, September 28, 2019.

"The conclusion": Scott, *Abbey Road to Ziggy Stardust,* 103–104.

"I listened to that stuff": Penna, "The Beatles Solo."

a note in Mal Evans's diary: Mal Evans, *Diaries,* July 28, 1970, Malcolm Frederick
    Evans Archives.

"the price will be too high": Betty Cantor-Jackson, interview with Cloud Surfing,
    March 20, 2010, www.cloudsurfing.gdhour.com/archives/tag/george-harrison.

"I listened to it": British Beatles Fan Club, archived at picboon.com/photo-video/B
    _J5m0oK2lQ.

"George Harrison used to pop into": Townsend, interview by Womack, December
    4, 2019.

"Eddie had a fine baritone voice": Leckie, interview by Kruppa, December 2, 2019.

"Dear Carol, Cathy, and Lucy": Swirsky, dir., *Beatles Stories.*

"never knew if he wanted": Scorsese, dir., *George Harrison;* see Barry Feinstein and Chris
    Murray, *George Harrison: Be Here Now* (New York: Rizzoli, 2020).

"Originally, when we took the photo": Kahn, *George Harrison on George Harrison,*
    534.

"definitely [be] a double": Feinstein and Murray, *George Harrison: Be Here Now,* 18.

"a black and white photo of you": "Original Painting for *All Things Must Pass* Poster,"
    Beatles Magazine, May 26, 2014, beatlesmagazine.blogspot.com/.

The East Indian style that Wilkes used: Roshni Subudhi, "Pattachitra: A Spectacular
    Folk Art Form from Odisha," *Culture Trip,* October 25, 2016, theculturetrip.com.

shadowy photo of Harrison: The photo of Harrison playing guitar would be used on
    the picture sleeve of the "What Is Life?" single the following year, while the dark
    close-up photo would appear on the sleeve of the single for "My Sweet Lord."

The bottom layer shows: Bruce Spizer, *The Beatles Solo on Apple Records* (New Orleans:
    498 Productions, 2010), 226.

"wanting to be some kind": Boyd and Junor, *Wonderful Tonight,* 122.

"No illicit sex": Wigg, *Scene and Heard.*

scrap the idea: Spizer, *The Beatles Solo on Apple Records,* 227.

"I picked 'My Sweet Lord'": See Badman, *The Beatles Diary, Volume 2.*

"a new stroke of light": Richard Williams, "Album Reviews," *Billboard,* December 19, 1970.

"*both an intensely personal*": Ben Garson, "*All Things Must Pass*," *Rolling Stone*, January 21, 1971.

"*the* War and Peace*"*: Alan Smith, "George Harrison: *All Things Must Pass*," *New Musical Express*, December 5, 1970.

"*somewhere along the line*": Christgau, "I.P.M.C."

"*and there was a friend of mine*": Harrison, *Crawdaddy*, February 1977.

"*Well, it's better than Paul's*": Wenner, *Lennon Remembers*, 18.

"*My idea in 'My Sweet Lord'*": George Harrison, interview by Mukunda Goswami, *Transcend*, September 4, 1982, www.transcend.org/tms/2020/03/george-harrison -25-feb-1943-29-nov-2001/.

Billy Preston's original: Apple released Preston's recording of the song as a single on December 3, 1970. It peaked at number ninety in February.

"*Every time I put the radio on*": Nicholas Schaffner, *The Beatles Forever* (New York: McGraw-Hill, 1978), 143.

would be nominated: Harrison lost the Grammy in both instances to Carole King, for "It's Too Late" and *Tapestry*, respectively.

"*was like a dead dog*": Kahn, essay and liner notes for *Layla*, 26.

"*unrelenting and monotonous press litany*": Harry Shapiro, *Eric Clapton: Lost in the Blues* (New York: Da Capo, 1992), 12.

"*from the magnificent*" through "*electric guitar*": Roy Hollingworth, "Derek and the Dominos: *Layla and Other Assorted Love Songs*," *Melody Maker*, December 12, 1970, www.rocksbackpages.com.

"*pointless and boring*": Ellen Sander, "Rock 1970: A Level of Excellence," *Saturday Review*, December 26, 1970, 38.

"*Eric's developing style*": Ed Leimbacher, "*Layla and Other Assorted Love Songs*," *Rolling Stone*, December 24, 1970.

"*even though this one*": Robert Christgau, "Consumer Guide (15)," *Village Voice*, January 7, 1971.

"*I remember George*": Kahn, essay and liner notes for *Layla*, 22.

"*Everybody wanted Eric*": Scapelliti, "An Oral History."

"*I had a call*": Clapton, *Clapton: The Autobiography*, 139.

"*It's one of my favorites*": Kahn, essay and liner notes for *Layla*, 37.

"*Paranoia was getting pretty heavy*": Kahn, 37–38.

"*Jim and Eric weren't talking*": Kahn, 37.

"*Drugs were the beginning*": Scapelliti, "An Oral History."

"*I was a bachelor*": Scapelliti, "An Oral History."

"*I think she was deeply touched*": Clapton, *Clapton: The Autobiography*, 139.

"*I don't think*": Boyd and Junor, *Wonderful Tonight*, 173.

"One day": Clapton, *Clapton: The Autobiography*, 140.

"I waited two years": Scapelliti, "An Oral History."

"George knew that Eric": Boyd and Junor, *Wonderful Tonight*, 174–175.

"I got to the sound check": Clapton, *Clapton: The Autobiography*, 147.

"Music should be used": Aronowitz, "Georgemania!"

Epilogue: Royal Albert Hall, November 2002

"he must have known": Sheff, *All We Are Saying*, 150.

Bright Tunes filed suit against Harrison: The long and winding legal battle involving "He's So Fine" and "My Sweet Lord" is covered in exacting detail by Soocher in his book *Baby You're a Rich Man: Suing the Beatles for Fun and Profit*.

"radio stations all over the country": Soocher, *Baby You're a Rich Man*, 178.

"Those bastards": In 1975, the Chiffons recorded a cover of "My Sweet Lord," dropping "He's so fine" into the lyrics at one point. See Joseph C. Self, "The 'My Sweet Lord'/'He's So Fine' Plagiarism Suit," web.archive.org/web/20020208074051/http://abbeyrd.best.vwh.net/mysweet.htm.

"So George was aware": Soocher, *Baby You're a Rich Man*, 181, 191.

"It is clear": Soocher, 190.

"I don't feel guilty": Harrison, *I, Me, Mine*, 176.

"It was difficult": See the liner notes for *All Things Must Pass*, thirtieth-anniversary remastered edition (Apple, 2001).

"So we're sitting there": Penna, "The Beatles Solo."

"I didn't include it": White, *"All Things* in Good Time."

no trace of his name in the credits: Eric Clapton was likewise not credited, though according to Harrison it was to avoid entanglements with their respective record companies at the time. This was the same reason Harrison had been credited as "L'Angelo Misterioso" on Cream's *Disraeli Gears* album.

"Really, Phil?" through *"play congas badly"*: Collins, *Not Dead Yet*, 73–74.

"A lot of people new to me": See the liner notes for *All Things Must Pass*, thirtieth-anniversary remastered edition.

"I felt that there": Kahn, *George Harrison on George Harrison*, 298.

"amazing collection": Ed Naha, "Review: *Layla and Other Assorted Love Songs*," *Circus*, September 1972.

"blues-rock guitar masterpiece": Greg Kot, "It's a Roller-Coaster Career from Blues to Pop and Back," *Chicago Tribune*, February 21, 1993.

"finest pickup band": Christgau, "Turkey Shoot," *Village Voice*, December 4, 1990.

"a masterpiece": Anthony DeCurtis, "*Layla and Other Assorted Love Songs*," *Rolling Stone*, January 27, 2005.

"*a make-believe band*": Scapelliti, "An Oral History."

"*I have done it the same*": Milton Lage, dir., *Eric Clapton: Unplugged* (Reprise, 1997).

"*I'm very proud of it*": "Eric Clapton: The Mike Hrano Interview," www.eric-clapton.co.uk/interviewsandarticles/reptileinterview.htm.

"*two guitars and two small amplifiers*": Boyd and Junor, *Wonderful Tonight*, 180–181.

Harold Bloom once observed: Harold Bloom, ed., *Alexander Pushkin: Modern Critical Views* (New York: Chelsea House, 1987), preface.

"*One Christmas Eve*": Clapton, *Clapton: The Autobiography*, 185.

"*Eric and I were playmates*": Boyd and Junor, *Wonderful Tonight*, 256.

"*Lory showed up*": Thomson, *George Harrison*, 452.

"*It was a fine program*": Clapton, *Clapton: The Autobiography*, 312.

"*relived the night*": Clapton, *Clapton: The Autobiography*, 312.

"*wasn't a burglar*": Thomson, *George Harrison*, 479.

Appendix: Sessionographies

"*orangy-brown*" *Weimaraner*: White, "*All Things* in Good Time."

"*I don't like*": Mal Evans, *Diaries*, September 18, 1970, Malcolm Frederick Evans Archives.

BIBLIOGRAPHY

Books

Abbott, Kingsley, ed. *Little Symphonies: A Phil Spector Reader*. London: Helter Skelter Publishing, 2011.

Babiuk, Andy. *Beatles Gear: All the Fab Four's Instruments, from Stage to Studio*. San Francisco: Backbeat, 2001.

Badman, Keith. *The Beatles Diary, Volume 2: After the Break-Up, 1970–2001*. London: Omnibus, 2009.

———. *The Beatles Off the Record: Outrageous Opinions and Unrehearsed Interviews*. London: Omnibus, 2001.

Beatles. *The Beatles Anthology*. San Francisco: Chronicle Books, 2000.

Bloom, Harold, ed. *Alexander Pushkin: Modern Critical Views*. New York: Chelsea House, 1987.

Boyd, Pattie, and Penny Junor. *Wonderful Tonight: George Harrison, Eric Clapton, and Me*. New York: Three Rivers, 2007.

Brewer, Jon, dir. *Cream: Their Fully Authorized Story*. Image Entertainment, 2005.

Brown, Mick. *Tearing Down the Wall of Sound*. New York: Knopf, 2007.

Brown, Peter, and Steven Gaines. *The Love You Make: An Insider's Story of the Beatles*. London: Macmillan, 1983.

Carter, Chris. *A Conversation with George Harrison*. Capitol Records, 2001.

Clapton, Eric. *Clapton: The Autobiography*. New York: Three Rivers, 2007.

Collins, Phil. *Not Dead Yet: The Memoir*. New York: Crown, 2016.

Conforth, Bruce M. *Up Jumped the Devil: The Real Life of Robert Johnson*. Chicago: Chicago Review Press, 2019.

Connolly, Ray. *The Ray Connolly Beatles Archive*. London: Plumray Books, 2018.

Doggett, Peter. *Abbey Road/Let It Be: The Beatles*. New York: Schirmer, 1998.

———. *You Never Give Me Your Money: The Beatles after the Breakup*. New York: HarperCollins, 2009.

Dowlding, William J. *Beatlesongs*. New York: Simon and Schuster, 1989.

Emerick, Geoff, and Howard Massey. *Here, There, and Everywhere: My Life Recording the Music of the Beatles*. New York: Gotham, 2006.

Epstein, Brian. *A Cellarful of Noise: The Autobiography of the Man Who Made the Beatles*. 1964. Reprint, New York: Pocket Books, 1998.

Evans, Mike, ed. *The Beatles Literary Anthology*. London: Plexus, 2014.

Everett, Walter. *The Beatles as Musicians: The Quarry Men through Rubber Soul*. Oxford: Oxford University Press, 2001.

Fawcett, Anthony. *John Lennon: One Day at a Time*. New York: Grove Press, 1976.

Feinstein, Barry, and Chris Murray. *George Harrison: Be Here Now*. New York: Rizzoli, 2020.

Greene, Joshua M. *Here Comes the Sun: The Spiritual and Musical Journey of George Harrison*. New York: Wiley, 2007.

Harrison, George. *I, Me, Mine*. 1980. Reprint, San Francisco: Chronicle Books, 2002.

Harrison, Olivia. *George Harrison: Living in the Material World*. New York: Abrams, 2011.

Howard, David N. *Sonic Alchemy: Visionary Music Producers and Their Maverick Recordings*. Milwaukee: Hal Leonard, 2004.

Huntley, Elliot J. *Mystical One: George Harrison after the Breakup of the Beatles*. Toronto: Guernica Editions, 2004.

Jackson, Andrew Grant. *Still the Greatest: The Essential Solo Beatles Songs*. Lanham, MD: Scarecrow, 2012.

Kahn, Ashley, ed. *George Harrison on George Harrison: Interviews and Encounters*. Chicago: Chicago Review Press, 2020.

Keys, Bobby. *Every Night's a Saturday Night: The Rock 'n' Roll Life of Legendary Sax Man Bobby Keys*. Berkeley, CA: Counterpoint, 2013.

Lage, Milton, dir. *Eric Clapton: Unplugged*. Reprise, 1997.

Leary, Timothy. *Psychedelic Prayers and Other Meditations*. Berkeley, CA: Ronin Publishing, 1997.

Leland, David, dir. *Concert for George*. Warner Home Video, 2003.

Leng, Simon. *While My Guitar Gently Weeps: The Music of George Harrison*. Milwaukee: Hal Leonard, 2006.

Lewisohn, Mark. *The Beatles Live!* London: Pavilion, 1986.

———. *The Complete Beatles Chronicle*. London: Hamlyn, 2003.

———. *The Complete Beatles Recording Sessions: The Official Abbey Road Studio Session Notes, 1962–1970*. New York: Harmony, 1988.

———. *Tune In: The Beatles—All These Years*. New York: Crown, 2013.

Longfellow, Matthew, dir. *Classic Albums: John Lennon, Plastic Ono Band*. Eagle Rock Entertainment, 2008.

MacDonald, Ian. *Revolution in the Head: The Beatles' Records and the Sixties*. New York: Holt, 1994.

Madinger, Chip, and Mark Easter. *Eight Arms to Hold You: The Solo Beatles Compendium*. Springfield, MO: Open Your Books, 2018.

———, and Scott Raile. *Lennonology: Strange Days Indeed—A Scrapbook of Madness.* Springfield, MO: Open Your Books, 2015.

Martin, George, and Jeremy Hornsby. *All You Need Is Ears.* 1979. Reprint, New York: St. Martin's, 1994.

Massey, Howard. *The Great British Recording Studios.* Milwaukee: Hal Leonard, 2015.

Meltzer, Peter E. *So You Think You Know Rock and Roll?: An In-Depth Q&A Tour of the Revolutionary Decade, 1965–1975.* New York: Skyhorse, 2017.

Miles, Barry. *The Beatles Diary, Volume 1: The Beatles Years.* London: Omnibus, 2007.

———. *Paul McCartney: Many Years from Now.* New York: Holt, 1997.

Moran, Johnny. *The Beatles Today.* BBC Radio 1, March 11, 1970.

Norman, Philip. *Shout!: The Beatles in Their Generation.* New York: Simon and Schuster, 1981.

Reid, Jan. *Layla and Other Assorted Love Songs by Derek and the Dominos.* New York: Rodale, 2006.

Ribowsky, Mark. *He's a Rebel: Phil Spector—Rock and Roll's Legendary Producer.* New York: Cooper Square, 2000.

Riesman, Bob. *I Feel So Good: The Life and Times of Big Bill Broonzy.* Chicago: University of Chicago Press, 2011.

Riley, Tim. *Lennon: The Man, the Myth, the Music.* New York: Hyperion, 2011.

Roberty, Marc. *Eric Clapton: Day by Day.* Milwaukee: Backbeat, 2013.

Rodriguez, Robert. *Fab Four FAQ 2.0: The Beatles' Solo Years, 1970–1980.* Milwaukee: Backbeat, 2010.

Ryan, Kevin, and Brian Kehew. *Recording the Beatles: The Studio Equipment and Techniques Used to Create Their Classic Albums.* Houston: Curvebender, 2006.

Sandercombe, W. Fraser. *The Beatles Press Reports: 1961–1970.* Toronto: Collector's Guide, 2007.

Sandford, Christopher. *Clapton: Edge of Darkness.* London: Da Capo, 1994.

Schaffner, Nicholas. *The Beatles Forever.* New York: McGraw-Hill, 1978.

Schumacher, Michael. *Crossroads: The Life and Music of Eric Clapton.* Boston: Little, Brown, and Company, 2020.

Scorsese, Martin, dir. *George Harrison: Living in the Material World.* HBO, 2011.

Scott, Ken. *Abbey Road to Ziggy Stardust: Off the Record with the Beatles, Bowie, Elton, and So Much More.* Los Angeles: Alfred Music, 2012.

Scott, Paul. *Motherless Child: The Definitive Biography of Eric Clapton.* London: Headline, 2015.

Shapiro, Harry. *Eric Clapton: Lost in the Blues.* New York: Da Capo, 1992.

———, and Cesar Glebbeek. *Jimi Hendrix: Electric Gypsy.* New York: St. Martin's Press, 1990.

Shapiro, Marc. *All Things Must Pass: The Life of George Harrison.* New York: St. Martin's, 2002.

Shaw, George Bernard. *Immaturity.* London: Constable, 1921.

Sheff, David. *All We Are Saying: The Last Major Interview with John Lennon and Yoko Ono.* Edited by G. Barry Golson. New York: Griffin, 2000.

Soocher, Stan. *Baby You're a Rich Man: Suing the Beatles for Fun and Profit*. Lebanon, NH: ForeEdge, 2015.

Southall, Brian. *Abbey Road: The Story of the World's Most Famous Studios*. Wellingborough: Patrick Stephens, 1982.

Spitz, Bob. *The Beatles: The Biography*. Boston: Little, Brown, and Company, 2005.

Spizer, Bruce. *The Beatles Solo on Apple Records*. New Orleans: 498 Productions, 2010.

Starr, Michael Seth. *Ringo: With a Little Help*. Milwaukee: Hal Leonard, 2015.

Sulpy, Doug, and Ray Schweighardt. *Get Back: The Unauthorized Chronicle of the Beatles' Let It Be Disaster*. New York: Griffin, 1997.

Swirsky, Seth, dir. *Beatles Stories*. Cinema Libre, 2011.

Thomson, Graeme. *George Harrison: Behind the Locked Door*. London: Omnibus, 2013.

Voormann, Klaus. *Warum spielst du Imagine nicht auf dem weißen Klavier, John?* Munich: Heyne Verlag, 2003.

Welch, Chris. *Cream: The Legendary Sixties Supergroup*. San Francisco: Backbeat, 2000.

Wenner, Jann S. *Lennon Remembers: The Full Rolling Stone Interviews from 1970*. New York: Verso, 2000.

White, Timothy. *George Harrison Reconsidered*. London: Larchwood and Weir, 2013.

Whitlock, Bobby, and Marc Roberty. *Bobby Whitlock: A Rock 'n' Roll Autobiography*. Jefferson City, NC: McFarland, 2011.

Williams, Richard. *Phil Spector: Out of His Head*. London: Omnibus, 2009.

Winn, John C. *That Magic Feeling: The Beatles' Recorded Legacy, Volume Two: 1966–1970*. Sharon, VT: Multiplus, 2003.

———. *Way Beyond Compare: The Beatles' Recorded Legacy, Volume One: 1957–1965*. Sharon, VT: Multiplus, 2003.

Wolfe, Charles, and Kip Lornell. *The Life and Legend of Leadbelly*. London: Da Capo, 1999.

Wright, Gary. *Dreamweaver: A Memoir—Music, Meditation, and My Friendship with George Harrison*. New York: Penguin, 2014.

Articles

"100 Greatest Guitar Solos," *Guitar World*, October 28, 2008. web.archive.org /web/20090831061616/http:/www.guitarworld.com/article/100_greatest_guitar _solos_14_quotlaylaquot_eric_clapton_duane_allman.

Altham, Keith. "Eric Clapton: Another Crossroad." *Fusion*, February 6, 1970. www .rocksbackpages.com.

Aronowitz, Al. "George Harrison: Why Is George in New York?" *Rolling Stone*, June 11, 1970.

———. "Georgemania!" *Blacklisted Journalist*, July 1, 2001. www.blacklistedjournalist .com/column61a.html.

———. "Staring Down Death: George Harrison and Me." *Blacklisted Journalist*, August 1, 2001. www.blacklistedjournalist.com/column62.html.

"The Beatles Have Unity Through Diversity and Are Unlimited." *New Musical Express* (March 14, 1970): 3.

"Bob Dylan's Secret Recording Session with George Harrison and Friends." *Rolling Stone*, May 28, 1970.

Bosso, Joe. "Alan White from Yes: What the Beatles Mean to Me." *Music Radar*, September 11, 2009. www.musicradar.com/news/guitars/alan-white-from-yes-what-the-beatles-mean-to-me-219747.

Budnick, Dean. "Delta Spirit: Rita Coolidge Reflects on Delaney & Bonnie, Mad Dogs & Englishmen, 'Layla,' and More." *Relix Media*, October 25, 2016. relix.com/articles/detail/delta_spirit_rita_coolidge_reflects_on_delaney_bonnie_mad_dogs_englishmen_layla_and_more/.

Buskin, Richard. "Classic Tracks: Derek and the Dominos' *Layla*." *Sound on Sound*, September 2006. www.soundonsound.com/people/classic-tracks-derek-dominos-layla.

———. "Classic Tracks: The Ronettes' 'Be My Baby.'" *Sound on Sound*, April 2007. www.soundonsound.com/techniques/classic-tracks-ronettes-be-my-baby.

Cantor-Jackson, Betty. Interview with Cloud Surfing. March 20, 2010. cloudsurfing.gdhour.com/archives/tag/george-harrison.

Christgau, Robert. "Consumer Guide (15)." *Village Voice*, January 7, 1971.

———. "I.P.M.C." *Village Voice*, September 1971.

———. "Turkey Shoot," *Village Voice*, December 4, 1990.

Clapton, Eric. "Eric Clapton: The Mike Hrano Interview." www.eric-clapton.co.uk/interviewsandarticles/reptileinterview.htm.

"Clapton and Bruce to Join Miles!" *Melody Maker*, June 5, 1970: 1.

Cooke, Deryck. "The Lennon-McCartney Songs." *Vindications: Essays on Romantic Music*. Cambridge: Cambridge UP, 1982.

DeCurtis, Anthony. "*Layla and Other Assorted Love Songs*." *Rolling Stone*, January 27, 2005.

Doyle, Tom. "Let It Roll." *MOJO*, June 2020. www.rocksbackpages.com.

"Duane Allman's Coricidin Bottle (Slide)." *Ground Guitar*, 2005. www.groundguitar.com/duane-allman-guitars-and-gear/duane-allmans-coricidin-bottle-slide/.

Fact or Fantasy. "Prayer and Meditation." BBC Television, April 26, 1970.

Frampton, Peter. "'Nothin's Gonna Keep Me from Playing' Peter Frampton on Preparing for His Farewell Tour." Interview by Tom Power, Q, Canadian Broadcasting Corporation, April 29, 2019. www.cbc.ca/radio/q/monday-april-29-2019-peter-frampton-rowley-irlam-and-more-1.5112767/nothing-s-gonna-keep-me-from-playing-peter-frampton-on-preparing-for-his-farewell-tour-1.5112895.

———. "Peter Frampton Talks Talk Boxes and Recording *All Things Must Pass*." Interview by Damian Fanelli. *Guitar World*, 2013. www.guitarworld.com/artists/interview-peter-frampton-talks-talk-boxes-and-recording-george-harrison-all-things-must-pass.

"Friar Park, Henley: The Residence of Frank Crisp, Esq." *The Gardener's Chronicle*, October 28, 1899.

Fusilli, Jim. "Clapton, Harrison, on the Bus." *Wall Street Journal*, August 14, 2010.

Gerson, Ben. "*All Things Must Pass.*" *Rolling Stone*, January 21, 1971.

Ghianni, Tim. "Nashville Starr: When Ringo Came to Town." *Nashville Scene*, July 3, 2008. web.archive.org/web/20080710100158/http://www.nashvillescene.com/Stories/Cover _Story/2008/07/03/Nashville_Starr/#.

Gilbert, Jerry. "Wolf Gathers His Flock in London." *Melody Maker*, May 16, 1970.

Giles, Jeff. "How Peter Frampton Met the Talk Box." *Ultimate Classic Rock*, September 9, 2014. ultimateclassicrock.com/peter-frampton-talk-box/.

Green, Douglas. "Pete Drake: Everyone's Favorite." *Guitar Player*, September 1973.

Harrison, George. "A Conversation with George Harrison." Interview by Mick Brown. *Rolling Stone*, April 19, 1979.

———. "George Harrison Interviewed." Interview by Timothy White. *Goldmine*, November 27, 1992.

———. "*Guitar World* Interviews George Harrison." Interview by Vic Garbarini. *Guitar World*, January 2001.

———. Interview. *Crawdaddy*, February 1977. www.beatlesinterviews.org.

———. Interview by David Wigg. *Scene and Heard*, BBC Radio 1, October 8, 1969. www .beatlesinterviews.org.

———. Interview by Howard Smith. New York City, April 25, 1970.

———. Interview by Mukunda Goswami. *Transcend*, September 4, 1982. www.transcend .org/tms/2020/03/george-harrison-25-feb-1943-29-nov-2001/.

Harrison Herald, April 1970.

Harrison Herald, July 1970.

Harrison Herald, September 1970.

"Harrison in Supersession." *Melody Maker*, June 13, 1970.

Harrison, Olivia. Interview with Dark Horse Radio, November 2018.

———. Interview with KSHE-95, December 26, 2018.

Havers, Richard. "Derek and the Dominos' Historic First Gig In London." udiscover-music, June 14, 2019. www.udiscovermusic.com/stories/derek-and-the-dominos -take-a-bow/.

Headlam, Dave. "Blues Transformations in the Music of Cream." *Understanding Rock: Essays in Musical Analysis*. Oxford: Oxford University Press, 1997.

"Henley Houses Plan Rejected." *Reading Evening Post*, October 4, 1968.

Hilburn, Robert. "Clapton Finds the Right Combination." *Los Angeles Times*, November 17, 1970.

———. "Tearing Down the Wall of Silence: Pop Legend Phil Spector Is Talking Comeback a Decade after Drawing the Curtain on His Life." *Los Angeles Times*, November 10, 1991.

Hollingworth, Roy. "Derek and the Dominos: *Layla and Other Assorted Love Songs*." *Melody Maker*, December 12, 1970. www.rocksbackpages.com.

"Home of the 'Sleeping Friars' to Be Bulldozed?" *Reading Evening Post*, February 9, 1967.

Jones, Cliff. "We're Waiting for the Beatles." *MOJO*, October 1996. www.rocksback pages.com.

Kot, Greg. "It's a Roller-Coaster Career from Blues to Pop and Back," *Chicago Tribune*, February 21, 1993.

Leimbacher, Ed. "*Layla and Other Assorted Love Songs*." *Rolling Stone*, December 24, 1970.

Levenson, Bill. "*Layla*'s 40th: The *Where's Eric!* Interview with Bill Levenson," *Where's Eric!* March 19, 2011. www.whereseric.com/eric-clapton-news/303-laylas-40th -wheres-eric-interview-bill-levenson.

Mann, William. "What Songs the Beatles Sang." *Times*, December 27, 1963. jolomo .net/music/william_mann.html.

Martin, George. "Listen to My Story: George Martin Interview with *Melody Maker*." Interview by Richard Williams, *Melody Maker*, August 21, 1971.

———. "The Producer Series, Part 1." Interview by Ralph Denver. *Studio Sound*, January 1985.

McConnell, Anita. "Crisp, Sir Frank, First Baronet (1843–1919)." *Oxford Dictionary of National Biography*. Oxford: Oxford University Press, 2007. www.oxforddnb.com.

Naha, Ed. "Review: *Layla and Other Assorted Love Songs*." *Circus*, September 1972.

Nightingale, Anne. "Pop Profile—George Harrison." BBC Radio 1, February 1977.

Norman, Philip. "The Great God Clapton." *Sunday Times Magazine*, March 1, 1970.

"Original Painting for *All Things Must Pass* Poster." *Beatles Magazine*, May 26, 2014. beatlesmagazine.blogspot.com/.

"Pattie Boyd Exhibits Pictures from Life with George Harrison." Sveriges Radio, September 16, 2014. sverigesradio.se/sida/artikel.aspx?programid=109&artikel=5966879.

Penna, Tris. "The Beatles Solo: *All Things Must Pass*." BBC Radio 2, September 28, 2019.

Sander, Ellen. "Rock 1970: A Level of Excellence." *Saturday Review*, December 26, 1970.

Scapelliti, Christopher. "An Oral History of Derek and the Dominos' *Layla*." *Guitar Player*, July 2, 2020. www.guitarplayer.com/players/an-oral-history-of-derek-and -the-dominos-layla.

Self, Joseph C. "'The 'My Sweet Lord'/'He's So Fine' Plagiarism Suit." web.archive.org /web/20020208074051/http://abbeyrd.best.vwh.net/mysweet.htm.

Senoff, Pete. "Spector on Pop Today." *Melody Maker*, October 11, 1969.

Sheffield, Rob. "And in the End." *Rolling Stone*, August 17, 2020. www.rollingstone .com/feature/beatles-inside-breakup-50-years-later-1042196/.

Simons, Dave. "Tales from the Top: George Harrison's *All Things Must Pass*." *Songwriter 101*, December 21, 2007. www.bmi.com/news/entry/Tales_From_the_Top _George_Harrisons_All_Things_Must_Pass.

Sinclair, David. "1966 – The Year That Built Rock: The Brit Blues Boom." *Louder*, January 22, 2016. www.loudersound.com/features/1966-the-year-that-built-rock-the-british-blues-boom.

"Sir Frank Crisp, Bt." *Proceedings of the Linnean Society of London, 1918–1919*. London: Burlington House, 1919.

Smith, Alan. "Beatle Single—By George!" *New Musical Express*, November 1, 1969. www.rocksbackpages.com/Library/Article/beatle-single--by-george.

——. "George Harrison: *All Things Must Pass*." *New Musical Express*, December 5, 1970.

Smullen, Madhava. "Devotees Say Their Goodbyes to Yamuna Devi at Alachua Memorial." ISKCON News, December 31, 2011. iskconnews.org.

Subudhi, Roshni. "Pattachitra: A Spectacular Folk Art Form from Odisha." *Culture Trip*, October 25, 2016. theculturetrip.com.

Welch, Chris. "Delaney & Bonnie: Out of the South Comes 'The Best Band in the World.'" *Melody Maker*, October 18, 1969.

White, Timothy. "*All Things* in Good Time." *Billboard*, January 8, 2001. www.billboard.com.

——. "A New *Yellow Submarine Songtrack* Due in September." *Billboard*, June 19, 1999.

Williams, Richard. "Album Reviews." *Billboard*, December 19, 1970.

——. "Ringo and the Nashville Cat." *New Musical Express*, August 29, 1970.

Author Interviews

Barham, John. Interviews by Jason Kruppa, June 16, 2020; July 11, 2020; August 12, 2020; February 2, 2021.

Harrington, Kevin. Interview by Kenneth Womack, February 3, 2021.

Kurlander, John. Interview by Jason Kruppa, August 31, 2009.

Leckie, John. Interview by Jason Kruppa, December 2, 2019.

Levenson, Bill. Interview by Jason Kruppa, June 18, 2020.

Parsons, Alan. Interview by Kenneth Womack, September 17, 2019.

Sarver, Cathy. Interview by Jason Kruppa, June 7, 2020.

Townsend, Ken. Interview by Kenneth Womack, December 4, 2019.

Voormann, Klaus. Interview by Jason Kruppa, December 5, 2019.

Webb, Nick. Interview by Jason Kruppa, November 6, 2019.

White, Alan. Interview by Jason Kruppa, June 1, 2020.

Miscellaneous

Bright Tunes Music Corp. v. Harrisongs Music Ltd. 42 Federal Supplement 177 (1976).

Davis, Andy. Liner notes for *Encouraging Words*, by Billy Preston. Apple, 2010.

Kahn, Ashley. Essay and liner notes for *Layla and Other Assorted Love Songs: 40th-Anniversary Super Deluxe Edition*, by Derek and the Dominos. Polydor, 2011.

INDEX